Management Accounting

Published in association with
the Chartered Institute of
Management Accountants

Other titles in the CIMA series

Management Accounting

Strategic Planning and Marketing

Stage 4

Patrick McNamee

For our sons: David and Stephen

Butterworth-Heinemann Ltd
Linacre House, Jordan Hill, Oxford OX2 8DP

PART OF REED INTERNATIONAL BOOKS

OXFORD   LONDON   BOSTON
MUNICH   NEW DELHI   SINGAPORE   SYDNEY
TOKYO   TORONTO   WELLINGTON

First published 1988
Reprinted 1989, 1991

British Library Cataloguing in Publication Data
McNamee, Patrick B.
  Management accounting: strategic planning
  and marketing
  1. Management accounting
  I. Title   II. Chartered Institute of Management
  Accountants
  658.1'511

ISBN 0 7506 0339 9

Printed and bound in Great Britain by
Redwood Press Limited, Melksham, Wiltshire

Contents

Preface

This book aims to show how contemporary strategic management can be used with creativity and control to steer an organization towards its goals. This aim reflects the author's belief that strategic management is most effective when, at one end of the spectrum it stimulates creative thinking: i.e. it helps planners to think in open-ended and divergent terms about their business environment, their organization, and those strategies which will bestow strategic advantage on it, while at the other end of the spectrum, it stimulates planners to see past the creative dimensions of strategy development and into the detail required for effective implementation, monitoring and control. The book attempts to do this through the medium of a comprehensive model which disaggregates the strategic process into a number of discrete units – assessment of the environment, assessment of the organization, assessment of the organization's current strategic position, the development of strategies, the implementation of strategies and finally the evaluation of strategies. It is hoped that this model will enable readers to see both the totality and the detail of the strategic management process.

Although the text focuses on strategic management and operations in a United Kingdom context, the discipline is essentially international and consequently considerable attention is given to the techniques of strategic management and examples of practice of other countries, especially the United States and Japan.

This book has been written to support the Chartered Institute of Management Accountants' Stage 4 syllabus 'Management Accounting – Strategic Planning and Marketing' and consequently the topics covered reflect this syllabus. These topics, however, are the broad range of topics that would be covered in many university or business school courses on strategic management/business policy and so the book should also be a suitable text for groups such as: final level undergraduate and MBA business policy students; practising managers who wish to develop their strategic perspectives, and management consultants.

The book has two major distinctive features which differentiate it from most other strategy texts: a strong marketing orientation and the provision of a computer-based strategy model which can be used to support the text.

There is a major section on marketing which reflects the author's view that the ultimate success of any organization is determined by the success of its products or services in its markets. Consequently, understanding the marketing environment, understanding alternative marketing strategies, understanding the marketing process and understanding how to evaluate marketing effectiveness are considered to be fundamental to effective strategic management. Thus the major aims of this section are to help develop readers' awareness of the importance of marketing and also to help integrate the discipline of marketing into the strategic management process.

The book has a computer-based strategy model which may be used to complement the text. Although computer-based strategy models have been available for many years, the building of these models has, generally, required a degree of specialist computer knowledge and skill which is normally outside the competence of strategic planners and accountants. However, with the advent of extremely powerful micro-computers and user-friendly spreadsheet software packages, strategic planners now have the tools to develop their own sophisticated models for strategic management. Accordingly therefore, a model has been produced which reflects these developments.

The model runs on an IBM PC* with at least 512k (or an equivalent compatible) and is built upon the software modelling package Javelin.† The Javelin software was chosen because, in the opinion of the author, it appeared to offer the most suitable medium for building this type of strategy model for the following reasons:

- It is very powerful.
- It can be understood easily by non-computer specialists: all the relationships in the models are written in English.
- It can handle automatically different time periods, i.e. it can convert weekly, monthly or quarterly data into annual data and vice versa.
- It can provide very high quality output, i.e. the output can be in colour and can be in tabular, graphic and chart form. This facility should aid the communication process.

Although the model which is shown in Chapter 20 is based upon a single hypothetical company, it can be tailored to particular organizational structures and strategies.

Now that this book is completed I would like to express my thanks to those many people who have been of such help to me in this task. First, at a personal level, I would like to thank my family – my wife Brid and

---

* IBM is the registered trademark of the International Business Machines Corporation.
† Javelin is the registered trademark of Javelin Software Corporation.

our children David and Stephen for their unfaltering support. Next, I would like to thank the following people who have all, in different ways, supported me in this work: Paul Deeney for developing such an effective and suitable computer model; Graeme Brown and Mark Wright of the CIMA for asking me to write the book and for their support; Professor Bernard Taylor of The Management Centre, Henley; David Hussey of Harbridge House; Professor Michael Thomas of the University of Strathclyde; and Peter Prince of the Strategic Planning Society in London, for their encouragement.

Finally, at the institutional level I would like to thank the University of Ulster, my colleagues and our students for providing me with an atmosphere and a physical environment conducive to this type of work.

Patrick McNamee
Centre for Research in Management
University of Ulster

Part One

1 Introduction and the model

What do the names on the list below have in common?

- Aerated Bread Limited
- Bell's Asbestos Limited
- Bodega Limited
- Brunner, Mond and Company Limited
- City Offices Limited
- Fley Brothers
- General Hydraulic Power Limited
- Gordon Hotels
- Milners Safe Limited
- Price's Patent Candle Limited
- Welford and Sons Limited

Most readers will not be able to recognize the companies or state the common link. The link is that the above companies were actively traded stocks on the London Stock Exchange in the first week of January 1900. For many people living at that time – stockholders, managers and employees of these companies – it must have appeared that the continuing and future success of these businesses was fairly certain. Yet today, around three generations later, virtually all of these companies have disappeared.

Why did they disappear? Is there a common strand connecting the demise of each company? Could this happen again to companies which are currently being actively traded on the London or other stock exchanges?

It could be argued that, irrespective of the specific reason for the failure of an individual company, all of them failed to survive because they failed in their *strategic management* and that today there are well-known, and apparently successful, companies which will also disappear because they are failing in their strategic management.

Strategic management in this book, is considered to be that type of management through which an organization tries to obtain a good fit with its environment. It is therefore concerned with those long-run and fundamental decisions about the organization's mission, scale of operations and spread of activities. The term 'organization' is used rather than firm or company as it appears to be the most general term. Thus in the context of this book, an organization can be taken to mean any type of work grouping: private sector or public sector; large or small; profit seeking or charitable; privately owned or publicly owned.

Thus for effective strategic management the strategic planner must have the knowledge, skills and vision necessary to:

1   Understand the environment in which the organization is operating with particular reference to the opportunities and the threats which are, or will be, present.
2   Understand the total organization, i.e. its goals, or objectives, its mission, its culture, its overall strategies, the lower level strategies and activities of the different functional areas, and the resources available.
3   Develop strategies which are appropriate to the organization and the environment in which it operates.
4   Implement chosen strategies.
5   Control, evaluate, and amend as appropriate strategies which have been selected.

This brief description is the core of the model of strategic management which will be employed in this book. Figure 1 makes the elements of the model explicit and each of these elements is introduced and then discussed in more detail below.

Exhibit 1:   Strategic management at Jaguar plc

A clear example of the effectiveness of this type of planning and leadership is provided by the influence of John Egan on Jaguar plc. From the early 1970s until 1980 Jaguar – the famous British luxury car – suffered a decline so severe that by 1980 its continuing existence began to appear to be doubtful. Jaguar experienced, in that decade, a steady decline in sales, a reputation for very poor quality, low productivity, a demoralized workforce and severe financial problems. In April 1980 John Egan was appointed Chairman and Chief Executive and under his leadership, as the table below shows, the company had by 1985 achieved a remarkable turnaround.

Summary of Jaguar's performance from 1980 to 1984

	1980	*1981*	*1982*	*1983*	*1984*
Vehicles produced	15,469	13,933	21,007	28,467	33,424
Value of sales (£m)	166.4	195.2	305.6	472.6	634.1
Profit (loss) (£m)	(46.0)	(31.7)	9.5	49.5	57.1
Cost per vehicle (£m)	13,621	16,228	14,067	14,807	15,173
Per cent exported	60	63	69	75	77

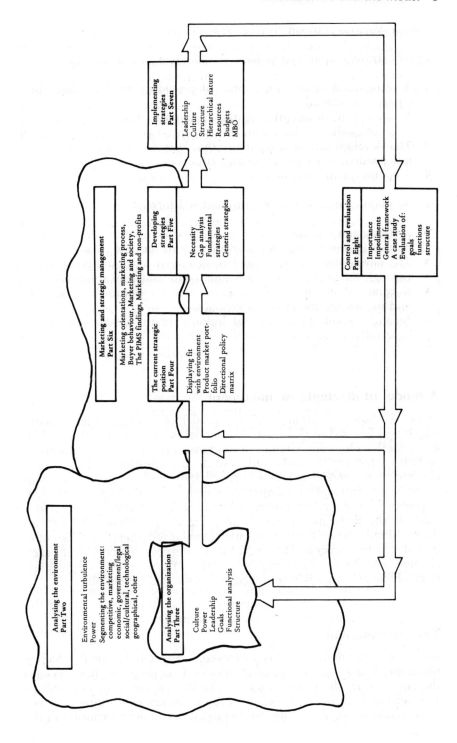

**Analysing the environment
Part Two**

Environmental turbulence
Power
Segmenting the environment:
competitive, marketing
economic, government/legal
social/cultural, technological
geographical, other

**Analysing the organization
Part Three**

Culture
Power
Leadership
Goals
Functional analysis
Structure

**Marketing and strategic management
Part Six**

Marketing orientations, marketing process,
Buyer behaviour, Marketing and society,
The PIMS findings, Marketing and non-profits

**The current strategic
position
Part Four**

Displaying fit
with environment
Product market port-
folio
Directional policy
matrix

**Developing
strategies
Part Five**

Necessity
Gap analysis
Fundamental
strategies
Generic strategies

**Implementing
strategies
Part Seven**

Leadership
Culture
Structure
Hierarchical nature
Resources
Budgets
MBO

**Control and evaluation
Part Eight**

Importance
Impediments
General framework
A case study
Evaluation of:
goals
functions
structure

Figure 1 *A model of strategic management*

Source: Various company annual statements

Egan's strategy appeared to have the following main strands:

1 A recognition of the importance of providing products that the customers wanted.
2 A strategy of differentiating the Jaguar car from others on the basis of quality, value for money and prestige.
3 The development of a company that was financially sound and independent of Government and BL.
4 A commitment to growth.

These main elements were operationalized through:

- A strong commitment to improving product quality which would be manifested in superior warranty terms for new cars.
- The development of increased productivity and quality of work through the development of harmonious industrial relations.
- Substantial investment in research and development to widen and modernize the range of vehicles.
- Strong marketing efforts and 'reform' of the dealer networks, especially in the US and Western Germany.

A model of strategic management

Figure 1 shows, schematically, the model of strategic management which will be used in this book. The model is concerned with developing a methodology for aligning an organization with its environment and also satisfying the stakeholders of the organization. Although each element in the model is set out sequentially, and for the purposes of analysis it is rational to examine each element in the order presented, in practice this neat delineation and sequencing will not always occur – many of the elements are overlapping and their analyses will be conducted simultaneously. Strategic management will therefore be an integrated <u>iterative</u> process. However, for the purposes of exposition, each element will be treated separately and will comprise a single part. Each of the elements is introduced and discussed briefly below.

The environment

In Figure 1 the environment is portrayed as an irregular block which is much larger than any of the other blocks. It is irregular, first because the environment faced by every organization is different and unique and second because each organization's unique environment is not static but is constantly changing due to the continuous variation in the intensity and mix of forces in it. Consequently a regular delineation is not appropriate. The environmental block is larger than the other blocks in order to emphasize its importance: *successful strategies are ones where the organization adapts to its environment and not vice versa.* Phrasing this slightly differently – those organizations which fail to adapt to their environment will not in the long run survive and will, like dinosaurs, disappear.

Exhibit 2:   The failure of Nexos[1]*

In 1979 the UK government, in an effort to develop a British presence in the very fast growing automatic/electronic office industry established a company called Nexos. Nexos, it was hoped, would become the leading UK office automation company and would act as a catalyst for the more general development of this industry in the UK.

In 1982 the company collapsed with a loss of more than £30 million.

A report carried out by Mr Russell Ford on behalf of the Public Accounts Committee (the UK parliamentary watchdog on government spending) showed that the company failed because of poor strategic management. The failure occurred because the management was overambitious and had built an organization which could not be justified by its level of business.

On Nexos's high trading losses the report says that to a great extent the losses represented the costs of the head office and central management organization together with the excess overheads of the sales organization. These were established or built up vastly in excess of the size required for the turnover it adds ...

Criticisms of the Nexos management include:

- Being critically dependent on the early success of a single product – the unproven 2200 word processor from Logica. The Nexos corporate plan was based on obtaining 25 per cent of the UK word processor market by the end of 1981.
- Failing to recognize and plan for the possibility that the 2200 might be late.
- Creating a much larger organization with higher outgoings than was justified by the sales levels.
- Trying to do too much too quickly in view of the amount of funding committed by the NEB.
- Committing substantial expenditure to the Delta project – a powerful telecommunications system being developed in the US by Dephi, a subsidiary of Exxon – without proper assessment of its then state.

Clearly Nexos did not align with its environment.

---

*   References are collected in sections at the end of each chapter.

The process of analysing the environment presents the strategic planner with a dilemma – if all those environmental elements which *could* have some influence on the organization are included then the analysis becomes extremely complex and unwieldy with the constituent elements being analysed to a relatively low level of resolution. Alternatively, if in the interests of reducing the level of complexity, certain environmental elements are omitted then, although the level of analytical resolution should be higher, certain crucial environmental forces may, in the process, be omitted from the analysis. In practice the appropriate balance between the width of the environmental analysis and its depth is frequently a function of the nature of the industry and requires knowledge, experience and judgement on the part of the strategic planner.

Part Two will examine the environment in detail. It will develop a methodology which will enable a strategic planner to understand the total environment in which his organization operates and then identify and analyse those elements or forces in the environment which will either be opportunities for the organization to exploit, or threats to its existence which must be counteracted. It is suggested that the environment can be segmented into a discrete number of broad forces which have been found by researchers to be the most common crucial ones. These forces are competitive, marketing, economic legal/government, social, technological, geographical and other.

Competitive

The competitive forces which buffet an organization frequently change over time and sensitivity to these changes is crucial. For example, one of the major competitive forces (see Part Two) is the entry of new competitors.

New entrants to an industry can come in a great variety of sizes and adopt a great variety of strategies. Two common types are:

- Large new entrants who have substantial resources and have leadership in other related industry sectors.
- New entrants who are small and flexible and enjoy cost advantages over existing competitors.

An example of an industry which has been 'squeezed' by these species of new entrants is the computer aided design industry in the US.

Exhibit 3:   Sensitivity to competitive pressures[2]

Some of the leading computer aided design companies have made a major strategic blunder in their battle for the world market for computer aided design and manufacturing (CAD/CAM), a leading specialist researcher believes.

Mr Charles Foundyller, of Daratech consultancy, who has just completed a major survey of the market which shows that the long expected shakeout in the industry is underway, believes something strange began to happen about the middle of last year.

Major American CAD/CAM companies such as Computervision and Applicon, which were starting to feel the squeeze and having to lay people off, started to emphasize computer integrated manufacture (CIM) to go for growth.

The future, they argued, lay not just in CAD, but in systems that integrated everything from inventory control, finance and design.

'The purchasing decisions started to move from the engineers to the data processing managers', Mr Foundyller believes. Engineers might know all about Computervision products but the data processing managers were more familiar with IBM.

'Suddenly companies like Computervision and Applicon started finding themselves competing with IBM on its home ground. In effect that strategy handed IBM the CAD/CAM market on a silver platter,' Mr Foundyller said.

At the same time as the traditional CAD/CAM companies were being squeezed at one end by integrated IBM systems they were facing trouble at the other by the increasing use of small personal computers for computer aided design at a fraction of the cost of large dedicated systems.

The effect of IBM's entry can be gauged by the sales of the major competitors as shown in Figure 2.

Keen sensitivity to competitive forces plus the ability to react effectively to them is a vital element in determining strategic viability.

Marketing

Overlapping with the competitive forces in the environment are the market forces, i.e. those fundamental factors which will determine whether the products or services offered by an organization will be ultimately purchased by consumers at a price acceptable to the organization. Frequently throughout the text the term 'product' will be used with the term 'service' implied. It is assumed that the strategic management of services can be undertaken using the same model. For example the services provided by a firm of accountants are considered to be the 'products' of that 'organization'. In this text the importance of organizations having a marketing orientation is strongly emphasized. Therefore only those organizations which adapt their products to the needs and wishes of consumers will survive in the long run. The arguments in favour of this view are advanced in more detail in Part Six. Among the more important market elements in the environment which will be considered are:

- The size and affluence of the market.
- The number of competitors and their sizes.

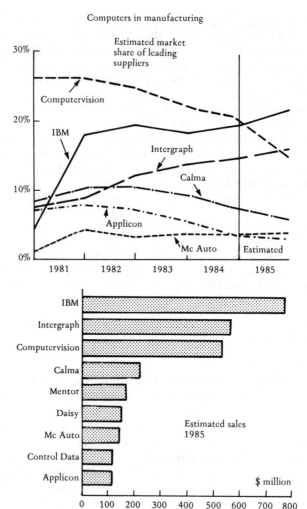

Figure 2 *Sales of computers in manufacturing*
Source: Daratech

- The growth rate of the market.
- The influences on buying decisions – prices, product features, methods of distribution, and methods of promotion.

Awareness of, and responsiveness to, market needs is a crucial aspect of strategic management and it is an area where, it is argued, Japanese companies have shown particular flair and reaped the rewards as Exhibit 4 shows.

Exhibit 4: Japanese marketing flair[3]

Between 1951 and 1984 Japan enjoyed the fastest rate of economic growth in the world, averaging almost 8 per cent annually. During that same period, Japanese GNP per capita grew from below 25 per cent of the British level to 25 per cent above it. The explanations offered for this phenomenon are many and inter-related ...

... but one aspect has attracted rather less notice – the quality of Japanese marketing ...

... to test the validity of these assumptions – and particularly how far they may account for Japanese marketing success abroad – interviews were obtained with the top marketing decision makers of fifteen leading Japanese companies operating within the UK; also for the sake of comparison, with their counterparts in fifteen major British competitors ...

... overall the results strongly support the initial hypotheses about Japanese marketing strengths. The British companies, by contrast, were too often finance- or production-oriented; and their strategies generally failed to reflect the dynamics of markets. Perhaps most importantly, many of them failed to recognize the dynamics of competition ...

Economic

Here the overall economic context in which the organization operates and how general economic performance will influence strategic planning are examined. For example, since the late 1970s many large UK multinational corporations have been disappointed by the performance of the UK domestic economy and have, as a consequence, given a greater weight to overseas investment.

This is illustrated through data taken from the UK's largest company ICI. ICI has, since 1980 at least, had a policy of developing its investments overseas. This is reflected in the numbers employed by the group in the different regions in which it operates as shown in Table 1.

Table 1 ICI'S employment according to region 1979–84[4]

	1980	1981	1982	1983	1984
UK	84,300	74,700	67,300	61,800	58,600
Continental W. Europe	10,800	10,600	10,400	12,500	13,200
The Americas	19,900	18,800	18,000	16,900	17,200
Australasia and E. Asia	15,500	15,700	15,300	14,100	13,700
Indian subcontinent	10,600	10,800	11,100	11,000	11,500
Other countries	1,900	1,800	1,600	1,700	1,400
Total	143,200	132,400	123,800	117,900	115,600

Legal/government

Frequently an organization's current and future operations are affected by legislation – national and international – over which the organization has no control. The development of the European Community, which has a tariff barrier erected against imports of products from non-member states has had a major effect upon the international investment policies of multinational companies. Thus, in order to have unrestricted access to this large market many non-European multinational corporations have set up manufacturing facilities within the Community. This can be seen in terms of the increase in foreign direct investment in Europe by US companies.

Table 2   US direct investment in Europe in the period 1970–81[5]

	1970	1975	1978	1979	1980	1981
Investment in Europe (Millions of US dollars)	25,255	49,305	70,647	83,056	96,534	101,318

Social

This element is concerned with an analysis of the major social influences which are affecting, or will affect, the organization. For example, in the late 1970s and early 1980s in many developed Western countries society in general became very concerned about health, diet and fitness. This social change provided market opportunities for industries and organizations that were aware of the change. Thus, Pineapple Dance Studios, which was founded in England in the 1980s by Debbie Moore, and was launched on the Unlisted Securities Market in 1983 had, for the financial year ending 31 July 1984 (in spite of some unexpected impediments to expansion,) taxable profits of £209,000 and a turnover of £1.73 million. This company responded to a social change which provided a market opportunity. The opportunity was the demand, mostly by younger women, for modern facilities for aerobic dance and fitness activities plus fashionable health and fitness clothes and associated equipment.

Technological

In many industries technological change has fundamental influences and in such industries, in order to survive, organizations must keep abreast of such changes. The European (and US) machine tools industry is an example of an industry which has paid particularly heavily for its failure to perceive the threat posed by technological developments of Japanese rivals as Exhibit 5 shows.

Exhibit 5: The technological environment and the machine tool industry[6]
Until the early 1970s, this was a mature industry with highly stable product technology, market structure and a competitive environment. The key elements of product technology were developed in association with rising industries early in the century (such as the automobile industry) and there had not been a change in product cycles. Indeed, we could find thirty to forty-year-old products as major 'breadwinners' in leading machine tool companies.

The pace of change was incremental and along established trajectories. In other words, this type of technical change (although improving machine performance) allowed existing competitors to exercise rivalry in an orderly way. Indeed, there was little mobility in the world league of leading competitors and new entrants rarely achieved high visible positions.

This relatively slow pace of progress changed dramatically in the 1970s. The machine tool industry was in a profound state of flux and disequilibrium and this presented considerable threats and opportunities for both incumbents and potential entrants.

Strategic change in the machine tool industry implies a 'new' economics of the industry. At the firm level, this requires the development of new management routines and skills and competitive behaviour, without which firms may well find that their survival is at stake. Changes in the economics of the industry have wide implications for corporate choices towards vertical integration, relative emphasis on marketing service and R & D, and the profile of distinctive competence.

Geographical

With the development of almost instant global information communication systems and the decreasing costs of physical transport, industry has in general become less restricted in its choice of manufacturing location. Many industries are no longer tied to natural factor endowments – for example sources of raw materials, or cheap labour, nor are they tied to being close to their markets. Instead industry's location is increasingly determined by a whole range of factors of competitive advantage or necessity which vary from industry to industry but which in advanced industries, according to Porter frequently include:

> human resources with particular skills, resident scientific infrastructure of appropriate types and access to sophisticated suppliers.[7]

As it seems likely that the locational freedom of industries will increase in the future, awareness of the true competitive advantages conferred by location will become an increasingly important element in the assessment of the environment.

Other

This is really a 'catch-all' category for any relevant environmental forces (should there be any) which are not captured in any of the other categories.

In summary, analysing the environment is concerned with isolating, and then understanding, the prevailing fundamental environmental forces and trends which affect a particular organization and then measuring their existing and likely future impact on that organization.

Finally, all the above information can be summarized and displayed graphically in an environmental assessment diagram as shown on page 89.

The organization

The organization is portrayed as an irregular box inside the 'environmental box'. Its irregularity is meant to indicate that the organization should be responsive to changes in its environment and should adapt its 'shape' to the 'shape' of the environment rather than vice versa.

Part Three will develop a methodology for making an assessment of the strategic health and potential of an organization. It will do this by showing how to identify and analyse the goals, leadership, culture, organizational structure and the relative strengths of each functional area in any organization. Implicit in this approach is the assumption that the overall strength of a organization is the sum of these parts, although in many instances this is not the case – there may be positive or negative synergy among the constituent elements which defies this type of analysis. By positive synergy is meant a situation in which the total strategic health or strength of an organization is greater than the sum of the strengths of the individual parts while negative synergy obtains in a situation in which the strategic health or strength of an organization is less than the sum of the strengths of the individual parts.

Goals

Understanding the goals* of the organization could be described as the fundamental starting point of strategic analysis. This analysis will be effected by commencing with an examination of who the top decision makers in an organization are and what value systems and goals they have. These are the corporate strategic goals of the organization and once they have been established then the analysis proceeds by an examination of how these goals are translated into strategies and then woven into the fabric of the entire organization.

* Frequently the word 'objective' is used instead of 'goal'. See page 111.

Leadership

Leadership can be a fundamental determinant in the success or failure of an organization (see Hosmer[8]). A very public demonstration of the power of leadership was given by Bob Geldof's success in raising money for famine-struck regions of the world, through the Live Aid Concerts held in London and Philadelphia in July 1985. It was a widely held view at the time that this phenomenally successful fund-raising activity would not have been possible without Geldof's leadership. Effective leadership can take many forms from, at one end of the spectrum, coercive and autocratic leadership to, at the other end, participative and democratic leadership. Leadership, in strategic management, is judged not according to style, but according to whether it is appropriate to the organization and its industry and also according to whether it is effective in successfully managing the organization.

Culture

The culture of an organization is assumed to be that somewhat nebulous but nonetheless real set of values and attitudes that somehow pervades all organizations and binds the people of the organization together in some common set of attitudes. For example, companies in traditional industries such as banking and insurance tend to have extremely conservative cultures while less traditional industries such as video promotions and advertising tend to promote a much more dynamic image.

Organizational structure

The formal structure of an organization can have profound effects upon its performance, all other things being equal. This section of the analysis will be concerned with establishing the appropriateness of an organization's structure to its goals, its strategies and its operations.

Functional strengths

Finally, the relative strength of each functional area will be assessed. In this part of the analysis a methodology for assessing the strengths and weaknesses in the functions of finance and accounting, marketing, production, personnel and management information systems will be made. In passing it is important to note that although it is frequently maintained that it is important to have balanced overall functional strength this is not necessarily always true. Thus, at the growth stage of a business it may be more important to have sales growth (and therefore strength in the marketing function) than control (strength in the finance and accounting function) and by way of contrast when an organization is in a period of retrenchment it may be more important to have control.

An analysis of all the above elements will be used to provide an overall picture of the strategic health and potential of the organization.

As was the case for summarizing the environmental influence impinging on a organization, an overall summary picture of the organization is provided by an organization assessment diagram as shown on page 138.

The current strategic position

In Part Four a methodology for assessing the current strategic position of the company will be developed. In this part of the model the environmental appraisal (of Part Two) is married to the company appraisal (of Part Three) to provide a locus for the company on its strategic map. This locus is the basis upon which future strategies will be developed. The rationale is that it is best to base future strategies upon the realities of the current position.

The current strategic position will be displayed graphically by relating the environmental assessment diagram to the company assessment diagram as shown on page 148. This approach has the advantage of not only providing an effective summary but also giving an immediate visual impact of the position.

Additionally in this chapter alternative methods of displaying this information – the Boston Consulting Group Matrix and the Directional Policy Matrix will be examined. These approaches rose to importance in the 1970s and although they are now subject to considerable criticism they are still regarded by many as tools which can provide valuable insights into strategic performance and potential.

Developing strategies

In many respects this could be regarded as the most creative part of strategic management. Here, assuming that a total profile of the organization's current strategic position – which includes an assessment of the environment and an appraisal of the organization's strengths and weaknesses – has been developed then a future strategy is formulated.

Prior to developing the actual strategy to be pursued, it is suggested that it may be appropriate for organizations to carry out a 'gap analysis'. A gap analysis aims to show the gap or discrepancy that would develop between the goals that have been set for an organization and the performance that would actually be achieved if the organization continued to follow its existing strategies: the larger the gap that is forecast to occur the greater will be the need for a change in strategic direction.

Although in any particular situation there is an infinite variety of strategies that could be developed, a two stage methodology which contains a limited number of strategies will be developed in Part Five.

The first stage is to decide upon a fundamental strategy for the organization. This decision will be determined by the goals of top management in the organization, the organization's current strategic position, the environmental prospects and the gap in goal achievement that is forecast should current strategies continue to be followed. In this model of strategic management it is assumed that there are just five fundamental strategies:

- **Conservative growth**
- **High growth**
- **Neutral**
- **Recovery**
- **Reduction**

In Part Five these fundamental strategies are further refined into more precise sub-strategies.

The second stage in the process is to develop, following Porter[9], an appropriate generic strategy. Porter suggests that there are just three generic strategies which will enable an organization to gain competitive advantage. These are:

High volume/low cost

Here the strategy is to gain competitive advantage through having lower costs and higher volumes than competitors. Organizations that have successfully adopted this approach include Black and Decker power tools and Toyota motor cars.

Differentiation

Here the strategy is to gain competitive advantage through differentiating the product from lower priced ones on the basis of some non-price factor such as quality. For example BMW has very successfully differentiated its cars from others on the basis of quality and performance.

Focus

This occurs where a producer concentrates on serving just one very narrow customer group or market segment and does not attempt to serve any others. Here the strategy is to offer a product which is so tailored to a very small market segment that the producer gains a competitive advantage either through volume advantages or through the willingness of purchasers to pay a premium price for a strongly differentiated product. A focused strategy can be either on the bases of 'high volume/low cost' or 'product differentiation.'

For example the Japanese sewing machine manufacturer Janome, through encouraging its parts suppliers to focus on producing just one, two or three items, (i.e. they were persuaded to follow a 'focus on high volume low cost' strategy) was able to defeat the Singer company which was then the world's leading sewing machine manufacturer:

> In anticipation of Singer's re-entry into Japan after World War II, Janome and three other leading sewing machine firms organized about 200 independent parts manufacturers and about 230 independent parts subcontractors to benefit from standardized parts specification. By having each parts manufacturer and subcontractor specialize in one-, two- or three-part items, each was able to reap the benefits of a manufacturing economy of scale, In around 1948 when Singer was trying to re-enter Japan, a typical Japanese part manufacturer was producing over 500,000 units of the same part per month, while Singer's largest production run of a single part item at that time was estimated to be at best around 40,000 units per month.[10]

By way of contrast a 'focus on product differentiation' strategy (where the emphasis is on serving very well a narrow market segment at a premium price) is the type of strategy that is employed by those record shops which have comprehensive collections of very narrow ranges of esoteric music. These types of shops can charge a premium price for their products as unfocused rivals will not be able to provide such an extensive range and will not have deep knowledge of the music.

Marketing and strategic management

The increased climate of competitiveness which, in general, has prevailed in the Western world since the early 1980s has caused many organizations to realize the importance of developing a heightened awareness of marketing in their strategic and operational management. For many organizations from all sectors of society – profit seeking, non-profit seeking, government institutions, educational institutions, the professions and charities – marketing has come to be recognized as a fundamental strategic lever which can be used to magnify their efforts and gain significant competitive advantage.

For example, in the UK the recent outstanding performance of the Burton Group of retail shops can be dated from the decision to have, as the kernel of their strategy, responsiveness to the needs of existing and potential customers. The financial effects of the development of this strong marketing orientation can be seen in the company's annual statements, and its physical manifestation in the major changes which have taken place in the layout and decor of Burton's shops and the range of products which they sell.

The marketing process is seen, in this book, as a fundamental complement to the strategic management process and is set out in detail in Part Six. It is portrayed in Figure 1 on a large and irregular block. This shape is intended to reflect first the importance which is accorded to marketing in this book and second the view that marketing influences are not regular but in a constant state of flux. In Part Six after considering the importance of having such an orientation in the industrial sector, the public sector, the non-profit seeking sector, and the professions, a four stage methodology for developing and implementing a marketing orientation in any type of organization is presented. The four stages are:

Market identification

In this stage the organization attempts to identify opportunities in its environment which it may be able to exploit successfully. This will normally involve market research to ascertain existing and potential consumers' needs so that the company can structure its products and services to meet these needs.

Market segmentation

In this stage the organization, having identified possible opportunities, attempts to refine this general information, gathered in the market identification process, into precise information on those specific market segments which appear to offer the best opportunities for the organization's products. Although there are many axes on which markets can be segmented just four major categories – demographic, geographic, social class, and product function – are considered.

Product positioning

When an organization has decided upon the target market segments in which it will sell its products or services, it must then determine how it can best position its products in relation to competitors' products so that it meets customers' needs in ways which are believed by customers to be superior.

Marketing mix strategies

The final stage of the process is to decide upon a range of specific marketing strategies which will enable the organization to position its products in desired locations in its target market segments and so achieve desired strategic/marketing goals. It is suggested that there are four fundamental strategies, known collectively as the marketing mix, which can be used to achieve this. These strategies are:

1 *Product strategy*: This is concerned with developing product features (for example, price, quality, style etc.) which distinguish an organization's product from others offered by competitors.
2 *Place strategy*: This is concerned with how and where the product will be sold and what channels of distribution will be used. (For example for a consumer product will it be sold through wholesalers to retailers, direct to retailers, by mail order etc?)

3 *Price strategy*: This is concerned with developing a pricing strategy
   (for example a relatively high price, a relatively low price, a price
   based on profit targets, a price based upon costs etc.) which will
   achieve marketing and strategic goals.
4 *Promotion strategy*: This final element in the marketing mix is concerned with deciding upon, and then using, the most appropriate
   means by which an organization communicates with, influences,
   and responds to its targeted market segments. (For example should a
   product be promoted by means of salespeople, television advertising, newspaper advertising, etc.)

The chapter concludes by considering those broader influences which
in general affect the behaviour of buyers, both consumer and industrial.
   Finally, the importance of integrating a marketing orientation into
the strategic management process has been succinctly expressed by
Alan Zakon of the Boston Consulting Group.[11]

The rules of strategy

Scripto is introducing disposable lighters in packages of four for $1.
Wilkinson is spending $23 million to support its Retractor razor.
P & G has spent $530 million to go upscale with new Pampers. The
$4,000 Yugo has a four-month waiting list, and Chrysler is planning its
Maserati product.

This is what competitive strategy is all about – targeting consumer
needs and outflanking entrenched competitors. Strategy is also backing
new leadership with advertising, R & D, distribution, and manufacturing to build advantage that will be sustainable well after the initial
success . . .

The rules of strategy: Summary

The essence of strategy is to create segments with sustainable competitive advantage. A segment is simply a group of consumers who prefer
your price/quality/feature package to other combinations, and a group
of competitors that themselves offer the marketplace a different mix.
Targeting a segment is as much choosing competitors as choosing customers.

And while there is no cookbook recipe to get there, the simple rules of

- Go around
- Create new value
- Plan for advantage

are a solid rewarding start.

Strategy implementation

In many businesses it is the case that the words of a strategy are more the reality than the actual activities. Part Seven will be concerned with developing an approach that should ensure that the implementation of a strategy is accorded an importance equivalent to its formulation.

Implementation of strategy is regarded as a crucial element in the strategic management process and considerable effort will be focused on developing a methodology that should ensure that the sentiments of a strategy are translated into business realities. For example, if the fundamental strategy of a business is 'to have real sales growth of 10 per cent per annum for the next three years' then the implementation of this strategy will involve actions to ensure that:

- The leaders of the organization are seen to be in agreement with this strategy and are capable of achieving the specified targets.
- There are adequate resources provided for each of the functional areas (which will have the task of achieving the results) to make the achievement of a 10 per cent growth target feasible.
- The structure of the organization is capable of supporting this increase in growth.

The methodology used will break the implementation process into the the following related elements.

1 *Leadership and implementation*: How appropriate for implementing the new strategy is the current leadership? More specifically, does it have the power, influence, and knowledge to ensure successful implementation?
2 *Culture and implementation*: Is the culture that prevails in the organization capable of implementing the strategy?
3 *Structure and implementation*: Does the current structure of the organization match the goals and strategies which are to be implemented?
4 *Implementation of functional policies*: Have overall organization strategies been translated into effective and feasible functional policies, targets and precisely delineated programmes and operations.
5 *Corporate and functional resources*: Are there sufficient resources at the corporate levels to ensure that strategies can be translated into actions?
6 *Information systems and procedures*: Are the organization's information systems sufficient to ensure that the strategy can be implemented, monitored, and amended if necessary.

In summary this section of the model is concerned with ensuring that verbal or written strategic aspirations which are often formulated by those at the apex of the organizational hierarchy, and which are frequently couched in broad financial or marketing terms, are transformed into effective material and measurable programmes for action at all levels throughout the organization.

Evaluation and control

This is the final element in the model and is concerned with monitoring how effectively the strategy which has been formulated has been implemented and triggering appropriate actions if the organization is failing to meet the goals which were set at the strategy development stage.

Part Eight will present a framework for monitoring how successful a chosen strategy has been and for making adjustments when deviations from the chosen strategy are found.

The methodology involves a consideration of:

- The behavioural aspects of the need to monitor.
- Mechanisms for ensuring objectivity, speed and accuracy in feedback.
- Criteria for the assessment of the success of operations.
- Mechanisms to ensure action on deviations from strategy targets.

This element is really a feedback and correction loop and provides information on the effectiveness of strategies being pursued.

Summary of the model

Thus, this model of strategic management attempts to provide a comprehensive integrated methodology for:

- Analysing the strategic position of an organization.
- Formulating future strategies.
- Implementing, monitoring and evaluating those chosen strategies.

As Figure 1 shows, the model is a closed loop and strategic management should therefore be regarded, not as an activity which takes place at certain specified times in the business calendar, but rather as a continuous process which is iterative and self-correcting and which is a fundamental part of the total management process.

References

1   Crisp, J., 'The Misplaced Ambition That Lured Nexos to Enlargement and Extinction', *Financial Times*, 17 July 1985, p. 9.
2   Snoddy, R., 'Blunder gave IBM a World Lead in Factory Automation Sales', *Financial Times*, 16 July 1985, p. 16.

3   Marsh, D., 'Japan Boosts Share of EEC Manufactured Goods', *Financial Times*, 6 December 1984, p. 5.
4   ICI Annual Reports.
5   Department of Commerce Bureau of the Census, Statistical Abstract of the United States, 1982–83, US Government Publishing Office, Washington DC, 1983.
6   Rendeiro, J. O., 'How the Japanese Came to Dominate the Machine Tool Business', *Long Range Planning*, Vol. 18, No. 3, June 1985, pp. 62–7.
7   Porter, M. E., *The Industrial Competitiveness of Nations: Beyond Comparative Advantage*, address to Irish Management Institute, Dublin, June 1986.
8   Hosmer, L. T., 'The Importance of Strategic Leadership', *Journal of Business Strategy*, Vol. 2, No. 2, Fall 1982, pp. 47–57.
9   Porter, M. E., *Competitive Strategy: Techniques for Analyzing Industries and Competitors*, Collier Macmillan, 1980.
10 Tsurumi, Y., *The Japanese are Coming*, Ballinger, Cambridge, Mass., 1976.
11 Zakon, A, The Rules of Strategy, The Boston Consulting Group, Perspectives series, No. 282, 1986.

2 Selected concepts in strategic management

This chapter examines concepts which are of core importance in strategic management: organizational structure, the product life cycle, strategic decision making versus functional decision making and the implications of strategic decision making for accountants.

Organizational structure

For effective strategic planning the system adopted must be matched to the structure and needs of the organization in which it is being employed. This means that an effective strategic planning system can range from the unwritten verbal plans of an entrepreneur to the large and detailed planning volumes of a multinational corporation. Neither of these systems is naturally superior; the important thing is that each system should be appropriate to its organization.

Although the selection of a planning system should not just be the mechanical matching of a system to an organization, there are, nonetheless, fundamental differences in planning systems which are a direct function of the structure of the organization. The section below introduces alternative forms of organization structure and relates each structure to an appropriate planning system.

Simple or small business structure

This is the most basic type of organizational structure and is shown in Figure 3. In this type of structure there is an owner or a manager who has a small number of employees who produce a limited range of products for a limited range of market segments. This structure is also known as 'entrepreneurial' as it is normally the type employed at the start-up phase of a business.

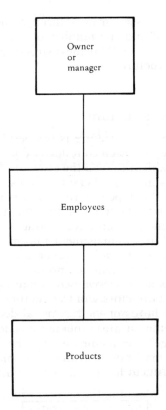

Figure 3 *Simple or small business structure*

In this type of structure strategic management tends to be informal and takes place at two levels – the business level and the operational level. The terms 'operational level' and 'functional level' are, in the context of this section, used synonymously. (See the section below on the functional business structure.)

At the business level the owner or manager devises strategies for the business.

At the operational level the employees, under the owner or manager's supervision, implement these strategies.

In this type of structure it is normally the case that the products, markets and the set of competitors are fairly fixed and the principal concern of strategic planning is competing effectively against rivals in existing, or extensions of existing, product lines. Thus the business is 'given' and the *major strategic issue is how to succeed in that given business*. An example of this type of business would be a local bakery where the range of products is limited, the customers are from the locality and the set and nature of competitors is fairly static.

This structure is really only effective for the smallest type of business and, normally, as businesses grow – through increasing the range of products manufactured and the number of personnel – specialization becomes possible and the small business structure tends to evolve into a functional business structure.

Functional business structure

As a business develops the structure is frequently changed in order to enable it to handle the increased complexity due to the increasing range of activities and to enable it to reap the economic benefits that additional staff bring. Figure 4 gives a schematic representation of a functional business structure. In this type of structure personnel are grouped into departments according to the function that the department carries out. Traditionally these functions are: accounting and finance; marketing; production; personnel and management information systems. Each of these departments has an overall manager who, as well as having the tasks of managing the department and promoting coordination between departments, also acts as a two-way coordinating link to the board of directors. The board of directors will frequently comprise the owners of the company plus the heads of the functional departments.

In this type of structure strategic planning is devised by the board of directors and is, largely, implemented by the functional managers. Therefore, as in the small business structure, planning takes place at two levels – at the business level and at the functional level.

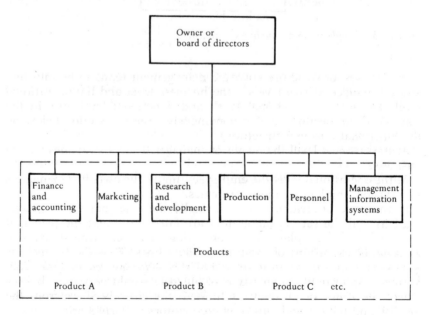

Figure 4 *Functional business structure*

At the business level, as is the case for the small business structure, it is assumed that the business area is given – i.e. the products, markets and set of competitors are already in existence and *the major task of the strategic planner at this level is to plan how the business can succeed against competitors who are in the same or similar businesses*. In most cases the company will have a range of products and a range of markets and strategic planners will, therefore, have discretion about altering the balance of the *portfolio of products* manufactured and also the range of markets in which the company competes, in order to achieve strategic goals.

Thus, for example, in the UK biscuit industry there are, as shown in Table 3, four dominant manufacturers of biscuits.

Table 3 Market shares in the UK of the major UK biscuit manufacturers[1]

Company	Market share (%)
United Biscuits	40
Huntley & Palmer	20
Nabisco	5
Burtons	11

In the biscuit divisions of these companies, it is assumed that the 'business' is given (i.e. the business is biscuits) and therefore in this context strategic decision making is concerned with competitors striving to gain competitive advantage through altering the range of products manufactured – Chocolate biscuit lines, other chocolate biscuits, sweet biscuits, semi-sweet biscuits, plain biscuits, savoury biscuits, crispbreads and others – and altering the marketing strategies supporting these products.

At the functional level the major task is to implement the strategies decided upon by the board of directors. Thus, at this level functional managers have the tasks of ensuring that those guidelines which were devised at the business level are implemented and ensuring that cooperation takes place across functions so that plans are implemented in a balanced fashion right across the organization.

Strategic planning in this type of structure is therefore simply an extension of strategic planning in the small business structure.

The divisional structure

Frequently, as a business grows, the functional structure becomes inadequate for its range of activities or inappropriate to its goals. This can be seen particularly clearly when an organization develops discrete ranges of products which are not directly related to each other. For example a motor vehicle manufacturer may have three discrete ranges of vehicles – specialist sports cars, volume cars and commercial vehi-

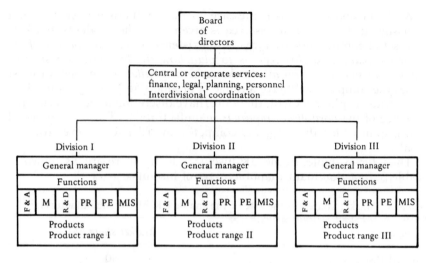

Figure 5   *Divisional business structure*

cles. Although the ranges are related there are clear distinctions between the nature of the products in each range, the market segments at which each range is aimed and the nature of the competition each range faces. Because of these differences in products, markets and competitors, different levels of resources, different skills and different business performance expectations apply to each range.

Frequently it is logical to structure such an organization to reflect these differences. This type of structure is known as a divisional structure and in the above case the divisions could be known as: specialist sports car division; volume car division and commercial vehicle division. A schematic representation of a divisional business structure is shown in Figure 5.

An example of a company which is organized on this basis is the UK automotive supply company AE plc. A diagrammatic representation of this company's structure is shown in Figure 6.[2]

In an organization which has a divisional business structure strategic planning is a conceptually different process from strategic planning in either the small business structure or the functional business structure. In the divisional business structure strategic planning takes place hierarchically at three levels:

- The corporate level
- The business level
- The functional level

The planning process for the business and the functional levels are as previously described. However, at the corporate level, strategic planning is concerned with the issue of deciding '*In what businesses should*

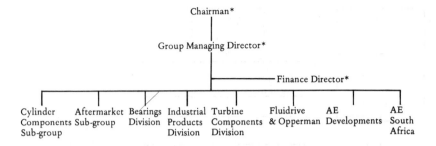

Chairman*

Group Managing Director*

Finance Director*

| Cylinder Components Sub-group | Aftermarket Sub-group | Bearings Division | Industrial Products Division | Turbine Components Division | Fluidrive & Opperman | AE Developments | AE South Africa |

* These and the present Managing Directors of the Cylinder Components and Aftermarket Sub-groups are executive directors

Figure 6 *AE plc: Group structure*

the organization be engaged?' This type of strategic planning is thus conceptually different from strategic planning for the small business structure and the functional business structure where the set of businesses is given and the issue is *how* to compete in the given businesses rather than the issue of what is the optimal *portfolio of businesses* which the organization as a whole should have. Although the definition of just what constitutes optimality will vary from organization to organization, in general this level of strategic planning will be concerned with developing a balanced portfolio of businesses either through expansion of existing businesses, acquisition of new businesses, or the disposal of businesses. The question of what constitutes a balanced portfolio will be discussed in the section 'the concept of the SBU' on page 32.

In a divisional business structure it is normally the case that the various divisions are managed, as largely independent businesses by division managers, within certain corporate parameters and with support from corporate services as required. The board of directors in this type of structure will frequently comprise of the owners of the business, top corporate managers and the managers of the divisions.

Matrix structure

In organizations where there are two (or more) dominant criteria for success it is important that these criteria are reflected in the organizational and power structures of the organization. For example, it may be the case that for a multinational food company to succeed it must have both effective product management and also be sensitive to the preferences of the various markets in which it sells. In other words the company will not succeed if, first, it does not manufacture effectively and, second, if it is not sensitive to local preferences. In such situations matrix structures have been developed.

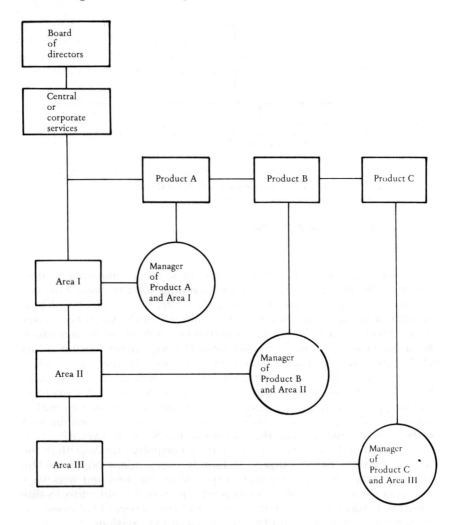

Figure 7   *Matrix structure*

A schematic representation of a matrix structure is shown in Figure 7. This example illustrates the structure for a multinational organization which manufactures three sets of product ranges – Product A, Product B and Product C – and sells the products in three areas – Area I, Area II and Area III. Effective product management and sensitivity to each area market are considered crucial to this organization. Therefore, the organization is structured in a two-dimensional matrix form with the axes of the matrix being 'product' and 'area'.

Along the 'product' axis there are three overall product managers – one for each product – while along the 'area' axis there are three area managers – one for each area. The product managers and the area managers are of equal status and power in the organization and each pair of product and area managers (for example Product A manager and Area I manager) reports to an overall product and area manager who has responsibility for both aspects of the business. Thus the structure explicitly recognizes the importance of both effective production and sensitivity to local tastes.

In this type of structure, as in the divisional structure, strategic planning takes place at three levels:

1 *The corporate*: Concerned with the portfolio of businesses and carried out by board of directors and corporate staff.
2 *The business*: Concerned with the portfolio of products and markets and carried out by the product and area managers.
3 *The functional*: Concerned with implementation and carried out by functional managers.

In the matrix structure there are two or more command systems which, in theory, have equal weight. For example, in the above food company example shown in Figure 7 there would be an equally strong command and information link from the manager of Product A and Area I and the Area I manager and the Product A manager. In practice, however, it is normally the case that one of the dimensions of the matrix becomes more important.

Holding company structure

Figure 8 shows schematically a holding company structure. This structure is similar in many ways to the divisional structure. The fundamental difference is the degree of independence exercised by the constituent companies. In this type of structure the holding company is really just a collection of separate companies which are held together by a financial control system. The management and strategic decision making of the constituent companies is carried out with minimal corporate interference or influence – the relationship between the constituent companies and the corporate headquarters is mainly financial and also there tends to be minimal coordination among the various businesses in the company.

In this type of structure strategic planning tends to be a lesser feature of the total organization than in other structures as the main corporate concern is financial management. However, it could be argued that strategic planning takes place at three levels in this structure:

1 *Corporate*: Mainly financial decisions, carried out by corporate staff.
2 *Business*: As before, carried out by the top management within each separate business.

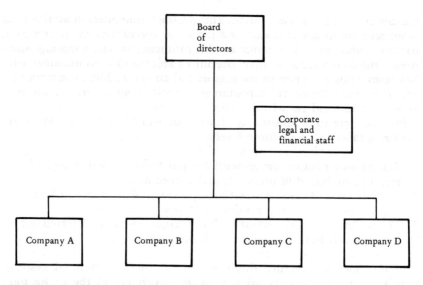

Figure 8   *Holding company structure*

3 *Functional*: As before, carried out by the functional managers in
  each separate business.

Although it has been argued that the holding company structure grew
out of the divisional structure – i.e. as a divisional company developed
there also developed increasing independence between the divisions
which led ultimately to the much looser holding company structure,
Channon has asserted that this is not the case in the UK.[3]

> In 1950 when most companies were only diversified to a limited degree
> their system of management was largely functional. As diversification
> occurred, so many of these functional structures gave way to holding com-
> pany organizations where acquired subsidiaries were left to run largely
> autonomously with little or no central coordination. During the 1960s and
> early 1970s first in manufacturing companies and later in service businesses
> these holding company structures gave way to divisional forms of organisa-
> tions.

The concept of the SBU

In large divisionalized or matrix organizations it can be the case that
the sheer number of separate activities or divisions is such that it can
be extremely difficult for strategic planners to have a meaningful concept of the overall strategic profile and posture of the organization. A
corollary of this problem is that, in such cases, it is impossible to
develop effective corporate plans for the future. These corporate plan-

ning problems may arise first because of the difficulties in analysing, assimilating and conceptualizing such a large quantity of diverse information and second because of the problems of coordinating and integrating such a range of diversity into a coherent corporate strategy. These problems are frequently manifested in the failure of corporate staff to provide appropriate resources for those businesses which are likely to grow and in withdrawing resources from those businesses which are likely to be unsuccessful. In other words there is a failure to develop a balanced portfolio of businesses which yield satisfactory results for the organization's stakeholders.

Although the balance of a portfolio can be assessed along many dimensions, the more frequent measures used are:

Growth

Has the organization a portfolio of businesses which are at different stages of growth*, i.e. are there:

- Businesses at the development stage which are likely to be net absorbers of cash today but may be cash contributors in perhaps three years time?
- Businesses at the growth stage which are currently cash neutral but which should be net cash generators in the immediate future?
- Businesses at the mature stage which are likely to be net generators of cash for some time to come.
- Businesses at the senile stage which are currently absorbers of cash and likely to remain so as long as they are supported?

Risk

Is the spread of businesses such that there are offsetting risk influences which minimize the overall risk of the portfolio? The principal dimensions of risk being economic, marketing, financial, geographical and political.

Cash flow and profitability

Is the combined flow of funds from the businesses in the portfolio in balance and are the stakeholders in the organization satisfied with their returns?

To help resolve the difficulty of coping with the problems of size and diversity and achieving overall balance in such organizations the concept of the Strategic Business Unit or SBU was developed. The concept of the SBU was orginally developed by General Electric (GE) of America. In the 1960s GE found that in spite of substantial growth in sales, its

* The stages of growth of a product or a business are discussed in the section 'The product life cycle' on page 42.

profits were not increasing correspondingly. GE's top management, after investigating the problem, recognized that one of the major causes of the inadequate profits was the the lack of balance in its portfolio of businesses. Accordingly, therefore in 1971, it restructured its 170 or so departments into just fifty Strategic Business Units. Since then the concept has been widely used in many large companies.

An SBU is a natural 'grouping' of part of a corporation. It is natural in the sense that, normally, it has the following characteristics.

- An SBU is managed by an SBU manager, largely, as an independent unit. The SBU manager also acts as a link between the SBU and the board of directors.
- The SBU has its own set of goals and strategies.
- The SBU's goals and strategies are within broad parameters and are largely set by the corporate or holding board of directors (or corporate planners).
- The SBU has a range of related products that share similar technologies or production processes.
- The products are sold in similar or related market segments.
- The products are sold against a well-defined set of competitors.
- The SBUs in any given organization are, as far as practicable, similar in size.
- Each SBU in a particular organization should be able to operate independently of any other SBU.

Additionally the SBU serves as an intermediate device for effectively linking corporate management with SBU (i.e. divisional), functional or product managers. Thus it enables *corporate management* to apply an overall corporate perspective and resolve such *corporate issues* as:

- What are the overall goals of this organization and are they being fulfilled?
- Are the organization's stakeholders being satisfied?
- In what businesses is the organization operating?
- Why is the organization in these businesses?
- What businesses ought the organization to be in, in five years time?
- Is the organization's portfolio of businesses balanced?

and then set guidelines within which SBU managers must operate.

Thus the corporate planners do not take part in the day-to-day management of an SBU, but are rather concerned with seeing how the individual SBUs, when taken together, constitute a corporation which fits together to form a balanced portfolio of businesses. Frequently the main device they use to help ensure that SBUs comply with corporate guidelines is corporate cash.

Thus SBU managers are able to concentrate on strategies at the business level which will enable their particular business unit to succeed against competitors, success being measured by the parameters

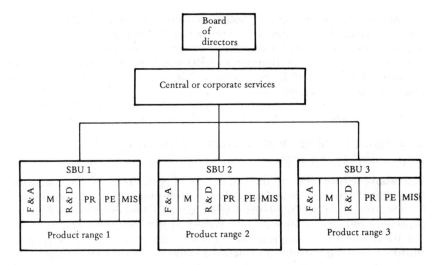

Figure 9 *An SBU organization structure*

given by the corporate planners. Consequently SBU managers will often have discretion over all the functions necessary to operate a full business and are thus much more than just managers of manufacturing units: they are strategic decision makers operating within broad corporate guidelines. Figure 9 gives a schematic representation of an organization structured on an SBU basis.

In summary the SBU type of organizational structure helps overcome some of the problems associated with size and diversity by breaking strategic planning into three levels.

1 *Level I – the corporate level:* At this level the fundamental task is to develop a balanced portfolio of businesses which will achieve the goals of the corporation and satisfy its stakeholders.
2 *Level II – the SBU level:* At this level the business, or set of activities is given, and the major task for the strategic planner at this level is for the business to succeed against competitors and also satisfy corporate success criteria.
3 *Level III – the functional level:* This is as described on page 26 for the functional business structure.

SBUs could therefore be said to provide the best of both worlds in a structural sense. On the one hand through interaction with corporate strategists the SBU managers are aware of overall organization goals and strategies while on the other hand because they have almost complete control of their unit they are free to pursue those strategies which they believe are optimal for their unit without the frustration of having to deal with (sometimes uninformed) corporate interference.

It should be noted that although the concept of the SBU and the concept of the division are very similar and are treated similarly in a strategic planning context they are not necessarily identical concepts. Thus it may be the case that an SBU may include more than one division. However, for the purposes of this book they will be treated as interchangeable concepts.

Strategic planning, organizational structure and responsibility centres

The above exposition of the influence of structure on the strategic management process may be too broad to provide the detail necessary for effective planning, implementation, control, and evaluation. Greater precision and practicality can be added to the structural concepts set out above by considering two other dimensions of structure: the responsibilities for which discrete structural elements within an organization can be held accountable, and the types of activities in which such elements engage.

Responsibilities

Recalling that a primary function of any organizational structure is to facilitate the planning, implementation, control, and evaluation of strategies, it follows that for these activities to be effective, precise responsibilities should be unambiguously attached to the managers controlling discrete structural units within an organization, so that precise monitoring of the managers' individual performances, and the performances of the units for which they have responsibility can be achieved. Because of this necessity of evaluating structural elements according to the responsibilities which they have, they are often known as responsibility centres, i.e. they are centres in organizations where responsibility can be seen clearly to reside. Because of variation in the degree of responsibility which centres can have, it can be useful to define them on a scale of responsibility.

Thus, when a centre has responsibility for all its decisions and activities concerned with fixed assets, current assets, revenues and costs then such a centre is defined as an *investment centre*. Consequently the performance of such a centre should be evaluated in terms of all the above activities.

When a centre has responsibility for all its decisions and activities concerning revenues and costs then such a centre is defined as a *profit centre*. Evaluation of the performance of such a centre should be made on the basis of just revenue and cost achievements.

In passing it should be noted that although the terms profit centre and investment centre are, by the above definitions, different, in practice the terms are often used interchangeably.

Finally, when a centre has responsibility only for the costs associated with its operations, it can be defined as a *cost centre*. Such a centre should be judged only on its cost control performance.

Activities

Responsibility centres can be established for a wide range of activities which can vary from the broad and comprehensive for example, the total set of planning, implementing, controlling, and evaluating activities for an investment centre or an SBU; to the narrow for example, the control of costs by a purchasing cost centre. There are no exact guidelines for deciding when it is optimal to have a centre set up in the form of an investment centre, profit centre or cost centre. The choice should be influenced by the nature and scope of the activities undertaken by the centre and the objectives which the centre is required to achieve. Figure 10 attempts to show the most commonly found types of responsibility centres. In Figure 10 those centres which are labelled profit centres could be either investment centres or profit centres: the broader label has been used to indicate that the exact level of responsibility depends upon the organization in which the centre is located. Each type of centre is briefly discussed below.

Centre defined by business

This type of centre is really the SBU which has been considered previously. It is most commonly found in larger diversified companies which have a variety of products which are serving a variety of markets and have a variety of customers.

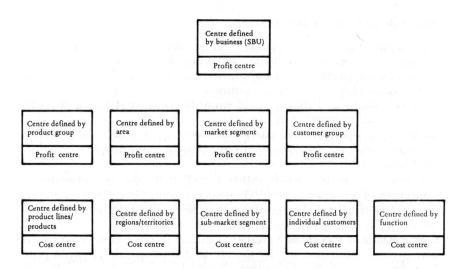

Figure 10 *The most common types of responsibility centres*

In spite of the prevalence of this type of structure today, it may be the case that using such a broadly defined centre does not provide sufficient detail for effective strategic and operational planning, and it is not uncommon to find more narrowly defined centres of the type considered below.

Centre defined by product group

When an organization has clearly defined product groups it may be strategically beneficial to structure its centres around them. Such centres may be profit or cost centres. At a further level of refinement centres based on product groupings may be sub-divided into cost centres based on product lines or individual products. Such refinement enables close attention to be paid to the development of detailed strategies for specific products and the detailed evaluation of their performance.

Centre defined by area

When an organization operates in a number of discrete geographical areas the planning and operations in each area may be facilitated by structuring its centres on this basis. For example, in many multinational corporations each country is defined as a profit centre and the planning and operations in each country are carried out relatively autonomously by country-based managers. Further insight into geographical performance can be achieved by establishing cost centres based upon sub-regional groups. For example a country may be designated a profit centre with the regions North, South, East, and West designated cost centres.

Centre defined by market segment

Organizations which serve distinct market segments may find that they can do so most effectively if they structure themselves around important market segments. For example an organization which served the following market segments: government, industrial, professional, and consumer might find that it could enhance its understanding of these segments and monitor their contributions most effectively if it structured its profit centres around them. Once again, additional insights could be acquired through sub-dividing such segments into smaller units and establishing cost centres based on these smaller units. For example, in the above case, the costs of serving the different professions – accountancy, medicine, architecture, and law, could be closely monitored by establishing cost centres based upon each profession.

Centre defined by customer group

This type of centre in some ways overlaps with the market segment centre above but is distinguished from it on the basis that customer group is defined by the sizes of customers' orders. Thus organizations having customers that could be divided into groups such as 'those who place large orders' and 'those who place small orders' may find that their most appropriate profit centres are based on these categories. As with the other axes of centre definition, additional insights may be gained by establishing cost centres based upon individual customers.

Centre defined by function

Centres which are defined by function – i.e. finance, marketing, production, personnel, management information systems, – are cost centres which enable planners to have insights into how the costs of each functional area are behaving.

Conclusions on responsibility centres

Responsibility centres are the structural foundation stones of organizations. Centres which are appropriately designed in terms of:

- Their responsibilities
- Their activities
- Their suitability in relating the organization to its markets

can provide strategic planners with two-way channels through which plans can be communicated and implemented throughout the organization and results can be fed back and evaluated.

The product life cycle and its role in strategic management

In spite of having been the subject of considerable criticism for many years (see Wasson[4] and Wells[5]) the product life cycle is still widely regarded as a fundamental tool of marketing and strategic management. In its simplest form this concept maintains that all products, in their commercial lives, go through a series of stages which collectively comprise 'the product life cycle' and the stage at which a product is at in its life cycle has major strategic and functional implications. The product life cycle theory asserts that the 'life' of a product can be divided into four distinct stages: development, growth, maturity* and decline. The stages are shown in Figure 11 and are discussed in greater detail below. In the description below it is assumed that there exists a 'model product' which fits a 'model product life cycle'. In practice, however, as will be shown in the section 'Limitations of the product life cycle', this will not normally be the case: products vary enormously in the shapes and durations of their life cycles. In spite of this

---

* There are those who suggest that the product life cycle has five stages – introduction, growth, maturity, saturation and decline.[6] Here, however, maturity and saturation have been combined to comprise the single stage maturity.

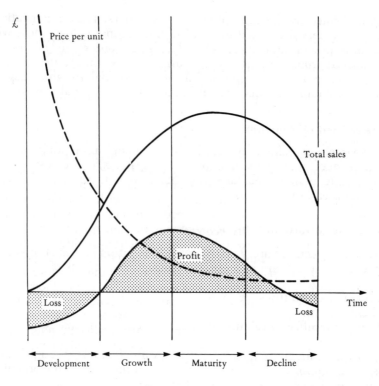

Figure 11   *The product life cycle*

caveat, the product life cycle remains a useful device for understanding market developments and relating these developments to strategic and functional policies and targets.

Development stage

This is the stage when a new product is introduced to the market. Typically, at this time, there will be a single pioneering organization or a small number of pioneers, prices of the product will tend to be high and sales volume will be low. The introduction of the product will tend to be regarded as 'risky', the riskiness stemming from two main sources.

Uncertainty about consumption
As the product is new there is no certainty that consumers will purchase it in the required volumes and at the required price. This fate befell the Sinclair C5 electric car. When this product was introduced into the UK market in early 1985 it was predicted by the manufacturer that in its first year production would be at a rate of 1000 vehicles per week. However, in July 1985, the production rate was just 100 vehicles per week. Shortly afterwards production ceased completely.

Uncertainty about fundamental strategies
The novelty of the product may mean that the competitive rules for success in the industry have not been established and consequently the fundamentals of potentially winning strategies have not yet emerged. (At this stage it is not yet apparent which of the fundamental and generic strategies are likely to be winners, nor, at a lower level of strategy, have the optimal methods of promotion, distribution etc. emerged.) Thus the competitive strategies employed by the manufacturers of personal computers changed dramatically between the introduction of these products in the early 1980s and the mid 1980s. Initially personal computers were a simple toy with limited memory and very limited capabilities without a wide range of proven software. Their appeal was primarily to children and to people with a technical interest or disposition. As the product developed – through improved and more powerful hardware and the development of high quality proven software – and the market grew, it began to segment into different sectors – among the more important of which were: the games sector, the education sector and the business sector. Consequently manufacturers began to manufacture, promote, price and distribute their products to give them specific sectoral appeal. For example the Acorn Model B was targeted strongly at the education sector, the Apple IIe was targeted at the business sector and the Sinclair Spectrum was targeted at the games sector. In the main, those brands which failed to have some competitive advantage in a specific sector tended to experience the greatest problems.

As well as being risky, the development stage tends to require relatively heavy investment for the following reasons.

1 The market must be developed, i.e., as the product is new there may be consumer resistance to it which must be overcome. This is normally achieved through investment in market promotion and the setting up of channels of distribution.
2 Production facilities must be constructed.
3 Personnel must be recruited and trained.

Generally, at the development stage, competitors tend to have two fundamental pricing strategies available – a skimming price strategy or a penetration price strategy.

A skimming price strategy
Here the objective is to maximize the returns to the organization as quickly as possible through setting a high price for the product. Such a pricing strategy makes the product appealing to the purchaser who is willing to pay a premium price for a novel or original product. The major benefit of this type of strategy is that super profits may be earned and the return on the investment will be maximized extremely quickly. However, such a strategy has the drawback that it will make participation in the industry a very attractive proposition to potential new

entrants, i.e. companies who are not manufacturing the product will be tempted to do so by the lure of the large profits that are being seen to be earned by the 'price skimmer(s)'. This aspect of pricing is considered in greater detail in Part Six.

A penetration pricing strategy
A company following this strategy sets the price of its product at a fixed percentage above its cost and then continues to reduce the price at the same rate as costs decline. Strictly speaking it is normally the case that the initial price is set below the initial cost and price is reduced only after break-even has been exceeded. The philosophy behind such a strategy is that market demand for the product will be strongly stimulated because of the relatively low price and also new entrants will be discouraged because the profits being earned are modest and the investments required by new entrants in order to be effective competitors are substantial. This type of pricing strategy is considered in greater detail in Part Six.

Growth stage

At this stage the product has been accepted by the market and a very rapid increase in market size is likely. Typically, new companies (imitators who have perceived the success of the pioneers) enter the, more and more certain, market with similar products. Complementing the accelerating increase in sales there is a rapid decrease in price levels – this is caused by two major factors:

1   In order to gain market share the increased number of firms engage in price competition.
2   Because of the increases in the volume of production that successful firms are enjoying, cost reductions, effected through economies of scale and experience effects, occur. (See page 205 for further information on economies of scale and experience effects.)

Additionally at this stage, in order to serve the rapidly expanding market, promotion and distribution require increased resources. Finally, it is in this stage that profits tend to reach a peak.

Maturity stage

At this stage, although sales may be continuing to increase, they are increasing at a slower rate while prices and profits are declining. The weight and resources given to promotion also tends to decline as consumers frequently, by this stage, have adopted particular brands and tend not to switch.

The number of competitors may decline as some companies leave the industry for brighter prospects elsewhere or alternatively takeovers or mergers may occur.

As the maturity stage continues and growth continues to decline consumer saturation develops and this further increases the downward pressures on prices as the competition among the remaining competitors intensifies in their efforts to maintain viable market shares. This competitive pressure is further exacerbated by those competitors who wish to increase their share of the market – as there is no growth in the market the only source of growth is to take market share from existing competitors.

An industry which appears to have entered this phase is the Western European car industry. In Western Europe market sales are fairly static and it is estimated (see Bhaskar[7]) that in 1984 there was an annual excess productive capacity, among European producers, of 2.3 million units or approximately 20 per cent. These circumstances have led to intense competition among producers and the development of many multicompany and cross-border production alliances.

Decline stage

At this stage saturation of the market has occurred and absolute sales of the product decline. (On occasions demand for the product will even disappear completely as has happened with the demand for hand-held LED calculators and LED digital watches.) Because of the ensuing overcapacity in the industry there is strong competitive warfare which is manifested in severe promotion battles (using price competition and advertising), declining profits and withdrawal from the industry by the less successful competitors. This phase is also frequently described as the shakeout phase and is characterized by an increasing concentration of competitors as they form alliances in the hope of remaining viable.

A good example of an industry which appears to have entered this phase is the European domestic appliance industry.

> The 300-odd European companies fighting for increased shares of a stagnant market are already in the throes of a shakeout. On present trends, after the process of absorption and extermination now under way, there will be four to five major international companies left in Europe with perhaps the same number of 'niche' producers in each country producing for local or specialist needs. Those with the nerve to bet on the outcome suggest that the international survivors – despite many difficulties, not all of which are connected with appliances – will be Electrolux-Zanussi, representing Italy, Philips-Bauknecht in a Dutch-West German combine, Thomson-Brandt of France and the Bosch-Siemens joint production company with AEG-Telefunken representing West Germany ...

> ... Most industry leaders suggest that Europe will follow the US where the number of washing machine makers has fallen from 60 to five in the past twenty-five years.[8]

These are the major stages of the product life cycle and a summary of the basic strategic and functional implications of the product life cycle is given in Table 4.

Table 4 The basic strategic and functional implications of the product life cycle

Stage in life cycle		Development	Growth	Maturity	Decline
Basic strategy:		Invest	Invest	Hold	Divest
Finance	Liquidity	Low	Improving	Improving	High
	Profitability	Losses	Greatest	Decreasing	Decreasing–losses
	Cash flow	Negative	Improving	Improving	Large–negative
	Leverage	High	High	Decreasing	Low
	Dividends	None	Small–increasing	Increasing	Large–none
Marketing	No. of competitors	Few	Increasing	Decreasing	Fewer
	Market size	Small	Growing	Stable	Declining
	Market share	Small	Growing	Stable	Declining
	Price	High	High	Falling	Low
	Expenses	High	High	Falling	Low
	Research	Intense	Reducing	Minimal	None
Production	Volume	Low	Increasing	Stable	Declining
	Costs	High	Falling	Falling	Stable–low
	Development	Continuing	Slowing	Minimal	None
	Technology	New	New	Established	Obsolete
Personnel	Numbers	Increasing	Increasing	Fewer	Fewer
	skills	Being developed	Developed	Developed	Developed
Risk implication		Very high	Decreasing	Low	Low

Functional implication

Limitations of the product life cycle

Reliance upon the product life cycle as a guide for strategic action must be qualified by the considerable criticisms which the concept has received. Prominent among the criticisms are the following.

The shape of the product life cycle

There is no one universal curve which applies to all products. Thus empirical studies (see Dhalla and Yuspeth[9], Rink and Swan[10] and Levitt[11]) and casual observation have shown that many products simply do not pass through the four stages that it is claimed comprise the product life cycle. For example certain products, frequently 'necessities of life' such as beer, soap and vehicles which have been purchased, in large volumes for decades, or even longer seem to be set permanently in the mature stage of the life cycle and show no signs of ever going into a decline phase. By way of contrast, some products, such as, for example, skateboards seem to just go through two stages – explosive growth and then rapid decline.

The level of aggregation

There is controversy about the level, or levels, of aggregation at which the product life cycle applies. Porter takes the view that the concept can apply at the industry level – i.e. all industries go through these stages. Dhalla and Yuspeth maintain that their research shows that although the concept may have some little validity at the product class level (i.e. it is classes of products that go through these stages – e.g. denim jeans) it has almost no validity at the brand level (i.e. branded products such as Levi jeans or Wrangler jeans do not follow product life cycles.

The product life cycle as a predictive tool

There is no evidence to suggest that the technique has any predictive power. Its chief power seems to be in the analysis of historical situations. Thus, because there is no single curve it is impossible to know exactly what stage a product is at, at any particular time, and therefore it offers little strategic guidance.* For example, if a product, which it is accepted, is in the mature stage, experiences a decline in growth it is impossible to know, at that time, if this is signalling the onslaught of the decline stage or is merely a temporary hiccup in a continuation of the growth stage.

Companies can alter the shape of the life cycles of their products

The product life cycle is not a law. It is a phenomenon which is frequently observed with the benefit of hindsight. Many companies

---

* See: Yelle, L. E., 'Adding Life Cycle to Learning Curves', *Long Range Planning*, Vol. 16, No. 6, December 1983, pp.82–7 and McNamee, P. B., Brief Case, *Long Range Planning*, Vol. 16, No. 6, December 1983, pp. 103–4.

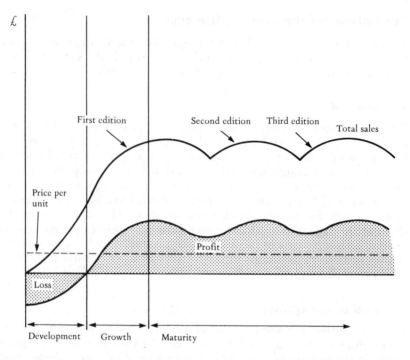

Figure 12   *Extending the maturity stage of a textbook though the introduction of new editions*

have been able to influence the shape of a life cycle through such devices as product innovation and effective advertising and promotion. This type of influence can be seen in the publication of textbooks. It could be considered that standard textbooks have a natural life after which they lose their appeal because they have become somewhat dated in relation to competing works. The maturity stage of textbooks can be, and is, extended through bringing out new editions which contain the latest material and thus extend the life cycle. This is shown diagrammatically in Figure 12.

Conclusions on the product life cycle

The product life cycle, especially when strategic and functional perspectives are applied, can be a useful vehicle for understanding the stages that products are likely to pass through in their lives and the implications that these stages have for performance expectations and resource requirements for each functional area within the company. It also helps strategic planners to see the age relationships that exist in a company's portfolio of products and also to see how their company's products are relating to overall market developments.

However, it must be remembered that there is no single unique curve which fits all products and this lack of rigour or universality makes its predictive powers minimal. A consequence of this is that strategists should be aware of the concept and integrate the information it provides with other sources of information and models, but they should be wary of basing firm strategic decisions on this type of analysis alone. Dhalla and Yuspeth have clearly indicated the dangers of overreliance on the doctrine of the product life cycle.

> The PLC concept has little validity. The sequence of marketing strategies typically recommended for succeeding stages of the cycle is likely to cause trouble. In some respects, the concept has done more harm than good by persuading top executives to neglect existing brands and place undue emphasis on new products.

Strategic decision making versus functional decision making

There is an important distinction to be made between the nature of decision making from a strategic perspective and a functional perspective.

When decisions are made in the context of a functional perspective such decisions will tend to be ones which reflect, and will be sustained by, the cultural context of the functional area. For example, decisions taken by accountants will tend to reflect concern about issues such as prudence, control and evaluation while those taken by marketing personnel will tend to reflect concern with issues such as growth of sales, market share, customer satisfaction, quality, price etc. If left to their own devices, especially in large organizations, each functional area would, increasingly, pursue strategies which would be in the interests of its own function but the sum of these strategies would rarely be the optimal strategy for the organization as a whole.

Ideally, strategic decision making should transcend functional bias and therefore the strategic decision maker should, as shown in Figure 13, be able to:

- Draw upon each functional area.
- Synthesise their contributions.
- See patterns and recognize threats and opportunities that a narrower perspective would not reveal.
- Take decisions which are in the best interests of the total organization rather than just a single function.

It is this wider set of perspectives that gives strategic decision making its currency and such an approach should not only make the organization more effective in terms of achieving its current goals and targets, but it should also (perhaps more importantly) help make it a 'winning' organization in the long run. In other words strategic perspectives should help free the planners from the natural bias engendered by their functional specialization and help them see the opportunities for their organization and the threats against it in a new and more creative light.

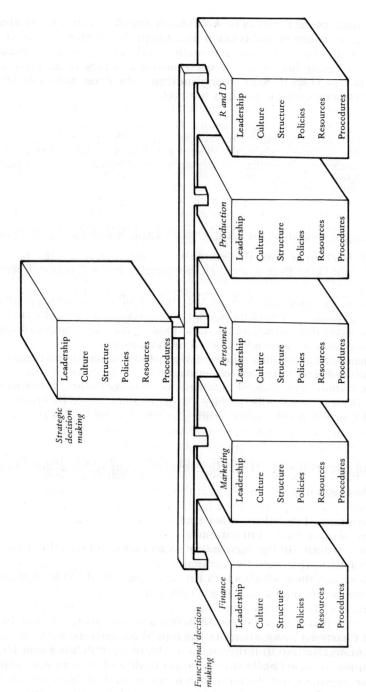

Figure 13 *Strategic decision making versus functional decision making*

The element of creativity is becoming an increasingly important aspect of strategic management as the following quotation shows.

Some companies continually invent new businesses, find new areas of advantage, and create more value than their competitors. Others do not. Since creativity is at least partly a function of intuition, it appears that some organizations, like some individuals, have more 'intuition' than others.

Creative, intuitive people see new patterns in the information to which they are exposed. These new patterns are the cornerstone, and often the major insight of innovation. Not only does creativity require the ability to see the new in the old, it also requires, fundamentally, exposure to all the information that gives rise to the new pattern.

Most organizations evolve naturally toward specialization. An organization of specialized people is more efficient, easier to direct, and easier to control than one in which everybody tries to do everything. Yet, specialization puts information into channels that eliminate the ability to see new patterns, and hence organizational intuition.

The organizational separation of research, marketing, engineering and manufacturing, for example, is a classic – and obvious – block to the ability to generate new products that fill a consumer need, that are priced to sell, and that are engineered for proper manufacturing costs. Each of these functions pursued on its own to optimize its individual priorities will never see the tradeoffs implicit between them. They cannot create something new that optimizes the system, rather than the elements.

Organizational intuition requires integration of organizational elements and is the essence of the creative enterprise.

The essential attributes (of intuition) are short lines of communication, individuals having a broad perspective, communication across functions, and the ability to put together disparate ideas in a new synthesis.[12]

The implications of strategic decision making for accountants

What has been written above about the increasing importance of having informed strategic perspectives for business in general equally applies to accountants. Like all the other professions the accounting profession is today being subjected to a greater variety and intensity of pressures than ever before. By the accounting profession is meant all the people who practise professionally as accountants whether they are in the private sector, the public sector or professional offices. This, in the UK is normally, members of: The Chartered Institute of Management Accountants; The Institute of Chartered Accountants in England and Wales; The Institute of Chartered Accountants of Scotland; The Institute of Chartered Accountants in Ireland; The Chartered Association of Certified Accountants and the Chartered Institute of Public Finance and Accounting. It seems likely that the magnitude and the unpredictability of these pressures will increase in the future and for members of the profession to benefit from (or indeed survive) these changes they must have a width of vision which will enable them to perceive the strategic implications of these pressures. The main causes of the turbulence which the profession has recently experienced can be grouped together under a number of headings.

The impact of the world recession

The world recession, which commenced in 1979, has had a relatively severe impact on the UK economy which has been manifested in record bankruptcies and numbers of people unemployed. The trauma of this experience has led to a general questioning by business of the role and importance of accountants and the sorts of services and information which they should provide. For example 57 per cent of the entrepreneurs questioned in a recent survey (1984) by *Your Business* magazine complained that their accountants had not played a constructive role in their business apart from auditing the annual accounts and only 27 per cent said that their accountants suggested, or helped them implement, business plans.

It seems likely that in the future accountants will be required not just to provide financial information in the traditional form, but, increasingly, they will need to provide financial and other information, tailored to the needs, experience and interests of a much wider set of constituents.

The rise in competitive pressure

Competition within the accounting profession and between the accounting profession and others who are capable of supplying the services accountants provide has been increasing. Thus, within the profession there has been a polarization, in terms of the size, of professional accounting offices. At one end of the spectrum there have been mergers of very large international accounting firms and the consequent creation of huge international 'accounting/management consulting' companies with enormous power and resources. This development has placed great pressure on the medium-sized professional office and has helped lead to the development of small specialist firms seeking competitive advantages in small niches of the profession where they can out-compete the major offices. (See Part Five for further information on niche or focused strategies.) Intensifying this 'internal' competition, in the UK, was the decision in October 1984 to remove the restrictions governing marketing and sponsorship by accountants. This decision has placed a very powerful strategic lever at the disposal of companies and it will result in an increasing level of intensity of competition.

From outside the profession accountants are facing increasing pressure from those who can provide comparable, or even enhanced, services. This, as Professor Bhaskar of the University of East Anglia has pointed out, can be seen easily in terms of the threat posed by practitioners of data processing, management services and computing services.

Although the ICMA has been much concerned with computers and information processing, the accounting profession as a whole has tended to be slow in reacting to the technological revolution. Consequently, a new functional area (data processing/management services/ computing) has arisen in business, taking over a role more traditionally associated with the finance function. Either the accounting profession must react and utilize the new facilities or another group may take over functions formerly associated with the accountant. The management accountant and his orientation on information are particularly vulnerable. This, if nothing else, should provide both the student and the qualified practitioner with the motivation to learn and harness the possibilities created by the information and the technological revolution now under way.[13]

The impact of information technology

Although the impact of information technology has already been referred to above, so profound is its impact likely to be that other aspects of its influence are now considered briefly.

Information technology within the organization

The increase in the scope, potential availability, speed, reliability and cheapness of information within an organization has been a feature of the information technology revolution. Integrated electronic information systems in companies now mean that many types and immense volumes of previously unobtainable information are now readily accessible. An additional feature of the revolution is that previously separated and discrete categories of information can now be merged and appraised. As well as enhancing the control and evaluation capabilities of managers the new patterns of information should help stimulate the creative aspects of management. This wealth of information means that decision makers now can now make decisions on the broader and more informed basis of information obtained from all the functional areas. This type of high quality information system has been found to be a feature of those European companies which are currently successfully competing with (much larger) US and Japanese competitors.

> A typical feature of all the (successful) companies is that they use information technology to speed up reporting of key figures from their subsidiaries and international outposts.
> Market share or market position (i.e. relative to the closest competitor) on the one hand and cash flow, the balance sheet or return on investment on the other are available in some cases at monthly intervals.
> The advance in fingertip control for the chief executive runs parallel with a decentralizing trend, pushing responsibility down the line in the organization.[14]

The influence of new information technology is reflected in this book in the software package Javelin.

Information technology outside the organization

The number of electronic data bases is rapidly increasing and access to them is becoming more open and less expensive. These fertile sources of information about the environment are increasingly important tools for the strategic decision maker.

Conclusions to Part One

Part One has laid the foundations for the later chapters in the book. Thus it has developed a general model of strategic management which can be used to appraise the strategic health and performance of a company. Additionally, selected concepts which are important for understanding the nature of strategic management, were introduced and finally the importance of informed strategic thinking for business in general and the accounting profession in particular was considered briefly.

References

1   McNamee, P. B., *The United Kingdom Biscuit and Savoury Snack Industry: A Case in Competitive Strategy*, forthcoming.
2   McNamee, P. B., *The United Kingdom Automotive Components Industry: A Case In Competitive Strategy*, forthcoming.
3   Channon, D., 'Industrial Structure', *Long Range Planning*, Vol. 15, No. 5, October 1982, pp. 78–94.
4   Wasson, C. R., *Dynamic Competitive Strategy and Product Life Cycles*, St Charles, Ill., Challenge Books, 1974.
5   Wells, L. (Ed.), The Product Life Cycle and International Trade, The Harvard Business School, Division of Research, Boston, Mass., 1972.
6   Day, G. S., 'The Product Life Cycle: Analysis and Applications Issues', *Journal of Marketing*, Vol. 45, Fall 1980, pp. 60–7.
7   Bhaskar, K. N., *Future of World Motor Industry*, Nichols, 1980.
8   Parkes, C., 'Why Just a Few Will Survive', *Financial Times*, 18 July 1985, p. 26.
9   Dhalla, N. D. and Yuspeth, S., 'Forget the Product Life Cycle Concept!' *Harvard Business Review*, January-February 1976, pp. 102–12.
10 Rink, D. R. and Swan, J., 'Product Life Cycle Research: A Literature Review', *Journal of Business Research*, September 1979, pp. 219–42.
11 Levitt, T., 'Exploit the Product Life Cycle', *Harvard Business Review*, November–December 1965, pp. 81–94.
12 Lochridge, R. K., 'Organizational Intuition', *Perspectives*, The Boston Consulting Group, 1985.
13 Bhaskar, K. N. and Housden, R. J. W., *Accounting Information Systems and Data Processing*, Heinemann, 1985.
14 Dullforce, W., 'How Small can be Beautiful in Europe', *Financial Times*, 8 July 1985, p. 8.

Part Two

3 Introduction to analysing the environment

A fundamental assertion made in Part One is that the primary function of strategic management is 'obtaining a good fit with the environment'. Part Two will examine, through the use of selected examples and research findings, the validity of this statement and will also develop a methodology for the effective analysis of the environment faced by any organization.

The importance to planners of being knowledgeable about, and sensitive to, the environment in which their organization is operating is illustrated below in two ways – first through examples of organizations and industries which were dramatically affected by environmental change and second through reference to research studies into how managerial commitment to environmental assessment tends to have affected organizational performance.

Examples of dramatic environment change

The decline and fall of the UK motor cycle industry is well documented. In summary, the UK motor cycle industry changed from being the world's leading producer of motor cycles in the early 1960s to a situation where in the late 1970s there were no major UK producers of motor cycles at all.

The demise of this, once world scale, industry was due to the failure of the industry to mount an effective strategic reaction to a major environmental change. The major environmental change was the emergence of the Japanese motor cycle industry. The Japanese producers planned their motor cycle industry on a world basis – i.e. they built factories which were designed to serve the world and not just their home market with the surplus being exported. Such a development was a major competitive and technological innovation to which the UK factories, with their much less automated production facilities and their more parochial vision of their markets, were unable to respond effectively. The shortcomings of their strategic response is illustrated by the selected production figures shown in Table 5.

Table 5 Productivity in the motor cycle industry[1]

Company	Unit output per year	Units/ man per year
NTV	20,000	15
Honda	2,000,000	174
Yamaha	1,000,000	200
Suzuki	800,000	114
BMW	25,000	20
R & D manpower		
NTV	100	
Honda	1,300	

This is a clear example of a UK industry which was extinguished by its failure to devise an appropriate strategic response to a major environmental change.

A major technological change which is currently taking place is the integration of telecommunications, financial services and retailing. One aspect of this change is manifested in the development of 'clever tills' or electronic point of sales (epos) systems. This development will render the traditional electrical or electronic cash till largely inappropriate for large retailing organizations and it is likely to be a boom market for those companies which have developed this type of technology and accompanying software.

Exhibit 6: 'Clever cash tills set for boom'[2]

The market for electronic point of sale equipment (epos) is set to grow dramatically over the next five years but there will be few business opportunities for companies which have not already established themselves in the field.

This is the chief conclusion of a new study by the market research consultancy International Data Corporation (IDC).

Most retailers think that electronic funds transfer at the point of sale (eft/pos) will be established in the UK by the end of 1987 and that it will boost opportunities for suppliers of epos equipment.

Epos and eft/pos are the key technologies which are behind moves towards the 'cashless society' and greater efficiency in retailing and wholesaling.

Epos implies the replacement of today's cash registers with electronic devices which handle ordinary cash transactions but will also provide price look-up capability, credit card validation and store trading information in a form in which it can be used to provide simple management reports.

The epos devices can stand alone but are more likely to be connected together into a network with an in-store computer providing the processing power and acting as switch to the company's headquarters mainframe.

IDC estimates there are only 25,700 epos terminals in action in the country at the present time (1985) but that the figure will grow to 290,000 by 1990. Even then the penetration will be only 40%.

More than 50 per cent of the growth in the market will come from existing accounts which are chiefly the larger companies. It means that most of the business will be collared by companies which have already installed equipment in the organizations, chiefly IBM, NCR, ICL and Data Terminal Systems (DTS).

Selected published research into the effectiveness of environmental assessment

There is a growing body of international evidence which tends to show that those organizations which are most committed to environmental assessment and strategic planning tend to achieve the best operating results.

Channon[3] has shown that one of the major strategic errors of British enterprise since World War II was its failure, by and large, to recognize that the post-war business environment was fundamentally different from the one which prevailed pre-war. Thus, from 1945 among the major changes were: the rise of new global competition; the demise of the seller's market and the rise of the power of the buyers; the fall of the British Empire and, with that, the loss of secure markets for British goods and the development of a freer system of world trade.

The first clear evidence of the benefits that can accrue from a systematic approach to strategic planning, and hence environmental assessment is a study which was conducted in 1965 by S. S. Thune and R. J. House[4] in the United States.

They found that those companies that engaged in formal long-range planning, when they were considered as a group historically, outperformed a comparable group of informal planners. Additionally they found that the successful economic results associated with long-range planning tended to take place in the rapidly changing industries and among the companies of medium size.

The importance of environmental assessment

1 It is a fundamental part of strategic management.
2 Planners in organizations must be sensitive to the environment and

scan it for the signals of change which will affect their industry in
general and their organization in particular.
3 Those organizations which are committed to it achieve better results
than those which do not.

The growth of discontinuity and turbulence

Today it is more important than ever for planners to be aware of the
increasingly turbulent and discontinuous nature of the environment
faced by business. An implication of turbulence is that the past is not a
good guide to the future. A consequence of this is that the traditional
extrapolative methods of forecasting may today have very little currency. Indeed, research by Spivey and Wrobleski[5] who examined past
studies of econometric models used in the US Government and for
industry planning found that non-econometric forecasts were at least as
good, and that in the period 1970 to 1975 US econometric models were
unreliable for three or more quarters into the future.

The difficulties in forecasting even one year ahead are well illustrated
by the attempts of the leading UK forecasters to make accurate forecasts of the likely state of the UK economy just one year ahead. In June
1985 the Financial Times published an alphabetical list of the forecasts
of selected indices of the UK economy which had been made approximately one year earlier by twenty-two leading forecasting institutions.
The results are shown in Table 6. As can be seen not only was there a
wide level of variation in the forecasts but all were incorrect. The major
factor which contributed to the general level of inaccuracy was the
coalminers' strike in the UK which occurred during this period: an
example of turbulence.

The authors of the article commented.

> Like the unfortunate weathermen, forecasters of the UK economy are equip-
> ped with large computers, huge amounts of data and a punter's instinct and
> still they get it wrong.[6]

This growth in environmental uncertainty has been documented well
by Ansoff[7] who asserts that there has been a general increase in the
level of turbulence since the start of this century. He maintains that the
degree of environmental turbulence can be expressed on a scale, as
shown in Figure 14, which goes from 'stable' at the year 1900 to 'creative' in the year 1990. Also helping to determine the level of turbulence
to which a company is subject are three other characteristics – the
familiarity of events, the rapidity of change and the visibility of the
future.

This increase in turbulence has been ascribed by Ansoff and others to
the following major developments:

• An increase in the speed of change.

Table 6 Forecasts for the UK economy made by twenty-two institutions

Forecasts for UK economy – how they fared percentage error from out-turn 1984

Forecaster	Date 1984	GDP	Consumer spending	Exports	Inflation	Unemployment	Average
Cambridge Econometrics	June	38	47	-17	13	-2	23
Capel-Cure Myers	June	25	80	-17	-9	0	26
CBI	March	17	100	-47	0	-3	33
City University	May	7			6	-3	5
Data Resources Incorporated	June	-11	-7	-6	13	-3	8
Grieveson Grant	June	90	127	-17	4	-6	49
Henley Centre	July	24	60	-20	4	-3	22
Hoare Govett	June	38	67	-11	52	0	34
Item Club	June	13	67	-9	0	-3	18
James Capel	July	4	27	-29	-4	-3	13
Laing and Cruickshank	June	50	27	-9	6	-6	19
Liverpool University	May	71			-27	-8	35
London Business School	June	-4	7	14	-2	0	5
National Institute	May	-30	7	2	25	-3	13
OECO	June	4	67	-20	3		24
Oxford Economic Forecasting	May	4	-7	-3	17	-3	7
Phillips and Drew	July	21	93	-2	2	-3	24
Rowe and Pitman	June	33	60	2	4		25
Simon and Coates	July	4	47	-18	8	0	14
Staniland Hall	June	8	27	-30	8	0	14
Treasury	March	29	127	-26	-6	0	47
Wood Mackenzie	June	21	67	-15	0	-6	22
Out-turn		2.4	1.5	6.6	4.8	3.1	

Note: Out-turn is real percentage increase year on year for GDP, consumer spending and exports. Inflation is twelve month rise in RPI. Unemployment is fourth quarter adult total in millions. Error: figures are percentage overestimate except negative figures which are underestimate. Errors are calculated as closely as possible from variables actually forecast, for example consumer prices rather than RPI.

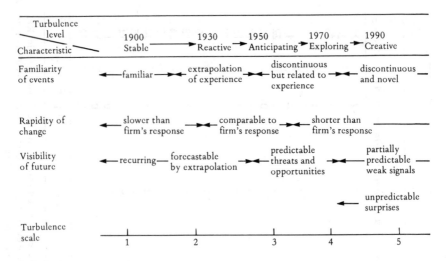

Figure 14   *Growing environmental turbulence*

- An increase in the novelty of change.
- An increase in environmental complexity.
- An increase in the level of interdependencies.
- The development of globalization.
- A general increase in size and scale.
- An increase in the levels of competitive pressure.
- A decrease in the life expectancy of industries and products.

Exacerbating the effects of the increase in the speed and magnitude of change has been a progressive decrease in the time *available* for firms to mount effective responses plus an increase in the time *required* for effective responses. Thus, because changes in the environment are happening more speedily, firms must be more speedy in their responses. However as businesses, through globalization and general increases in scale, have become larger, and therefore more prone to the inflexibility that size generally engenders, so the time needed to generate an effective response to a major environmental change has increased.

A consequence of this increase in environmental turbulence and the decrease in time available for an adequate response is that today firms must, in their assessment of their environments, rely less on traditional means of forecasting the future and must develop their ability to be sensitive to weak signals of forthcoming change. One method of doing this is scenario planning.

Power and strategic management

Power and its role in strategic management can be considered in two main dimensions: the power relationships that exist between the firm and the environment in which it exists, and the power relationships that obtain within the firm. The first of these relationships is considered below and the second is considered in Part Three.

The power relationships between the firm and the environment

In this context power could be considered as the degree to which the firm can influence the environment or the degree to which the firm is influenced by the environment. The changing nature of this relationship is considered below under a number of headings.

The development of the 'firm'

The general power relationship between the firm and the environment, or more specifically the society element of the environment, has changed considerably over the past one hundred years and is likely to continue to change. Thus the development of the modern 'firm' can be divided into a number of broad stages:

1 The initial small businesses which were run by the founders in an owner/manager capacity. In this stage because their economic and social power was limited firms tended to be dominated by their environment.
2 The evolution of small businesses into large corporations. These business empires, which were frequently owned and autocratically controlled by just one individual, often had enormous economic, political and social power vested in the hands of the owners. Perhaps the most publicized example of such power are the exploits of the 'Robber Barons' in the United States from the late nineteenth century to the 1920s, one of the most famous of whom was J. Pierpoint Morgan.

> The power of Morgan was unequaled. It was said of him by journalist Lincoln Steffens, 'In all my time, J. P. Morgan sat on the American throne as the boss of bosses, as the ultimate American sovereign'. Cras wrote of Morgan, 'For nearly a generation, Morgan rivalled kings and presidents as an object of interest, respect and hate'. Among his achievements were the rescue of the US monetary system in 1895 and the prevention of a banking collapse of 1907. On both occasions, US presidents sought his counsel and followed his directions explicitly. Morgan was also responsible for the creation of such industrial giants as General Electric, International Harvester, and American Telegraph and Telephone. However, he also nearly destroyed the financial structure of the country in an incident which led to the first antitrust dissolution decision of the US Supreme Court.[8]

3 The dispersal of ownership and the rise of the professional management class. As firms grew in size and complexity there developed a separation of ownership and management. On the one hand the ownership of firms became more dispersed through the development of a heterogeneous shareholding class and, on the other, there developed a class of professional managers who managed all aspects of the firm's activities. So there was, in general, a diminution of the

power of owners (shareholders) and an increase in the power of managers.

Social attitudes towards business

In the early part of the twentieth century, especially in the US there was a prevalent societal acceptance of the maxim that what is good for business is good for society. A consequence of this attitude was that the legitimacy of the firm was not really questioned and that firms frequently were free to pursue their objectives (which were usually assumed to be profit maximizing) with a laissez faire attitude on the part of government and acceptance on the part of society.

Particularly since the 1970s this maxim has been strongly challenged as various interest groups have questioned such an attitude. Thus there has been a rise, especially in Europe and the US of interest groups who are concerned with issues such as:

- The rights of shopfloor workers and their rights to membership of the strategic-making board of the company and company information.
- The environmental effects of polluting industries.
- The protection of the rights of the consumer from unscrupulous business practices.
- The guaranteeing of equal rights in industry for minorities.
- The protection of the rights of shareholders.
- The morality of trading with politically unacceptable regimes.

The influence of technology

As industries have become more technologically sophisticated so power has shifted to the technocrats upon whose skills the industry often relies. Thus in high-tech industries in which success depends upon highly skilled and much sought after people, power has shifted to this type of person – the business cannot function without them and frequently because their skills are in short supply they often have the choice of joining other rival companies, or developing their own businesses.

This power is not confined to high-tech industries but is also present in other industries which rely increasingly upon the technical and professional skills of people such as information systems professionals and accountants.

The influence of government

Government in most societies is playing a larger role than before. Complementing this is the development of the power of government as a major force which shapes the industrial development of a nation. Perhaps the best example of the intervention of government in industrial development is provided by the intervention of the Japanese government, through its Ministry of International Trade and Industry (MITI), in the development of post World War II Japan.

With the confirmation in the 'New Long Term Economic Plan' (1957) and the 'National Income Doubling Plan' (1960) in which the aim of government policy was the development of the heavy and chemical industries, industrial policy was carried out in the following way. MITI first designated within the heavy and chemical industries those categories which were to be promoted. These included oil refining, petrochemicals, artifical fibres, motorcars, industrial machinery, aeroplanes, electronics and electrical appliances. These categories were then provided with absolute protection and developmental assistance. Initial measures to provide protection from competition from foreign enterprises included the limitation of imports by imposing quotas on foreign currency, directly limiting the amount of imports by such measures as the introduction of an import licensing system and indirectly regulating imports by such means as imposing a high protective tariff on imports and introducing a preferential commodity tax for domestically produced goods ...

... In Japan to be deserted by the government is to be relegated to being a second-rate enterprise.[9]

The power relationship between a firm and its environment will depend strongly upon the individual firm, the nature of the industry, and the nature of the environment and it will range from the firm being the dominant partner in the relationship to the firm being the supine acceptor of the environmental circumstances.

References

1 Boston Consultancy Group Ltd, *Strategic Alternatives for the British Motor Cycle Industry*: A report prepared for the Secretary of State for Industry, 30 July 1975.

2 Cane, A., 'Clever Cash Tills Set for Boom', *Financial Times*, 12 September 1985, p. 35.

3 Channon, D., *The Strategy and Structure of British Enterprise*, Macmillan, 1973.

4 Thune, S. S. and House, R. J., 'Where Long Range Planning Pays Off: Findings of a Survey of Formal, Informal Planners', *Business Horizons*, Vol. XIII, August 1970, pp. 81–7.

5 Spivey, A. W. and Wrobleski, W. J., *Surveying Recent Econometric Forecasting Performance*, Reprint 106, American Enterprise Institute, February 1980.

6 Wilkinson, M. and Cassidy, J., 'Pit Strike Proves a Handicap for Economic Forecasters', *Financial Times*, 3 July, 1985, p. 9.

7 Ansoff, H. I., *Implanting Strategic Management*, Prentice-Hall International, 1984, p. 12.

8 Sturdivant, R. V., *Business and Society: A Managerial Approach*, Richard D. Irwin, 1981, p. 117.

9 Tsurumi, Y., *The Japanese are Coming*, Balinger, Cambridge, Mass., 1976.

4 A methodology for analysing the environment

Just as the environment faced by all individuals is unique to each individual so the environment faced by every organization is unique to it and this makes it difficult to formulate a general methodology for understanding and analysing the environment – if each organization's particular environment is so unique how can any generalized approach be of any value?

Research, and the experience of company planners, indicates that it is possible to make an effective judgement about the environmental prospects faced by an organization by using a three stage approach.

Stage 1: Segmenting the environment The first stage is to divide the environment into a number of discrete segments which generally will be important for most organizations.

Stage 2: Analysis of the segments The second stage is then to analyse in detail each segment and make an assessment of the threats and opportunities that each segment represents for the organization under analysis.

Stage 3: Attributing weights to each segment The third stage is to attribute a weight to each segment which will reflect the segment's anticipated impact – in terms of opportunities for the organization to exploit, or threats against it which must be countered – upon the organization under analysis.

In selecting the segments for analysis and in the actual analysis of each segment it is important to realize that not all industries will require all the environmental segments to receive an equal depth of analysis. For example, if the organization being considered was a company engaged in the manufacture and sale of vodka then the environmental analysis for this company would be biased towards a rather detailed examination of segments such as the level of competition, the marketing environment, and the advertising environment, as these three elements are of crucial importance in the vodka business. By way of contrast, if the analysis were concerned with a company engaged in the manufacture and sale of jet aircraft engines then in addition to analysing the competive environment, considerable emphasis would probably be placed upon an analysis of the technical environment, with particular reference to the technical developments of rival companies and the technical requirements of prospective customers.

Finally, all environmental analysis is placed within the context of uncertainty which now prevails for many industries. A diagrammatic representation of the approach is shown in Figure 15. Each of the stages of the environmental analysis is now considered in detail.

Stage 1: Segmenting the environment

Here it is assumed that the environment comprises the following segments:

- Competitive
- Marketing
- Economic
- Legal/government
- Social/cultural
- Technological
- Geographical
- Other

Although each of the segments is separated above, in practice they will be overlapping and the distinction between each of them will not always be clear. For example it will frequently be somewhat artificial to separate the 'economic' and 'government/legal' segments as they are so closely intertwined. The segment 'other' has been included as a catch-all or new category for environmental influences not captured by the other segments named in the list. Just what this segment contains, if it is used at all, will be determined by the particular circumstances which the organization under analysis is facing.

How each of these segments is appraised is now considered.

Stage 2: Analysis of the segments

The various segments into which the environment has been sub-divided are now analysed using the methodology given below.

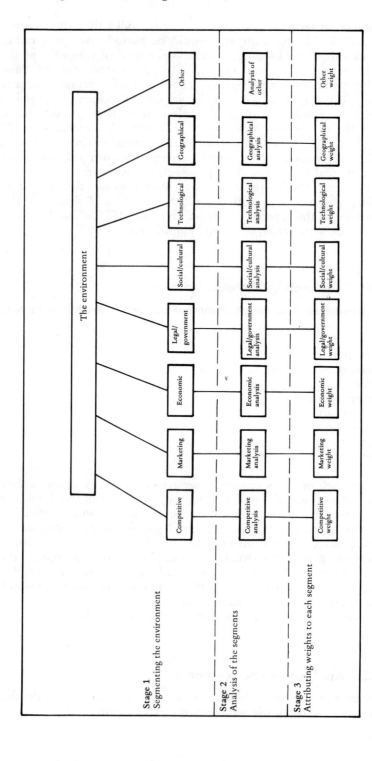

Figure 15   *A three stage approach to analysing the environment*

The competitive segment

In 1980 Professor Michael Porter of the Harvard Business School published his seminal work *Competitive Strategy: Techniques for Analyzing Industries and Competitors*. This work was the first rigorous analysis, exposition and publication of the fundamental competitive forces that prevail in all industries and that determine their levels of profitability. This section summarizes some of the basic findings of Porter's work and indicates how an assessment of the competitive environment, which an organization faces, may be made.

Porter asserts that the competitive climate which prevails in an industry is not just a matter of luck or fortune. Rather, there are five fundamental competitive forces – threat of entry, threat of substitutes, power of buyers, power of suppliers and the level of rivalry among current competitors – and that the combined strength of these forces determines the profit potential of an industry. The power of these forces varies from industry to industry and therefore to understand the strategic position and potential of any organization, a strategist must understand the competitive context of the industry in which it operates. This can be achieved through an analysis and understanding of each of the five competitive forces and then developing a strategy which will enable an organization to best defend itself against these forces or influence them in its favour.

The five competitive forces are shown in Figure 16[1] and each of them is now discussed in greater detail below.

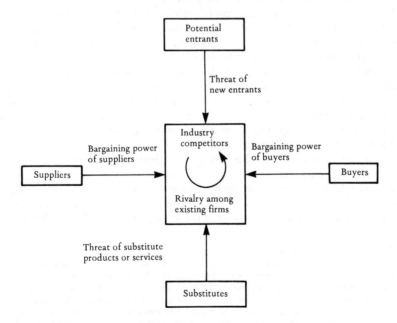

Figure 16 *Forces driving industry competition*

Threat of entry
When new competitors enter an industry by definition, they make it more competitive – there are more 'players' competing in the market. More specifically, new entrants have the effects of increasing overall industry capacity and will probably be active – through, for example, price competition and advertising – in their efforts to gain market share. Therefore, from the point of view of existing competitors, efforts should be made to minimize this threat.

The strength of the threat of entry depends upon two major factors – the barriers to entry that existing competitors have erected, plus the anticipated reaction from existing competitors. In general the higher the entry barriers and the stronger the likelihood of adverse reaction by existing competitors, the smaller will be the threat of entry.

Porter lists six main barriers to entry.

- Economies of scale
- Product differentiation
- Capital requirements
- Switching costs*
- Access to distribution channels
- Cost disadvantages independent of scale
- Government policy

The height of the barriers to entry will vary from industry to industry and two contrasting examples are provided.

The major players in the world motor industry have now erected entry barriers which would seem to preclude the entry of any new independent competitors. Just two of the more important entry barriers are capital investment and lead time.

It has been estimated that, in 1985, the average cost of designing and tooling for a new car was in the region of $800 million and this acts as a major barrier to entry. In fact no country, except Japan, has been able to develop, since World War II, a world scale domestic motor industry without the partnership of a multinational producer.

An additional problem for new entrants is that the minimum lead time for the development of a new car is around five years – a remarkably long lead time for a consumer product. It may be the case however that CADCAM may offer car manufacturers the opportunity to reduce the costs of introducing a new model and also speed up the process.

The height of these barriers to entry is well illustrated by the doubts

---

* These are the costs incurred by a consumer of a product or service who switches from one brand of product to another and in certain industries these costs can be extremely high. For example an accounting firm which has installed a certain brand of computer cannot easily switch to another brand even though the alternative may be in every respect a superior model. The switching costs are not just the costs of changing the hardware and the software but also involve changing existing records and data bases onto the new system, staff retraining and perhaps a change in the format of the information provided by and for, clients. It is these latter costs which are the major impediments to switching.

surrounding Malaysia's efforts to develop an indigenous motor industry:

Malaysian car takes to the road

Malaysia's industrialisation efforts enter a new but uncertain phase today when the country's National Car, the Proton Saga, rolls off the production line for the first time. The M$560m (£177m) project is the brainchild of Dr Mahathir Mohamed, the Prime Minister. . .

. . . Partnering the Government–owned Heavy Industries Corporation of Malaysia (Hicom) are Mitsubishi Motors and Mitsubishi Corporation, both of Japan . . .

. . . From the start the Proton project, the centrepiece of a wider heavy industrialisation programme, has been shrouded in controversy because of doubts whether a small country like Malaysia (population 15m) can support an indigenous car industry without heavy protection and costly subsidies . . .

. . . Dr Mahathir admitted earlier this year that the first 7,500 units being produced in 1985 will cost M$35,000 (£11,000) each. They are to retail at around the same elevated price as the Saga's nearest competitors' $20,000.

'We expect to lose money for the first three to four years,' says Datuk Wan Nik Ismail, the project's executive director.[2]

By way of contrast an industry with minimal barriers to entry is the 'retail stamps' segment of the UK philatelic industry. This industry is concerned with selling postage stamps and covers (i.e. postage stamps on envelopes which have passed through the post) to collectors. It is characterized by very large number of dealers who operate on a part-time basis, have low overheads, and market their products, at relatively low levels of expense, through the philatelic press.

The threat of substitutes

Although it could be argued that all the products produced by rival companies in a particular industry are substitutes for each other, this is too narrow a view. Substitutes also include products from outside the industry which are capable of performing a function previously carried out by products of the industry. For example, the laser disc, although designed to provide an alternative to the video recorder, has also been developed as a device for storing information for computers. It therefore represents a substitute method of data storage for computers and could therefore be considered as a rival to computer disks. In general, the greater the number of alternatives the greater will be the threat of substitutes.

Porter suggests that those substitutes which should be monitored most closely are:

- Those products which are providing a better performance/price standard than the industry standard.
- Products produced by industries earning high profits.

The power of buyers

The greater the power of buyers the more they can adversely affect an industry's profitability and its room for strategic manoeuvre. Porter has found that power of a buyer group seems to be strongest when the following conditions apply.

- It is concentrated or purchases large volumes relative to seller sales.
- The products it purchases represent a significant fraction of the buyer's costs or purchases.
- The products it purchases from the industry are standard or undifferentiated.
- It faces few switching costs.
- It earns low profits.
- Buyers pose a credible threat of backward integration.
- The industry's product is unimportant to the quality of the buyer's products or services.
- The buyer has full information.

The strength of the buyer group vis-à-vis the supplier group will vary from industry to industry and again two contrasting examples are given.

In the defence industry it is normally the case that the government is the only buyer. Even when defence industry products are purchased by foreign governments it usually requires approval by the government of the country in which the product is manufactured. In the UK, government defence acquisitions are made by the Ministry of Defence Procurement Executive (MOD PE) and this committee has the power to unilaterally set terms and conditions of contracts.

In contrast to this extreme concentration of buyer power, organizations or indeed individuals, purchasing water from a local water authority of utility have little power – they must accept the terms or conditions of the supplier or go without.

Although it will frequently be the case that a company will be disadvantaged when faced by a powerful buyer, in practice this will not always be so. For example, in the UK, it is commonly asserted that those (relatively small) companies which supply the large retail multiples are severely disadvantaged because of the enormous disparity in their power vis-à-vis the buyer. In fact, many of these smaller supplying companies have benefited substantially, both commercially and in terms of their strategic behaviour, from such associations as Exhibit 7 shows.

Exhibit 7:   How to deal with the big fish[3]

Pinney's of Scotland, David Stapleton's company, is the only supplier of smoked salmon to Marks & Spencer. It has become twice the size of its nearest rival, and expects to see its turnover rise from £5m to more than £7m in the year (1985) to September.

Based in Dumfriesshire, Pinneys is an example of the way in which it is possible to turn a cottage industry into a leader in its field by applying techniques perfected by much larger businesses, like production and cost control. It also shows that while a high exposure to one customer (M & S accounts for half of Pinney's sales) has its drawbacks, such dependence can actually help the supplier make its business more efficient and widely based.

The M & S link has been important both because of the technical help the store has offered in developing new products like smoked salmon pâté or salmon roulade and because of the flexible attitude it can afford to take over pricing.

If the price of any particular ingredient suddenly shoots through the roof, for instance, M & S can minimise the damage to sales of that product by spreading the increase across all five of Pinney's M & S lines. 'Much of what we have achieved would not have been possible without M & S', admits Stapleton.

The power of suppliers

The power of suppliers tends to be the opposite to the power of buyers. Thus powerful suppliers can, through their supplying policies determine the profitability, and room for strategic manoeuvre, of the organizations they are supplying.

The main determinants of suppliers having power over an industry occur, according to Porter, when:

- It is dominated by a few companies and is more concentrated than the industry to which it sells.
- It is not obliged to contend with other substitute products for sale to the industry.
- The industry is not an important customer of the supplier group.
- The supplier's product is an important input to the buyer's business.
- The supplier group's products are differentiated, or it has built up switching costs.
- The supplier group poses a credible threat of forward integration.

A good example of supplier power is afforded by OPEC, the cartel of petroleum exporting countries. Even though the power of this cartel has diminished somewhat in recent years, it is still a formidable force and it exerted enormous power in the 1970s.

Rivalry among current competitors

Different industries enjoy different levels of rivalry among the various competitors – the level of rivalry among the professions such as for example accounting firms – tends to be less intense than the rivalry that prevails among life insurance sales people.

According to Porter rivalry is intensified by the following factors.

- Numerous or equally balanced competitors.
- Slow industry growth.
- High fixed or storage costs.
- Lack of differentiation or switching costs.
- Capacity augmented in large increments.
- Diverse competitors.
- High strategic stakes.
- High exit barriers.

In the UK the big four clearing banks – Lloyds, National Westminster, Barclays and Midland – have for many years enjoyed a relationship with each other which has had a relatively low level of rivalry. The four banks offered almost identical services to customers at almost identical costs and had relatively stable market shares. However, with the development of a greater degree of deregulation, the internationalization of banking, the convergence of the services offered by banks and other non-banking institutions (such as, for example, building societies) and the entry of new competitors it seems that the intensity of rivalry will increase.

Surveying and analysing the competitive map which all industries have is a crucial step in environmental assessment. After determination of the overall competitive forces that prevail in the industry the second step is to determine just where the organization under analysis is located on the overall map and which competitive forces it can either take advantage of, or defend itself against.

When the analysis of the competitive environment has been completed the threats and opportunities which prevail should then be weighted as shown in Stage 3.

The marketing segment

Overlapping with, and complementing the, competitive segment of the environment is the marketing segment.* The marketing segment could be described as the potential demand for the goods and services which the company offers. Although, throughout this section, the goods and services will be couched in terms of consumer goods and services the same general analytical approach can also be applied to industrial goods and services. Also, when the potential demand is being considered, reference will be made to the population which makes this demand. The term 'population' is used in the statistical sense and refers

---

* Because of the importance to accountants of understanding the perspectives that a marketing orientation can give in strategic management a separate chapter on marketing has been included in this book. Thus, Part Six will provide additional techniques for analysing the marketing segment of the environment. Consequently this section on appraising the marketing segment of the environment should be read in conjunction with Part Six.

to the potential total number of consumers of the products and services whether the consumers are people or other businesses.

The fundamental determinants of potential demand
There are a number of environmental indicators which, it is usually agreed, are frequently the fundamental determinants of the potential level of demand for goods and services. Depending upon the scale of operations of the company under consideration and the nature of the industry, these indicators can be considered in a national and/or an international context.

The size and affluence of the market
Fundamental to the potential demand for a product is the absolute size and affluence of the population which may demand the product. This importance can be illustrated by reference to the world's most prosperous market – the US. The size of the US population combined with its high level of affluence has made it almost essential for would-be world competitors to have success in this market if they wish to become global companies. Thus Porter has concluded:

Access to the US market

In many industries, globalization has hinged critically on foreign firms having access to the US market because of its uniquely large size. Recognizing the strategic nature of the US market, foreign firms have pressed for innovations in order to gain access to it.

In contrast to the continuing importance of the US market, has been the decreasing importance, in world terms, of the UK market. This can be seen in many UK industries which, as their absolute domestic market has declined, in order to survive, have focused their operations increasingly on overseas markets. A typical case of this phenomenon is the UK car components industry which had traditionally been heavily dependent on UK engine manufacturers for sales.

Although the UK demand for components products has been strongly affected by the slump in OEM production, it has been even more adversely affected by the slump in UK output of engines. The largest manufacturers of engines in the UK are Ford and BL. The major UK independent engine manufacturers are Perkins Engines Group Limited (part of the Massey-Ferguson corporation), The Hawker Siddeley Group plc, Rolls Royce Limited and The Cummins Engine Company Limited.[4]

Table 7, shows how the output of engines using the industry's products has slumped over the period 1972 to 1982.

Over this period components manufacturers tried to offset the reduced demand from the home market by increased exports but were not completely successful in this effort.

Table 7   UK engine production 1972–82 (000 units)[4]

Type of engine	1972	1974	1976	1978	1990	1982
Car	2,020	1,617	1,402	1,305	1,807	1,034
Commercial vehicle	309	320	303	303	306	202
Tractor	309	297	341	259	271	181
Industrial/marine	246	241	253	282	246	186
Total	2,884	2,475	2,299	2,149	1,910	1,603

The trends in the market

A crucial sub-set of indicators of market potential are the trends which are occurring in the market. Thus although it was stated above that absolute size and affluence of the market is a fundamental primary demand factor, the trends that are occurring must also be considered. The more important trends tend to be the following:

Total population trends: Is the total population growing, static or declining? It is frequently advocated that markets which are growing are the most fruitful ones in which to operate. Although this is often the case this observation must be strongly qualified. Fast-growing markets often tend to be subject to very high levels of competition with business failure being a frequent occurrence. For example in the UK two very fast-growing sectors in 1985 were computers and electronics. Yet these sectors were among the worst performing (in terms of profitability) sectors of all with relatively poor performances from computer companies such as Acorn, Sinclair, and Apricot and from electronics companies such as Plessey, Racal and GEC (electronics divisions). In fact many traditional and apparently less glamorous industries had much superior performances.

Trends in segments of the population: Products are, in the main, targeted at various segments of the population (market segmentation is dealt with in greater detail in Part Six) rather than the total population and it is therefore important to know how the different target segments within the total population are changing. An illustration of this is provided by the steady increase in the UK of the proportion of the population over the age of sixty-five years with the increase in life expectancy being particularly marked for women.

These trends have obvious marketing implications for those companies in businesses such as: the provision of sheltered accommodation for older people; the provision of holidays for older people and the marketing of food products for older people.

Income trends: Is the overall level of income in the population increasing, static or declining and how is the distribution of income among the various segments changing? Thus, in the UK since the passage of the Equal Pay and Sex Discrimination Act in 1970 there has been a steady decrease in the differential between male and female wage rates and earnings so that today it tends to be the case that there is equal pay for equal work. This represents a significant change in the

Table 8 Changes in the proportion of the UK population aged over sixty-four years.[5]

Year	Males over sixty-four years (millions)	Females over sixty-four years (millions)
1901	0.8	1.0
1911	0.9	1.3
1921	1.2	1.6
1931	1.5	2.0
1941	1.9	2.5
1951	2.3	3.2
1961	2.4	3.8
1971	2.8	4.5
1980	3.2	5.0

distribution of income. Other important changes in income distribution which have occurred and are occurring are: the shift in income distribution towards the professional classes; the relative and increasing disparity in income distribution between the employed and the unemployed, etc.

Stage in the industry/product life cycle
The concept of the product life cycle has already been discussed in some detail in Chapter 2. From a marketing perspective it is important for planners to be informed about the stage which their industry is at in its product life cycle (for example the car industry in Europe is considered to be at the mature stage) and where the particular products made by the company under analysis are, in their own life cycles (for example in the late 1970s many of the cars manufactured by British Leyland were considered, relative to European rival cars, to be at the decline stages of their life cycles).

Measuring the market potential
The potential of a market can be measured by market research and forecasting to measure in the total population and the relevant segments indices such as sizes, growth rates, price senstivity etc. Some of the techniques of market research and the measures which can be used are discussed in Part Six. When the market potential has been quantitatively and qualitatively assessed it can be assigned as weight.

The economic segment

For most organizations the economic segment of the environment is fundamental and will require detailed analysis. Because of the necessity of understanding national economic goals and how these goals are translated into policies which can have material effects upon organizations.

The economic environment, for the purposes of strategic analysis, can be divided into two broad areas: the world economy and the national economy.

The state of the 'world economy'
Because of the influence of global economic events (for example the world price of oil) it is usually inadequate to consider national economic policies without taking cognisance of this broader global economic context in which, to a greater or lesser extent, all national economies must exist. This broader economic context can include an assessment of such fundamental indices as the performance of the major industrial countries* in their:

- Rates of inflation.
- Real growth rates of GNP.
- Current account balances.
- Levels of employment.
- Interest rates.

Such an appraisal should enable a judgement to be made about the general state of the world economy and its stage in the 'business cycle'.

Consideration of world economics should also include information on, and analysis of, other global issues such as:

- The economic development and performance of other nations.
- Global efforts at monetary reform.
- The behaviour of the currency markets.
- The international capital markets.
- Commodities.
- Trade talks.
- Activities of the International Monetary Fund.
- Activities of the World Bank.
- Third World indebtedness.

The state of the national economy
The analysis of the global economy can form the economic context within which the natonal economy can be appraised. This can be done on a hierarchical basis as shown below.

The economic goals of the government in power and the overall thrust of its economic policy: In this section the top economic goals of the government are assessed. The information for this can be obtained from party manifestos, government statements, budget statements etc. For example, current economic issues which tend to receive most attention

---

* In the appraisal of the 'world economy', frequently particular attention must be focused on the US economy. This is because this economy is so large and such a powerful influence on the performance of many other economies that such attention may be warranted. Of course, special attention should also be paid to the economies of other major trading partners.

from governments include: does the government place a higher priority on controlling inflation or increasing employment?; is the government expansionary in its stance or deflationary? etc.

The specific policies advocated and implemented to achieve these goals: These policies fall under the following main headings:

- Fiscal policies – what is the overall level of government spending and what are its policies on taxation? For example, is government, through public expenditure attempting to raise the level of demand and hence reduce unemployment? Is the government's tax strategy designed to increase investment or increase public spending power?
- Monetary policies – how tightly are monetary measures such as the money supply and the PSBR being constrained?
- Inflation policies – what is the government's attitude towards inflation and what does it believe are its causes? What steps is it taking to influence the level of inflation?
- Foreign exchange and balance of payments policies – what is the government's attitude towards stability in the value of the national currency? How do changes in the value of the national currency affect the economy in general and the organization under analysis in particular.
- Unemployment policies – how committed is the government to having full employment and what policies does it use to achieve its employment goals?
- Privatization policies – how strongly committed to the privatization of nationalized industries is the government? What is the objective of privatization – to increase competitiveness, to raise revenues for the government, to prove an ideological theory etc?
- Regional policy – how committed is the government to strong regional policies to prevent the concentration of industry and commerce in favoured locations.

Note on inflation
Irrespective of the underlying causes of inflation the rate of inflation that prevails can be a significant environmental influence on an organization's performance and expectations. High rates of inflation are generally portrayed as being 'bad' for organizations and therefore are generally regarded as an environmental threat, while low rates of inflation are generally portrayed as being 'good' for organizations and therefore are considered as an environmental opportunity. This view of the likely impact of inflation is, however, too narrow. Different organizations and industries are affected in different ways by inflation and it may be the case that some organizations are actually advantaged by periods of high inflation. Therefore, it is difficult to make a judgement about the performance of an organization in a period of inflation if conventional accounting data alone is used. This is because inflation tends to act as a 'tax' on current assets and as a 'subsidy' on fixed asssets and consequently the effects of inflation on different organiza-

tions are influenced by the proportion of current to fixed assests. Thus, for example, banks, whose assets are skewed towards money and other similar products must, in periods of inflation, earn a return on equity which is at least as great as the rate of inflation: otherwise their net worth is being eroded by inflation. By way of contrast, organizations which have a very high proportion of fixed assets – property companies for examples – may find that the value of these fixed assets is understated on their balance sheets during a period of inflation. Such companies may earn a return on equity which understates the full value of the assets which will be realized when the asset is eventually sold.

Therefore, in a period of inflation, it is important for strategic planners not just to take cognisance of the actual level of the inflation rate, but also to understand the strategic and operating implications of inflation for their industry and their organization. The Boston Consulting Group has clearly expressed the importance of understanding this aspect of inflation.

> One day we may return to a world of low or at least stable rates of inflation. Until then, managers must expand their planning activities to include continuing, detailed evaluation of the impact of inflation on their businesses. This requires much more than inflating a revenue or cost stream according to simple pricing or cost increase assumptions. Business need not passively accept the invisible redistribution of wealth brought about by inflation. By actively seeking out the second and third order effects of inflation, managers can avoid its ravages and perhaps turn it to their advantage.[6]

The operation of most of the economic indicators can be quantitatively assessed as there tends to be good statistical records for them publicly available. Once the overall impact of the economic segment has been assessed, it can be weighted as shown in Stage 3.

The legal/government segment

Government at all levels – regional, national and international – is becoming increasingly involved in society. In the section on the economic segment the role of the national government in formulating and implementing economic policies was considered, but it is also important to take cognisance of the other pervasive roles that governments can play.

It is convenient, for the purposes of environmental analysis, to divide the role of government into two categories – government acting as an aid to business and government acting as an impediment to business. Although it will often be the case that government will be simultaneously an aid and an impediment to business.

When an analysis is being carried out it is important to consider the level of the government influence. Thus it can be, for example: regional – the role of a local development office in the provision of packages of assistance for local start-up businesses; national – the role of the central government in determining the level of taxation, or international – the role of the European Community in determining the levels of tariffs to be imposed upon foreign imports. For the purposes of this exposition, however, the national or central government will be the principal level of aggregation.

Government as an aid to business

Government can act either deliberately or unintentionally as an aid to business. Some of the main ways in which it does this are outlined below.

Government as a buyer: Government is frequently a major purchaser of goods and services and, generally, is regarded by business as an excellent customer because it will not default on payment and also because government purchases, as well as being a mark of approval, also are frequently relatively large. For example the construction industry in the UK, particularly in the area of civil engineering – road contracts and bridge contracts, relies heavily on government purchases. Accounting and consulting companies also tend to regard government contracts in a favourable light.

Government as a sustainer of R & D: In many industries today the costs of engaging in the R & D necessary for the successful development of new products is frequently beyond the financial capabilities of individual companies. In such circumstances it may be the case that government underwriting of the costs may be the only way in which it is feasible to undertake the research. This is especially true in the defence and aerospace industries.

Government as the provider of protection: Frequently government will protect an industry which is threatened by a foreign competitor. This is usually done in a number of ways – through the provision of subsidies to the threatened industry, through the erection of tariff barriers against foreign products, through the erection of quotas against foreign goods and through the exercising of preferential procurement practices. For example, in Europe, in general, most shipbuilding yards tend not to be commercially viable. Yet, the strategic importance of having an indigenous shipbuilding facility is high, so most governments tend to provide aid for their shipbuilding industries.

Government as an aid to control wage costs: Governments frequently introduce incomes policies. These policies ease the difficulties of businesses in meeting wage demands which they believe to be excessive.

Government assistance in training: There are many government schemes which help reduce the full cost of training through rebates, tax relief and grants.

Government assistance for start up businesses: In regions of high unemployment especially, governments frequently have generous schemes which can significantly reduce the cost of starting up and then running a business in such a region. These schemes operate at both national and regional levels.

Government as a provider of new business opportunities: In the UK and, indeed, in many other Western countries as well, since the late 1970s there has been a general tide which favours the privatization of state industries and generally a climate of deregulation. This new climate will provide many opportunities which were previously unavailable. For example, the liberalization of the monopoly of the post office as a postal carrier has permitted the development of private carriers.

Government as an impediment to business

The development of the 'web of regulation':   A complaint of business in general has been that as the involvement of government in society has increased so has the amount of legislation and regulation which attends that involvement so that today business suffers large, and frequently hidden, costs in conforming with regulations which, from a business perspective, seem to be pointless. A good example of this costly exasperation is provided by the difficulties in meeting the regulations to transport goods from one state to another in the European Community. The charge is often made by intra-European transporters that as the Community has developed so have the cross-border regulations and that today it is actually more difficult to transport goods between European Community states than before the European Community was founded. The long queues of trucks which are often seen at the borders of member states are a testimony to the truth of this claim.

Government as a controller of prices: Incomes policies are also frequently complemented by prices policies. These policies are generally regarded by industry with some hostility. The argument tends to be that it is impossible for governments to have the knowledge and skills to legislate for all the pricing situations that obtain in industry and that statutory price controls build in rigidities which go against market trends and may unfairly penalize companies.

Government as a protector of the environment: In the 1960s and the 1970s there developed in most Western nations a greater awareness of the long-term costs of industrial pollution. This led to the development of legislation to curb the activities of companies which it was believed were causing pollution. Many industries feel that they are unfairly penalized because they are made by government to bear the costs of avoiding pollution while their foreign competitors may not have such costs.

Government as the guarantor of health and safety at work: Government, through legislation, has in the 1970s especially, taken a much more active role in ensuring the health and safety of people at work. This concern is manifested in legislation to ensure such issues as: standards of mechanical and electrical safety; standards of hygiene; maximum working hours per day and per week etc. All of these elements are regarded by certain businesses on occasions as costs they should not have to bear and also an intrusion by government into the privacy of the organization's workplace.

Government as the guarantor of equal opportunity: Conforming to equal opportunity legislation (i.e. equal rights to employment and promotion without regard to sex, age, race or religion) throughout Europe has been largely regarded by business as a cost.

Government as the defender of competition against monopoly: In the UK, through the Monopolies and Mergers Commission, government seeks to ensure that industries do not become monopolized. Although this is regarded as desirable from a social point of view, and also from the point of view of the smaller firms in the industry, the operation of monopoly legislation is regarded somewhat negatively by larger firms in certain industries. With the development of global markets and global competitors there is a body of opinion which says that for a company to be internationally competitive it may well need to be a national monopoly in order to have the necessary critical mass.

Government as the defender of the rights of the consumer: Most Western governments have enacted legislation to protect the consumer against unscrupulous business practices. This legislation ranges from laws on consumer credit, to laws on advertising standards, to laws on the honest labelling of goods, to laws on the safety and health standards of products. The more extensive these laws are, the more hostile business tends to be towards them.

Government as the decider of industry location: Frequently it will be the case that government may coerce an organization to locate in a region which it does not favour. This can be achieved through differential levels of assistance or more coercively through withholding planning permission for construction in one region and granting permission in a location which it favours.

The above are just the main influences which the government/legal sectors have on business in general. Any specific analysis will, of course, be tailored to the circumstances of the organization under analysis. However, irrespective of the organization and irrespective of whether a regional, national or international perspective is taken, it should be possible for strategic planners to make an assessment of the impact of government and then weigh this impact as shown in Stage 3.

The social/cultural segment

Although it could be argued that the social and the cultural segments of the environment are separate, in this analysis it is considered that they are so overlapping that they are grouped together to form a single segment. The social/cultural segment is considered to be that undefined, but nonetheless very real, set of values, beliefs and attitudes that somehow expresses the general attitude that society has towards life and work. The social/cultural segment of the environment can be thought of in two broad areas – how it affects the products and services of business and how it affects employee attitudes towards their work.

How social/cultural factors affect products and services
The degree of attention which planners need to give to the analysis of this factor is a function of the industry. For example planners engaged

in such fast-changing and socially sensitive industries as fashion, television, records, and advertising need to be extremely sensitive to social changes whereas planners in industries such as quarrying, coal delivery and civil engineering do not need the same levels of sensitivity.

Although it is impossible to give an exhaustive list of all the social/cultural elements in the environment of which planners should be aware, the following are indicative of the types of elements which should be considered.

Education: The level, availability and participation rate in education can have major implications for many products and services. Thus, for example, in Western Europe, as the general level of education has increased, so the sophistication of products and the promotion strategies of products have developed.

Health and fitness: There has been, in Western Europe, an overall increase in people's concern about health and fitness. This has been manifested in the increased participation rate in many sports, the development of restaurants and foods which are geared to this market, adverse publicity for products (such as alcohol and tobacco) which are considered injurious to health and the development of sports people as ideal role models for young people. This cultural/social change has implications not just for sports related businesses, but also for how non-sports related products and services are promoted and how potentially 'unhealthy' products overcome their image. For example, the tobacco industry is a major sponsor of sporting events.

Family size: Family size has generally decreased since 1945 and today, in most Western countries, the average number of children per family is less than three children. This has implications not just for the suppliers of children's goods (such as, for example baby food, prams, clothes etc.) but also for seemingly unrelated products such as houses and cars where design and size is frequently a function of family need.

Family units: Family units have generally become less stable – there has been an increase in the level of divorce and an increasing tendency for young people to leave home and live apart from their parents. This has implications for promotion, packaging etc.

Religion: There has been an overall decrease in the power of churches and their appeal, especially to young people. This has had a major influence on such issues as: how poeple spend their leisure; the types of moral attitudes that are socially acceptable and retail opening hours.

Geographical mobility: The advent of cheap international travel has increased greatly the scope for international travel both for business and for pleasure. It has also greatly increased people's knowledge of foreign environments and tended to make goods and services more 'cosmopolitan'. For example, the increase in the growth of ethnic restaurants.

Domestic mobility: The development of mass motoring has meant a major social change not just in recreation but also in retailing. Thus, many retailers have moved from downtown sites to out of town shopping centres with good car parking facilities. A further complementary social factor in retailing has been the rise in the incidence of freezer ownership which has led to the weekly shopping trip as opposed to the 'daily' necessity of shopping which used to be prevalent.

The role of women in society: With the great increase in the proportion of women working outside the home and the development of equal opportunity legislation, there has been a change in society's attitude towards the role of women and also a change in the attitude of women towards their own role. Thus, there has been a diminution of the domestic role of women and an increase in their broader role in society.

How social/cultural factors affect attitudes towards work
There is a wide diversity in the attitudes, managerial and shop floor, that prevail towards work and business. This diversity is most easily seen when international comparisons are made, although, it has been claimed that regional comparisons within countries are also observable. Perhaps the clearest example of differing attitudes towards work can be seen when the Japanese work ethic and the Western European work ethic are compared. A report by the Japanese External Trade Organisation (JETRO) showed the width of the gap:

Divisions over the work ethic

The Japanese notion of overtime, for example, does not go down well in Europe. While about 75 per cent of the companies surveyed said they asked their employees to work overtime, getting them to agree to the request, they said, was much more difficult than in Japan.

Reasons for the difficulty in ordering overtime ranged from 'the employees give too much emphasis to their private lives' to local labour laws. Some 40 per cent of the companies said that employees had refused to obey orders when told to do overtime work.

The study is directed at Japanese businessmen contemplating their own moves into Europe, so it includes some touching descriptions of labour conditions in Europe. These go some way toward explaining why many Japanese management practices cannot be happily transplanted to European soil.

For example, the study notes: 'Western Europe is more advanced compared with Japan in social security systems. Local employees, unlike Japanese employees, do not consider their work to be the centre of their lives. If push comes to shove, they consider work something they have to do to live. This is where the difficulty lies in expecting local employees to contribute as much to their companies as Japan.[7]

At a national or regional level, with the development of a permanent class of long-term unemployed people, there is increasing government concern in many European countries that such people will, because of the effects of such enforced unemployment become completely unemployable in any capacity.

Finally, as with the other segments of the environment, strategic planners should be aware of the important elements of social change for their industry and their business and be able to assign a weight to the importance of this environmental influence.

The technological segment

As indicated on page 58, the world is in an era of unprecedented technological change and strategists must incorporate this dimension of the environment into their analyses. Although, at one level, technological change is all pervasive – for example all industries are to some extent affected by the microcomputer/information technology revolution – at another level, it is important to realize that some industries will be much more affected by technological change than others.

For example, companies engaged in a traditional industry such as the delivery of coal to domestic customers, although they need to have up-to-date information systems and methods of handling coal, do not need to be constantly scanning their environment for technological advances which will threaten their existence. By way of contrast, companies engaged in the hardware aspects of office automation must be constantly aware of new developments which may be threats or opportunities. In this industry there has been a fusion of what were once disparate technologies – printing, optics, telecommunications, electronics and computers and future technological developments are highly uncertain.

Not only will these changes in the environment have fundamental influences on manufacturing industry but they will cause major changes in the service sectors. For example, with the advent of relatively inexpensive and widely available electronic information data and information transmission those accounting and consultancy firms which fail to embrace this new technology may be disadvantaged.

Business takes to the latest fax machines

British companies are taking to facsimile (fax) for business communications with a new enthusiasm. There are already more fax machines installed in the UK than anywhere else in Europe, and the number is growing at about 50 per cent a year.

New figures from British Telecom International suggest that Britain will have 48,000 fax installations by the end of 1985 compared with Japan's 850,000 machines and 550,000 for the US. The comparable figure for the whole of Europe is 120,000.

A major factor in the more extensive use of fax has been the new technology. The earliest fax machines (group one) besides being expensive took around six minutes to send a single page of a document. The latest generation of machines – group three – besides being much smaller and cheaper can scan and transmit a page of an A4 document in less than 60 seconds.[8]

It is important to realize that technological change affects not just final products but also the production methods and indeed the raw materials. Thus Henry Ford's adoption of the production line to produce the Model T Ford was a technological change in the production process which, temporarily, gave the Ford company enormous competitive advantage over its rivals and changed the 'rules of the game' for the manufacture of automobiles. Similarly, the development of the integrated circuit and sophisticated chips have changed the 'raw materials' which industries such as the computer industry and the watch industry use.

Although it is difficult to measure, except with hindsight, the importance of technological change to an industry, two measures which may give a reasonable indication are suggested.

The first is some measure of the amount that the industry spends on R & D. This could be either an absolute amount or it could be a relative measure such as R & D expenditures as a proportion of sales.

Another measure, which strictly speaking does not measure the rate of technological change in an industry but may, nonetheless, be a good surrogate, is the PIMS* measure of innovation (see Part Six). This measure defines the level of innovation as the proportion of revenues that accrue from products which have been introduced in the last three years. The measure does give a good indication of the relative importance to the industry of new products.

When the analysis of the technological environment has been completed the threats and opportunities which prevail should then be weighted as shown in stage 3.

The geographical segment

Since the 1960s especially the internationalization of business, at all levels, has accelerated so that today, increasingly, the products of business are globally homogenized, sold to world markets and made with inputs which are sourced globally. This 'sea change' has altered the 'rules of the game' for business strategy and this additional perspective must be integrated into environmental analysis.

The trend towards the internationalization of business with marketing, production, finance and personnel strategies planned on, or at least taking cognisance of, the global dimension has been, and will continue to be inexorable.

It is easy to see the importance of having international perspectives in those industries which are clearly perceived to be global – for example television set manufacture, vehicle manufacture and aircraft manufacture. In the case of vehicle manufacturers a predominantly global view is now taken in this industry. This has led to the development of world cars (i.e. cars whose sourcing, manufacture and sales are planned and implemented on a global rather than on a national basis – for example the General Motors (GM) world car the Corsa/Nova is assembled from parts sourced from many European countries.

> GM has put new component capacity into Cadiz (steering columns, steering gears, front-wheel-drive axles) as well as a Logrono (seat trim covers, headliners, instrument panels, consoles and bumper fascias) in Spain.
>
> Other components are made in Northern Ireland (seat belts, exterior mouldings), England (steering columns, exhaust valves) France (batteries and heaters) and Portugal (rubber and plastic vehicle components).
>
> There is also major investment in Austria where new engine transmission

* See Chapter 13

plants are made side by side. They will supply not only the Corsa, but other Opel vehicles.[9]

Increasingly, these global perspectives are becoming important even in industries which have traditionally enjoyed parishes of protection. An industry's parish can be considered to be that area in which it enjoys substantial protection from globally prevailing competitive forces. These parishes are frequently delineated by geographical, political and cultural boundaries and are sustained by geographical distance and official regulations. Today, parish boundaries are being continuously eroded. This can be seen even in the accounting profession which, in the future, will be subject to increasing global competition.

> The pressure to build strong international firms is steadily increasing as clients become more international. Geographical boundaries no longer have much relevance today for many forms of business, and accountants that cannot provide an international service – even for comparatively small clients – are condemning themselves to a small-time future . . .
>   The international firms are now vast enterprises. New information about their scope has recently been released in the US to the Dingell congressional sub-committee on the accountancy profession. Arthur Andersen had total worldwide partners' capital of $342m at August 1984, within total capital employed of $639m. Its fee income was $1.4 bn . . .
>   . . . And the big challenge will be to put in place management systems that can control sometimes jealous professionals in several continents and scores of countries. Some of the so-called international firms are loose associations designed for little more than mutual business reference, rather than integrated businesses. That may not be good enough to hold them together as competition intensifies.[10]

In summary, in most industries today, strategic planners must, more seriously than in the past, analyse the potential threats and opportunities that the globalization of business now provides. The reality of globalization is illustrated in Exhibit 8 through reference to the shoe industry

---

Exhibit 8:   Globalization of the shoe industry – an industry wrongfooted by the pace of change[11]
When President Reagan decided recently not to impose further barriers on imports of shoes into the US the sighs of relief in traditional European manufacturing centres such as Northampton, Alsace and Florence were almost audible.

Had the President bowed to pressure from the American industry and blocked imports, the rapidly growing output in countries such as Brazil, Taiwan and South Korea would almost certainly have been diverted to Europe.

With the exception of Italy, which has become the most important producer of leather shoes in the world, Europe has taken too much of a battering to welcome further low-cost imports. German production has dropped from 151m pairs in 1972 to 92m last year, British from 184m pairs to 127m and French from 240m to 195m.

The centre of gravity of the shoe industry has shifted from the developed world to the Far East. Europe, especially Italy, remains the centre of the leather side, but the vast increase in numbers of non-leather shoes – trainers, flip-flops, casuals of all sorts – has come about as a result of industrialization allied to low wage rates in the Far East and changing fashion.

This shift of emphasis has spurred the growth of large shoe empires in the Far East, and more recently, Brazil. Taiwan employs around 200,000 people in its industry and South Korea 105,000 – but Britain is now down to 47,000.

As recently as 1978 Brazilian exports amounted to no more than 39m pairs. Today, it exports more than the production of either Germany or Britain and soon will export more than both make. Its shoes are good quality and attractively designed. With its low wage rates, high capital utilization and solid marketing the Brazilians can make leather shoes to European standards at Far Eastern prices.

Despite the fierce competition Mr Michael Feilden, director general of the British Footwear Manufacturers Federation, believes the European industry can survive – but only if it is willing and able to invest.

'There have been enormous improvements in design, production, engineering and factory organization. Computer-assisted design has been complemented by the use of numerically-controlled machines. The chain from supplier to customer is more efficiently administered, so that the industry has the ability to survive.'

The Anglo American Trend:

	US		UK	
	Import penetration (%)	Numbers employed	Import penetration (%)	Numbers employed
1970	30	213,600	28	93,000
1971	33	200,600	31	91,000
1972	36	193,300	33	88,000
1973	39	182,900	31	85,400
1974	37	172,400	34	83,900
1975	41	157,700	35	75,300
1976	47	164,200	41	73,000
1977	47	156,900	44	73,000
1978	48	158,400	43	69,900
1979	51	148,900	43	69,900
1980	49	143,600	47	64,300
1981	51	146,400	54	57,400
1982	58	135,100	55	52,700

| 1983 | 63 | 127,400 | 56 | 49,600 |
| 1984 | 71 | 120,700 | 60 | 49,800 |

When the geographical segment has been appraised it is weighted as shown in Stage 3.

Stage 3:   Attributing weights to each segment

In this stage of the environmental analysis the segments of the environment, which have been selected in stage one of the process and analysed in stage two, are given weights which summarize the impact which each segment is expected to have on the organization under analysis. The weights are calculated as follows.

The *importance* to the organization under analysis, of each segment of the environment which has been analysed, is ranked on an ordinal scale which goes from 0 to 5. Thus, if a segment is considered of crucial importance to the organization it merits a score of 5, if it is of average importance it merits a score of 3 and if it is of no importance at all it scores zero. For example, in the office automation hardware industry (see page 84) the technological segment of the environment is of crucial importance and would probably score 5, while in the delivery of domestic coal industry (see page 84) the technological segment is of minimal importance and would probably score zero, or perhaps 1.

Once the importance of each factor has been determined the *strength* of each factor in the period under analysis is then ranked on an ordinal scale from −5 to +5. −5 indicates that this factor is likely to have as strong a negative influence on the organization as possible. For example, it is likely that today most European shipbuilders would assign a score of −5 to the segment 'the competitive environment'. In contrast, a score of +5 indicates that the segment under consideration is likely to have as strong a positive influence on the organization as possible. For example, when a company which has a profitable proprietary product is faced with excess demand and is obliged to ration its sales, then the market could be assigned a score of +5. Finally a score of 0 indicates that the factor does not have any strength at all.

When the importance and the strength of each factor have been determined these two numbers are multiplied and an ordinal overall score for each relevant segment in the environment is obtained. Note that the values obtained may not be summed: all each value indicates is the likely relative overall imapact that each segment is likely to have on the organization. Finally, the score for each segment can be shown graphically on an environmental assessment diagram, as shown in Figure 17. The advantage of the graphical exposition is that it tends to make the analysis more 'alive' and more easily understood by a group.

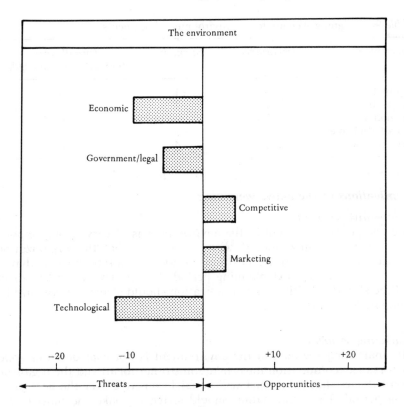

Figure 17 *Environmental assessment diagram*

A hypothetical example to illustrate how the stages of the environmental analysis are carried out

Stage 1: Segmenting the environment For this organization, it was decided that the segments of the environment which were most relevant were: economic, government/legal, competitive, marketing and technological

Stage 2: Analysis of the segments A detailed analysis of the segments selected in Stage 1 was carried out for the period immediately prior to the date of the analysis and also projections about the future trends in each of the segments for the next planning period or period of analysis of the organization were made.

Stage 3: Attributing weights to each segment After each segment had been analysed the following weights were assigned.

Table 9 Assigning weights to the environmental segments

Segment	Importance	Strength	Overall score (importance × strength)
Competitive	4	+1	4
Marketing	1	+3	3
Economic	5	−2	−10
Legal/government	2	−3	− 6
Technological	3	−4	−12

Implications of the above weighting

Competitive segment
The competitive segment of the environment is of very strong importance to this organization. However, it is seen that this organization
appears to be in a strong position vis-à-vis its competitors in that it
feels that over the next planning period the competitive environment
will be slightly positive. The organization should strive to maximize its
competitive advantages.

Marketing segment
The marketing segment of the environment is not considered of great
importance (competition must take some other form) and the organization believes that its impact will be fairly positive over the next planning period. The organization should strive to make the most of the
opportunity which the marketing segment of the environment is presenting.

Economic segment
It would appear that the economic climate is particularly important for
this organization and that in the next planning period it is not very
conducive. It must regard the economic segment as a 'threat' and
consider what actions it can take to minimize this threat.

Legal/government segment
Although the government/legal segment is generally a threat in the next
planning period, its importance is not considered to be so great, and so
efforts to minimize this threat will probably be less than for the other
two threats.

Technological segment
Similarly, although the technological environment is considered not to
be quite so important in the environment, in the next planning period it
appears that the organization will be confronted with major technological threats.

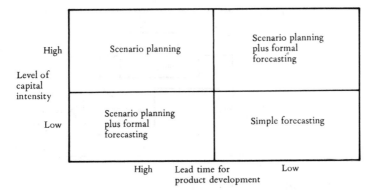

Figure 18   *The relationship between the forecasting method and the industry type*

Scenario planning

As asserted on page 58, today, because of the turbulence of the environment an overreliance on formal forecasting methods – such as times series analysis, regression analysis and exponential smoothing – may be unsound. Here it is suggested that such formal methods should, in appropriate industries, be complemented with a scenario planning approach to forecasting.

It is important to note that accurately forecasting the future is more important in some industries than in others. Thus, industries which are characterized by high levels of capital intensity and a long lead time for product development apply greatest efforts to forecasting the future. Typical industries are the extractive industries such as oil and mining where there is a very large capital investment and it may be twenty years before the financial rewards of a successful investment are reaped. Figure 18 aligns the type of forecasting method with the industry.

An approach to scenario planning*

There are many approaches to scenario planning – it can be highly quantitative or highly qualitative, it can extend over a relatively short period of time into the future or it could extend up to twenty years or more, it can comprise just a single scenario of the future or multiple scenarios.

Here it is assumed that a scenario is an integrated and consistent set of possibilities that somehow describe the future. This scenario is evolved out of a process of group discussion and decision making based on quantitative and qualitative data. Central to the idea of the scenario is that the past is not a good guide to the future and that valuable insights into the future may be obtained through qualitative and open-ended discussion about the future.

*   In this section an approach to scenario planning is summarized. This topic is examined to a greater depth in Chapter 7 of *Tools and Techniques for Strategic Management*.[12]

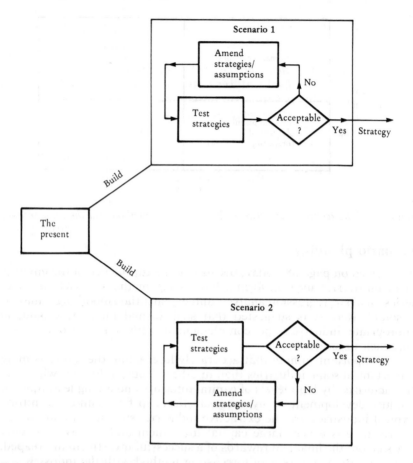

Figure 19   *Evaluating strategies in two scenarios*

Normally scenario planning involves building a number of scenarios and then testing the impact of each scenario upon the organization's plans. The Shell Company, which is a prominent practitioner of scenario planning, advocates that scenario planners try to devise just two scenarios – a best case scenario and a worst case scenario and the organization's strategies can then be tested in these situations. This approach is shown diagramatically in Figure 19.

A practical approach to scenario planning

The approach comprises six discrete steps.

Step 1:   Develop a data base
In this step two data bases – one for the organization and one for the environment are built. These data bases will provide the scenario

builders with the information they may need when constructing the scenarios.

Step 2: Develop a strategic profile of the organization
In this step all the crucial features of the organization are integrated to form a profile. (This is similar to developing a picture of the organization's strengths and weaknesses, see Part Three).

Step 3: Develop a profile of the environment
Here a profile of those segments of the environment which are relevant to the future of the organization is developed.

Step 4: Testing the likely impact of each environmental element upon each organizational element
The objective of this step is to assess the impact the environmental element is likely to have upon each organizational element.

Step 5: Further analysis of the key organizational and key environmental factors identified in Step 4
The key organizational elements and the key environmental elements which were revealed in Step 4 receive further analysis in this step and their likely impact is re-assessed.

Stage 6: Assessing the likely impacts of the different strategies under the two starkly different scenarios.
In this final step the the likely impact of the proposed strategies is examined in detail and the strategies are agreed or amended in the light of the likely impact.

Although scenario planning may appear from the above description to be insufficiently precise to warrant credibility, this approach has been found, in certain industries, to yield superior results to the traditional methods.

References

1 Porter, M. C., *Competitive Strategy: Techniques for Analysing Industries and Competitors*, Collier Macmillan, 1980.
2 Sherwell, C. and Sulong, W., 'Malaysian Car Takes to the Road', *Financial Times*, 9 July 1985, p. 6.
3 Dawkins, W., 'How to Deal with Big Fish', *Financial Times*, 5 July 1985, p. 14.
4 McNamee, P. B., *The United Kingdom Automotive Components Industry: A Case in Competitive Strategy*, Forthcoming.
5 Sadler, P. and Barham, K., 'Demographic and Social Trends 1970–80', *Long Range Planning*, Vol. 15, No. 5, October 1982, pp. 52–77.

6   The Boston Consulting Group, *Inflation's invisible hand, perspectives*, No. 1, 237, 1981.
7   Rappaport, C., 'Divisions Over the Work Ethic', *Financial Times*, 2 December 1985, p. 18.
8   Cane, A., 'Business Takes to the Latest Fax Machines', *Financial Times*, 4 September 1985, p. 22.
9   McNamee, P.B., *European Cases in Competitive Strategy*, Forthcoming.
10 'Accountancy', *Financial Times*, 25 November 1985, p. 38.
11 Moreton, A., 'An Industry Wrongfooted by the Pace of Change', *Financial Times* 2 October 1985, p. 12.
12 McNamee, P. B., *Tools and Techniques for Strategic Management*, Pergamon, 1988.

Part Three

5 Analysing the organization

Introduction

The counterpart to the analysis of the environment is the analysis of the organization. As was stated in Chapter 1 the organization should adapt its shape to the shape of the environment. Part Three is concerned with developing a methodology which will enable a judgement to be made about the overall shape or profile of any organization being analysed. This analysis uses a three-stage approach similar to the methodology used in the analysis of the environment.

Stage 1: Division of the organization The first stage is to divide the organization into a limited number of discrete sections which tend to be the major and important sections of most organizations.

Stage 2: Analysis of the sections The second stage is to analyse in detail each section of the organization and to make an assessment of the strengths and weaknesses of each of these sections.

Stage 3: Attributing weights to each section The third stage is to attribute a weight to each section which will reflect the section's strength or weakness.

When selecting the sections of the organization for analysis and when conducting the actual analysis of each section the generalized methodology given below must be tailored to the particular circumstances facing the organization under analysis. For example, if it were a 'leading-well-established' competitor in the 'manufacture of bricks' business, then it would be expected that the analysis would be biased towards considering elements such as production efficiency, control and costs as this is a mature industry with relatively little product differentiation where competitive advantage may be based on factors such as price, delivery, and quality. By way of contrast, an analysis of an organization engaged in the provision of 'collectors' investment port-folios' such as portfolios of rare stamps, coins, paintings, sculptures etc. would be biased towards an examination of the culture of the organiza-tion with particular reference to the skills of the personnel – skills in their knowledge of the investments and the markets and in their abili-ties to deal with clients.

A diagrammatic representation of the approach is shown in Figure 20.

Although there are many axes along which an organization can be divided, here it is assumed that there are three major ones: behavioural, structural and functional.

The behavioural analysis

The behavioural axis of an organization is placed first because there seems to be evidence to show that in understanding the functioning of any organization it is important not to regard it simply as a black box which receives various inputs from the environment and by a resource conversion process transforms them into goods and services which the environment demands. Instead it is considered to be more realistic if a less mechanistic view is taken and consequently this part of the analysis attempts to capture the major behavioural forces which prevail in all organizations. In other words, in the analysis below it is assumed that in order to understand the strengths, weaknesses, and potential of an organization a crucial first step is understanding its behavioural climate.

The behavioural climate in any organization is considered to be that set of 'non-concrete', and frequently not defined, behavioural elements that play a fundamental role in moulding an organization's goals*, strategies, attitudes, and actions. Below, this climate is considered under three main headings: culture, power and leadership. It is further assumed that out of these behavioural characteristics grow the orga-nization's goals. This is not meant to imply that this is the process in which the behavioural climate of an organization is established. In reality the behavioural climate that prevails in an organization does not develop in the structured and orderly way that the above may suggest. Instead these four elements – culture, power, leadership and goals – operate simultaneously in multiple directions and normally it is im-possible to separate them discretely: the multiple arrows in the be-havioural section of Figure 20 are meant to imply this. Therefore their separation in this chapter is advocated purely to facilitate analysis. Each of the above behavioural elements is now considered.

Culture

Ackoff has shown that in their strategic behaviour, individuals in organizations strive not just for results but also for certain styles of

* The related terms goals, mission and objectives are defined and discussed on page 113.

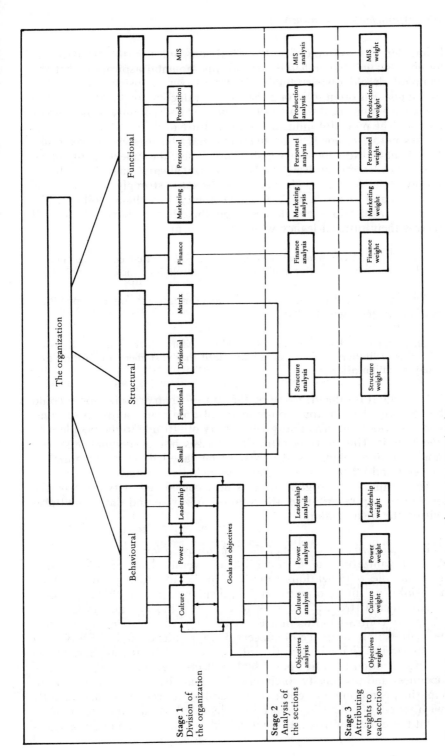

Figure 20 *A three-stage approach to analysing an organization*

99

behaviour. For example, family-owned companies frequently have the (often unstated, but nonetheless real) fundamental aspiration that the company should always remain as a family-owned business. This cultural influence is often so strong that it is not uncommon for the owner to allow such a business to fail rather than surrender family ownership or control. The powerful influence of the culture of the organization is not always negative, nor is it confined to family businesses. For example, one of the world's most successful companies, the American high-tech electronics company Hewlett-Packard has always had the cultural stamp of its founders, Hewlett and Packard, strongly visible in its activities and its products. Thus, the company has always followed the founders' aspirations and today, even though they have left, it still retains their cultural legacy which makes it a:

> people-oriented company with management policies that encourage individual creativity, initiative, and contribution throughout the organization.[1]

This type of culture has caused the company to have a product-market strategy which has:

> concentrated on developing quality products, which make unique technological contributions and are so far advanced that customers are willing to pay premium prices.

Although it is difficult to define the culture of an organization it could be considered to be that common set of dominant values, traditions, and behaviour patterns that gives a unity of attitude to the people who comprise it. This unity of attitude polarizes into archetypal organizational cultural extremes which may be labelled 'go-go/dynamic' at one end and labelled 'stodgy/conservative' at the other.

The culture of an organization is now considered at two levels: the overall corporate culture of the total organization and the sub-cultures within the organization.

The overall corporate culture of the total organization

Many organizations tend to exhibit an overall characteristic culture. For example, organizations which are in the advertising industry tend to exhibit an image of extroversion, display keen sensitivity to recent environmental trends, and seek to convey a modern and progressive image. In contrast to this image, organizations in the banking business tend to exhibit an image of conservatism, prudence and stability.

Ansoff[2] has characterized the different cultures that can characterize an organization on a five-point scale reflecting an increasing degree of openness and propensity to change. The scale is: stable, reactive, anticipating, exploring and creative. Generally, in order to fit successfully with its environment, the more turbulent and changeable the environment the more towards the 'creative' side of the scale an organization's cultural locus ought to be. For example, those companies who are leaders in a fast-changing industry such as information technology ought to have a culture which could be described as anticipating or exploring or creative while those companies which are in established industries which are subject to little change – for example the delivery of domestic coal – ought to have a 'stable' culture. Thus the extent of an organization's success or performance may be strongly influenced by the extent to which its culture is appropriate to the nature of its industry.

The sub-cultures within organizations
In many organizations, particularly large diversified ones which are structured on a divisional or SBU basis, it is often the case that there is not a universal homogeneous culture. Instead, there exist a variety of cultures which reflect the activities and aspirations of the sub-divisions and often these cultures are a function of the technology or work of the divisions or the SBUs.

At levels below the SBU level these sub-cultures also often obtain, particularly, within functional departments. Thus, it is not unusual for the culture of the accounting department to be somewhat different from that of the production department or that of the marketing department. Although each of these sub-cultures often considers its particular perspectives to be the crucial ones for the success of the total organization this is rarely the case and, indeed, the unbalanced dominance of a single set of functional cultural values can be disastrous as was shown in the case of Rolls-Royce just prior to its collapse in 1971. At this time the dominant power group in the company was the engineers and consequently the dominant culture was engineering. This led to a functionally unbalanced top management team in which the decisions were strongly influenced by engineering considerations with a neglect of the financial aspects. The inspectors who afterwards analysed the reasons for Rolls-Royce's collapse certainly considered that this was one of the factors which contributed significantly to it.

> While strongly rejecting the theory that Rolls-Royce failed because of poor accounting information, they (the inspectors) do agree that, as with so many companies, the information system was deficient. In particular, the board were given two documents at each meeting, a green folder and a red folder. The green folder contained all the important matters to be discussed and was compulsory reading for all directors. All the financial data – masses of it in great detail – were in the red folder, i.e., the voluntary one, which few of the directors would have had time to absorb. The other reason was that 'the personalities on the financial side were out-gunned and out-numbered by those on the engineering side'. (For example, in 1969 the DED* board had 22 members of whom only one was not an engineer.)[3]

---

* DED stands for the Derby Engine Division which was responsible for developing the RB211 engine.

The case of Rolls-Royce also illustrates the importance of power in the behavioural climate. This aspect is considered next.

Power

Understanding the power structure and the power process in an organization are fundamental to understanding its strategies, its operations, and behaviour. Power could be described as the ability of an individual or a group to influence other individuals or groups. (In this chapter, it will be assumed, unless otherwise stated, that it is held by a group.) Although power is not usually clearly defined or explicitly and formally publicized in most organizations (except as expressed through organization charts) its presence is real, and its effects are significant and therefore any comprehensive strategic analysis of an organization ought to include a consideration of its power dimensions.

The strong influence that the power of a single group can have over a whole industry can be illustrated by reference to the UK newspaper industry. A crucial challenge facing this industry in the late 1970s and early 1980s was to change over from the traditional manual craft composition of newspapers (by craft union employees) to single stroke, computerized electronic composition by journalists. This changeover, which by the mid-1980s had been successfully effected in many other industrialized countries, was considered by newspaper owners and managers to be vital to the future of the industry. Yet it was not until 1986, in spite of having had, for many years, the necessary resources and technology, that national newspapers such as *The Times* and *The Sunday Times* were able to impose their wish to change over to new technology. The major impediment to the changeover was the power of the craft union – the National Graphical Association (NGA) and the union Sogat 82.

> The affairs of Fleet Street have been a national disgrace for at least four decades. While newspapers have continually lectured the rest of British industry on its inadequacies, Fleet Street itself has remained a microcosm of Britain's industrial malaise at its worst: ridiculous overmanning; absurd restrictive practices; pusillanimous management; top-of-the-league pay levels which bear little relation to the work done or the skills involved; and the technology of the 19th century. Three royal commissions and countless other government and private inquiries over the past 40 years have all pointed the same finger, and urged Fleet Street to put its shameful house in order. But the arrogance of print-union power and the abdication of managerial control have always conspired to keep things as they are.[4]

Within any organization power can accrue to, or be accumulated by, individuals or groups either through official or unofficial means. The important consideration in any analysis of the power structure and process in an organization is the practice that actually prevails and not whether it is official or unofficial. Thus, when an organization which has an explicit and clear official power structure (typically expressed through an organization chart) which is not followed, and yet an un-official set of power relationships is followed, it is the unofficial power structure that should be analysed.

In general, in any organization, individuals or groups can obtain power, formally or informally, officially or unofficially from a number of sources. The main sources are given below.

Power over resources
Those individuals or groups who exercise control over resources which are scarce and important to the organization tend to accumulate power. The scarcer the resource and the more important the resource is to the organization the greater will be their power.

Traditionally, the most important resource in Western-style organizations has been considered to be money and this has led to a predominance of people with a financial background becoming the most powerful group in many Western organizations.

The power of the finance function is seen clearly in the case of General Motors – the world's largest vehicle manufacturer. Table 10 shows the chairmen of General Motors since 1917 and their functional backgrounds. As can be seen the dominant function is finance.

Table 10 The names and functional backgrounds of the chairmen of General Motors[5]

Name	Years	Background
P. S. DuPont	1917–1929	Finance
L. DuPont	1929–1937	Engineering/finance
A. P. Sloan	1937–1956	Finance
A. Bradley	1956–1958	Finance
F. G. Donner	1958–1967	Finance
J. M. Roche	1967–1972	Operations/engineering
R. C. Gerstenberg	1972–1975	Finance
T. A. Murphy	1975–	Finance

In contrast to the dominant influence of the finance function in Western companies, Japanese companies tend to regard money or finance as just one of many critical resources necessary for success. Consequently the composition of their decision-making boards tends to be functionally much broader than Western boards reflecting the power accorded to each of the functions.

The power of knowledge or skills
Those individuals who possess knowledge or skills which are crucial to the organization and who would be difficult to replace tend to accumulate power. This source of power is particularly noticeable in those new high-tech industries where the viability of such organizations is frequently determined by the quality and efforts of the technocrats, i.e. the

engineers and other technical staff. In such industries people with these technical skills tend to have real power as their skills are crucial and are often in short supply.

The power of reward or punishment

Those individuals or groups who are in a position to offer rewards or deal out punishments tend to accumulate power. Their influence is often considered fundamental by other groups for career advancement and this belief confers power on such groups.

The power of personality

The personality or charisma of an individual can have fundamental power effects. Those individuals who have the ability, and the skills to exercise this type of power can, and do, have material effects upon the directions taken by organizations. The personal characteristics which a survey of managers considered necessary to be an effective source of power are listed in Table 11.

Table 11   Reported characteristics of effective political actors[6]

Characteristic	Per cent of respondents mentioning
Articulate	29.9
Sensitive	29.9
Socially adept	19.5
Competent	17.2
Popular	17.2
Extrovert	16.1
Self-confident	16.1
Aggressive	16.1
Ambitious	16.1
Devious	16.1
'Organization man'	12.6
Highly intelligent	11.5
Logical	10.3

Pfeffer[7] has asserted that there are four main personal characteristics that determine the power of an individual in an organization. These are:

1 *Verbal skills and articulateness*:   Generally the more skilful the individual is in this respect, the more likely he is to be able to achieve power.
2 *Diagnostic skills*:   The better an individual is in diagnosing where power lies in an organization the more capable he is of aligning himself and hence allying himself with the groups or factions that will be successful.
3 *Understanding the rules of the organization*:   The better an individual understands the rules by which decisions are made in an organization

(whether, in making the decisions, the rules followed are the formal ones of the organization or whether they are informal) the more likely is the individual to accumulate power.

4 *Personal belief in oneself*:   The more an individual has confidence in his own skills and abilities the more likely he is to develop himself as a source of power.

Power configurations
Organizations exhibit different power configurations ranging from the highly autocratic centralized power structures (where, typically, great power is concentrated in the hands of the Chairman or Chief Executive Officer) to distributed power structures where power is disseminated throughout the organization. The type of power configuration that obtains, generally, will be a function of the environment faced by the organization (this was discussed in Part Two), the nature of the industry in which the organization operates, and the traditions and culture of the organization. Usually, those organizations which are most homogeneous in their work and their beliefs will tend to adopt a centralized power structure while those that have the greatest degree of variety in their work will tend to adopt the most distributed types of power structures.

For example, in the multiple retail chain-stores business, where each store tends to be built to, and operate on, a standard formula, power tends to be concentrated at the centre with little real power being delegated to the individual stores. Such a configuration is appropriate as the fundamental task is 'control of each store according to a formula'.

In contrast to this, businesses which have great heterogeneity in their work – for example conglomerates which have a high degree of unrelated diversification – tend to have a much more distributed power structure, with power being passed down to the individual strategic business units (SBUs). Again, this type of configuration is appropriate to this type of organization as the characteristics of the business in which each SBU is engaged may be so different that success can only be achieved by allowing the manager of each SBU the freedom to set and pursue strategies which are constrained only by the broadest of corporate parameters.

Heterogeneity in organizations is engendered not just by work variety, but also by functional variety. Thus, although the different functional departments in organizations may share the same top level corporate goals (this is further discussed on page 330) frequently they will pursue lower level functional objectives which are incompatible: it is not unusual for the finance function of an organization to place a high priority on issues such as the control of costs and for a marketing department to place a high priority on an issue such as the expansion of sales. This functional heterogeneity leads to interdepartmental conflicts which are resolved through the use of power, with the most powerful departments having the greatest influence.

Japanese companies have long recognized the harmful effects that such interdepartmental power struggles can have. They have sought to mitigate these effects by de-emphasizing functional importance and emphasizing the importance of a generalist approach. Thus in Japanese companies there is a strong emphasis on functional rotation throughout managers' careers so that when managers arrive at senior management positions they have had experience in all the functional areas. This approach helps top managers to develop multifunctional perspectives on problems and issues and helps develop organization-wide homogeneity and reduce the power tensions caused by monofunctional blinkers.

The exercise of power

The process by which power is exercised in an organization is a function of the nature of the industry, the way in which power is distributed, and the traditions or culture of the organization. The processes used to exercise power can be divided into three main groups – consensus, trade-off and autocratic.

Consensus: The benefits that can accrue to an organization when power is exercised in a consensual fashion are well demonstrated by the success of Japanese companies. In the main, Japanese companies seek to have strategies at all levels implemented by the power of consensus. The rationale of employing this process is that when such a consensus obtains then the power of such an agreement helps build a very high commitment to the strategy adopted and this commitment is ultimately reflected in superior corporate performance. The principal drawback of this process of implementation is that it can be extremely time consuming. Thus, the time needed to achieve genuine consensus and commitment from all the interested power groups may be so long that implementation of the company's consensual strategy may be too slow for optimal results.

In general, therefore, the greater the homogeneity in the organization, or department, and the longer the time available for decisions, the greater will be the opportunity for consensual implementation of strategies.

Trade-off: This occurs when there are a variety of individuals or groups within the organization who all have positions of power so that no single individual or group is dominant overall. In this situation political trade-offs are negotiated among the various power holders and compromise agreements reflecting the power configuration of the groups are adopted.

Autocratic: This process is used when organizations are strongly centralized and power is held at the centre. Such a process tends to be used in those organizations which are homogeneous in the nature of their work and where decisions may need to be taken relatively quickly. Although this method of exercising power suffers from the drawback that it may be coercive and therefore not likely to command the commitment that a consensual approach to implementation would, it does have the major attribute that it allows decisions to be made and implemented very quickly and therefore tends to be an appropriate method in those organizations which require speedy responses to challenges.

Power shifts
Changing the power structure in any organization is extremely difficult – the existing holders of power have a vested interest in retaining their power and usually will be most unwilling to surrender it. Ansoff asserts that a major shift of power can only occur in an organization when there is an organizational crisis so severe that its very survival is threatened. Under such conditions the various power groups will unite in their common goal of saving the organization. The old leaders of the organization, because they have failed, will be dismissed and a new leader (the 'saviour of the organization') will be brought in. This new leader will enjoy a honeymoon period in which he will be granted, by most power groups, the right to behave autocratically, and impose previously unacceptable strategies in the interests of the organization's survival. The UK electronics company Thorn EMI experienced such a situation in 1985.

Exhibit 9:   Survival crisis and power shift at Thorn EMI[8]
A fully-blown crisis hit Thorn EMI last summer when the once cash-rich business built on the pillars of TV rental and lighting began to run out of money. Peter Laister, chairman and chief executive, resigned and Sir Graham Wilkins, Thorn's deputy chairman and former chairman of the Beecham Group, immediately took over and announced a substantial reorganisation of its two biggest trouble spots, Inmos, which makes microchips, and Ferguson, the television manufacturing subsidiary ...
   ... The new regime has cut head office staff, installed new management systems, fired over one-third of the top 150 managers and made substantial changes in some of the more troubled parts of the business including Inmos, Ferguson and Capital, the north American music subsidiary.
   The new team paints a remarkable picture of a company which lacked basic business controls and market research and which had done little to rationalise the multitude of companies acquired over the years in the UK and overseas. These criticisms, and comments, made when the company's interim results were published earlier this month are clearly intended to blame the former management for the group's present woes.

Assessment of power in an organization
There is no single appropriate power configuration or process for the exercise of power in an organization. The appropriateness of these two

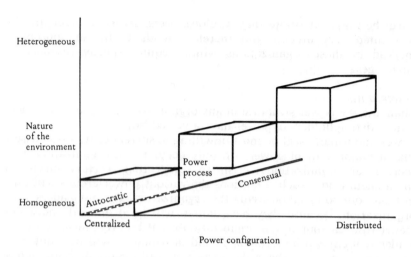

Figure 21   *The relationship between the power process, the power configuration, and the time required for an adequate response*

aspects of power is determined by the environment which the organization faces, the nature of the industry(ies) in which the organization operates, and its cultural climate. Once again Thorn EMI provides an example of an organization whose power structure seemed inappropriate:

> Thorn EMI's present problems – at once highly diversified and centrally run and having a high proportion of business in the UK – date back to the days of Sir Jules Thorn ...

Finally, the power dimensions of an organization can be presented as a three dimensional 'power map' as shown in Figure 21. This map attempts to align the 'power configuration', the 'exercise process of power', and the 'nature of the environment' so that any organization should be able to judge how appropriate its configuration is for its circumstances. Each of the axes of the power map is an unquantified continuum.

Leadership

The importance of good strategic leadership is not really questioned. Confirmation that good leaders tend to be in short supply is manifested in the constant search for such leaders in which many organizations – public sector as well as private sector – engage. However, the nature of just what good leadership actually is, is a more complex issue. Broadly speaking the views as to what constitutes good leadership polarize into two main camps – the 'task view' of leadership and the 'people view' of leadership.

The task view stems from the work of Taylor[9] and it suggests that the most effective leaders are those people who have the qualities necessary to achieve the tasks of the organization in the most efficient way possible. Thus, in this view of leadership the primary concern is with efficiency and consequently the human problems that may be generated in achieving high levels of efficiency are given minimal attention. In other words, the people in the organization are just a factor of production and should be used as efficiently as possible.

The alternative people view, which stems largely from the work of Mayo[10], asserts that the way to successfully achieve an organization's objectives is through the commitment of the people who comprise the organization. Therefore, a leader's primary objective is not the efficient carrying out of tasks, but the motivation of groups of people to carry out the tasks. In other words, when people are sufficiently motivated they will wish to and, will indeed, carry out the tasks efficiently.

In this book both of these leadership attributes are assumed to be of importance, the importance varying with the organization, the nature of its work, and its culture and that leadership is most effective when the mix of 'task' and 'people' strategies is in the proportions appropriate to the organization.

An examination of the leadership in an organization is therefore concerned with an analysis of the processes of leadership used by those individuals who have the ability to cause other groups to conform to their wishes. It is important to realize that leadership exists in organizations not just in the hierarchical sense, but leadership may be exercised horizontally and also unofficially. It is not unusual to find, in organizations, individuals who, although the organization chart does not accord them any leadership status, do, for various reasons effect leadership.

Although there is no checklist of the attributes necessary for good leadership, some or all of the attributes listed below are frequent requirements.

Personality and charisma
Frequently leaders exude an exceptional personality or aura of charisma. Such people are often able to influence others to adopt their views and are often extremely adept at communicating their ideas and infecting others with their own enthusiasm.

Intellect
Leadership may be based upon knowledge. This type of leadership is frequently seen in industries such as 'high-tech' sectors and knowledge industries such as the professions. Such leaders gain and maintain their positions by means of their superior knowledge.

Vision
At the strategic level, perhaps the most important attribute that leaders can have is that of vision. Leaders with vision have the dual ability to

see the organization as an entity and develop strategies which will be in the long-term interest of the entire organization and they also have a clarity of vision about the future which is often at variance with most other contemporary observers.

Legitimacy

Leaders can only continue to lead as long as they are the 'legitimate leaders' in the eyes of the group or groups that they are leading. This legitimacy is measured in terms of the attributes – charisma, intellect and or vision – necessary for successful leadership and legitimacy is most frequently questioned after failure. The fundamental question being 'Does the leader have the qualities necessary to lead?' If the group being led is of the opinion that the leadership does not possess the required qualities, then, power conditions permitting, the leadership will change.

Leadership in a survival crisis

When an organization is confronted with a survival crisis there is frequently a power shift and a change of leadership. It is at such times that leadership receives its most severe test. If, after a crisis, there is a power shift and the new leader fails to resolve the crisis, he too will be replaced. Alternatively, even if he succeeds in removing the crisis, once the organization feels that the crisis has been removed, then there will be attempts to re-structure the organization back to its old pre-crisis behaviour patterns and strategies. Resisting such forces is a major test of leadership.

Conclusion on leadership

Clearly, appropriate leadership is a crucial element in assessing the strategic health of an organization. It has been suggested, as the following quotation shows, that the reason why the performance of many European companies lags behind that of their American and Japanese counterparts, is because of leadership.

> Such leaders are giving their companies a new sense of direction, generally stripping them back to their basic businesses and then grafting on a set of new activities which have been more carefully chosen than past diversification. Equally important, the new breed has begun to cut through decades of accumulated bureaucracy, and to alter managerial attitudes quite dramatically – its member have, in the fashionable jargon, set about changing the corporate culture ...
>
> ... But the list of challenges is a daunting one, and overall, the auguries for Europe are decidedly uncertain.
>
> • Overriding all else will be top management's ability to develop a clear vision of where the company should be going and by which route and to communicate this through the organisation in the form of an explicit set of objectives ...
>
> • In creating this corporate vision, top management must recognise that

competition is already international, and in many markets is going global. Strategies and structures will have to be changed accordingly and alliances forged with foreign partners.
- Companies must improve the sophistication of their marketing, especially their customer segmentation and the differentiation of their products and services ...
- Having built competence in particular functions, companies must develop the ability of managers at all levels to think more clearly and strategically.

Three main factors make it difficult for some European companies to rise to these challenges:

1 Leadership. As Maucher, Harvey-Jones and Co. have shown, Europe's sleeping giants are in need of more incisive leadership, not only at the top, but at various levels in the organizations ...
2 Managing ambiguity. For a multinational to achieve the ideal balance between centralisation and decentralisation, tightness and entrepreneurship, it needs to be able to operate with a flexible mixture of what *In Search of Excellence* called 'loose-tight controls'.
3 Managing complexity and diversity under pressure. A welter of factors is increasing the complexity of business management, and the pressures under which companies must operate. They include globalisation; growing interdependence (technological, market, or otherwise between previously distinct parts of the company; the shortening of product life cycles; and the need radically to improve the co-ordination of research, development, marketing and production.[11]

Goals

Two examples of publicly stated company goals are given below.

Example 1
Matsushita Electric, the Japanese electrical and electronics company has stated that:

The company Creed expresses the basic business philosophy of Matsushita Electric which defines the direction of the company. The Creed translates as follows: 'Through our industrial activities, we strive to foster progress, to promote the general welfare of society and to devote ourselves to furthering the development of world culture.'[12]

The company has also stated that:

Our goal is the creation of a corporate structure so strong that it will enable Matsushita Electric to achieve long-term earnings growth regardless of the external climate. At the same time, we intend to increase emphasis on overseas production by transferring more of our technologies, adhering to our basic policy that our activities must be welcomed by all peoples of the world, with a view toward achieving continuous healthy growth as an international corporate leader.[13]

Example 2

The Chairman of United Biscuits (Holdings) Ltd., the UK biscuit and savoury snack manufacturer has stated that:

> I think the time has come to include with my statement the long-run corporate objectives which our company strives to achieve. These are designed to give security of employment and the highest possible standard of living to our employees, the best possible value for money to the consumer and consistently reward the investor at a level which fully recognises the element of risk, while ensuring that the business remains internally competitive.

Later in the same report it is stated that the objectives are as follows:

1 *Return on capital employed*
   Objective:
   Profit before interest and tax to be not less than 20 per cent of capital employed with a target of 25 per cent on an historical cost basis. Capital employed is defined as the total of shareholders' funds plus long- and short-term borrowings.
2 *Sales and profit*
   Objective:
   At least to maintain the increase in profits in line with the increase in sales, i.e. to maintain net profit margins.
3 *Capital expenditure*
   Objective:
   To maintain the quality of existing assets by investing not less than 5p per sales annually and to make new investment at rates of return applicable to the risk involved to meet the group's targeted return on capital employed.
4 *Dividends*
   Objective:
   That the return to shareholders should grow in line with the growth in net profit.
5 *Loans*
   Objective;
   That loans should not exceed 40 per cent of capital employed unless required for exceptional circumstances of a short-term nature.
6 *Overseas assets and liabilities*
   Objective:
   That foreign currency assets and liabilities are matched.[14]

The above quotations are taken directly from company literature and they express what is often called 'the corporate goals or corporate objectives' of the companies. These public statements, presumably, are designed to enable the readers to see just what the long-run intentions of each corporation are. However, the dissimilarity of each set of statements provokes the following observations:

There appears to be a substantial qualitative difference between each company's statements. Thus Matsushita's aspiration 'to foster progress, to promote the general welfare of society and to devote ourselves to furthering the development of world culture' seems to be a much broader, much more altruistic, and much longer term sentiment than United Biscuits' objective of having 'profit before interest and tax to be not less than 20 per cent of capital employed'. Is one of these sets of statements 'better' or 'worse' than the other?

In another vein if, in the future, Matsushita were only able 'to foster progress, to promote the general welfare of society and to devote ourselves to furthering the development of world culture' at the expense of 'the creation of a corporate structure so strong that it will enable Matsushita Electric to achieve long-term earnings growth regardless of the external climate' would the company be disappointed or pleased with that achievement? Or conversely if, in the future, Matsushita were only able to create 'a corporate structure so strong that it will enable Matsushita Electric to achieve long-term earnings growth regardless of the external climate' at the expense of 'fostering progress to promote the general welfare of society and to devote ourselves to furthering the development of world culture' would the company be disappointed or pleased with that achievement?

The above company statements, and the observations made about them, help to illustrate that there is a considerable degree of variety in the ways in which companies describe their long-term aspirations about their futures. Part of the reason for this variety and consequent confusion as to just what the appropriate level of resolution for 'long-term aspirations' ought to be is caused by disagreement over the definitions of terms used. The main terms used to describe the above aspirations are mission, goal, and objective. These terms are frequently used interchangeably by writers and practitioners and indeed it is not unusual for exactly opposite definitions to be used. Thus Lorange[15] has written that:

> Objectives, as referred to in this book, are more general statments about a direction in which the firm intends to go, without stating specific targets to be reached at particular points in time. A goal, on the other hand, is much more specific, indicating where one intends to be at a given point in time. A goal thus is an operational transformation of an objective; typically a general objective often gets transformed into one or more specific goals.

while Hofer and Schendel[16] have written that:

> We consider goals to be the ultimate, long-run, open-ended attributes or ends a person or organization seeks, while we consider objectives to be the intermediate-term targets that are necessary but not sufficient for the satisfaction of goals.

Mintzberg[17] who has researched and written very extensively in this area, has recognized the necessity of clarifying just what is meant by the various terms and has defined them in the following ways:

1 *Mission*: An organization's mission is its basic function in society

and it is reflected in the products and services that it provides for its customers or clients. For example, although all publishers are in the business of publishing and selling books to readers, there is within this industry a great variety of missions which publishers follow. For example, the UK publishing house Virago has a fundamental mission, which is the dissemination of 'women's views' on life through the publication of books by women for women. Consequently books selected by Virago for publication are based on their currency as well-written literary vehicles of 'women's views' rather than their market potential. This is a somewhat different mission than that followed by the publishers of cheap, mass market paperback books. Thus the mission of an organization is essentially a long-term – many years – view of its fundamental reasons for existence.

2   *Goals*:   An organization's goals are the intentions behind its decisions or actions. Goals will frequently never be achieved and may be incapable of being measured. Thus, for example, the United Biscuits goal of giving 'the highest possible standard of living to our employees' is a goal which will be difficult to realize and measure. Thus, although goals are more specific than a mission statement and tend to have a shorter number of years in their time scales, they are not precise measures of performance.

3   *Objectives*:   Objectives are goals expressed in a form in which they can be measured. Thus, the objectives given in the second quotation from the United Biscuits statement – for example, 'profit before interest and tax to be not less than 20 per cent of capital employed . . .' – are all capable of precise measurement.

These are the definitions which will be adhered to in this book.

The goals that organizations follow can be analysed along a number of axes. The principal axes of analysis are now considered.

Single goal versus multiple goals.
In traditional economic theory the role of goals can be understood quickly and easily: in this theory it is assumed that the rational economic man who controls a business has a single goal – profit maximization – and he resolutely pursues this goal to the exclusion of all others. Unfortunately, for economists, there has accumulated considerable evidence to show that, generally, this does not accord with reality.

Even in the smallest and most entrepreneurial businesses, where it would be thought that profit maximization would be most likely to prevail, there is evidence to show that the classic 'economist's entrepreneur' may pursue a goal other than profit maximization or may pursue multiple goals and that his goals may change over time. Thus, it is not unusual to find that entrepreneurs have, in addition to the profit goal, such goals as 'feelings of autonomy', and 'feelings of achievement'. Indeed Cromie[18] in his empirical investigations into the reasons why people start businesses found, as shown in Table 12, that entrep-

Table 12 Reasons given by founders for establishing their enterprises

Reason	Frequency
Autonomy	58
Achievement	46
Job dissatisfaction	46
Money	35
Career Dissatisfaction	26
Child rearing	14
Outlet for skills	9
Offer employment	8
Market opportunity	6
Job insecurity	6
Entrepreneurship	6
Inheritance	4
Status	4
Others	8
	276

(Based on a sample of 72 respondents)

reneurs had multiple motives and also that 'money' (i.e. profit maximizing) was ranked only fourth as a motivating factor.

In more complex organizations, where, frequently, there is more than one top decision influencer, the case for the single goal profit maximizing model of business becomes even more untenable.

Therefore, in this book, all organizations are considered to have multiple goals and they strive to satisfy these goals in a variety of ways. Multiple goal organizations normally will not be able to satisfy all goals simultaneously. (For example, the multiple goals of increasing marketing expenditure and reducing costs are mutually exclusive.) So the process by which such organizations satisfy, or fail to satisfy, their goals becomes important. There are three main views as to how this is achieved.

The first view is that not all goals are equally important – i.e. that organizations may have a hierarchy of goals and the more important a goal is considered to be then the more likely it is to be satisfied. For example, many US companies consider an increase in quarterly net earnings to be at the apex of their hierarchy of goals and strive for this with subordinate attention given to other goals. By way of contrast many Japanese companies consider the maintenance of life-time employment of their personnel to be a much more important goal and if a choice has to be made between paying a dividend and sacking personnel, will forego the dividend payment. When an organization has multiple goals of differing importance, it is assumed that they are satisfied in a hierarchical fashion.

A second view on how the problem of multiple goals is resolved has been put forward by Simon.[19] He has asserted that organizations which have multiple goals do not, in practice, maximize any of their goals, but rather, the goals act as constraints on decision making and therefore it is not goal maximizing that such organizations practise but goal satisficing. In other words, the goals are seen as minimum levels of performance which must be achieved rather than targets.

A third view has been formulated by Cyert and March[20] who have asserted that organizations really consist of a coalition of different groups with each group having its own preferences and beliefs and that goal incompatibility is resolved through trade-offs, based on power relationships, among the various interest groups. They assert that it is often the case that goals are satisfied sequentially and that the order of the sequence will change over time. When this is the case, then, in the longer term, no one goal is maximized, but instead a series of goals are maximized. For example, most organizations are affected by business cycles, i.e. there are times of growth and times of consolidation, and it seems likely that the goals which are maximized are a function of the stage in the cycle with goals such as 'sales maximization' being dominant in the growth stage of the cycle and goals such as 'control of costs' being dominant in the trough of the cycle.

Which of the above methods of the satisfaction of multiple goals occurs in an organization can be inferred from analysis of the historical practice of the organization.

Research appears to indicate that organizations derive their goals from three main sources: the people who comprise the organization, the organization itself and the environment.

Source 1:   The people who comprise the organization
Cyert and March have asserted that organizations are not inanimate structures. Rather, organizations are comprised of people and people have personalities, needs, aspirations, loves, hates etc. and this human aspect of organizations is the major source of an organization's goals.

People in organizations are grouped together according to many criteria such as: status, function, location, age, etc. and therefore it may be more correct not to regard an organization as a single entity, but to regard it as a coalition of interest groups. Each of these interest groups will tend to strive after goals which are most important to its particular value system. Therefore, the corporate goals which an organization has develop out of the trade-offs between the different groups which comprise the coalition. The interest groups will use such devices as power, politics, status, and tradition to impose their value systems and goals upon the organization.

The interest group which will often, though not always, be the dominant group in the formulation of goals will be the top management, i.e. the group responsible for the strategic decisions of the organization. Top management will vary from a single individual alone, to a group of managers. The value system of this top group frequently will be the major determinant of the goals and therefore the strategies of the organization. (Although the term top group is used, in practice, the influential set of values could come from just one person in the group (the leader) or from a sub-group or faction within the top group.) Consequently, understanding the value systems of the top group and the influences that motivate them are often crucial prerequisites to understanding the strategic behaviour of the organization. An example of the influence of one person on a company's goals is provided by Dr Edward Land, the founder of the instant photograph company Polaroid.

Exhibit 10:   Polaroid and the influence of Dr Land

In the 1960s the Polaroid company sought technical help from Kodak (the world's largest photographic company) to develop colour instant film. However, Polaroid lost its monopoly in the instant photographic market when, in 1976, Kodak launched its first instant photograph camera. Six days after the Kodak camera was available in the shops Polaroid sued Kodak on the grounds that during the years of their cooperation Kodak had stolen Polaroid's proprietary secrets and infringed their patents. The dispute between the two companies cost Polaroid $10 million in legal fees, lasted for 10 years and was finally settled, in Polaroid's favour, in January 1986. A major factor influencing Polaroid's decision to fight the much larger Kodak so tenaciously was the value system of Dr Land. Land was 'a near-fanatic in protecting Polaroid's intellectual property' and was outraged by Kodak's actions. A goal of the company became the return of the intellectual property.

Polaroid had the goal of commitment to excellence through innovation implanted in its culture by Dr Land.

Source 2:   The organization
Not only do the people who comprise an organization have goals which they bring to their organizations, but the organizations themselves have goals which they transmit to their employees. That is, the organization can be regarded as having a 'life of its own' and it influences the people who work there. The power of organizations to transmit its goals to its people is illustrated by reference to IBM. In spite of heterogeneity prior to employment in IBM, their salespeople, after some time in the company, tend to be regarded as rather homogeneous in their business attitudes and appearance. They absorb the organization's value systems and goals and are often recognized, by people they have never met, as IBM people – they have absorbed part of the organization.

Source 3:   The environment
The influence of the environment on the organization has already been discussed in Part Two. An additional way in which the environment influences organizations is in goal formulation. Goal formulation in organizations is influenced by the power that the environment has over the organization. In general, the stronger the external influences are on

an organization, the more influential outside forces are likely to be. Thus, prior to its privatization, British Airways was a government-owned airline which enjoyed monopolies on many domestic routes. Its state status and monopoly position effectively insulated it from many competitive realities on these routes and the goals which were pursued reflected this privileged position. With the deregulation of domestic air routes in the early 1980s and the proposal to privatize the airline, it became more dependent on its external competitive environment and this change of dependency was reflected in the goals which were then pursued. Perhaps the most noticeable of the changes was the goal of becoming more competitive through giving priority to the passengers. This was manifested in improvements in the areas of: punctuality of flights; the provision of in-flight meals and refreshments; and a more flexible fare structure.

In analysing the goals that an organization is following it is necessary to establish the sources of the goals as this will strongly influence their nature.

Recognizing organization goals

Recognizing just what the goals of an organization are is not always an easy task in that the goals which are stated by an organization to be its 'official' goals may not, in practice, be the ones which it actually follows. Thus, for example, a university which proclaims that one of its primary goals is the pursuit of academic excellence through empirical research and yet does not provide the resources to support such research cannot be regarded as pursuing that goal. If it were, appropriate resources would be made available for research activities and the nature of the work of the staff would reflect the pursuit of the goal. Thus, in trying to ascertain what the goals of an organization are a dilemma may arise if there is a discrepancy between its official goals and its unofficial goals. The dilemma is: which set of goals – the official or the unofficial – is the true set of goals of the organization?

The true goals of any organization are those ones which in practice are followed whether they are official or unofficial and the test of which goals are being followed is the willingness of the organization to devote resources to them. For example, if an organization has as a primary goal 'the pursuit of quality' and it fails to give resources to this goal (through failing to promote staff responsible for quality improvement; through paying staff in the quality improvement function less than staff in other functions; through lack of investment in the training of staff in the quality function) then this goal is only a paper aspiration and is not a true goal.

The goals that organizations follow

Although there is a wide diversity in the goals which organizations have and how they measure them, there are certain classes of goals – generic goals – which appear to have some influence on all organizations.

Survival: The primary generic goal appears to be survival. This is the fundamental goal for all organizations because the consequence of not meeting it is the extinction of the organization. The importance of this goal is demonstrated in periods of severe crisis when an organization's survival is threatened. In these conditions all other goals are temporarily discarded and all strategies and actions are directed to weathering the survival crisis. The case of Thorn EMI referred to on page 107 is an explicit example of this goal receiving public prominence.

Growth: For many organizations growth appears to be a naturally sought after generic goal. Perhaps this is because growth, apart from the material benefits which it bestows upon the stakeholders of an organization, also facilitates solving difficult management problems. Thus, when there is growth managers who are successful can be rewarded through promotion and increased benefits and managers who are relatively unsuccessful can be 'moved sideways'. However, in times of no growth, managerial frustrations develop in the successful managers in that their efforts do not appear, to them, to be receiving adequate recognition and the relatively unsuccessful managers may be fired – an action which tends to cause general fear and discontent. In short, growth helps organizations cope with strain.

Control and efficiency: Most organizations place some emphasis on these related goals. Perhaps the goals are best seen in Japanese companies. Mikami[21] has asserted that a fundamental reason for the outstanding success of Japanese business has been the goal of efficiency.

Of the top ten management strategies selected by Japanese managers as being of great importance over the next five years, rationalization, labor saving, and energy-saving problems related to increased productivity ranked second.

At the same time, Japanese managers expressed the intention of strengthening those activities in the years ahead.

In addition to the above generic goals, which apply to most organizations, the main goals, according to a survey carried out by Bhaskar and McNamee[22] in 1979, which the largest companies in the UK pursue are shown in Table 13.

There is no general rule for knowing in advance just what goals an organization is following. They can be divined by noting the organization's statements on its mission, goals and objectives and then analysing how it allocates its resources.

Setting goals and objectives
From the above it follows that the goals and objectives in an organization are set by the dominant power group (or coalition of groups) and Ansoff has suggested that this is done in a hierarchical fashion. That is, the primary goals and objectives are set by the dominant power group and then these goals and objectives 'cascade' down through the orga-

Table 13 Frequencies given to goals by major UK companies

Goal	Total number of responses
Profitability	115
Market value	57
Company growth	104
Turnover ratios	64
Depth of skills	70
Age of assets	74
Liquidity	91
Flexibility	70
Risk	93
Image	67
Government	64
Environment	76
Other goals	34

nization, with progressively more precision being added as they percolate downwards to the lowest levels in the organization. For example, a diversified holding company which had the mission of 'increasing the wealth of its shareholders could have, as its primary goal, the achievement of a satisfactory return on investment (ROI). This could then be refined into an objective of an ROI of 16 per cent, and then further refined, at a functional level, into a 'net profit to sales' ratio of 4 per cent and a 'sales to assets' ratio of 4 per cent. These ratios could finally be further refined into operating targets, i.e. value of assets, prices, costs and sales targets necessary to achieve these results. These 'operating targets' are then turned into budgets and targets for departments and individuals.

In summary this method of setting goals and objectives suggests a filtering through the organization, as shown in Figure 22 with a progressive refinement, a shortening of the time scale and less discretion for deviation as the aspiration cascades downwards in the organization. This method assumes that it is the official goals which prevail. Should the situation be one where unofficial goals are the prevailing ones then the process can be similarly traced from the power group which sets the goals to the operating targets.

Characteristics of goals
When official goals are effective they are followed. Some of the general characteristics which help goals to be effective are set out below.

Consistency   Goals ought to be consistent in two directions – vertically and horizontally. Thus, in the hierarchy – mission, goals, objectives and operating targets – there should be a vertical consistency so that each level in the hierarchy dovetails with the other levels. Similarly, in any stratum in this hierarchy there should be horizontal consistency such that the targets or goals can coexist. For example, if three goals of

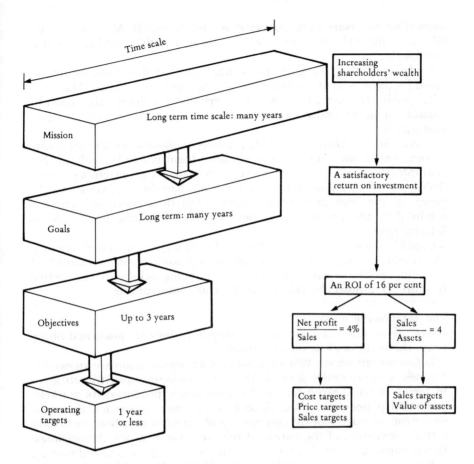

Figure 22 *How operating targets derive from a mission statement*

an organization are lifetime employment for all employees, the introduction of the latest labour-saving technology and the improvement of
return on investment it is unlikely that these goals will all be simultaneously achievable without very great expansion of sales. Such a set
of goals may well be inconsistent and unrealizable.

Feasibility: Any goals that are followed by any organization should
be feasible, otherwise they will not be taken seriously in the organization and will become meaningless paper sentiments or, even worse,
may lead to disaster. Carroll[23] has shown that a small company which
has the goal of being a leading world force in a high-tech industry, in
which there are already in existence major competitors, is unlikely ever
to realize this goal. His research shows that the goal is not feasible
because the small company is not of sufficient size, and therefore lacks
the resources, to engage in the degree of research and development and

marketing necessary to be competitive and profitable. Most companies who have these characteristics will fail to realize this goal because it is not feasible.

Understandable: For goals to be implemented they must be understood by those who are responsible for their implementation. Therefore when goals are enunciated – whether verbally or written – they must be capable of being understood and, as a corollary, be effectively communicated.

Acceptability: Goals must be acceptable to those groups in an organization whose power of veto would cause them not to be realized. For example, the goal of many Fleet Street newspaper proprietors of introducing new printing technology in the 1980s had this goal vetoed by the power of the craft print trade unions until their power of veto was removed by the activities of Rupert Murdoch (the proprietor of News International).

Capable of measurement: At the level of objectives it should be possible to measure achievement. Failure to have some measure means that it is impossible to say if an objective is being achieved. The United Biscuits (Holdings) objectives are all clearly measurable.

The functions of goals

There are several main reasons why organizations set goals and objectives, the main ones being that goals:

Define the business: When the goals of an organization are known the business is more easily defined. Thus, if a business explicitly sets goals in terms of its: desired financial performance; products; its markets; personnel polices and research and development activities, then it is easier for employees of the company, and external stakeholders to have a true conception of the nature of the business in which the organization is engaged. Explicit goals define the business for interested parties.

Send signals to outside stakeholders: Explicitly stated objectives are used by organizations to send signals of their intentions to outside stakeholders. (Of course these signals need not necessarily be honest – they could be 'bluff' signals designed to mislead competitors.) Thus, when a package tour holiday company declare a goal of 'providing the lowest cost foreign holidays ever' this is a signal to potential customers that they will obtain excellent value-for-money holidays from this company and it is also a signal to competitors that the competitive instrument this company will use will be price.

Give direction: Goals help give an organization a sense of overall direction. Thus, when Nabisco Inc., the international food company stated that it would be 'the lowest cost producer while maintaining its reputation of high quality products' this statement helps give a direction to the strategies and operations that the various personnel in the company ought to follow.

Knit the organization together: When goals are consistent and effectively communicated they should have the effect of unifying the organization behind common purposes. This 'knitting' should take place in a vertical and a horizontal direction.

Thus when John Egan became chairman of Jaguar Cars plc he made it clear that a primary goal of the company was the improvement of the quality of its cars. The explicit statement of this goal, and its continuous reinforcement, helped unite all people in the company into a common purpose and its effect was manifested in record sales since 1985.

Set targets: As well as giving directions, goals and objectives also have the effect that they present targets for all levels in the organization so that success and failure can be measured. The role of goals as targets was discussed above in the context of United Biscuits' (Holdings) objectives.

Conclusion on mission, goals and objectives

Understanding the mission, goals, goal structure, and objectives is a fundamental first step in understanding why an organization is following particular strategies. An understanding of an organization's goals should also reveal what it is likely to do in the future. Goals are essentially of the future and not the present or the past and so they are targets at which the organization will be aiming and could be described as the driving forces which cause the organization to go in a particular direction or directions.

References

1 Glueck, W., *Business Policy and Strategic Management*, McGraw Hill, 1980.
2 Ansoff, H. I., *Strategic Management*, Macmillan, 1979.
3 Argenti, J., *Corporate Collapse: The Causes and Symptoms*, McGraw Hill, 1971.
4 'Putting our House in Order', *Sunday Times*, January 19 1986, 69.
5 Selnick, P., *Leadership in Administration*, University of California Press, 1984.
6 Hensey, P. and Blanchard, K., *Management of Organizational Behaviour*, Prentice Hall Inc., Englewood Cliffs, NJ, 1982.
7 Pfeffer, J., *Power in Organizations*, Pitman, 1981.
8 Crisp, J., 'Striving to Revitalise its Core', *Financial Times*, 29 January 1986, p. 16.
9 Taylor, F. W., *The Principles of Scientific Management*, Harper and Brothers, New York, 1911.
10 Mayo, E., *The Social Problems of an Industrial Civilization*, Harvard Business School, Boston, 1945.
11 Lorenz, C., 'Sleeping Giants Begin to Stir', *Financial Times*, 5 July 1985, p. 14.
12 Matsushita Electric, Annual Report, 1984.

13   Matsushita Electric, Public Relations Information.
14   United Biscuits Annual Report, an extract from the Chairman's statement, 1977.
15   Lorange, P., *Corporate Planning, an Executive Viewpoint*, Prentice-Hall Inc., Englewood Cliffs, N. J., 1980.
16   Hofer, C. W. and Schendel, D., *Strategy Formulation: Analytical Concepts*, West Publishing Company, 1978.
17   Mintzberg, H., *Power in and Around Organizations*, Prentice-Hall Inc., Englewood Cliffs, N. J., 1983.
18   Cromie, S., Unpublished Ph.D. thesis, University of Leeds, 1986.
19   Simon H. A., 'On the Concept of the Organizational Goal', *Administrative Science Quarterly*, 1964, pp. 1–22.
20   Cyert, R. and March, J. G., *A Behavioural Theory of the Firm*, Englewood Cliffs, N. J., Prentice-Hall, 1963.
21   Mikami, T., *Management and Productivity in Japan*, JMA Consultants, Tokyo, 1982.
22   Bhaskar, K. N. and McNamee, P. B., 'Multiple Goals in Accounting and Finance', *Journal of Business Finance and Accounting*, Vol. 10., No. 4, Winter 1983, pp. 595–621.
23   Carroll, C., *Building Ireland's Business; Perspectives from PIMS*, Irish Management Institute, Dublin, 1985.

6 The functional analysis

Introduction

This section is concerned with analysing the functional strengths and weaknesses that an organization may have. Its purpose is to ascertain what are the current 'functional coordinates' of the organization which will enable an assessment to be made of its current and potential functional strengths. It is also concerned with analysing how well the overall goals of the organization are translated into feasible functional targets and how effectively each of the functions is managed in terms of achieving overall, organizational goals.

In the functional analysis it is *relative* strengths and weaknesses that are important, not absolute measures of functional performance. Thus, the analysis is concerned with ascertaining the functional competitive power of the organization in relation to its existing and potential competitors. Consequently, it is important to realize that the functional strengths or weaknesses of an organization must be related to the nature of the industry in which it is located, i.e. there is no universal pattern of functional strength which is applicable to all organizations but rather there are particular patterns which are appropriate to particular industries.

For example, in the vodka industry where the tenchnology needed to manufacture and distribute vodka is well known and generally available, the primary functional strength which is required is that of 'strength in marketing'. Most vodkas are not clearly differentiated on the basis of taste or strength so vodka manufacturers often devote extremely high levels of resources to marketing. They hope, through heavy marketing, to differentiate their product from rival products and develop brand loyalty in the hope of removing the 'commodity status' which endangers such products. Products have commodity status when purchasers do not perceive differences in the products offered by rival manufacturers. For example, household lightbulbs could be regarded as having this status as there does not appear to be consumer loyalty to particular brands. Commodity status tends to depress the price that can be charged for a product and consequently adversely affects its margins. Products which may have the attributes of commodity status can be raised to the status of differentiated products through effective marketing. Thus, companies which are in the vodka industry must have expertise in the marketing function plus the financial resources necessary to support a heavy commitment to marketing. By way of contrast, in the missile industry the crucial functional requirements appear to be technology and the resources necessary to support the very high development costs. Abstracting from the issues of political influence, defence equipment tends to be bought on the basis of technical specification subject to costs. Thus, successful companies in the missile defence industry must have superior technical expertise plus the financial resources necessary to support heavy research and development programmes.

Therefore in appraising the functional strengths or weaknesses of an organization regard must be paid to the industrial context in which the organization is located.

For the purposes of functional appraisal it is assumed that all organizations can be functionally divided into the following areas – finance, marketing, production, personnel, and management information systems (MIS)* and that the strengths or weaknesses of each of these areas can be assessed under the following headings:

- *Resources*:   What are the total resources that the organization has allocated to each functional area?
- *Efficiency*:   How efficiently is each functional area managed?
- *Planning*:   How good is the planning in each functional area?
- *Control*:   Is control exercised effectively in each functional area?
- *Balance*:   Within each functional area is there internal consistency and is there consistency with the other activities of the organization?
- *Measures*:   What are the measures that can be used to indicate the quality of the performance of each functional area?

Using these headings each of the functional areas will now be considered.

Finance

Traditionally the finance function has as its primary goal, within the overall top goals of the organization, the maximization of stakeholders'

---

* Although MIS is not a functional area in the accepted sense, its role has become such a fundamental factor in determining the strategic and operating health of many organizations that in this chapter it is given a weight which reflects this importance.

wealth subject to such constraints as scarce resources and risk minimization. The finance function pursues this goal through three main
and interrelated sets of strategies:

The investment strategies

This set is concerned with deciding which new investments the organization should undertake and how its current portfolio of investments
in fixed and current assets should be managed in the long term and the
short term so that the goals and strategies of the organization are
fulfilled.

The financing strategies

This set is concerned with determining the optimal mix of finance
which will maximize the organization's goals. It is therefore concerned
with such issues as capital budgeting, (raising finance), capital structure (determining the mix of debt and equity), and working capital
management (the levels of working capital, debtors, creditors and in-
ventories that should prevail).

The dividend strategies

This set is concerned with determining what is the optimal amount of
money that should be paid to shareholders as dividends so that the
goals of the organization are realized.

Thus the finance function is concerned with developing optimal
strategies for the above and the general management, administration,
and control of financial and accounting matters in the organization.

In many respects the finance function is a uniquely powerful function
– most of the activities of most organizations can be measured, ultimately, in financial terms, so this is often the one and only universal
organization-wide indicator of performance. Also, because of this, the
finance function is often privileged to receive more information about
the organization than any other function and so it appears that it
should receive special attention. Finally, it is frequently the case that
financial information is the only information about the industry in
which the organization operates, so a knowledge of finance is important
for an understanding of the industry.

The finance function is now considered under the headings given on
page 126.

Resources

What are the total financial resources, long-term and short-term, that
the organization has?
How many people are employed in the finance area, what is their
quality and in what way are the finance personnel regarded by the rest
of the organization?

Costs and efficiency

What are the sources of outside funds available to the organization?
What are the costs of these funds?
What is the rate of return which the organization is earning on these funds?
What is the capital structure of the organizations and is it optimal?
What is the level of working capital and is it optimal?
What are the levels of debtors and creditors and are these optimal?
What is the level of dividend payment and is it appropriate to the goals of the organization?
What is the tax position of the organization?

Planning

What is the overall quality of financial planning in the organization?
Are the plans flexible and capable of adaptation to changing circumstances?
How effective are the capital budgeting procedures?
What is the level of financial risk to which the organization is exposed and is it appropriate?
How effective is the management of working capital?
How effective are the budgeting procedures?
How effective are the auditing procedures?

Control

In what way is the organization's accounting/finance system structured and is it effective in terms of control?
What is the reporting system?
What is the speed and accuracy of the system?
What are the procedures which are used when variances from plans arise?

Balance

Are the financial goals, strategies, and operations consistent with overall organization goals?
Are the financial goals, strategies, and operations internally consistent?
Are the financial goals, strategies, and operations consistent with the goals, strategies and operations of other functional areas?

Measures of performance

Although there are many possible measures of performance which could be used to assess how effectively the finance function is operating some of the more frequently used measures and the core financial strategies to which they most closely relate are given below.

Measure	Core financial strategy
Return on investment	} Investment
Return on capital employed	
Debt to equity ratio	
Creditors ratio	} Financing
Debtors ratio	
Return on equity	} Dividend
Payout ratio	
Current ratio	} Liquidity
Quick ratio	

Marketing

The marketing function has the overall goal of ensuring that the capabilities of the organization are utilized in such a way that the products or services which it produces meet the needs and wants of customers in a manner that enables the organization to realize its goals. For profit seeking organizations these goals will often be measures of profitability, but for non-profit seeking organizations the goals could include measures such as heightening public awareness of an issue (for example a health campaign), developing public allegiance to a political point of view etc. Because the marketing function is dealt with comprehensively in Part Six, only a brief outline, following the same format used for assessing the other functional areas, is presented below.

Thus, it is suggested that a judgement can be made about an organization's marketing effectiveness through assessing its performance in the areas of:

- *Market identification* How effective has it been in identifying markets which it has been, or will be, able to exploit?
- *Market segmentation* How effective has it been in dissecting markets into segments in which it has gained or will gain competitive advantage?
- *Product positioning* How effective has it been in positioning its products in its desired market segments?
- *Marketing mix strategies* How effective has it been in its product, distribution, pricing and promotion strategies in ensuring that marketing and corporate goals have been achieved.

The marketing function is now considered under the headings given on page 126.

Resources

What is the total value of the annual sales of the organization?
What is the mix and range of products that the organization has?
What is the balance of the product life cycles of the organization's products?

What are the market shares or relative market shares that the organization has for its products?

What degree of patent protection does the organization have for its products?

What methods of distribution are used for the various products and markets served?

What are the market segments for the organization's products according to geography, customer type, age, sex, etc?

Does the organization enjoy any cost or quality advantages which are integrated into its marketing process?

Does the organization enjoy any promotional advantages which it is able to exploit?

What is the image of the organization and its products?

How many people are employed in the marketing area, what is their quality and in what way are the marketing personnel regarded by the rest of the organization?

Costs and efficiency

Of the organization's total sales what percentage is contributed by each product?

What is the extent and quality of the distribution network?

What is the spread of sales by region?

What is the spread of sales by customer type (size)?

What are the total costs of marketing?

What are the margins that are realized on each product?

What are the margins that are realized on each channel of distribution?

What are the margins that are realized in each geographical market served?

What are the margins realized from each customer type?

Planning

What is the overall quality of the marketing planning in the organization?

Are the plans flexible and capable of adaptation to changing circumstances?

What is the extent and quality of market research?

How effective is the product range planning?

How effective is distribution planning?

What pricing strategies are followed and are they appropriate?

How well is product promotion planned?

Control

In what way is the organization's marketing and distribution information system structured and is it effective?

What is the quality of the sales and market data in terms of timeliness, comprehensiveness and cost?

What information and measures are used to provide information about product performance in the marketplace, quality of distribution, differences in the performances of different market segments, customer segments and channels of distribution, contributions of alternative methods of promotion?

What are the procedures which are used when variances from plans arise?

Balance

Are the marketing goals, strategies and operations consistent with overall organization goals?

Are the marketing goals, strategies and operations internally (i.e. within the marketing function) consistent? Are the marketing goals, strategies and operations consistent with the goals, strategies and operations of other functional areas?

Measures of performance

The main, and most easily extracted measures of marketing performance are given below.

Overall marketing performance

Measure	Core marketing strategy
Sales per employee	Overall effectiveness
Total sales volume	
Total sales value	
Total gross profit margin	Effectiveness of overall
Total contribution margin	product pricing strategies
Total net profit margin	
Net profit margin	
Promotion costs as a percentage of sales	Promotion strategies
Selling and distribution costs as a percentage of sales	Distribution strategies

Specific areas of marketing performance

1 *For each product line:*
Gross contribution margin — Profitability by product line
Product controllable margin to sales

2 For each channel of distribution:
Gross contribution margin — Profitability by channel of distribution
Product controllable margin to sales

3 For each sales region
Gross contribution margin — Profitability by sales region
Product controllable margin to sales

Production

The production function attempts to satisfy the overall goals of the organization through producing the highest quality goods demanded by customers at the lowest possible costs. This set of goals is pursued through the following core strategies:

- *Cost reduction strategies*:   This set of strategies is concerned with arranging the production facilities so that the products are produced at the lowest possible cost.
- *Quality maximization*:   This set of strategies is concerned with ensuring that the relative product quality of the organization's goods is as high as possible. Quality is judged on the basis of relative product quality rather than absolute quality. (See the PIMS findings on page 126.)
- *Capacity flexibility*:   This set is concerned with ensuring that the plant and equipment are such that the capacity utilization is always optimal.

Resources

What is value of the facilities and equipment?
What is the age of the facilities and equipment?
What is the capacity of the production facilities and is there flexibility?
Where are the facilities located and are the locations optimal?
Does the organization have good access to raw materials or supplies?
What is the degree of vertical integration?
How many people are employed in the production area, what is their quality and in what way are the production personnel regarded by the rest of the organization?

Costs and efficiency

What are the costs per unit produced?
What are the raw material costs?
What are the inventory costs?
What is the level of capacity utilization?
How good is quality control?

Planning

What is the overall quality of the production planning in the organization?
Are the plans flexible and capable of adaptation to changing circumstances?
What is the extent and quality of innovation and research and development?
How effective is the product range planning?
Is there design scheduling?
Is there product redesign?

Is there continuous process improvement?
What is the quality of maintenance?
How flexible are the production systems?

Control

In what way is the organization's production information system structured and is it effective?
What is the quality of the production data?
What are the wastage rates?
What are the reject rates?
What is the level of quality?
What are the inventory levels?
What is the reporting system?
What is the speed and accuracy of the system?
What are the procedures which are used when variances from plans arise?

Balance

Are the production goals, strategies and operations consistent with overall organization goals?
Are the production goals, strategies and operations internally consistent?
Are the production goals, strategies and operations consistent with the goals, strategies and operations of other functional areas?

Measures of performance

The principal measures of performance which can be used to assess how effectively the production function is operating are given below.

Measure	*Core production strategy*
Unit costs	Cost reduction
Fixed asset turnover ratio	
Capacity utilization	
Investment intensity	Cost reduction/flexibility
Fixed assets to total assets	
Sales to net current assets	
Inventory turnover ratio	
Relative product quality	
Reject rates	Quality
Wastage rates	

Personnel

The personnel, or human relations function, has the task of contributing to overall corporate goals through providing appropriate personnel who will enable corporate goals to be achieved. Therefore the personnel function is primarily concerned with strategies in the following areas.

- *Recruitment and training strategies*:   This set is concerned with those strategies which will ensure that the organization has the appropriate numbers of personnel with the appropriate skills.
- *Compensation strategies*:   This set is concerned with ensuring that there are patterns of career development within the organization which will make personnel maximize their efforts on the organization's behalf.

The personnel function is now considered under the headings given on page 126.

Resources

Does the organization have high quality staff?
How many people are employed in the personnel area, what is their quality and in what way are the staff in personnel regarded by the rest of the organization?
Does the organization have training and development programmes which will develop quality staff appropriate to the tasks?
Does the organization have a motivating career planning and compensation system?
Does the organization have good access to high quality potential staff?

Costs and efficiency

What are the unit labour costs?
What is the level of productivity?
What is the rate of labour turnover?
What is the level of absenteeism?
What is the rate of days lost through labour problems?
What is the attitude towards change and flexibility?

Planning

What is the overall quality of the personnel planning in the organization?
Are the plans flexible and capable of adaptation to changing circumstances?
What is the extent and quality of the training and development planning?
What is the quality of the recruitment policies?
What is the quality of the promotion policies?
What are the compensation policies and how effective are they?
What is the degree and nature of unionization?

Control

In what way is the organization's personnel information system structured and is it effective?

What is the quality of the personnel information data?
What are the staff evaluation procedures?
What are the staff development procedures?
What is the reporting system?
What is the speed and accuracy of the system?
What are the procedures which are used when variances from plans arise?

Balance

Are the personnel goals, strategies and operations consistent with overall organization goals?
Are the personnel goals, strategies and operations internally consistent?
Are the personnel goals, strategies and operations consistent with the goals, strategies and operations of other functional areas?

Measure of performance

Some of the leading measures which can be used to assess the effectiveness of the personnel function are given below.

Measure	Core personnel strategy
Unit labour costs	
Labour turnover rate	
Absenteeism	
Days lost	Productivity
Sales per employee	
Value added per employee	
Degree of unionization	

Management information systems

The goals of the MIS is to provide the information that the personnel in the organization need in order to run it effectively. It is important to note that although MIS systems are increasingly computerized, a computerized system is not a necessity. The system should be appropriate to the organization. Thus, for a very small business with a small number of customers and transactions, it may well be the case that a manual system is superior to a computerized one.

Resources

What is the value of the MIS equipment?
What is the age and quality of the MIS equipment?
How extensive is the MIS system within the organization?
How well is the MIS linked to outside systems and how sensitive is it to environmental changes?
How many people are employed in the MIS area, what is their quality

and in what way are the MIS personnel regarded by the rest of the organization?

Costs and efficiency

What are the general and administrative costs?
What is the quality of information?
How extensive are the systems?
How well are the systems integrated?
What is the reliability of the system?

Planning

What is the overall quality of the MIS planning in the organization?
Are the plans flexible and capable of adaptation to changing circumstances?
How extensive is the MIS planning?

Control

In what way is the organization's MIS structured and is it effective?
What is the quality of the information data?
What is the reporting system?
What is the speed and accuracy of the system?
What are the procedures which are used when variances from plans arise?

Balance

Are the MIS goals, strategies and operations consistent with overall organization goals?
Are the MIS goals, strategies and operations internally consistent?
Are the MIS goals, strategies and operations consistent with the goals strategies and operations of other functional areas?

Measure of performance

Among the measures of performance which could be used to assess how effectively the MIS function is operating are the following.

Measures	*Core MIS strategy*
Administrative costs as a percentage of sales	
System breakdowns	
Security	Efficiency
Speed	
Accuracy	
Extensiveness	

Attributing weights to each section

In this stage of the appraisal of the organization the various sections which have been selected in Stage 1 of the process, and analysed in Stage 2, are given weights which reflect their strength or weakness. The weights are calculated in the same manner as the weights for the environmental analysis in Part Two were calculated. The method is summarized below.

The *importance* of each section which has been analysed is ranked on an ordinal scale from 0 to 5. Thus, if strength in a certain section is considered to be of crucial importance to the organization then this section merits a score of 5; if it is considered to be of average importance it merits a score of 3 and if it is considered to be of no importance at all it scores zero. For example, in the vodka industry the functional segment 'marketing' is of crucial importance and would probably score 5, while for a company in the 'missile defence' industry the marketing segment would be, relatively, less important and therefore likely to score less than 5.

Once the importance of each section has been determined then the *strength* of each section is ranked on an ordinal scale from −5 to +5. −5 indicates that this section is likely to have as strong a negative influence on the organizations as possible. For example, if an organization needs great expertise in the marketing function yet it does not develop or intend to develop such expertise then a high negative number could be assigned to this section. In contrast a high positive score indicates that the section under consideration is likely to have as strong a positive influence on the organization as possible. For example, when an organization has a strong technical team and has a major technical lead in an industry where technical superiority is the crucial internal factor then such a factor could be assigned a score of +5. Finally a score of 0 indicates that the section does not have any strength at all.

When the importance and the strength of each section have been determined these two numbers are multiplied and an ordinal overall score for each relevant section in the organization is obtained. Each of these scores indicates the relative strength or weakness that the organization appears to have in each section. Finally, the score for each section can be shown graphically on an organization assessment diagram, as shown in Figure 23. The advantage of the graphical exposition is that it tends to make the analysis more 'alive' and more easily understood.

A hypothetical example to illustrate how the stages of the organization analysis are carried out

Stage 1: *Division of the organization*

This organization was divided into the following sections: culture, leadership, structure, corporate resources, finance, marketing, production, personnel, and MIS.

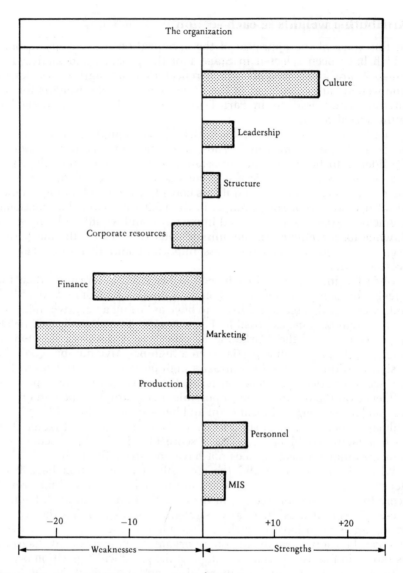

Figure 23   *An organization assessment diagram*

Stage 2:   Analysis of the sections

A detailed analysis of the sections selected in Stage 1 was carried out.

Stage 3:   Attributing weights to each section

After each section had been analysed the weights shown in Table 14 were assigned.

Table 14 Assigning weights to the sections of the organization

Section	Importance	Strength	Overall score (importance × strength)
Culture	4	+4	+16
Leadership	4	+1	+4
Structure	1	+2	+2
Corporate resources	4	−1	−4
Finance	5	−3	−15
Marketing	5	−4	−20
Production	2	−1	−2
Personnel	2	+3	+6
MIS	3	+1	+3

Implications of the above weighting

Culture
In this analysis the culture of the organization is considered to be extremely important and in this case the culture of the organization appears to be an element of considerable strength – it has a score of +16. This implies that the culture which prevails must be well suited to the organization and also appropriate to the industry in which it operates. This organization must have a culture which is significantly more suitable than its competitors.

Leadership
Leadership is considered to be extremely important to this organization. However, the quality of leadership which the organization has is considered to be a mild strength. This could indicate that there is room for the development of those aspects of the leadership which are causing it to have such a mild positive influence.

Structure
The structure of the organization is not considered to be of great importance and in this case it has, overall, a small positive effect of +2.

Corporate resources
The corporate resources – finance, personnel and image which the 'centre' of the organization supplies are considered to be very important. In this case it is felt that the support of such resources is a mild weakness, i.e. if only further resources could be obtained this could become a strength of the organization.

Finance
Although strength in the finance function is considered to be vital, unfortunately, for this company, it is considered to be rather weak in this area – it has a score of −15. Implicit in this score is the message that those weaknesses which have been revealed in the finance function must be reduced.

Marketing
The health of the marketing function is similar to that of the finance function: strength in marketing is considered to be vital and this organization has an extremely low score (−20) in this function. Clearly steps must be taken to correct the faults that have been found in the marketing function.

Production
The analysis suggests that the production function is of lesser importance to the organization and this organization has some slight weaknesses in this area. However, these weaknesses are of lesser importance than the other functional weaknesses.

Personnel
The personnel function is considered to be of below average importance and in this case the organization is quite strong in this area.

MIS
MIS is of average importance to this organization and its MIS system has been found to be a mild strength.

Conclusions to Part Three

Analysing the organization is the complement to analysing the environment. It enables an assessment to be made of how well the organization has adapted its internal profile to the environment in which it is operating. On completion of the analysis the strategist should be able to make judgements about those sections in the organization under analysis which display particular strengths and are likely to confer advantage and those sections in which it is relatively weak and which will leave the organization vulnerable if no remedial action is taken.

Finally, Table 15 attempts to summarize the approach to analysing the internal strengths and weaknesses of an organization which was the subject of Part Three.

Table 15 An overview of assessing the internal strengths and weaknesses of an organization

Function	Finance	Marketing	Production	Personnel	MIS
Resources	Total finance resources Number of staff Quality of staff	Annual sales Mix and range of products Markets Balance of product life cycles Market shares or relative market shares Distribution methods Patent protection Market segments Cost/quality advantages Promotional advantages Image Number of staff	Value of facilities and equipment Age of facilities and equipment Capacity Location of facilities Access to raw materials Degree of integration Number of staff Quality of staff	Quality of staff Number of staff Development programmes Motivation Access to good staff	Value of equipment Age of equipment Internal extensive External extensive Number of staff Quality of staff
Costs and efficiency	Sources of capital Cost of capital Capital structure Rate of return Working capital Debtors and creditors Dividend payments Tax situation	Percentage sales by product Distribution quality Sales spread Marketing costs Margins	Costs per unit Raw material costs Inventory costs Capacity utilization Quality control	Unit labour costs Productivity levels Labour turnover Absenteeism Days lost Attitudes to change	General and administrative cost Quality of information Extensiveness of systems Integration of systems Realiability of systems

Table 15 (cont.)

Function	Finance	Marketing	Production	Personnel	MIS
Planning	Overall finance planning	Overall marketing planning	Overall production planning	Overall personnel planning	Overall MIS planning
	Flexibility	Flexibility	Flexibility	Flexibility	Flexibility
	Capital budgeting	Market research	Innovation and R & D	Training and development planning	Extensiveness
	Risk	Product range planning	Product range planning	Recruitment policies	
	Working capital planning	Distribution planning	Design scheduling	Promotion policies	
	Budgeting	Pricing strategies	Product redesign	Compensation policies	
	Auditing	Promotion planning	Process improvement	Unionization level	
Control	Accounting system	Information system	Production information system	Personnel information system	Effectiveness
	Reporting system	Sales & marketing data	Quality	Data quality procedures	Quality of information data
	Speed and accuracy	Product distribution segment	Wastage rates	Staff evaluation procedures	Security
	Variance procedures	Promotion data	Reject rates data	Staff development procedures	Reporting system
		Variance procedures	Quality levels	Reporting system	Speed and accuracy of system
			Inventory levels	Speed and accuracy	Variance procedures
			Reporting system	Variance procedures	
			Speed and accuracy		
			Variance procedures		

	Finance	Marketing	Production	Personnel	MIS
Balance	Consistency with corporate plans Internal finance consistency Consistency across functions	Consistency with corporate plans Internal marketing consistency Constancy across functions	Consistency with corporate plans Internal production consistency Consistency with other functions	Consistency with corporate plans Internal personnel consistency Consistency with other functions	Consistency with corporate plans Internal MIS consistency Consistency with other functions
Measures of performance	Return on investment Return on capital employed Debt to equity Debt coverage Return on equity Creditors ratio Debtors ratio Return on equity Payout ratio Current ratio Quick ratio	Sales per employee Total sales volume Total sales value Total gross margin Total net profit margin Promotion as percentage of sales Selling and distribution as percentage sales Gross contribution by product Gross contribution by channel Gross contribution by region	Unit costs Fixed asset turnover Capacity utilization Investment intensity Fixed assets to total assets Sales to net current assets Inventory turnover Relative production quality Reject rates Wastage rates	Unit labour costs Labour turnover rate Absenteeism Days lost Sales per employee Value added per employee Degree of unionization	Total administrative cost Administrative costs to sales System breakdowns Security Speed Accuracy Extensiveness

Part Four

7 The current strategic position

Introduction

The primary aim of this chapter is to develop a methodology which will enable the current strategic position of an organization to be clearly displayed. Once the current position has been understood, then it is rational to use this as a starting base upon which to develop future strategies.

Three methods of displaying the current strategic position are considered – the approach developed in this book, the Boston Consulting Group Product Market Portfolio Matrix approach, and the Shell Directional Policy Matrix approach.

Irrespective of which method is being considered, they all approach the problem in the same way – each model attempts to align the organization with its environment and on the basis of the alignment make the judgement. Additionally, each model attempts to resolve a fundamental problem – how to adequately display the current position with the minimal amount of data. One of the problems in judging the current position and potential is that if all the data and information which has been generated in the 'analysis of the environment' and 'analysis of the organization' stages of the process are employed, then there tends to be a surfeit of data and this may actually hinder effective decision making. Therefore, each model has the goal of summarizing and simplifying the data available.

A model for displaying the current strategic position

This model integrates the information which has been gathered in Parts Two and Three so that a comprehensive total view of the organization's total current strategic position can be obtained. Thus the environmen-

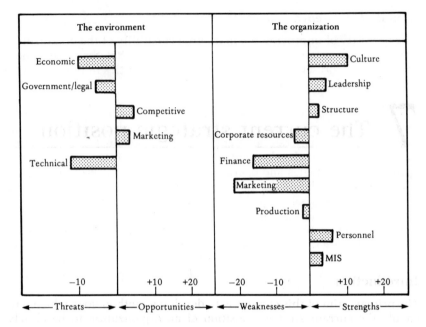

Figure 24   *Summarizing the current strategic position*

tal assessment diagram and the organization assessment diagram are joined as shown in Figure 24 to provide a summary of the current strategic position.

This method of display not only facilitates a judgement about the current strategic position of the organization but it also enables fundamental plans or strategies for the future to be developed. Thus in the case shown in Figure 24 it would appear that the following issues should be considered:

Appraisal of the organization

The organization appears to have considerable strength in its culture, leadership and personnel functions – its behavioural dimensions. Therefore, from the point of view of the overall quality of the management and personnel, the organization is strong. Consequently for the forthcoming planning period the question could be asked: 'In what ways can these important strengths be used to confer advantage on the organization, or at least overcome its weaknesses?'

The organization appears to be very weak in its marketing function and also in the finance function. These weaknesses must receive priority attention and action must be taken to redress them. The causes of the weaknesses will have been revealed in the earlier analyses.

Appraisal of the environment

The necessity of improving the marketing capability of the organization becomes even more pronounced when it is seen that the environment appears to be presenting at least limited opportunities in the marketing and competitive segments.

Thus using this very simple example, a total view of the current strategic position of the organization is provided and also some fundemental strategy developments are suggested. Just how these fundamental strategy developments are translated into precise organization-wide strategies and operations is considered in Part Five.

In passing it should be noted that the above organizational and environmental assessments are merely very short summaries of extensive supporting analyses, and it is suggested that the presentation of an appraisal such as the above should proceed first with the above general view on the organization's strengths and weaknesses and the opportunities and threats in the environment and then it should proceed through reference to the specific and detailed supporting quantitative and qualitative analyses.

Other models

Even though the above approach is a general one which may be used for simple, single products, small business-type organizations or complex multidivision, multiproduct companies, it does not explicitly make provision for the diversity of products and markets which many organizations have. In such multiproduct organizations, it is necessary to consider not just the absolute strategic position of each product, but also the total portfolio of products and the relationships which the products have to each other within the portfolio. For example, an organization could have four product ranges with cash and market characteristics for each product range as shown in Table 16.

Table 16 Cash and market characteristics for four hypothetical products

	Product 1	*Product 2*	*Product 3*	*Product 4*
Cash flow position	Negative	Negative	Neutral	Positive
Market share	Low	Low	High	High
Market growth rate	Low	High	High	Low
Stage in product life cycle	Decline	Growth	Growth	Maturity/ decline
Number of competitors	Few	Many	Fewer	Very few

In assessing the current strategic position of this organization, it is not sufficient to assess the position of each product in isolation as such an approach may develop an incomplete, and consequently false, impression of the strategic position of the total organization. Thus, in the above case, if such a single product view is taken, then Product 2 may be considered to be in a rather weak position and not to be contributing to the organization's performance. However, as will be seen on page 154 Product 2's performance is the 'normal' performance which should be expected from a product operating under such competitive circumstances. Furthermore, taking a single product view ignores the question of whether the total portfolio of products that a company has is 'balanced'.

Two major approaches which attempted to handle this type of complexity – The Product Market Portfolio Matrix and The Directional Policy Matrix – were developed in the 1970s. Each of these approaches is now considered briefly below. (The expositions of the Product Market Portfolio, and the Directional Policy Matrix given in this chapter are somewhat limited – for a much more rigorous analysis of their operations see McNamee[1] Chapters 4, and 5.)

The Product Market Portfolio Matrix

The Product Market Portfolio approach to strategic planning was developed by the Boston Consulting Group in the early 1970s and it quickly came to prominence as an original and fundamentally different way of developing a strategic assessment of an organization. In this model it is assumed that there is a multiproduct company operating in a variety of markets and the objective of the model is to enable the company to maximize the performance of each of its products while keeping the overall cash flows in balance. This is not the only level of aggregation at which the model can be used. For example, frequently the level of aggregation is set at the SBU level rather than the product level. The objective in such a situation becomes maximizing the performance of each SBU while keeping its overall cash flow in balance. The level of aggregation depends upon the requirements.

The factors determining strategic position

The strategic position of each product in the portfolio is assumed to be determined by three major factors – the growth rate of the market, the product's relative market share and the value of the annual sales of each product.

The growth rate of the market
When the growth rate of each product's market has been ascertained it is plotted, as a percentage, on an arithmetic scale on the vertical axis of the matrix as shown in Figure 25.

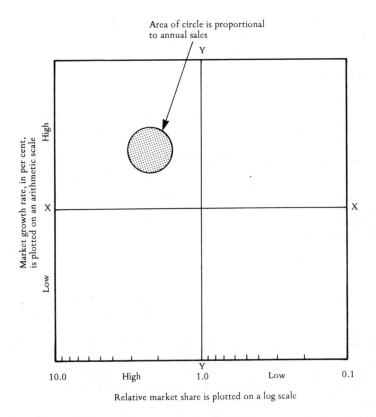

Figure 25 *Constructing a product market portfolio matrix*

The product's relative market share

There is considerable evidence (see page 201) to show that the financial benefits that accrue from a product are directly correlated with its market share, i.e. those products which have the largest market shares should, all other things being equal, enjoy the greatest positive cash flows. Expressed slightly differently, the more powerful a product is in its market, the greater the financial benefit to the company will be. The Boston Consulting Group[2] has suggested that the best measure of market power is relative market share, which it has defined as: 'The product's share of the market divided by the share of the next largest competitor.' Relative market share rather than simple market share is used because it is believed that this measure more accurately reflects a product's true competitive position. For example, if it is known that two firms A and Z have market shares of 25 per cent and 35 per cent of their respective markets this information alone does not enable the true competitive position of each firm to be assessed. On the basis of this information alone Z would appear to have a superior competitive position.

Table 17   Actual and relative market shares for A and competitors

	A	B	C	D	E	F	G	H	I	J
Actual market share (%)	25	15	10	10	10	8	8	8	5	1
Relative market share	1.7	0.6	0.4	0.4	0.4	0.3	0.3	0.3	0.2	0.04

Table 18   Actual and relative market shares for Z and competitors

	Z	Y	X	W
Actual market share (%)	35	40	20	5
Relative market share	0.9	1.1	0.5	0.1

However, when the industry figures, as shown in Tables 17 and 18 are considered, it can be seen that A has a much stronger competitive position than Z.

Thus A has a *relative market share* of 1.7 (obtained by dividing its actual share of 25 per cent by that of its next largest competitor, B, which has an actual market share of 15 per cent indicating that A's sales measured by volume are 1.7 times those of its nearest rival, B. In contrast, Z has a *relative market share* of 0.9 (obtained by dividing its actual share of 35 per cent by that of its next largest competitor, Y which has an actual market share of 40 per cent) indicating that Z's sales measured by volume are just 0.9 times those of its largest rival Y.

It should be noted that if any industry has a clear market leader this leader, by definition must have a relative market share of more than 1.0. In a situation where a company has a relative market share of 1.0 this indicates that the company is a *joint industry leader*, i.e. there is at least one other firm which has an equal volume of sales. In this type of situation it is likely that there will be intense competitive pressure as joint leaders vie with each other in their attempts to achieve outright leadership.

When each product's relative market share has been ascertained, it is plotted on a log scale on the horizontal axis of the matrix as shown in Figure 25.

Thus market growth rate and relative market share are the two coordinates which are used to locate each product on the matrix.

The value of the annual sales of each product
The final factor which is assumed to determine strategic position is the monetary value of the annual sales of *each* product. This is plotted on

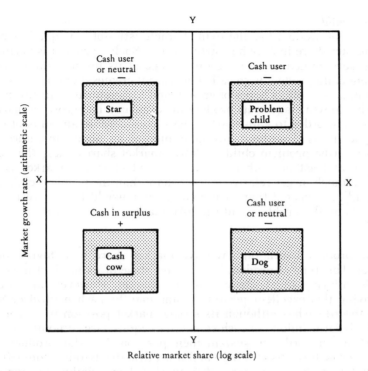

Figure 26 *The cash characteristics of each quadrant and the generic product types.*

the matrix as a circle whose area is proportional to the value of the annual sales and the circle is located at the coordinates of relative market share and growth rate of the market.

When a company has plotted these elements for each of its products on a matrix, then a judgement can be made about the prospects for each product, the current strategic health of the overall portfolio of products which the company has, and strategies that ought to be followed to achieve corporate goals.

Interpreting the matrix

The two dividing lines **XX** and **YY** divide the matrix into four quadrants and each of these quadrants tends to have the cash characteristics which are displayed in Figure 26.

The Boston Consulting Group has suggested that products can be branded as particular generic types, depending upon where they are located in the matrix. The generic types of products are 'problem child', 'star', 'cash cow', and 'dog' and their locations on the matrix are displayed in Figure 26. Their characteristics are discussed below.

Problem child
This type of product has the twin characteristics of having a low relative market share in a high growth market. Such a product is normally at the development or early growth stage of its product life cycle. A problem child product is so called because it creates great problems for the planner – it offers hopes of growth and high returns in the future (it is at the growth stage of its product life cycle in a fast growing market) however, in order to gain market share considerable amounts of cash must be invested without any guarantee of an adequate return: by definition (the problem child's relative market share is less than one) there is at least one other competing product in the market which enjoys a much larger relative market share than the problem child and it would be expected that such a competitor would fiercely resist any attempts by the problem child to take market share from it.

Star
A star product has a high relative market share in a high growth market. This type of product is in a later stage of its product life cycle and is enjoying the leadership of the market. However, in spite of occupying this excellent position a star may be cash neutral or may even absorb cash – although its strong market position will generate relatively large inflows of cash stars often require large amounts of cash to be spent in order to sustain their position. For star products the market growth rate is still high and it is attractive to other competitors who will be seeking to increase their market shares. Failure to support a star sufficiently strongly, may lead to the product losing its leading market share position, slipping eastwards in the matrix and becoming a problem child type of product. However, in spite of its possibly poor cash contribution, a star represents the best future prospects for the company. As the market growth rate for a star slows, it will drop vertically in the matrix into the cash cow quadrant and its cash characteristics will change.

Cash cow
This type of product has a high relative market share in a low growth market and should be generating substantial cash inflows. The period of high growth in the market has ended – the product life cycle is in the maturity or decline stage – and consequently the market is less attractive to new entrants and existing competitors. Additionally the cash cow product will be seen by existing and potential competitors to be so dominant in this unattractive market that strong competitive confrontation is not a rational strategy. Consequently cash cow products tend to generate cash in excess of what is needed to sustain their market positions. This excess cash can be used to pay dividends, overheads, etc., and, perhaps most importantly, to fund investments in other parts (problem children and star products) of the company's product portfolio.

Dog

The dog product has the twin traits of having a low relative market share in a low growth market. Such a product, tends to have a negative cash flow which is likely to continue. There is really only one way in which a dog product could improve its position – it could attempt to wrest market share from other competitors who are enjoying higher relative market shares. However it is unlikely that dog products will be able to do this – the other competitors, which have the advantage of having larger market shares, are likely to fiercely resist any attempts to reduce their shares of a low growth or static market. Consequently, in the view of the Boston Consulting Group, a dog product is 'essentially worthless' and should be liquidated. Failure to dispose of such a product may lead to the dog product causing the company to have a permanent and progressively worsening cash haemorrhage called by BCG a cash trap.[3] BCG has suggested if an organization has products which are dogs or cash traps, they must be disposed of if the organization is to survive. The harshness of treatment which the Boston Consulting Group has suggested ought to be meted out to dog products has received considerable criticism. The principal criticisms are: there are many examples of dog products which are successful; by definition in a period of recession most of the businesses in Europe (which tend to be smaller than their Japanese or US competitors), could be classed as dogs; frequently there are political impediments to such a harsh strategy; it is too simplistic to make strategic decisions to dispose of a business just on these two criteria. These and other criticisms have caused BCG to take a less stark view of how such products should be treated.[4]

Movement in the matrix

Two classes of movement are considered to be important in the matrix – movements of products and movements of cash. Ideally products and cash should move as shown in Figure 27. Thus products should move from being problem children to star to cash cow while the cash throw-offs from cash cow products should not be returned to these products, but rather should be directed to problem child or star products. Cash cow products are in the mature/decline stages of their product life cycles and have limited future prospects, while those products which are in the problem child or star categories, although they may be currently absorbing cash, represent the best hopes for the future. Consequently they should receive cash.

Strategies

In the Product Market Portfolio model therefore there are two levels of strategy formulation:

- Strategies for the portfolio of products.
- Strategies for the individual products.

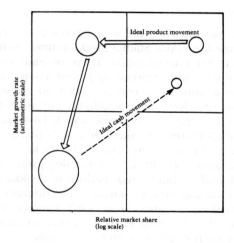

Figure 27   *Ideal movements of products and cash in the product market portfolio*

The strategies for the overall portfolio of products are concerned with the issue of balance, i.e. is the portfolio of products balanced internally in terms of the following?

- Are there a sufficient number of cash cows (or are the cash throw-offs from cash cows sufficient) to support those other products in the portfolio which are at stages of their life cycles when they require cash?
- Are there problem children which have reasonable prospects of becoming future stars and which do not, at present, constitute a disproportionate drain on the current cash flow?
- Are there an appropriate number of stars which will provide sufficient cash generation when the current cash cows are no longer able to fulfil this role?
- Are there any dogs and if so why?

At the level of the individual products there are four main strategies which tend to arise – build, hold, harvest and withdraw.

Build
This type of strategy is concerned with building the competitive power of the product. Although competitive power can be built in many ways (for example technological development, quality improvement etc.) in the context of this model it is normally taken to mean the development of market power. This can be achieved through marketing strategies such as price reductions, increased quality at the same price, increased promotion expenditure, and marketing. This type of strategy is usually most appropriate for products in the problem child quadrant.

Hold
This type of strategy is concerned with actions which are necessary to preserve the existing competitive power of a product against attacks by competitors. Again, in the context of this model, competitive power is often regarded as power in the market, and consequently holding strategies will often involve the commitment of resources to marketing and promotion. As this strategy implies that a product is already occupying a competitive position of some strength, it is often employed when a product is in the star or cash cow quadrant.

Harvest
When harvesting a product, a company attempts to maximize its short-term earnings from the product. It can do this by not committing resources to promote it and also by not reinvesting in fixed assets to support it in the future. This type of strategy is often appropriate for a product in the cash cow or dog quadrant – because such types of products are in the final stages of their life cycles, they may have rather poor futures and it is economically rational to maximize their contributions as quickly as possible.

Withdraw
When a company sees no prospect of a product making a positive cash contribution and is experiencing net cash outflows – as is often the case for dog products – it may decide that the most appropriate strategy is to withdraw completely from the market.

Limitations of the approach

Although the Product Market Portfolio approach has enjoyed considerable popularity it has also received considerable criticism. Its admirable simplicity – most people can easily grasp the fundamentals of the approach – is also the cause of much of this criticism. Thus, it could be argued that it is rather unrealistic and naive to base major fundamental strategic decisions, such as 'build' or 'harvest' on just two measures – relative market share and market growth rate. Surely more information is required to make an effective strategic decision than just two coordinates.

Second, there is an assumption that high growth markets are usually the best markets to enter. This may or may not be true. Thus the UK personal computer market was, in the early 1980s, an extremely fast growing one. It was not however a particularly fruitful one for many manufacturers – Sinclair, Acorn, Apricot.

Third, the positive correlation between relative market share and cash flow (or return on investment) is not a law. There are many examples of businesses where lower market share competitors have enjoyed substantially better financial returns than their larger peers. (See Fruhan.[5])

However, in spite of these, and other criticisms, the approach still has

many advocates and it remains as a particularly clear method of showing the importance of linking market share, market growth and financial returns.

The Directional Policy Matrix

The Directional Policy Matrix (DPM) was developed by the Shell oil
company (see Robinson, Hichens and Wade[6]) and, like the Product
Market Portfolio, it attempts to show graphically the overall strategic
balance of a company's portfolio of businesses, and what are likely to be
appropriate strategies for the individual businesses. As was the case
with the Product Market Portfolio model the level of aggregation used is
determined by the requirements. The Directional Policy Matrix can be
used at the product level or the SBU level. In this section it will be
assumed that the level of aggregation is at the SBU or business level.
The Directional Policy Matrix is rather similar to the Product Market
Portfolio in that it asserts that strategic position is determined by three
major factors – the business sector prospects, the business position and
the value of annual sales of the SBU.

The business sector prospects

Instead of asserting, as the Product Market Portfolio approach asserts,
that the prospects for a business are determined by the market growth
rate, the DPM asserts that there is no single, or indeed general, measure
which indicates the prospects. Instead, each business has a certain set
of business sector prospects and these prospects are determined by a set
of factors which are unique to the particular business or industry in
question. Because of this there can be only the broadest general rules
about what determine the prospects for a business. The broad categories of determinants which are most frequently instrumental in determining sector prospects are similar to the 'environmental factors' given
in Part Two – competitive, marketing, economic, social, geographical,
political, etc. When the various business sector factors have been determined, they are scored and the total score for the business sector
prospects faced by each business is recorded on the vertical scale of the
matrix as shown in Figure 28. It is normal to divide this axis into bands
which indicate the relative attractiveness of the business sectors. The
bands are 'attractive', 'average' and 'unattractive'.

The business position

Again, unlike the Product Market Portfolio approach, which asserts that
the power of a business is determined by the single factor, relative
market share, the DPM approach suggests that the business position of
each SBU is determined by a set of factors unique to that business and

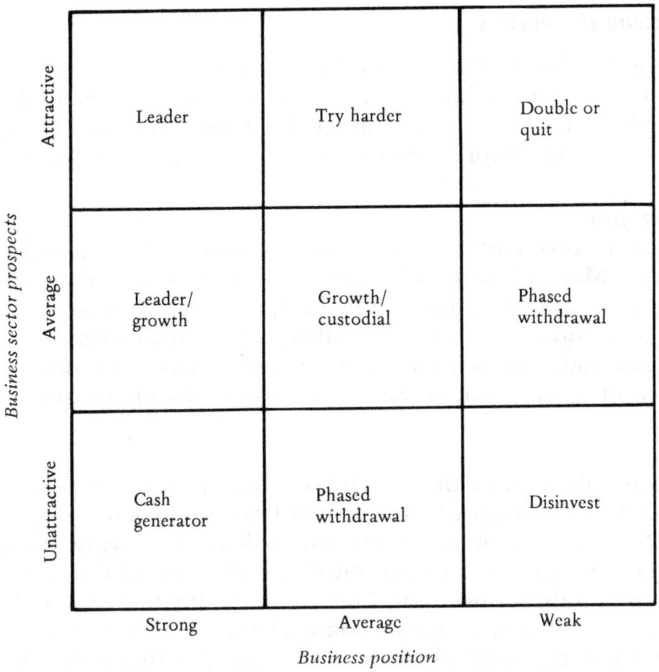

	Strong	Average	Weak
Attractive	Leader	Try harder	Double or quit
Average	Leader/ growth	Growth/ custodial	Phased withdrawal
Unattractive	Cash generator	Phased withdrawal	Disinvest

Business sector prospects (vertical axis label)

Business position (horizontal axis label)

Figure 28   *Constructing a directional policy matrix*

therefore any realistic portrayal of this must be tailored to the business which is being analysed and so cannot be inferred from a preordained measure or set of measures. Those broad categories which are frequently the most common determinants of business position are similar to those 'organization assessment factors' given in Part Three – culture, leadership, power, structure, finance, marketing, personnel, production, MIS etc. Once each factor has been analysed it is scored and the scores for each business are then summed to give a single overall score for the strength of each business's position. The score so obtained is then plotted on the horizontal axis of the matrix as shown in Figure 28. It is normal to divide this axis into bands which indicate the relative strengths of the business positions. The bands are 'strong', 'average' and 'weak'.

The value of annual sales of the SBU

As with the Product Market Portfolio the value of the annual sales of the SBU are plotted on the matrix as a circle whose area is proportional to the annual sales and which is located at the coordinates of business sector prospects and business position.

Interpreting the matrix

As Figure 28 shows, the matrix has been divided into nine squares and each square has a label which indicates the fundamental strategy that should be considered, initially at least, for a business lying in that square. The policy implications of each square are now considered.

Double or quit

A business in this square is somewhat similar to the problem child of the Product Market Portfolio Matrix. By 'double or quit' the formulators of the matrix mean that such a business, although it enjoys good sector prospects is much weaker than other competitors and may require substantial resources (with no guarantee of success) in order to achieve a position of some strength. Hence the name 'double or quit'.

Leader

A business falling into this square is similar to the Product Market Portfolio star. Although the leader will have advantages over the other competitors, the sector prospects will still appear attractive to other rivals and therefore the leader must invest considerable resources in order to maintain its position. Consequently, for this type of business, there may not be a substantial financial return at this stage in its life cycle. In passing, a good example of the power of this matrix to display the true power of a product is provided by the example of the launch of the IBM personal computer in the UK in the early 1980s. When it was introduced, this product, by definition, had a low relative market share, and hence would have been displayed on the Product Market Portfolio as a problem child. However, because of the power of IBM it was not really in this type of weak position; the other elements determining the strategic strength of a product's position – corporate resources available, corporate image, corporate marketing power, quality and width of software, all helped this product to occupy a leader position from its earliest days.

Try harder

The try harder business could be described as somewhere between a problem child and a star. Although such a business will be weaker than the leader it is, however, substantially stronger than some other competitors and may therefore be more worthy of considerable support.

Cash generator

A business in this square will have a strong business position in an unattrative business sector and will thus be similar to the cash cow product. Because of the unattractiveness of the sector and the business's dominance in it, it is unlikely that there will be strong competitive pressure and consequently strong positive financial returns should be expected from this type of business.

Leader/growth
This type of business could be described as being somewhere between the star and cash cow products. Here, the sector prospects are dimming, and consequently the sector is becoming increasingly unattractive to followers. However, because of the leader/growth's strong position, it should still be able to realize substantial financial returns.

Disinvest
This type of business has a weak business position and is in an unattractive sector and is therefore similar to the dog product of the product market portfolio. Such businesses tend to lose money and the matrix suggests that the only rational strategy in this situation is to disinvest.

Phased withdrawal
This type of business can occupy two squares on the matrix – it can have an average position in an unattractive sector or it can have a weak position in an average sector. Irrespective of which square such a business actually occupies, the strategic advice is the same – phased withdrawal.

Growth/custodial
This type of business is in the centre of the matrix and has an average position in an average sector. Such a business should receive considerable strategic attention as appropriate measures may move it westwards in the matrix to the leader/growth square, whereas inappropriate measures (which include 'doing nothing') may allow it to drift eastwards and become a continuous cash absorber.

Movement in the matrix

As in the case of the Product Market Portfolio there are two classes of movement which are considered to be important – movements of businesses and movements of cash. Ideally businesses and cash should move in the same direction as in the Product Market Portfolio.

Strategies

As in the case of the Product Market Portfolio strategies for the DPM are formulated at two levels:

- Strategies for the portfolio of businesses.
- Strategies for the individual businesses.

The same strategic issues of balance and strategies for individual businesses arise. However, the strategies which are often appropriate to particular positions in the matrix are indicated by the names of each square.

Limitations of the approach

Perhaps the most serious limitation of the approach is the inherent subjectiveness of the coordinates which are used to fix the business in a particular strategic location. No matter how strenuously efforts are made to preserve the objectivity of the analyses, some subjectivity is inevitable and this may lessen the power of the matrix, especially if it is used over a number of years.

Conclusions to Part Four

Irrespective of how the current strategic position is displayed at this stage in the analysis it should be possible to provide answers to the following questions.

- In what business or businesses is the organization operating?
- If it is a multibusiness organization is there balance among the various businesses?
- What are the current strengths and weaknesses of the organization and what are the environmental threats and opportunities?
- What strategies have been employed by the organization in the period of analysis?
- How successful and consistent have these strategies been in relation to:

  (a)   the mission and goals of the organization?
  (b)   The internal organization?
  (c)   The organization's external environment?

Qualitative and quantitative answers to these questions should provide a base for the development of future strategies which is considered in Part Five.

References

1   McNamee, P. B., *Tools and Techniques for Strategic Management*, Pergamon, 1985.
2   Henderson, B., 'The Product Portfolio', *Perspectives*, No. 66, The Boston Consulting Group, 1970.
3   Henderson, B., 'Cash Traps', *Perspectives*, No. 102, The Boston Consulting Group, 1972.
4   Boston Consulting Group, *Annual Perspective*, 1981
5   Fruhan, W. E., 'Pyrrhic Victories in Fights for Market Share', *Harvard Business Review*, Vol. 50, No. 5, Sept/Oct 1972, pp. 100–107.
6   Robinson, S. J. Q., Hichens, R. E. and Wade, D. P., 'The Directional Policy Matrix – Tool for Strategic Planning', *Long Range Planning*, Vol. 11, June 1978, pp. 815.

Part Five

8 Introduction and issues in developing new strategies

This part is concerned with the most exciting, risky and creative aspect of strategic management – the generation of those strategies which will determine the future fate of the organization. This stage in the strategic management process has the above characteristics because of the inherent uncertainty in making strategic choices about the future. On the one hand, the decision to embark upon a bold new strategy, which is a major break with the past, will have the excitement and appeal of novelty and perhaps the prospect of great rewards but may also carry with it a high level of risk and the possibility of total failure. On the other hand, the decision to continue following the same traditional strategies that have always worked in the past provides the comfort of knowing that the proposed future strategies have already been tried, tested and found to have been successful and are therefore likely to be low risk. However, the success of such strategies depends upon the environment remaining static. If this is not the case, then this approach may also, through ultra-conservatism, plunge the company into total failure. Two examples illustrate how this polarity of vision can be disastrous.

One well-documented (see Argenti[1]) cause of corporate failure occurs when a company embarks upon a new, relatively large project which later develops problems. Slatter[2] has given numerous examples to illustrate this, with one of the best known being Burmah Oil. In 1973 Burmah Oil was the twenty-fifth largest company in Britain with sales of £496 million and profits of £49 million. Yet within one year the company was totally insolvent. Slatter points out that among the major causes of its demise were:

- Financing of the Signal Oil acquisition – a major project which developed financing difficulties.
- A sharp drop in tanker rates due to the OPEC oil crisis.

Burmah had engaged in massive expansion of its tanker fleet and developed severe financial difficulties when tanker rates collapsed.

In contrast to the boldness of the Burmah strategy, there are many examples of organizations and industries which, because of their failure to develop imaginative strategies to cope with their changing environments, have failed. A clear example is provided by the specialist steel industry of Sheffield in the UK – an industry which has almost disappeared.

In 1958 there were 105 special steel producers in Britain and by 1984 there were fewer than ten makers of tool and high speed steel with none of them enjoying a significant market share. Additionally employment in the industry fell from 18,000 in 1970 to under 2,000 in 1984. Over the period 1970 to 1982 import penetration had increased from approximately 9 per cent to 64 per cent.

In contrast to this situation France's Commentryenne, which in 1984 was among the three largest producers of high speed steel in the world, was, in 1956, a small alloy steel re-roller which was on the point of closing. At that time new management came in and engaged in a strategy of heavy investment and specialization in high speed steel used in drill bits, saw blades etc. In addition the company also perceived a market need for high speed steel in coil form and ultimately became the world leader in coil sales.

UK manufacturers, however, failed to concentrate their efforts on specialist lines – a necessary precondition for obtaining the economies of scale necessary to reinvest in plant and development. The steelmakers of Sheffield clung to the 'ways of the past' and failed to adapt to their new environment.

As it is future strategies that determine the fate of the organization this part could be regarded as the most important element of the model of strategic management in the book. No amount of analysis of the past will, alone, ensure the future of an organization – the analysis of the past is merely part of the foundation upon which the future plans should be built. Therefore, this part is concerned with generating strategies which will fit well with the environment the organization faces, build upon its strengths and weaknesses, be appropriate to the organization's resources and culture, and satisfy the organization's stakeholders and decision makers.

As was pointed out in Part One (see pages 24–39) the nature of strategic management is, among other things, a function of organizational structure and this is particularly apparent when new strategies are being developed. At this stage the goals and the nature of the strategy generation process will be influenced strongly by the organizational structure.

This chapter will be concerned mainly with the development of strategy for the functionally structured business, i.e. at the SBU level.

The need to develop new strategies

It could be argued that if an organization is satisfying its stakeholders (i.e. achieving its goals) there should be no necessity to generate new strategies. After all, if success is being achieved, then why expend valuable managerial effort on generating new strategies?

The fundamental reason for the development of new strategies is that the environment faced by all organizations is constantly changing and organizations can only ensure their continued existence (or success) by successfully tracking their changing environment and adjusting their strategies and structures in response to these changes.

Because of the enormous variation in the rates at which the environments faced by different industries change, there is, consequently, great variety in the amounts of adjustment which successful competitors, in different industries, need to make. The required adjustment will vary from the dramatic and fundamental change of strategy to the fine-tuning of existing strategies. For example, an industry which was subject to extremely rapid change was the US civil airline industry in the years immediately after its deregulation after the passing of the Airline Deregulation Act in 1978. A consequence of the passage of this act was that the industry became much more open and turbulent. Thus there developed an influx of new and innovative competitors, an unprecedented rush of price cutting and aggressive pursuit of passengers, and a series of failures and mergers as competitors attempted to align themselves with their new environment. The importance of appropriate alignment is illustrated by the contrasting fates of two US airline companies. In March 1986, Eastern Airlines, the long established and third largest airline company in the US was taken over by Texas Air Corporation – a relatively recent arrival in the airline business and just half the size of Eastern. It was widely agreed by industry observers (see Hall and Taylor[3]) that, in contrast to Texas, Eastern had failed to generate and implement the dramatic strategies essential for survival in this new deregulated era.

In contrast to the volatility of the airline industry in the US is the relative stability of the environment faced by the legal profession in the UK. In this industry, through strong official regulation, the environment faced by barristers and solicitors has been relatively stable with new strategies requiring relatively little effort.

In addition to this universal necessity for tracking the environment there are other specific triggers to the development of strategies which are directly related to the circumstances faced by individual organizations.

A fundamental trigger causing a change of strategy occurs when an organization fails to meet its key goals. Thus, if an organization traditionally attaches great importance to goals such as:

- An increase in the real value of sales.
- An increase in the earnings per share.
- An increase in the return on investment.

and it fails to achieve these goals, then new strategies to correct this failure will be developed. A clear example of this trigger to change is provided by the US conglomerate ITT.

ITT's overall performance, as shown by some selected items from its 1984 Annual Report, are given in Table 19. The table shows that since 1980 there has been an annual decrease in sales and that in 1984 most measures of performance were less satisfactory than in previous years.

This failure to achieve traditional key performance goals led to a strategic change – asset redeployment and the sale of assets – which was referred to in the Chairman's opening statement of the 1984 Annual Report:

> The year 1984 was strategically critical for ITT. We took actions that were necessary for the future success of the company. ITT is different today, more competitive.
>
> Sales and revenues for the Corporation increased during 1984 but net income declined. Net income for the year totaled $448 million, or $2.97 per share, down from $675 million, or $4.50 per share, in 1983. Sales and revenues totaled $19.6 billion, up from $18.6 billion the year before.
>
> In 1984, we accelerated our ongoing asset redeployment program; continued to reduce staff at headquarters in New York and Brussels and at key units; continued to lower debt, and re-evaluated and revised our dividend policy. Our dividend is in line with our current earnings and allows us to continue our substantial research and development and meet our capital needs.

The trigger to develop new strategies is strongest when an organization's failure is so severe that its very survival is threatened. In these circumstances, the new strategies will tend to be most dramatic and will tend to exhibit the greatest departure from past strategies.

In summary, in order to survive, all organizations must be cognisant of the necessity to generate new strategies and these 'new' strategies will be on a continuum which ranges from 'minimal change from past strategies' – fine tuning to 'radical departure from past strategies' – dramatic change. The extent of the change will be determined by the nature of the industry and the environment it faces, the success of past strategies, the goals of the top decision makers and the resources available.

Resistance to new strategies and change

In the previous section the development of new strategies was presented as a logical step in the strategic management process which will arise, almost naturally, as a result of an effective assessment of the current strategic situation. In practice this may not be so. There are often cultural impediments to change. Frequently, people in established organizations will prefer to follow historical strategies and behaviour patterns rather than embrace the new. The past strategies have become familiar to them and they feel more secure and comfortable with them

Table 19 Selected items from the summary data of ITT's 1984 Annual Report as reported in the ITT Annual Reports for the respective years[5]

Dollars in millions except per share	*1984*	*1983*	*1982*	*1981*	*1980*	*1979*	*1978*	*1977*
Results for year								
Sales and revenues	$ 12,701	14,155	15,958	17,306	18,530	17,179	15,261	13,146
Return on stockholders equity	7.4%	11.1%	11.5%	11.1%	15.0%	6.8%	12.4%	11.5%
Dividends declared per common share	$ 1.88	2.76	2.70	2.62	2.45	2.25	2.05	1.82
Plant, property and equipment (net)	$ 4,701	5,295	5,361	5,540	5,387	5,210	5,130	4,629
Long-term debt: Excluding insurance and finance subsidiaries	$ 2,589	2,783	2,890	3,336	2,847	2,964	2,872	2,350

and any new strategy which is a break with the past may appear threatening.

Therefore, when new strategies are being considered, particularly any strategy which is a major break with the past, it is important to take cognisance of the cultural acceptability of the proposed new strategy. Too great a divergence from past strategies may generate a degree of hostility and non-cooperation which will render the introduction of the new strategy impossible. The importance of the behavioural dimensions of strategy development and implementation received particular attention in the 1980s and the necessity for addressing the cultural dimensions of strategy was well expressed by Seymour Tilles of the Boston Consulting Group:

> It is an inescapable fact that the shared values, beliefs, and behaviors of a company – its culture – change only slowly. Yet rapid change is frequently required to meet an environmental or competitive challenge. How does one actually change behavior in a corporation when all the unwritten rules may work to keep it the same?
>
> The most dramatic way to change the corporate culture, and one frequently invoked, is to change the chief executive. Indeed, many experienced people believe that having the right person in the top job will resolve any difficulty.
>
> While changing the chief executive can be effective, it is always a major risk and cannot be done very often in any one company. In any case, the new CEO will face an organization that retains many of the same barriers to change that were there before, although he may deal with them differently.
>
> While a committed CEO is necessary to achieve a change, any effort to accelerate change must address fundamental cultural variables: the status system, rituals and taboos, and the reward system. The challenge is to ensure that these cultural variables are consistent with the emerging needs of the company rather than past requirements ...
>
> ... it is important to remember that a culture that is inconsistent with a strategy dooms the strategy to failure. Changing the culture is part of changing the strategy.[5]

Therefore, the successful generation and implementation of strategies must accommodate the existing cultural context of the organization and must also include appropriate provisions for ensuring the support of the key people within it.

Gap analysis

One approach which can be of considerable help to organizations in both developing an awareness of the need for strategic change and in providing guidance in the selection of appropriate strategies is gap analaysis.

Gap analysis was devised by Argenti[6] and, in summary, the approach proceeds by providing information on the changes in strategies or policies which an organization must effect if it is to achieve its specified goals or targets. Thus, for example, if an organization has a goal of generating profits of £1 million in the forthcoming planning period, gap analysis could be used to reveal the strategic actions necessary to achieve this.

The objective of the analysis is to show the gap or discrepancy that would develop between the goals or targets that have been set for the organization and the performance that would actually be achieved if the organization continued to follow its existing set of strategies. If no gap is forecast to develop, then existing strategies are satisfactory and no strategic change is necessary. However, if a gap is forecast then this indicates that targets will not be achieved, and strategies should be sought and developed which will close the projected gap. The process of gap analysis can be carried out in the following linked steps:

The process of gap analysis

Step 1: Goals or targets are set
These are the performance levels which are desired by the end of the planning period. Generally the higher the level in the organization at which the planning is taking place the longer will be the planning time period.

Step 2: Current performance is extrapolated
Using environmental data and internal revenue and cost data, the organization's performance at the end of the planning period is forecast. These forecasts are based upon the existing strategy continuing with no substantial change, except for amendments to incorporate changed environmental or internal circumstances. For example, if an organization had been pursuing a strategy of steady organic growth of 10 per cent per year in volume terms then, in a gap analysis, the rate of growth would be assumed to continue with adjustment for changes in variables such as rate of economic growth in the markets for the product, changes in the costs associated with manufacturing and marketing the product, etc.

Step 3: The forecast gap is measured
Once the forecast has been made, then the difference between it and the goal or target can be measured. The difference is an indication of the size of the strategic adjustment that will be necessary to achieve goals or targets. Generally, the greater the gap the greater will be the required change in strategic direction necessary to close it.

Step 4: Develop strategies to close the gap
Strategies which will enable the gap to be closed are developed.

The generic nature of gap analysis

Gap analysis can be considered to be a generic approach to strategy development in that it can be tailored to any level in the organization

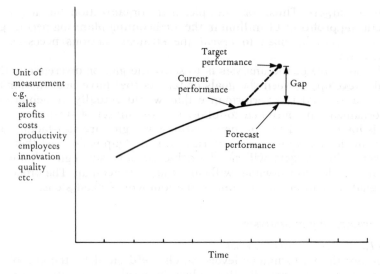

Figure 29   *A generic gap analysis diagram*

and the units by which the gap is measured can be determined by the objectives of the analysis and needs of the user.

Thus, at the corporate level, where goals are often set in relatively long-run broad financial and marketing terms, strategies will tend to set in similar terms, and consequently any projected gaps will tend to be measured in such units.

At the SBU level, where the goals tend to be for shorter time periods, and are usually more specific, any projected gaps will be measured in units which reflect this orientation.

Finally, at the functional level, where targets are set as specific functional numbers – for example, typical functional targets for an organization could include: annual sales of at least £500,000 for Product 1 and £300,000 for Product 2: 60 per cent of sales to be through Distribution Channel 1 and the remainder through Distribution Channel 2: the total number of employees not to exceed 125 full-time equivalents: etc. – projected gaps are measured in these units.

Thus, the generic nature of gap analysis is reflected not just in the process but also in the units which are used to measure projected gaps. Although monetary units – profit levels, value of sales etc. – are the units which are most commonly employed, other units of measurement such as productivity, numbers employed, speed of service, level of innovation, quality of service, etc., may be used. The choice of unit should be determined by the objectives of the analysis.

In the generic gap analysis diagram shown in Figure 29 the forecast is portrayed as a single line. This type of single forecast may cause an often unwarranted degree of trust to be placed in its accuracy. However, business forecasts, especially those which are long range, tend to be prone to error and a single line extrapolation does not reflect the range of possible results. This element of uncertainty in the forecast can be introduced into gap analysis through the use of probability distributions. This can be effected in two ways – through incorporating probability distributions into the above type of gap analysis diagram and/or by developing a risk/performance diagram. Both these diagrams are now illustrated through the use of a case example.

A case example to illustrate gap analysis

A simple case is set out below to illustrate how gap analysis may be employed to help see, and then bridge, the gap between a company's target annual sales and its sales forecast. In the analysis it is assumed that past conditions, internal and environmental, will continue to prevail and that future sales growth will continue to follow the historical pattern.

Company A is a manufacturing company that wishes to carry out a gap analysis to compare its target sales over the period 1987 to 1989 with its forecast performance. The company has been following a fundamental strategy of conservative organic growth through the sales of its current product range and its historical performance is as follows:

Year	1980	1981	1982	1983	1984	1985	1986
Sales (£000)	100	120	140	173	200	250	293

A gap analysis can be carried out as follows.

Step 1: Goals or targets are set
It is assumed that the planners in the company have set the following sales goals or targets for the next three years:

Year	1987	1988	1989
Sales (£000)	330.0	420.0	500.0

Step 2: Current performance is extrapolated
Current performance is extrapolated through analysing past trends and then building the forecast upon these trends. On the assumption that Company A's future sales will continue to increase in line with past performance it appears that the company's sales have been following a linear regression pattern. Therefore simple linear regression will be used to forecast the expected levels of sales over the planning period. A linear regression forecast has been used because this is merely an illustrative example. The same principles would apply should more sophisticated forecasting techniques such as nonlinear regression, multiple regression, time series or exponential smoothing be used.

The calculation of the linear regression equations is set out below. (Information on the mechanics of these calculations can be found in most elementary business statistics books.)

Year	X	Sales Y	X²	XY	Y²
1980	1	100	1	100	10,000
1981	2	120	4	240	14,400
1982	3	140	9	420	19,600
1983	4	173	16	692	29,929
1984	5	200	25	1,000	40,000
1985	6	250	36	1,500	62,500
1986	7	293	49	2,051	85,849
	28	1,276	140	6,003	262,278
	$= \Sigma X$	$= \Sigma Y$	$= \Sigma X^2$	$= \Sigma XY$	$= \Sigma Y^2$
	$n = 7$				

The linear regression equation for the above data can be calculated from the standard linear regression formula:

$$Y = a + bx$$

Where $b = \dfrac{n \, \Sigma XY - \Sigma X \, \Sigma Y}{n \, \Sigma X^2 - (\Sigma X)^2}$

and $a = \dfrac{\Sigma Y}{n} - \dfrac{b \Sigma X}{n}$

Thus in this case

$$b = \frac{7(6003) - 28(1276)}{7(140) - (28)^2}$$

$$= \frac{6293}{196}$$

$$= \underline{32.1}$$

and $a = \dfrac{1276}{7} - 32.1 \left(\dfrac{28}{7} \right)$

$$= 182.3 - 128.4$$

$$= \underline{53.9}$$

Therefore the regression equation for Company A is:
$Y = 53.9 + 32.1x$ (£000)

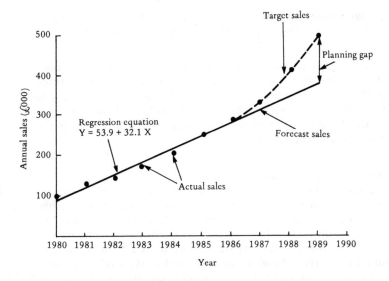

Figure 30   *The planning gap for Company A's sales over the period 1987–9*

This regression equation can be used to forecast future sales of Company A over the planning period if there were no change in strategy or forecasting conditions. On this basis, Company A's sales are forecast to be:

For 1987:   Y = 53.9 + 8 (32.1) = 310.7 (£000)
For 1988:   Y = 53.9 + 9 (32.1) = 342.8 (£000)
For 1989:   Y = 53.9 + 10 (32.1) = 374.9 (£000)

Step 3:   The forecast gap is measured
The gap between the target sales and the forecast sales can be seen to be as follows:

Year		*1987*	*1988*	*1989*
Target sales	(£000)	330.0	420.0	500.0
Forecast sales	(£000)	310.7	342.8	374.9
Gap	(£000)	19.3	77.2	125.1

The planning gap is shown in Figure 30.

Step 4:   Develop strategies to close the gap
The analysis indicates that Company A is going to fail, by progressively larger amounts, to meet its sales targets. If the company still wishes to pursue the above targets, i.e. close the gap, it must change from its current fundamental strategy of conservative organic growth to a fun-

damental strategy of high growth. The latter fundamental strategy*
could be achieved by one or more of the following sub-strategies:

1   *Internal high growth*:   This could be achieved through one or more
    of the following: increased sales of existing products; internal con-
    centric diversification; internal conglomerate diversification.
2   *External high growth*:   This could be achieved through one or more
    of the following: external concentric diversification; external con-
    glomerate diversification; merger.

Incorporating probability into the analysis
As indicated on page 58 the type of mathematical forecast in the
previous section may generate an unjustifiably strong feeling of faith
in its accuracy. However, experience and research (see Spivey and
Wrobleski[7]) indicates that, even when conditions remain stable, it is
extremely unlikely that mathematical forecasts will turn out to be
completely correct. An element of uncertainty, and hence greater reality, can be introduced into the exercise through setting up confidence
limits for the forecasts. In the above case this can be effected through
using the regression equation's standard error of estimate.
    The standard error of estimate (which can be considered as equiva-
lent to a standard deviation) can be computed from the formula:

$$S = \sqrt{\frac{\Sigma Y^2 - a(\Sigma Y) - b(\Sigma XY)}{n - 2}}$$

and in this case

$$S = \sqrt{\frac{262{,}278 - 68{,}776.4 - 192{,}696.3}{5}}$$

$$= \sqrt{\frac{805.3}{5}}$$

$$= + \sqrt{161.06}$$

$$= 12.7 \; (\pounds 000)$$

This standard error can be used to set confidence limits for the
predictions or forecasts as follows. Because the sample size is small (the
number of sets of data points upon which the forecasts are made is just
seven) at distribution rather than a normal distribution must be used
to set up the confidence limits.

* The selection of appropriate strategies and sub-strategies is dealt with more completely
on pages 181–222.

The 95 per cent confidence limits* for Company A's forecasted sales can be found using the formula:

$$\bar{Y}_p \pm t(.95, (n-2)) \cdot S \sqrt{\frac{1}{n} \frac{(X - \bar{X})^2}{\Sigma(X - \bar{X})^2}}$$

Where:

$\bar{Y}_p$ is the predicted value of Y (the annual sales) for any selected value of X (the year)

X is any selected year

$\bar{X}$ is the mean of the actual values used in the calculations

S is the standard error of estimate

t(.95, (n − 2)) is the value of t with (n − 2) degrees of freedom for a 95 per cent level of confidence

The 95 per cent confidence limits for the predictions for Company A's annual sales for 1987, 1988 and 1989 are as follows:

$$\bar{Y}_p \pm t(.95, Sdf)S \sqrt{\frac{1}{n} + \frac{(X - \bar{X})^2}{\Sigma(X - \bar{X})^2}}$$

For 1987:

$$= 310.7 \pm (2.571) \, 12.7 \sqrt{\frac{1}{7} + \frac{(8-4)^2}{28}}$$

$$= 310.7 \pm (2.571)(12.7)(0.84)$$

$$= 310.7 \pm (2.571)(10.7)$$

$$= 283.3 \text{ to } 338.1 \text{ (£000)}$$

For 1988:

$$= 342.8 \pm (2.571)(12.7) \sqrt{\frac{1}{7} + \frac{(9-4)^2}{28}}$$

$$= 342.8 \pm (2.571)(12.7) \sqrt{1.04}$$

$$= 342.8 \pm (2.571)(12.954)$$

$$= 309.5 \text{ to } 376.1 \text{ (£000)}$$

* A 95 per cent level of confidence was chosen for this example because it is a commonly employed level. Other levels of confidence can be calculated equally easily.

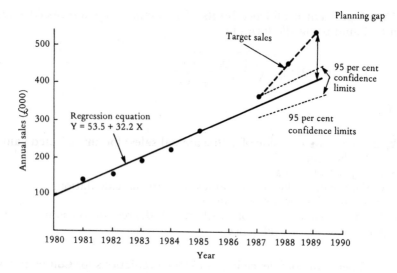

Figure 31   *The planning gap for Company A's sales over the period 1987–9 with confidence limits incorporated*

For 1989:

$$= 374.9 \pm 2.571(12.7) \sqrt{\frac{1}{7} + \frac{(10-4)^2}{28}}$$

$$= 374.9 \pm 2.571 \, (12.7) \sqrt{1.43}$$

$$= 374.9 \pm (2.571)(15.19)$$

$$= 335.8 \text{ to } 414.0 \, (\pounds 000)$$

These confidence limits are drawn on the planning gap graph shown in Figure 31.

As can be seen the 95 per cent confidence limits indicate that it is extremely unlikely that if current strategies are pursued targets will be met – the only sales target that shows any possibility of being met is that for 1987 (it lies inside the 95 per cent confidence limits) while the other two target sales lie outside the 95 per cent confidence limits. Thus for the 1988 and 1989 targets there is less than a 2.5 in 100 (the confidence limits which have been set are two-tailed) chance of meeting the set targets.

An alternative way to view the challenges posed by the above analysis is to draw each forecast in the form of a t distribution and then ascertain the probability of each target being met or exceeded using t tables. Figure 32 shows the t distribution for the 1987 forecast and the probability of the forecast being met or exceeded is computed below.

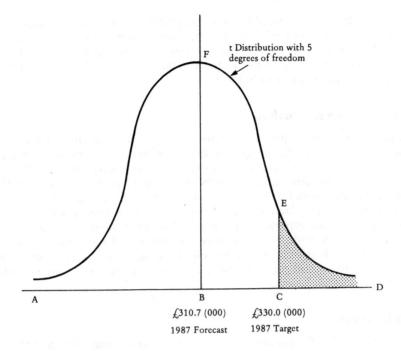

Figure 32 *A t distribution around the forecast for Company A's sales for 1987*

Recalling that:

the 1987 forecast for sales is
$\bar{Y}_p = 310.7\ (\pounds000)$
and the 1987 sales target is
$Y = 330.0\ (\pounds000)$

Then the shaded area CDE in Figure 32 shows the probability that the forecast will be met or exceeded. This area can be calculated by transforming the distribution shown into a standard t distribution, calculating the value of t corresponding to the point C and finding the area CDE using t tables. Thus the t value corresponding to point C is:

$$= \frac{Y - \bar{Y}_p}{S_{YX} \cdot \sqrt{\dfrac{1}{n} + \dfrac{(X - \bar{X})^2}{\Sigma(X - \bar{X})^2}}}$$

$$= \frac{330.0 - 310.7}{(12.7)(0.84)}$$

$$= 1.81$$

From t tables, the area CDE, i.e. the probability that with 5 degrees of freedom t will exceed 1.81, can be found, using interpolation, to be 0.14. Therefore the probability of Company A meeting of exceeding its 1987 sales target is 0.14. Therefore the risk of failing to meet this target must be extremely high.

Conclusion on gap analysis

Gap analysis can be particularly useful as a neutral device for showing the extent of strategic change necessary to achieve corporate goals or targets and can thus act as a stimulant to effecting change. Of fundamental importance to the quality of the analysis is the quality of the forecasts upon which it is based and in today's turbulent environment long-run accurate forecasts are the exception rather than the rule. However, the widespread availability of sophisticated computer-based information technology has enabled the process of forecasting and the speed at which it may be carried out to be greatly enhanced and this development should promote the frequency and quality of gap analysis.

References

1   Argenti, J., *Corporate Collapse: The Causes and the Symptoms*, McGraw-Hill, 1976.
2   Slatter, S., *Corporate Recovery*, Penguin 1984.
3   Hall, W. and Taylor, P. 'Falling, Prey to Reg of Deregulation', *Financial Times*, 5 March 1986, p. 22.
4   ITT Annual Report for 1984.
5   Tilles, S., 'Culture: Barrier to Change', *Perspectives*, No. 253, The Boston Consulting Group, 1983.
6   Argenti, J., *Corporate Planning: A Practical Guide*, George Allen & Unwin, 1968.
7   Spivey, A. W. and Wrobleski, W. J., 'Surveying Recent Econometric Forecasting Performance', Reprint 106, American Enterprise Institute, February 1980.

9 Developing new strategies 1

The base upon which new strategies are developed is the current strategic position which was considered in Part Four. It is suggested here that new strategies are developed using a two stage methodology which is shown schematically in Figure 33.

The first stage is to decide upon a fundamental strategy for the organization. It is assumed that there are just five fundamental strategies:

- Conservative growth.
- High growth.
- Neutral.
- Recovery.
- Reduction.

The second stage is to develop, following Porter[1] an appropriate generic strategy. It is assumed that there are three possible generic strategies:

- High volume low cost.
- Differentiate.
- Focus.

Each stage is now considered in greater detail.

Stage 1: The fundamental strategies

Because of the distinction which this model of strategic management makes between conservative growth and high growth, some bench-

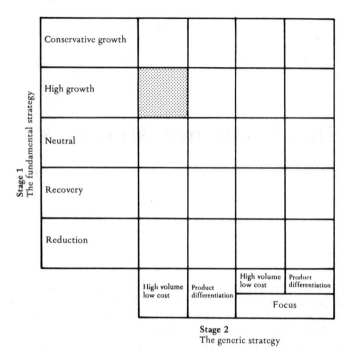

Figure 33 *A two stage methodology for developing strategies*

marks for distinguishing between each case are necessary. Growth is assumed to have three fundamental dimensions:

1 Actual growth rates of the performance measures (for example, sales, profits earnings per share, etc.) quantitatively expressed.
2 The growth in the range of products which an organization provides.
3 Growth in the range of markets served.

Conservative growth strategies

Generally, an organization could be described as following a conservative growth strategy when:

- Its growth rate is similar to the industry average.
- Its growth rate is similar to its own historical performance.
- It continues to serve the same or related markets with similar or related products.

Within the overall context of a conservative growth strategy there are various sub-strategies which may be employed.

Greater internal efficiency

Growth in performance can be achieved without altering the product-market scope of the organization but by improving its performance through stretching the gap between revenues and costs. The type of activities which would promote this could include the following:

- Reduction of costs.
- Improvement of quality.
- Price increases.
- Better human relations.
- Rationalization of production methods, products and markets.
- More efficient organizational structure.

The successful pursuit of increased internal efficiency has been a feature of the recent strategies employed by Japanese companies in general. In the 1970s after the two oil shocks, when the price of oil increased in real terms by a factor of approximately four, Japanese industry and society faced a serious threat to its continued growth – the cost of oil. Because of its extremely heavy dependence on imported oil (in 1981, Japan imported 99.8 per cent of its oil (see Mikami[2], page 2). The increase in energy costs threatened to destroy Japanese industry's growth aspirations. However, Japanese industry successfully responded to this challenge by improving its internal efficiency through increasingly focusing its fundamental research efforts on areas such as 'energy saving', 'labour saving, 'resource saving'. Thus, the Japanese Management Association (JMA) has shown how the objectives of research changed between 1970 and 1980 to reflect this concern with increasing internal efficiency. Selected statistics from the JMA findings are given in Table 20.

Table 20   Objectives of scientific and technological research

Year	Labour saving (%)	Resource saving (%)	Energy saving (%)
1950	9	5	2
1960	10	5	3
1970	11	8	5
1980	8	18	18

The fruits of this research were ultimately reflected in productivity rates and production costs which now bestow a strong competitive advantage on many sectors of Japanese industry.

This was an example of a strategy of greater internal efficiency practised on a national scale.

Deeper penetration of the same markets with the same products

Here the emphasis is placed on improving the quality of the marketing of the existing products in the existing markets. It is therefore rather similar to internal efficiency strategy except that the focus lies outside the organization in its markets. This type of strategy is concerned with more effective promotion and could involve activities such as advertising campaigns, warranty improvements, price reductions etc. which attempt to cause existing purchasers to purchase in greater quantities; attracting customers from rival products, or developing customers who previously were not consumers of the product.

Conservative growth was the strategy adopted by British Leyland in the UK in the early 1980s when it attempted to increase its market share of the UK automobile market. 'Armed' with a somewhat outdated range of models, the company attempted to retain existing customers and attract new ones, through marketing campaigns which featured special warranties and reduced prices.

This was an example of a strategy of attempting deeper penetration of the same markets with the same products.

The same products in new markets

Here the emphasis is placed upon developing further markets for the organization's existing products. These new markets can be divided into two main groups – additional segments within existing markets and new geographical markets – usually international or overseas.

The additional segments will arise when new uses can be found for existing products or when new segments can be persuaded to purchase the products. Appealing to a greater variety of segments was one of the elements leading to the success of the Japanese motorcycle companies in their penetration of European motorcycle markets. Their smaller motorcycles were promoted on the basis of their appeal to potential female motorcyclists – a segment which had been largely ignored by the UK and other manufacturers.

For organizations whose domestic market appears to offer limited or difficult future prospects, growth may be sought in foreign markets. An excellent example of an organization which has grown consistently, through its overseas operations, is the US multinational company Crown Cork and Seal. Crown Cork and Seal is a major manufacturer of crown corks and cans and has, since the 1960s, invested heavily overseas, especially in developing countries. It has frequently used outmoded US equipment for its overseas operations and has experienced a disproportionate contribution to profits from its overseas operations.[3] Thus this company has exploited new geographical markets with existing products.

New related products in the same markets

An alternative to market development is product development where the growth is achieved by developing the product in some fashion so that its market appeal is extended. This type of strategy is a feature of the strategies of manufacturers of DIY electric drills such as Black and Decker and Bosch. Once an electric drill is introduced onto the market there frequently follows a series of related products – attachments for polishing, sanding, sawing etc. – this is a strategy of new related products in the same markets.

New related products in new markets

This is really a combination of the two strategies considered immediately above. In this case there is both market development (which can be domestic or international or both) and product development. Again, Black and Decker provides an example of this type of strategy. Not only has the company introduced new related DIY products, but it has sought to extend its market segments by expanding into other domestic activities by developing ranges of gardening and household appliance products.

Circumstances appropriate to a conservative growth strategy

Like all the fundamental strategies considered in this chapter there are no absolute guidelines for determining when each of them is the correct strategy for an organization to follow. There are, however, general considerations which ought to sway decisions about the choice of a fundamental strategy. Among the more important considerations are the following.:

The environment
The conservative growth strategy tends to be appropriate when the current and future environments are considered to be relatively stable and there is modest growth – when there is modest growth in the economy it may be prudent to pursue a strategy which reflects this.

The competition
When there is competitive stability this type of strategy may be most appropriate. Competitive stability means that the major competitors which the organization under analysis faces are not jostling for competitive advantage but, in the main, are satisfied with the status quo i.e. they are earning returns which they consider to be satisfactory; there is a low level of rivalry; there are no strong threats of substitutes or new entrants, and the power of buyers and suppliers is not regarded as excessive. In this type of situation modest aspirations may be the most appropriate as attempts at aggressive growth may upset the relatively comfortable status quo through provoking fierce competitive reaction with consequent depressed returns for all competitors. For example, in the UK, because of the liberalization of the laws relating to the advertising of the professions, especially accountancy and law, it seems likely that the status quo which persisted until the 1980s will be upset and

some companies will pursue 'aggressive growth' strategies – pursued for example through advertising – which will put increased competitive pressure on many legal and accounting practices and may lead to lower average levels of profitability.

Resources

Any strategy must be related to the resources which the organization has available in order to support it. For organizations which have somewhat limited resources there may be no 'growth alternative' to conservative growth. For example, because of its limited resources, in absolute terms and in relation to its major competitors, British Leyland really did not have any alternative to attempting a conservative growth strategy in the early 1980s.

In addition to the restrictions upon growth rate imposed by an organization's resources relative to its competitors, there are also growth restrictions imposed by the absolute levels of a company's resources. Thus Argenti[4] and Slatter[5] have pointed out that for smaller businesses especially, overtrading, i.e. growing too quickly can be a fundamental cause of company failure:

> Overtrading is the process by which a firm's sales grow at a faster rate than the firm is able to finance from internally generated cash flow and bank borrowings. The failure of Brentford Nylons was due very largely to this factor. Overtrading can occur as a result of poor financial control, in which case the lack of adequate control is more accurately the cause of the decline. Very often, however, there is another factor at work: the firm is going after sales growth, regardless of whether or not is is profitable. Margins are reduced to increase volume and unprofitable customers are added just increase sales volume. Overtrading is a characteristic of growth firms.

The goals of the organization

Of crucial importance to the fundamental strategy adopted are the goals of its top decision makers. If these decision makers have had modest goals in the past and have been largely satisfied with modest growth in the past then such strategies are likely to persist in the future.

The culture of the organization

In choosing a strategy care must be taken to ensure that it either fits with, or can be fitted to, the culture of the organization. As pointed out on page 168 the culture of an organization is frequently a major impediment to strategic change. Thus the decision makers in organizations which have been accustomed to rapid growth in the past will find it difficult to adjust their behaviour and actions to a strategy of conservative growth. In contrast, decision makers who have become accustomed to a strategy of conservative growth will also find it difficult to come to terms with a strategy of, say, aggressive growth.

In summary those new strategies which represent the smallest break with the cultural past will probably have the best prospects of subsequent successful implementation.

High growth strategies

From a quantitative perspective a company could be described as following a high growth strategy when one or more of the following conditions obtain:

- Its growth rate is significantly greater than the industry average.
- Its growth rate is significantly in excess of its own historical performance.
- The previously accepted levels of its historical measures of performance need to be adjusted.

In addition to these quantitative measures high growth could also be said to be occurring when the company is adding to its portfolio of products or its portfolio of businesses, i.e. it is diversifying into new areas.

There are two main methods of achieving high growth – through internal or organic means and through external means – and each of these approaches may be pursued sequentially, or simultaneously. Strategies to achieve internal high growth can be sub-divided into two main categories:

- Increased sales of existing or related products.
- Sales of unrelated products.

Internal high growth achieved through increased sales of existing or related products

The strategies which may be employed to achieve this are really the same as the various sub-strategies which were suggested when conservative growth was the fundamental strategy: greater internal efficiency; deeper penetration – same markets, same products; same products in new markets; new related products in same markets; new related products in new markets. The only real change for high growth being that the expected *level* of growth should be higher.

When new related products are added to the existing range of products which the company offers, this strategy is frequently described as growth through *internal concentric diversification* because the growth is:

- *Internal* as it is generated from within the the company.
- *Concentric* as the new products are in some way related to the existing product range – they will probably be in similar industrial classifications.
- *Diversification* as the products are extensions to the existing range.

An example of the pursuit of high internal growth through the increased sales of existing and related products is provided by the recent history of the Minolta Camera Company Ltd of Japan. Table 21 shows the total revenues and contributions made by the products 'cameras and related equipment' and 'copying machines and other equipment' for this company over the period 1981 to 1985.

As Table 21 shows the company, which has traditionally been regarded as a camera manufacturer, now derives more than half of its revenue from non-camera products. Minolta, because the overall camera market is relatively flat and extremely competitive, has concentrically diversified from cameras, into other technologically related products whose growth prospects are superior. Judging from the 1985 annual report, this successful strategy of internal concentric diversification is likely to continue:

> Having built extensive businesses in cameras and business machines we are eager to expand the scope of our operations. The high-quality imaging on which we have established our reputation encompasses optics, microelectronics, precision machining and other technologies. Combinations of these technologies have yielded successful products in many areas, including photometry, medical equipment, and planetariums, and we will continue to apply our technological strengths to diversify our business activities.[6]

Internal high growth achieved through increased sales of unrelated products

This type of strategy is followed when an organization introduces new products which are unrelated to its existing range. The level of aggregation in this exposition is at the product level but it should be noted that diversification can also be achieved of course, at the business level by an organization adding to its portfolio of businesses. Because of the unrelated nature of the products it will normally be the case that the markets will also be new markets or new market segments.

An example of the successful adoption of this strategy is provided by the Lockheed Aircraft Company. This company, whose main business was in the manufacture of aircraft and related products, developed electronic data bases to help in their manufacturing processes. These data bases were so comprehensive that outside organizations started to make use of them and ultimately the Lockheed Aircraft Company diversified into the unrelated business of the commercial provision of electronic data base services on a world basis.

When new unrelated products are added to the existing range of products which the organization offers, this strategy could be described as growth through *internal conglomerate diversification* because the growth is:

- *Internal* as it is generated from within the organization.
- *Conglomerate* as the new products are not related to the existing product range.
- *Diversification* as the new products are extensions to the existing range.

Table 21 Earnings of Minolta Camera Co. Ltd 1981–5

	1985		1984		1983		1982		1981	
	Mn. ¥	(%)	Mn. ¥	(%)	Mn. ¥	(%)	Mn. ¥	(%)	Mn. ¥	(%)
Cameras and related equipment	106,843	44	98,535	46	93,751	49	94,553	49	95,473	55
Copying machines, microfilm equipment and others	138,010	46	115,356	44	98,843	51	99,817	51	78,562	45
Total sales	244,853	100	213,891	100	192,594	100	194,370	100	174,035	100

In passing, it should be noted that conglomerate diversification is usually not achieved by internal means – it is more usual for it to be pursued through external means. This type of strategy is discussed below.

External high growth is achieved by an organization extending its operations through some form of involvement with another organization. The main forms of involvement are mergers, acquisitions, take-overs, and joint ventures. For the purposes of this book, each of these forms of involvement will be described as a merger. There are four main strategies which may be employed in the pursuit of external high growth.

External concentric diversification

External concentric diversification occurs when an organization acquires, either in part or in total, another organization making the same or related products, i.e. products which have a similar industrial classification. The sub-strategies which can be employed to achieve this type of diversification are often described as integration strategies.

Integration is the process whereby the organization grows through strengthening its position in its given industry through developing forwards, backwards or horizontally.

Thus a strategy of *forward integration* occurs when an organization acquires totally, or in part, a business which distributes its output. For example in the UK brewing industry most of the major competitors – Bass, Allied Lyons, Whitbread, Grand Metropolitan, Scottish and Newcastle, and Courage – have large numbers of public houses and other types of retail outlets. Over time they have integrated forwards from manufacturing into retailing in order to guarantee sales.

Backward integration occurs when an organization acquires totally, or in part, a business which is a supplier. For example many major motor vehicle manufacturers have sought to reduce the power of their component suppliers either through backward integration or the threat of it.

Finally, *horizontal integration* occurs when an organization acquires a competing business which is engaged in the same or similar activities. For example when, in 1985, the Italian computer manufacturer, Olivetti, took over the British computer manufacturer, Acorn.

External concentric diversification can be achieved by employing one or more of the above types of integration.

Integration, as a high growth strategy, appears to be most appropriate when the future prospects of the industry in which the organization is operating appear to be positive, or if an organization feels that its size (and therefore its power) in the industry is so small, relative to its competitors, that its performance is being adversely affected.

In summary, it could be argued that when a strategy of external concentric diversification is followed successfully then in addition to the growth which such a strategy, by definition, imposes, it has the additional advantage that it can confer upon the organization a much stronger competitive and strategic position because of a relative diminution in one or more of the following determinants of competitive position:

- The power of buyers (this may occur if forward integration was the strategy followed).
- The power of suppliers (this may occur if backward integration was the strategy followed).
- The intensity of rivalry (this may occur if horizontal integration was the strategy followed).

Additionally the economic worth and the return on investment of the organization should be increased as the 'value added' aspect of the organization's operations ought to increase.

External conglomerate diversification

External conglomerate diversification (which is often called simply 'conglomerate diversification') occurs when an organization acquires totally, or in part, another organization whose area of business is not related to the acquiring organization's existing business interests.

A well publicized UK company which has practised this strategy is the conglomerate Hanson Trust plc. Starting out in 1964 as a family-run transportation company in England, Hanson Trust has developed, mainly in the UK and the US, into a company whose businesses now include: bricks; department stores; duty free goods retailing; dry cell batteries; electrical and gas equipment; the distribution and hire of construction equipment; speciality textiles; shoe manufacture and re-tailing; meat processing; the manufacture of garden and industrial hand tools; lighting fixtures; furniture; building materials and industrial products; typewriters, paints and foods. Hanson Trust quickly built up this portfolio of mainly unrelated businesses largely through a strategy of conglomerate acquisition to achieve high growth. Thus, in the period 1973 to 1985, its turnover and profit grew from £51.7 million to £2,674 million and £0.4 million to £131.7 million respectively.

Circumstances appropriate to a high growth strategy

The general considerations which ought to sway decisions about the choice of a fundamental strategy of high growth include the following.

The environment

The high growth strategy tends to be appropriate when the current and future environments are thought to be changing rapidly and/or the economic environment is growing quickly. In a rapidly changing environment, such as for example, domestic electronics, it may be the case that the speed of change is so rapid that those companies which do not grow rapidly will find their products obsolete before they have generated acceptable financial returns.

The competition

When the industry as a whole is at the growth stage and rivals are growing very quickly it may be the case that those organizations which fail to match or exceed the average industry growth rate will find their competitive position eroded. This is certainly the case in experience-related industries such as standard personal computers – those organizations which do not generate certain threshold sales levels will fail as they will not have sufficient volume to permit them to price competitively.

Resources

Organizations may pursue high growth strategies because their resources are underutilized. Underutilization of assets can be manifested in a number of areas which include the following:

Underutilized physical assets: In times of low economic growth or recession, it may be the case that an organization develops excess capacity, i.e. its physical plant and buildings are greater than it requires to serve its markets. Or indeed, even in times of economic growth, an organization may expand its physical operations to an extent that it cannot run its plants at full capacity. PIMS has shown empirically that excess capacity, or as PIMS calls it, investment intensity, is the largest single influence upon a business's return on investment. (See Figure 34.) In order to reduce the harmful effects that investment intensity may have on an organization's profits, a strategy of high growth i.e. volume grabbing with a lesser regard for price may be followed. (For further information see Schoeffler.[7])

Underutilized financial resources: Organizations which have been operating profitably may become cash rich and may develop large cash reserves on which they believe they can achieve the highest return through re-investing either in the organization itself or outside it. This process tends to promote a strategy of high growth and the development of relatively large reserves of cash may have been one of the factors which led UK tobacco companies to engage in conglomerate diversification in the 1970s.

Underutilized human resources: Where organizations have a policy of lifetime employment for all personnel, as automation and increased efficiency reduce the need for manpower the only means of sustaining the size of the workforce may be through pursuing a strategy of high growth. This is certainly a factor which influences large Japanese companies to pursue high growth strategies.

Underutilized marketing resources: Irrespective of the aspect of the marketing resources which is underutilized – sales personnel, distribution channels etc. the utilization of such slack capacity, through a strategy of high growth, should bring enhanced economic benefit.

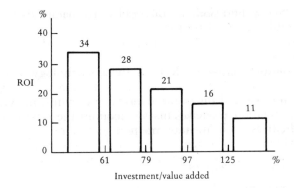

Figure 34   *Investment intensity is the largest single drag on profitability*

The goals of the organization

A fundamental driving force in the adoption of high growth as a strategy is the past success of the top managers in the organization. Managers who have had a record of success, and have fulfilled high growth goals, are unlikely to be satisfied by modest aspirations irrespective of the economic climate. When the economic environment is not conducive to a particular industry the growth strategy adopted is most likely to be through external means i.e. through merger and diversification.

The culture of the organization

This is closely related to the goals of the organization. Those organizations which have experienced high growth in the past, and have a growth orientated culture will wish this to continue.

The strategy of merger

Because of the great increase in the number of mergers in the 1980s in the UK and the US particularly, a special subsection on mergers is included in this section.

A merger could be said to occur when two or more separate companies* fuse to form a single new company. This fusion may take place in a number of ways:

- One company may acquire the other company(ies)' assets and liabilities in exchange for cash or shares or both.
- Both companies may be dissolved and the assets and liabilities joined together and a new company formed and shares in the new company issued.

* Because the mergers most relevant to strategic planning are those concerning companies or firms, the term 'company', rather than 'organization' will be used in this section.

Mergers, like integration can take place in various ways:

- Concentric mergers: Forward merger, backward merger and horizontal merger.
- Conglomerate mergers: No product or technology relationships.

Mergers are also known as takeovers, acquisitions, integration, joint ventures etc. For the purposes of this book all these types of company formations will be described as mergers.

The effectiveness of mergers

There is conflicting evidence about the effectiveness of mergers – there are those proponents of mergers (see Goldberg[8] and Doz[9]) who argue that merger activity is essential for the development of strong global competitors and confers economic benefit on both the parties concerned and society as a whole, while there are those (see Constable[10] and Stapleton[11]) who argue that merger activity confers little economic benefit.

Perhaps the most comprehensive and longest term analysis of mergers in the UK is the study, by Newbould and Luffman[12] of the strategies employed by 302 of the largest 500 companies in the UK in the 1960s and 1970s. The authors investigated the strategies employed by these companies over, approximately, a ten-year period and how these strategies had affected the four principal interest groups, as defined by them – the shareholders, the managers, the employees and the economy in general.

In terms of the effects of acquistitions upon each of the interest groups they found that:

> One group directly affected by acquisition are the shareholders of companies. The results of this study were fairly clear for shareholders: they received a lower rate of return on their investments and made larger capital losses on their shares the more committed companies were to the policy of acquisition ... Consequently, the conclusion must be that acquisitions were an unequivocal detriment to shareholders.
>
> Equally unequivocal was the fact that managers gained hugely from commitment to acquisition. The companies they controlled gained significantly in size, whether measured by sales, capital employed, or employees, the more their commitment to acquisition, the profits became more stable and there was a general reduction in the variability of success. The commitment to acquisition had no measurable impact on net cash flow.
>
> The section on the economy in general did not have such clear results as the two previous sections ... The balance then is that acquisition was detrimental to the interests of the economy in general.
>
> For employees, average remuneration worsened, and its variability increased as the commitment to acquisition increased, while the other measures showed no patterns. Again the conclusion, while not strong, must be that acquisition did not serve the measured interests of the employees.
>
> On balance then it appears a straight conflict between managers and the

other three interest groups. Since it is managers who formulate the policy on acquisition and then put the chosen strategy into effect, it appears that management must be prepared to put forward some very convincing explanation, not related to their personal needs of prestige and security, to justify a strategy which includes acquisitions.

In other words, in their findings, the only group which benefited was management.

More recent confirmation of the Newbould and Luffman findings has been provided by Constable[13] who has examined, empirically, the process of diversification in the UK economy and its effects.

Constable has shown that, between 1950 and 1980, the UK, when compared with the US, Germany and France, had moved from having the highest percentage of companies in the single and dominant business category (i.e. non-diversified) to having the highest percentage of companies in the diversified categories.

He suggests that the motives behind this trend towards diversification and acquisition are the aggressiveness of top management and a defence against being taken over.

The economic consequences of this activity, do not appear to Constable to have been beneficial:

> ... the propensity of engagement in merger and acquisition activity in the UK has done nothing to alleviate the decline and indeed may have been a significant cause of the decline.

Constable points out that most of the major studies into the effects of merger activity conclude that mergers tend to have the following effects.

- The merged companies are less profitable after the merger.
- Synergies tend not to be realized.
- Profitability tends to be less than prior to the merger.
- Selling shareholders tend to gain, but overall, in the long run shareholders do not.
- Profits attributable to internal investments would have been greater.

He concludes that in the case of the UK among the major consequences of merger activity are:

- There has been an illusion of growth rather than real growth.
- There has been too great an emphasis on the financial aspects of mergers with a neglect of the operational aspects.
- A disproportionate amount of top management time has been spent on merger activity.
- There has been a diversion of funds for internal investment into mergers.

The conclusion therefore, for the UK anyway, appears to be that generally the benefits which mergers bring are, at least, questionable to all groups except top managers.

Although there can be many reasons behind companies' decisions to pursue merger strategies, and the actual motives must be determined in each particular situation being analysed, those motives which have been most commonly found to be behind such merger strategies are set out below under a number of headings. The headings and the list of motives are not exhaustive and are not mutually exclusive, i.e. some motives which have been placed under the heading 'management driven', could equally well appear under the heading 'competition driven' and vice versa.

Management driven motives for merging

High growth

High growth tends to have an inherent appeal to most top managers – it rewards them. Consequently a strategy of merger, as shown on page 198, is often a quicker and 'more effective' way of achieving high growth than organic means. The rewards that high growth confers on managers are not just financial (although the practice of linking managers' financial rewards to performance, one aspect of which is often growth, is becoming increasingly common) but include such intangible rewards as increased power and feelings of success or accomplishment. There is considerable evidence to show (see Newbould[14]) that managers are often strongly motivated by power – it is a commonly held view that the larger the company the more important and powerful are its managers. Therefore, the managerial urge for a company to grow rapidly in such areas as: number of subsidiaries; value of sales, range of products; range of markets and numbers of employees is extremely strong. All these areas commonly are taken as explicit measures of the power of the top managers and, indeed, so strong may be the desire to achieve growth in one or more of these areas that managers may forgo profitability in order to achieve it.

In addition to the power that high growth is often assumed to confer, it is also often regarded by many of the stakeholders in companies as an indicator of success. This tendency to equate growth with success is demonstrated in the summaries of annual statements which most public companies publish in the financial press. These statements usually include information under headings such as: growth of earnings; growth in earnings per share; growth in ranges of products and markets etc., and generally, the higher the growth figure the more successful the company is judged to be.

High growth also tends to help engender a positive behavioural climate within a company. Thus when a company enjoys a sustained period of high growth, not only does it help develop a feeling of security among employees, but it also acts as a performance motivator as it enables personnel, at all levels, to map out and follow upwardly-moving career patterns within the company. Additionally, high growth provides an opportunity for ambitious managers to utilize their skills and realize their ambitions in ways which are beneficial to the company and themselves. To illustrate this last aspect of the effects of high growth – when companies are stagnating, or in decline, it is not unusual for top management to develop their status and power through internal political manoeuvring which may be beneficial to the managers themselves, but may be costly to the company. The negative effects that a low growth rate can have was illustrated well by Pascale and Athos in their description of the type of top managers that the US banking and financial services corporation Citicorp employs and the change of behaviour which a period of relatively low growth can provoke in these managers:

> ... The term we use around here is 'tiger' and it is not a negative image. The attributes sought are naked ambition, tremendous flexibility, willingness to change and an assertive kind of 'meeting macho' where you verbally punch your points home and spear those who disagree. Problems arise, however, when an organization can't expand fast enough to absorb that kind of aggressive energy. Then the tigers turn into sharks ... all swimming around in a confined space ... waiting. The quicker students who attend these courses on the niceties of man-management are watching out of the corner of their eye to see who the managers are who are going to survive and thrive. 'Interpersonal virtue' is no match for the powerful force of role models who consistently exemplify aggressiveness and hustle.

In times of stagnation or recession, ambitious, growth-orientated managers face a problem – how can they achieve their growth goals in a period of low or negative growth in their industry. The solution often is to use mergers.

Just how high growth can be achieved through a strategy of merger, even when the economy is stagnant and no organic growth in the merging companies is occurring, is illustrated below using a hypothetical example.

Although Company A has been a fast growing and successful company in the past (as is reflected by its PE ratio of twenty-two) the environment it now faces is static with no real growth at all expected over the next year and yet the company wishes to continue to grow quickly. How can this objective be achieved?

The solution is conglomerate diversification and the 'magic' leverage of a high PE ratio. So the company decides to acquire two companies in the next year and use the leverage of its high PE ratio to effect this growth. The criteria for deciding upon the companies to be acquired are their size and financial performance with particular reference to their PE ratios, which must be less than that of the acquiring company. The industries in which the companies to be taken over operate are irrelevant: hence the mergers are conglomerate. The first company to be taken over is Company Z. Company Z's statistics are given in Table 22. As can be seen, although its annual sales and earnings per share are as high as Company A's, its PE ratio is only eight and this results in a

Table 22   Company A bids for Companies Z and Y

Company	Earnings (£ million)	Number of shares (million)	EPS (£)	PE ratio	Share price (£)	Value of bid per share (£)
A	0.5	2.0	0.25	22	5.50 *3A FOR 5B*	
Z	0.5	2.0	0.25	8	2.00	3.30
A'	1.0	3.2	0.28 *0.31*	22	6.28 *6.82*	
Y	1.0	3.2	0.31	8	2.48 *1A for 24*	3.41
A''	2.0	4.8	0.42	22	9.20	

much lower quoted share price. Company A makes the following paper bid for Company Z: three shares in Company A (value £16.50) for every five shares in Company Z (value £10.00) which is equivalent to paying a price of £3.30 for every £2.00 share in Company A – an attractive offer. It is assumed that the offer is accepted by all the shareholders in Company Z and a 'new' company – A' – is formed.

This new company, A', then makes a bid for Company Y. Again Company Y, although it is of the same size and has the same earnings per share as Company A', has a PE ratio of only eight which results in a share price of only £2.48. Company A makes a paper bid for Company Y: one share in Company A' (value £6.28) for every two shares in Company Y (value £4.96) which is equivalent to paying a price of £3.14 for every share in Company Y – an attractive offer. It is assumed that the offer is accepted by all the shareholders in Company Y and a new company Company A'' is formed.

The report of the new company, A'', at the end of this period might include the information shown in Table 23.

Table 23   A summary of changes in Company A'' in the past year

	One year ago	Now	% change
~~Sales~~ *Earnings*	£0.5 million	£2.0 million	300
Ordinary shares	2 million	4.8 million	140
Earnings per share	£0.25	~~£0.48~~ 0.42	~~48~~ 68
Share price	£5.50	£9.20	67

These summary figures show that in the past year, in spite of the static economy, Company A has had an outstanding performance and if Company A's management has its rewards tied to growth performance substantial benefits should accrue.

A good example of merger strategies based on differing motives was provided in 1986 when, in the UK's biggest ever takeover bid (£2.8 bn), two rival bidders – United Biscuits (a major UK food product company) and Hanson Trust (an industrial conglomerate) sought to take control of the Imperial Group (a tobacco to brewing conglomerate).

Exhibit 11: Signs point to a nail-biting finish[15]
There is also a classic symmetry in the clash of cultures between the protagonists and the future they offer Imperial: United Biscuits holds aloft a banner labelled 'long term industrial logic' and Hanson one proclaiming simply its proven management skills for making under-performing assets sweat ...

... Battle was first joined in early December when, in the space of a week, first Imperial and United unveiled plans for a merger (in the form of an Imperial bid for the smaller United) and then Hanson bid for Imperial, claiming that the merger was merely a defensive pact between the two bid targets ...

... Imperial and United insist that a marriage of the two makes great sense: for Imperial, it would mean a much reduced dependence on tobacco (which would account for about 33 per cent of the combined group's 1985 sales, against 29 per cent for brewing and leisure and 38 per cent for food). For United it would mean access to the strong cash flow from the cigarettes business to help fund its expansion as a major international force in the foods business ...

... Certainly, Hanson has said remarkably little about its intentions for Imperial. It argues that there is little point coming up with solutions until it has won and taken a close look at the problems of the business. Essentially, it is standing on its record, and it can compare its 33.9 per cent annual growth in earnings per share over the past five years with 9.2 per cent recorded by United.

'We have greater experience of acquisitions of this size and have proved we can inject new life into companies,' says Lord Hanson ...

... It (Hanson Trust) stands accused of generating remarkably little organic growth and being dependent on making ever larger takeovers to sustain expansion. Its relatively low level of capital investment (£59m last year) is contrasted with that of Imperial (£193m) and United (£94m). Hanson replies that its return on capital employed is double Imperial's. 'They believe it is virile to invest money. We believe it is virile to get a return.'

Speculative gain
It is not unknown for mergers to be motivated by the prospects of speculative gains by the management side which instigates the merger. Thus, Newbould and Luffman have shown that, in the UK in the 1960s – a period when there was a substantial amount of merger activity – shareholders and those with privileged information could gain speculatively, from high levels of bids at the time of the merger, but that overall, in the longer term, shareholders' returns were reduced when

their companies pursued strategies which had a strong commitment to a policy of acquisition.

Entrepreneurial versus professional management skills

There is some evidence to show that the types of managerial skills required to start up a company successfully are somewhat different from the skills required to effectively manage an established company. Therefore established companies often take the view that the 'entrepreneurial-start-up' phase of a business is best undertaken by managers who have this particular type of skill and that once this stage has been passed and the business is seen to be established then a bid is made and a takeover is effected. This approach has the additional advantage to the company effecting the takeover in that the, frequently highly risky, start-up stage is borne by outsiders.

In passing it should be considered that this type of takeover is not necessarily against the best commercial interests of the company which is taken over. Often the people who possess those special entrepreneurial skills so necessary in the start-up stage of a business do not possess the required managerial skills or the resources necessary for sustaining the later development of the business.

Use of surplus cash

It is not unusual for companies to become cash rich i.e. their business operations are so financially successful that they generate positive cash throw-offs which are so high that the company does not have a sufficient number of internal projects to absorb it, and so the cash is invested, usually suboptimally, in safe liquid interest-bearing investments. In such a situation a company may 'hunt' for suitable companies to acquire so that it may more profitably use its excess cash.

Displace existing management

Elements of the existing management in a company may be performing unsatisfactorily but they may be in such powerful positions that the only way in which they can be dislodged is through the company merging with another. In the new post-merger situation, 'rationalization' may make the displacement of such personnel easier.

Competitive driven motives for merging

Market power

A company may engage in merger activity in order to increase its power in the market. This can be achieved in a number of ways. For example: increasing its market share through horizontal merger; extending its channels of distribution through forward integration merger; extending it power over suppliers through backward integration.

Large market share: One of the aims of a merger based on horizontal diversification is that it should increase the company's relative market share. This should have a beneficial effect upon the profitability of the

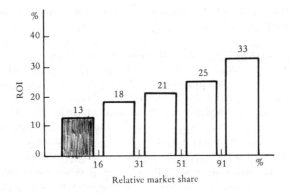

Figure 35 *Market position boosts profitability*

company. There is considerable empirical evidence to show that economic benefits i.e. return on investment are directly related to market share. Thus a fundamental finding of the PIMS studies, as shown in Figure 35[16], is that those companies which are most dominant in the marketplace, i.e. have the highest relative market share, tend, on average, to have the highest returns on investment. This finding clearly illustrates the importance behind pursuing a strategy which attempts to enable the company to grow in order to make it dominant in the market – the reward should be the highest return on investment. This was the strategy adopted by Texas Instruments in all its activities in the early 1970s (see page 205). When companies engage in horizontal diversification, apart from the proven advantages that larger volumes bring, there is also the competitive advantage conferred by the fact that such merger activity, by definition, helps to reduce the variety and the degree of competition which may give enhanced opportunities for pricing and profits reflecting a movement towards monopoly. Indeed the power and benefits that accrue through concentration through merger are so great, and felt by many interested parties to be so much against the public interest, that this is the reason for the existence of the Monopolies and Mergers Commission in the UK and similar bodies in other countries. This concern is reflected in the activities and decisions of the UK Monopolies and Mergers Commission. Thus in the UK between 1980 and 1985, a period during which there was a considerable degree of merger activity a total of forty-two proposed mergers were referred to the Monopolies and Mergers Commission and only eight resulted in successful mergers – eight were abandoned during the investigation, fifteen were blocked by the Commission and the others failed for other reasons.

Extending the channels of distribution: When companies expand through merging to extend their channels of distribution this move ought to give them greater power in the market and so enhance their profitability prospects. The importance of having effective channels of distribution is particularly important in export sales. Thus one of the crucial elements in successful exporting to the US is having access to appropriate channels of merger in order to achieve this. (The benefits of forward integration have already been discussed on page 190.)

Backward integration: A merger based on backward integration should give a company increased power over its suppliers. (This has already been discussed on page 190.)

Market expansion: Merger is often regarded as an effective way to expand a company's markets – either through the addition of new products or through the addition of new geographical segments. In respect of the latter in particular, this is often regarded as a relatively cheap and less risky method of entering a new market rather than developing a 'greenfield' operation. A substantial amount of foreign direct investment in the UK today is in the form of merger.

Insufficient market demand: There are two main ways in which this type of situation can develop – the absolute size of the market itself may be stagnant or falling because the product is in the decline stage of its life cycle, or the market may be suffering from excess capacity. Both of these sets of circumstances are major stimuli to merger. For example in the automotive components industry in the UK in the early 1980s GKN, a major competitor, attempted to take over AE plc, another major competitor. One of the motivating factors behind this bid was the shrinking of the absolute size of the UK automotive components market. Similarly, in the European truck industry there have been, since the late 1970s, a series of mergers – perhaps the best known one being the Iveco merger of Fiat, Magirus, Unic (and later Ford) – which were partly motivated by the overcapacity in that industry (see Doz[17]).

Cost position
A company may merge in order to increase the scale of its operations and thereby reduce its costs. Thus, in many industries today, the process of globalization has allowed a limited number of companies to develop scales of operations which yield cost positions which national producers are often unable to match. For example food multinational H. J. Heinz is quite explicit about its achievements and ambitions in this area. (See Exhibit 12.)

Exhibit 12: Dramatic changes signal growth initiatives at Heinz[18]
This is our 23rd consecutive year of new financial records. It was also a year of dramatic changes, many of which flowed from your company's quest of low cost operator status in each of its operating subsidiaries ...

The low cost operator programme has evolved into the creation of a new entrepreneurial spirit within the universe that is Heinz. We continue to pursue vigorously an acquisition search for middle-sized companies that fit comfortably into niches within our present structure and that are attuned to ever changing consumer needs ...

As for the future – always the concern of an alert management – I believe company shareholders have every right to be optimistic. Our core business is strong and growing while new products and line extension multiply in response to consumer needs. We back all our brands with ever-larger marketing expenditures. We pursue our policy of niche acquisitions with diligence.

Critical mass
Related to the relative size of a company in its market is the 'mass' of the company in the industry. In many industries there is a certain 'critical mass' in terms of functional resources, channels of distribution, advertising power, access to capital etc. and if a company does not reach this size it is competitively disadvantaged. For example, in the soft drinks industry, unless a national manufacturer is of a certain critical size it will be so disadvantaged that it cannot effectively compete. The advantages that large size can confer in the area of advertising costs is well illustrated by the case of the Coca Cola Company.

Figure 36 shows the advertising expenditure incurred by several well-known manufacturers of soft drinks.[19] As can be seen, in spite of having the largest total advertising budget, The Coca Cola Company enjoys the lowest advertising cost per case. In order to compete against such companies a certain critical mass is necessary. Companies may merge to achieve this size.

Risk reduction
Risk reduction is often put forward by advocates of conglomerate diver-. sification mergers as one of the main benefits that accrue. In theory, just as it is possible to reduce risk by having a portfolio of shares so also, when a company acquires, through conglomerate mergers, a portfolio of disparate businesses it should have reduced its risk of failure because its interests will be spread across many industries. Indeed, this was one of the fundamental motives behind the diversification strategy of the US conglomerate ITT during its most active period of acquisition when it was guided by the legendary Harold Geneen.

> Many of these corporations were searching for stability, not true internal growth. Geneen observed that by spreading risks over several industries in different parts of the world, he was minimizing the dangers of a single or even of multiple failures at ITT as a whole and protecting his corporation from some of the hazards of the business cycles. A recession in one area in which the corporation had products might be balanced by expansion in another. Diversification is, in short, an 'insurance policy' for orderly future growth and thus has important positive values as a concept in itself. Moreover only a stable firm such as this could afford to take risks.[20]

Related to this motivation is the motivation of the reduction of cyclical elements faced by companies. Thus a company which feels itself vulnerable to vicissitudinous cyclical economic forces, may attempt

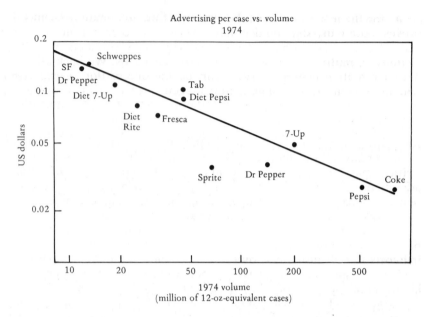

Figure 36 *Advertising expenditure for the Coca Cola Company and others*

to reduce their impact through having a portfolio which smoothes the effects of such forces.

It should be noted that a strategy of conglomerate diversification also carries with it a risk increasing element. In conglomerate diversification there is an assumption that the nature of the businesses being acquired is largely irrelevant – it is assumed that the managerial skills of the managers of the diversifying company are so effective that they can be universally applied to any business. In other words the nature of the business being acquired doesn't matter, what does matter is the managerial skills of the managers effecting the takeover. In practice this has not always been observed to be the case.

Synergy
One of the most commonly quoted reasons for advocating a merger strategy is that substantial economic benefits can accrue because of synergy. Synergy is defined here as the benefit that arises when the total economic contribution obtained from the new entity comprising two or more previously separate parts, is greater than the sum of the individual contributions from the previously separate parts. For example, when a company, which is in the leather tanning business merges with a company which is in the leather garment business, synergy would be said to have occurred if the economic performance of the new (combined) company was greater than the sum of the economic performances of the two companies before they merged. Although in theory

such benefits are easily seen, in practice their realization frequently proves more elusive.

Gaining expertise
A major motive behind mergers can be the acquisition of expertise, whether it is in the area of general management, technical or functional management. For example, in 1983, the American telecommunications company AT & T bought 25 per cent of Olivetti's shares with an option to take their stake to 40 per cent in 1988 – a major motivation, on Olivetti's part, was the acquisition of technical expertise:

> By the link with AT & T Olivetti has also gained access to some of the best telecommunications technology in the world. 'At the moment,' said Piol, 'that technology is not very important for the office automation business but, in five years' time, it certainly will be.'[21]

Offensive and defensive mergers

Finally, another dimension to the motivation to engage in merger activity is whether it is inspired by defensive or offensive motives.

Defensive motives arise when a company feels threatened either by the overall prospects in the industry (perhaps low growth and the prospects of poor returns or even bankruptcy) or by an individual competitor in the industry. Thus companies may merge to prevent an unwelcome takeover. Perhaps the best recent example of this motivation was the successful takeover of Distillers plc by Arthur Guinness in 1986 – a merger which took place, at Distillers' request, in order to block the unwelcome bid for Distillers from Argyll.

Offensive motives arise when a company perceives the opportunity to become dominant through high growth and it aggressively pursues this strategy with the ultimate aim of reaping the economic benefits that size confers. This was the motivation behind Texas Instruments strategy in the late 1960s and early 1970s.

> Texas Instruments, the market leader among some 50 or more calculator makers in 1974 with an estimated $225 million in calculator sales, relied upon experience curve pricing as its main marketing strategy under a sharply focused corporate objective of becoming the dominant producer in each field it entered.[22]

Reduce environmental uncertainty

One method of reducing the level of environmental uncertainty is through altering the boundaries of the organization. This can be done through merger activity – whether forward, backward, horizontal or conglomerate. In each of these types of merger, the company effecting the merger has changed, or expanded its boundaries with the environment and may reduce its risk exposure.

Conclusion on merger strategy

Large-scale merger activity is a major facet of strategic life today and therefore an understanding of the nature of merger activity, which includes the motives behind it and its likely effects, is an essential dimension of strategic management.

Neutral strategies

A neutral strategy could be described as one where there is no significant deviation from the past strategy i.e. the goals achieved, the organization's activities and its current competitive position have been historically satisfactory and similar achievements in the future would also be considered satisfactory. Therefore in this type of strategy no change is proposed. In the analyses of cases, many students find it difficult to accept the neutral strategy of 'no change.' They often feel that, somehow, even in organizations that are manifestly well run, it is better to suggest changes rather than to accept the evidence that the organization is performing well. It is almost as though they equate a strategy of action with evidence of their own industriousness. In those cases where the organization has discovered the 'formula for success' tampering with that formula may be a mistake.

Circumstances appropriate to a neutral strategy

Apart from the general circumstances outlined above, the following situations may help an organization decide upon a neutral strategy.

Environment

If the organization's planners anticipate that the environment facing the organization will change little in the next planning period, and as the achievements of the organization in the past have been found to be satisfactory, there would appear to be little incentive to change.

The competition

If the organization has achieved a satisfactory competitive position then, rather than upset this by introducing a change of strategy which might provoke hostile competitive retaliation which could leave the organization worse off, it may be better to have no change.

Resources

If the organization only has the resources to continue the same strategy as it followed in the past, then it has no choice.

Goals

If the goals of the organization have been satisfied by the achievements of the past strategy then it is likely that the goals will be satisfied by a similar strategy in the future.

Culture

From a cultural point of view, this is the easiest strategy to implement. People are familiar with it, it tends to be of little threat, and it requires little additional effort.

Although the neutral strategy is, for the reasons given under culture above, often very attractive to management, the simple re-application of the 'formula that brought success in the past' has great dangers. As many organizations have found out to their cost, the assumption that the particular environment faced by a particular organization is not changing is indeed a large one. The perception of 'no change' may be caused by 'organizational blinkers' and not reflect reality.

Recovery strategies

In spite of the painful business experiences which many business people had in the late 1970s and 1980s, there are many who still consider business crisis or failure to be a unique and unexpected occurrence. It is not. It is as normal an occurrence in business as illness is in the average human being. In all industries there is a dynamic of change and adjustment and there will always be a certain proportion of businesses that are experiencing crises or failing. Although the levels and impact of business failure tend to be most severe in the types of recessionary times which the UK has recently experienced, it should not be thought of as a phenomenon which is determined exclusively by recession. Thus, in the case of Japan, Mikami[23] has shown that over the period 1970 to 1979 because of the severity of competition, the rate of bankruptcies in Japan was two to three times greater than in the US.

These comments are not intended to detract from the seriousness of business crisis or failure, but rather to put such events in the context of a 'normal' business occurrence and so increase the weight given to the importance of considering strategies which will prevent failure i.e. strategies of recovery.

There is a continuum in the severity of the crisis which may require the instigation of a recovery strategy. At one end of the continuum is the immediate prospect of insolvency and bankruptcy – naturally the strongest trigger – and at the opposite end of the continuum is dissatisfaction with the achievement of the organization and a feeling that remedial action must be taken if even more unsatisfactory results are to be avoided. For the purposes of this section it will be assumed that a recovery strategy is appropriate when the organization is in a crisis which is not going to cause immediate failure, but will certainly cause failure to occur if remedial action is not taken immediately.

The aim of any recovery strategy ought to be at the least to minimize the losses that are occurring and, if possible, to change a declining organization which is generating unsatisfactory returns into one which achieves satisfactory returns for the organization's stakeholders and to develop as far as possible a long-term sustainable competitive position.

Although it is axiomatic that any successful recovery strategy must be tailored to the causes of the crisis in the organization under consideration there are, however, a number of fundamental general activities which appear to be appropriate in most recovery situations. Therefore the exposition of recovery strategy given below will be as follows: general activities for recovery (these are activities which can be applied in most recovery situations) and then causes of failure and how to recover (in this section the most frequently found causes of corporate failure, and how to deal with each of the causes are considered.

General activities for recovery

In almost all recovery strategies one or more of the following activities will help in the development of a successful strategy.

Early action
In general, the earlier in the developing crisis that action is taken the more time and scope there is for manoeuvre and the greater is the likelihood of a successful recovery. Ensuring early action means having the managerial motivation to act upon adverse signals coming from the organization's information system. The types of signals which tend to indicate that a crisis may be developing are given in the following section.

Related to the need for early action is the time dimension of recovery strategies. Because recovery strategies generally require urgent action if failure is to be avoided, it is normally the case that the planning horizon for these types of strategies is much shorter than is normal. For example, instead of being concerned with such issues as long-term market potential, future competitive strategies of competitors etc., the necessity for urgent action focuses attention on such issues as increasing cash flow and quick methods of reducing costs and assets.

Reducing costs
Organizations in crisis are often there because of a failure to control, or even know about, their costs. Therefore any recovery strategy, should, as a starting point, consider how existing costs can be reduced or at least controlled.

Reduce the assets
Frequently, in a crisis, an organization may have too large an asset base

for the sales and profits which it is generating. In these circumstances, a reduction in the value of the assets automatically increases the return on equity and additionally the proceeds of the sales may be used to reduce the level of debt or increase the proportion of equity.

Increase the revenues
A more positive way to lead an organization out of crisis may be to increase its revenues. This may be achieved through a variety of means – price changes, better marketing, new markets etc.

Change the top management
Perhaps the most crucial element in the development of a successful recovery strategy is having appropriate top management, particularly the chief executive officer or managing director. Frequently it is the case that a successful recovery can only be effected if the top management is replaced. As the incumbent top management is normally aware of this threat, it is not unusual for them to attempt to mask a forthcoming crisis in order to help them preserve their positions as long as possible.

A good example of the typical types of strategies taken to effect recovery are the actions that have been taken to try to turn round the UK electronics and computer company STC. In 1985 STC developed severe financial difficulties and then embarked upon a series of actions, outlined below, that were designed to return the company to profitability.

> Twelve months ago when Sir Kenneth Corfield, the then chairman of STC, the telecommunications and computer group, addressed the annual meeting he said 1985 would be a year of consolidation and the longer-term outlook was highly encouraging.
> Three months later STC was in the throes of a grave financial crisis and he was ousted in a boardroom coup.
> Lord Keith of Castleacre, prime architect of that coup and the man who has temporarily taken over the chairmanship, is likely to be rather more circumspect in his remarks today to STC's 1986 AGM.
> Nevertheless, after eight months of internal upheaval he will be able to point to substantial progress in getting the group back on to a sounder financial footing.
> There has been a major programme of cost-cutting, debt reduction and asset disposals and the strategic emphasis has switched from grandiose long-term planning to immediate profits and positive cash flow.
> The message the company is trying to put across is that the worst is past, the corner has been turned.
> ... A great deal has changed in personnel terms. Most obviously, much of the board is new, with a chief executive arriving last September in the form of Mr Arthur Walsh, formerly head of GEC-Marconi.
> Over the past year the company has cut some 8,000 to 9,000 jobs – with 6,000 of those going since August – reducing total employees to 43,000.
> ... There is less emphasis on peripheral businesses and the manufacture

of components, which must make a reasonable return to the rest of the group. Over the past year STC has raised more than £100m from the disposal of some 18 subsidiaries ...[24]

Causes of failure and how to recover

There has been a considerable amount of empirical investigation into the causes of decline and failure and this research has resulted in a number of methods of predicting corporate failure. It could be argued that the predictors of corporate failure can be divided into two approaches. The first approach, as represented by researchers such as Altman[25] and Taffler[26] asserts that corporate failure is reflected by, and can therefore be predicted by, financial and other published operating data provided by companies. The other approach, as represented by researchers such as Argenti[27] and Slatter[28] asserts that for an effective prediction, in addition to the financial and operating data, it is also necessary to include a consideration of the broader managerial and environmental circumstances in which the organization operates. This latter approach is considered below under a number of headings which group together the most frequently found causes of decline and failure. After each cause of failure has been considered an appropriate strategy for dealing with the cause is given. It should be noted that in most situations of decline and imminent failure there is not usually just one single cause. Rather, there will usually have been a variety of contributing factors, each of which must be dealt with if a successful recovery is to be achieved.

Management causes

Managerial failure is one of the most frequently cited causes of corporate decline. This type of failure can be manifested at one or more of the following levels.

Dominant and powerful chief executive or small caucus

When an organization is controlled in all its significant strategic aspects by just one person, or a small caucus, this concentration of autocratic power can lead to idiosyncratic decision making which may not be in the best commercial interests of the organization. Argenti suggests that when the chairman of a company is also its managing director, that it tends to concentrate an excessive amount of power in the hands of one person. Argenti argues that such power structures have, in a number of the failed companies he has analysed, contributed to their demise. It is rather paradoxical that the influence of a dominant chief executive has often been found to be a major factor contributing to the decline of companies as it is frequently the case that the dominant chief executive who autocratically leads his company into decline is the same person who actually built the company into its successful state. In such situations it may be that his strengths, which are so essential for building the company, become weaknesses when different strategic problems are encountered: such people help cause decline and failure because they themselves fail to change in line with changed circumstances.

Recovery strategy: The top management ought to be replaced. It should be noted, however, that normally this will be feasible only when all other strategies have failed and the crisis is so severe that the prospect of bankruptcy of the company is imminent.

Poor board of directors
When the board of directors fails to discharge its duties properly this may be a contributing factor to future failure. Poor performance by a board of directors can be expressed in a number of dimensions including:

- Lack of skills and knowledge i.e. the board does not have balanced functional expertise or is ignorant of the competitive realities of the business and its industry.
- Lack of communication i.e. there is little effective communication among the members.
- Lack of assertiveness i.e. rather than acting as a forum for the informed debate of fundamental strategic issues concerning the organization, the board may act as a rubber stamping agency for the chief executive officer, or some other dominant personality, and may, in a supine and uncritical fashion, continuously accede to his wishes.

Recovery strategy: The removal of those members of the board who have failed to make worthwhile contributions and their replacement with personnel who do have the necessary skills and knowledge, or augmenting the board with additional talent.

Diffusion of managerial effort
It is not unusual to find, particularly for organizations which have engaged in diversification, that strategic managerial effort may be absorbed by new and unrelated projects with the consequently costly neglect of the fundamental businesses of the organization. In passing it is instructive to note that one of the major criticisms of those companies which have been recipients of hostile takeover bids by predatory financiers is that a disproportionate amount of top management's time is absorbed in defending the organization against such bids rather than creative strategic planning and implementation. However, diffusion of managerial effort does not necessarily come from outside the company. It can be the case that the skills of management are spread too widely so that it fails to perform its core functions adequately. This was the major problem for ICL in its crisis years in the early 1980s. The com-

pany regarded itself as a serious competitor to IBM (which had sales fifty times greater than ICL) and consequently it tried to offer the wide range of services and applications that IBM offered. It did not have the capability to do this, and under the recovery strategy of Robb Wilmot redefined its business from being a competitor of IBM into being a producer of specialist machines for specific functions.

Recovery strategy: A restriction on the range of the activities in which top management is engaged. This may involve the disposal of parts of the business and 'getting back to basics'.

Functional causes

Although all the functional areas can contribute to decline, researchers of the causes have found that the following are the most frequently occurring causes.

Finance

1 *Poor financial control:*   This is a most frequent contributing factor to decline and is often exhibited when organizations have poor or non existent:

    - cash flow forecasting systems, and/or
    - budgetary control systems, and/or
    - cost control systems.

2 *Poor financial structure:*   The overal financial structure of the organization may, especially when there is a period of stagnant or reduced growth, impose strains. This frequently occurs when the amount of debt which the organization has is too large relative to its equity (see page 387).

Recovery strategy: The introduction of effective financial information and control systems. This will often include introducing the following:

- An accurate cash flow forecasting system.
- An effective budgetary control system.
- An effective cost control system.

Improving the financial structure through:

- Reducing the amount of debt. This could be achieved through the sale of assets and using the proceeds of such sales, or by leasing rather than purchasing assets.
- Increasing the amount of equity in the organization. This could be achieved through asking existing investors for additional funds or attracting new investors, or being taken over.

Overtrading
When the rate of the organization's growth is high and its consequent level of sales relative to its assets is very great, then overtrading, as described on page 186 can occur with disastrous consequences.

Recovery strategy: Reducing the rate of growth of sales of the organization and consolidating sales to relate them more closely to the size of its assets.

Marketing
When the effort made by those concerned with marketing is poor, as measured by the various marketing indices referred to on page 131 then failure is likely.

Recovery strategy: There is a great variety of possible strategies which can be selected from those detailed on pages 208–10. It is instructive to note that a 'reformation' of marketing strategies was one of the key ingredients of the UK computer company ICL's recovery strategy in 1985. One of the key elements in their recovery was a realization of their inadequacy in the areas of market segmentation, product positioning and other basic marketing techniques.

Production
When the costs of production become high, relative to competitors, this is frequently an indicator of failure. The Japanese concentration on production efficiency has been so effective that the production costs of many western companies are now no longer competitive.

Recovery strategy: If possible reduce the costs of production. This could be through improving the quality of the production equipment, acquiring additional production staff and expertise, shifting the location of production to a lower cost area, product redesign with the objective of lowering production costs, improving the quality of the product and reducing production costs. Although not in danger of failure the power tool division of the West German automotive and communications company Robert Bosch was, in the late 1970s and early 1980s, concerned about its inability to compete against Japanese competitors' prices. It embarked upon a campaign of cost engineering with the objective of reducing price without sacrificing quality. The results were impressive:

> The concept of cost engineering proved difficult for many to accept. Practising engineers, for example, tended at the start to state 'it can't be done' and to ask management which components they wanted taken out.
>   Management insisted. Helped by the campaign, the price of the company's 2 kg hammer has been brought down from DM800 to DM300 with no loss of quality. Annual sales have increased 20-fold in the past few years, Lungerhausen (the managing director of the division) boasts. It is now the division's main line and sets a price and quality standard for the rest of the world to match.[29]

Major strategic errors

Two types of major strategic error seem to be the most frequent cause of failure.

The big project
Argenti has documented well how a single large project which goes wrong can have the most disastrous consequences for an organization, with perhaps the best example being the decision of Rolls-Royce to develop the RB211 jet engine. The problems associated with this huge project helped contribute to the company's collapse in 1971. A consequence of this finding is that a project which is large, in relation to the total size of the organization, should be embarked upon only with the greatest degree of caution.

Recovery strategy: In this type of situation, depending upon the scale of the crisis, there are a number of possible strategies:

- Abandon the project altogether. In spite of the money which has been sunk into the project, if it shows no signs of becoming viable, it may be better just to abandon it and stop the haemorrhage of resources which it is absorbing.
- Sell the project. There may be another competitor, or business anxious to acquire the project.
- Seek additional funding/resources to enable the project to continue. If it appears that the project will ultimately be commercially successful and that the crisis it is causing can be weathered if sufficient additional resources are made available, then this may be a viable option.

Acquisition
Although acquisition is frequently seen by top management as the most attractive and frequently a relatively low risk method of growth (see page 196) it has also been, for many companies, a fundamental cause of failure. This failure can be due to a number of reasons including: absorption of top management time in developing the acquired company; paying too much for the acquired company; and simply acquiring companies which are poor performers and whose poor performance only becomes apparent after the acquisition.

Recovery strategy: Reduce the rate of acquisition and/or divest some of the more troublesome acquisitions.

External causes of decline

Although there can be many external causes of decline here they are grouped under two main headings – competitive pressure and market or economic recession.

Competitive pressure
When the competitive pressures become particularly severe, then failure can be expected. For example, in the Western European textile industry there have been many cases of textile companies failing because of the severe competitive pressures caused by the advent of new low cost entrants from the Far East.

Recovery strategy: The prospects for recovery are linked to the severity of the competition – the level of competition may be so severe that recovery is impossible. Assuming that the competition is not as severe as that, the company should attempt to structure itself so that it can profitably differentiate itself from its competitors.

Market or economic recession
A decline in the total market demand for a product could be due to either a change in demand for the product because of the stage it has reached in its life cycle – for example the demand in Western Europe for electro-mechanical cash registers is now relatively small as this product has been superseded by electronic cash registers – or because of a general decrease in the level of demand for all products caused by economic decline. For example in the UK in the late 1970s and 1980s there was a severe increase in the number of bankruptcies in the construction industry. This was due, in a large part, to a fall off in demand which reflected the general economic recession in the country.

Recovery strategy: If the products manufactured by the organization are in the death stages of their life cycles then they should either be abandoned, or if feasible and economically sensible, they should, in some way, be restructured so that their life cycles are extended. If the causes of the decline in demand are due to economic recession, then the appropriate recovery strategy, would be to reduce the scale of operations of the organization – which could include range of activities, range of products, range of markets, assets and personnel to match the reduced economic circumstances. Alternatively, and more positively, if the recession applied just to the organization's domestic market, then new sales could be sought in foreign markets.

The most common causes of business decline

Finally Table 2 shows the causal factors of decline which Slatter has found in his empirical investigations into this topic.

Circumstances appropriate to recovery strategies

As the tenor of this section on recovery indicated, when certain conditions prevail, an organization will frequently have a stark choice – liquidation or a recovery strategy. Therefore the circumstances determining when a recovery strategy is appropriate are somewhat different

Table 24   Frequency (in %) of causal factors of decline in forty UK recovery situations

Causal factor	Total sample	Successfully recovered	Failed to recover
(Sample size)	(40)	(30)	(10)
Lack of financial control	75	73	80
Inadequate management:			
chief executive	73	67	90
other	12	7	30
Competition:			
price competition	40	20	100
product competition	18	17	20
High cost structure:			
operating inefficiency	35	36	40
high overheads	30	20	50
scale effects	28	17	70
Changes in market demand:			
cyclical	33	40	30
secular	18	17	20
pattern of demand	7	6	10
Adverse movements in commodity market	30	30	30
Lack of marketing effort	22	17	40
Financial policy	20	20b	20
Big projects:			
capital	17	20	10
revenue	15	20	10
Acquisitions	15	13	20
Overtrading	–	–	–

– it may be more true to assert that recovery strategies are triggered by the prospect of crisis rather than any managerial aspiration towards any particular style of strategy.

Reduction strategies

An organization could be said to be following a reduction strategy when there is a curtailment of the overall level of business activity of the organization and one or more of the following situations obtains:

• A decline in the absolute value or volume of sales.
• A reduction in the range of products.
• A reduction in the range of markets served.
• A reduction in the total assets of the organization.

The conditions under which a reduction strategy is appropriate are in many ways similar to those which trigger the necessity of following a recovery strategy and are briefly considered below under two linked sets of causes – environmental causes and internal causes. As with the conditions which cause a recovery strategy to be followed, one or more of the conditions given below, may cause a reduction strategy to be appropriate.

Environmental causes

If the environment changes to an extent that the organization cannot cope with, then there may not be any alternative to reduction. This change could occur in any of the environmental segments considered in Part Three. Examples of such change could include the following:

- The *advent of severe competition* – the competition faced by British Leyland has caused it to follow reduction strategies since the mid 1970s;
- *Changes in the nature of marketing* – the effective marketing of furniture and other related household products in the UK by large out-of-town stores, such as MFI, has caused smaller, more traditional retailers to adopt reduction strategies.
- *The effects of general economic depression* – the negative economic conditions that prevailed in the UK in the late 1970s and early 1980s caused a reduction in the scale of most industries.
- *Legal/government decisions* – the US federal government in 1983 legislated that the world's largest company (A T & T which was the almost monopoly supplier of telephone services in the US) be broken into local telephone companies.
- *Social/cultural attitudes* – the hostile social attitude that a significant proportion of the propulation has developed towards nuclear energy has caused, in the US especially, a reduction in the level of activity of those organizations involved in the construction of nuclear power stations and the dumping of nuclear waste.
- *Major technological change* – the development of electronic watches caused a severe dimunition in the volume of traditional mechanical watches made in Switzerland.

Environmental triggers leading to reduction strategies are generally more serious than internal triggers in that the environmental changes are normally outside the control of the organization and all it can do is attempt to develop an effective response to the pressures.

Internal reasons

The internal conditions which determine whether or not a reduction strategy is appropriate may be related to external or environmental pressures – for example poor financial performance may be due to strong competitive pressure – or they may be due to poor or inadequate internal skills or resources. The main causes of a reduction strategy being necessary include:

- *Poor financial performance with little prospect of the achievement of acceptable performance* – a reduction strategy may be triggered when an organization is achieving unacceptable levels of profitability or is making losses, or there are available opportunities for obtaining better returns for shareholders' funds. For example the Singer company of Connecticut, USA, mainly because of severe Japanese competition, in the 1970s and 1980s experienced severe erosion of its profits in its once main line of business – sewing machines. In 1986 Singer decided to restructure its business by spinning-off its sewing machine and furniture businesses and moving into the aerospace and defence businesses. In May 1986, Singer sold (i.e. spun-off) its controls division to Eaton, a Cleveland engineering and components group.
- *Portfolio incompatibility* – when the activities of an SBU becomes incompatible with the organization's other activities this may cause the organization to divest itself of these operations. (This same argument could, of course, apply at the level of the 'product' as well as the level of the SBU.)
- *Strategic importance* – if the activities of the SBU are seen as strategically unimportant to the organization as a whole, and it is feasible to divest the organization of that SBU without harming its other activities, then reduction may be considered.
- *Inadequate resources* – when the level of resources of the organization are not sufficient to sustain its current level of activities – for example when key personnel who are difficult to replace leave – then a reduction strategy may be appropriate.

Methods of achieving reduction

Reduction may be achieved through two main methods: divestment and liquidation. Each of these is now considered.

Divestment

Divestment is a generic term which is usually taken to mean the sale of part of an organization to another party. However, within the context of divestment there are a variety of means of achieving this. The main one being a spin-off.

This could be said to occur when a part of the organization, usually an SBU, is severed from the main activities of the organization, made operationally independent, and then either:

- *Managed as an independent organization:* In this situation, in the new organization there may or may not be an ownership interest by the parent organization.

- *Sold to an independent buyer:* In this case the severed SBU is put on the market as an independent organization and is sold to the most attractive bidder.
- *Management buy out:* Here, the severed SBU is sold to the existing management who then become the owners and the managers.
- *Franchise:* This occurs when a complete business package or system is licensed to a number of independent users. (Franchising is considered in greater detail in Part Six.)

Liquidation

Liquidation occurs when the organization ceases trading, its assets are sold and the proceeds, if any, are divided amongst those who have first claim on the assets. There are two situations when this type of strategy is appropriate. First when the break-up value of the organization's assets exceeds any returns which the operations of the organization are likely to generate, then the financial interests of the shareholders of the organization are best served through liquidation.

Second, there may be no choice about liquidation. If the organization is heading towards bankruptcy and will soon be, or indeed is, trading illegally, then liquidation may be inevitable.

Circumstances appropriate to a reduction and a recovery strategy

Reduction strategies are generally not sought. They are usually triggered by some of the circumstances given on pages 210–16.

When a company is faced with imminent bankruptcy there may be no alternative to some type of involvement with another party, sale or liquidation.

However, frequently reduction strategies and recovery strategies are linked sequentially, i.e. it is often the case that the first step in a recovery strategy is reduction. This was the strategy sequence employed by Robb Wilmot in the successful recovery that he effected at the UK computer company ICL. Under Wilmot's leadership and guidance ICL changed from having a loss of around £50 million in 1981 to having a profit before tax, in 1985, in excess of £50 million and also saw its turnover increase in the same period from over £600 million per annum to over £1 billion per annum

> ... Dr Robb Wilmot, who had been brought in from Texas Instruments 19 months before at the age of 36 in a last ditch attempt to rescue ICL, had administered a particularly strong dose of the company doctor's classic formula: swingeing cuts in employment at all levels (down by a third, to 22,000); a slashing of inventory; the injection of new management blood and the imposition of tough new budgetary and management controls.
>
> But Wilmost possessed vision as well as a scalpel. With an eye on more than just the immediate future, he had accompanied the scrapping of

Table 25 Alternative strategies, their goals and consequent activities

Fundamental strategy	Goal (s)	Activities	Terminology
Conservative growth	To increase established measures of performance – sales, profits, etc, through the same or related businesses	Greater internal efficiency	
		Deeper penetration: –	
		same products in same markets	
		same products in new markets	
		new related products in same markets	Concentric diversification
		new related products in new markets	Concentric diversification
High growth			
1 Internal high growth:			
• Related products	Major increase in performance measured through sales of related products	Greater internal efficiency	
		Deeper penetration:	
		same products in same markets	
		same products in new markets	
		new related products in same markets	Concentric diversification
		new related products in new markets	Concentric diversification
• Unrelated products	Major increase in performance measures through sales of unrelated products	New products in same markets	Conglomerate diversification
		New products in new markets	Conglomerate diversification
2 External high growth:			
• Concentric diversification			
• Related products	Major increase in performance measures through sales of related products	Acquiring a company making related products	

Backward integration		Acquiring a 'supplying' company	Concentric diversification
Forward integration		Acquiring a 'buying' company	Concentric diversification
Horizontal integration	Major increase in performance measures through sales of unrelated products	Acquiring a competitor	Conglomerate diversification
• Unrelated products			
• Conglomerate diversification		Acquiring any company with perceived potential	Conglomerate diversification
Neutral	To maintain historical levels of performance	Minimal change from past activities	Depends on past strategies
Recovery	To survive	Change top management Reduce assets Reduce costs Increase revenues Amend/scrap big project Challenge the competition New partner(s) New markets New products	Turnaround
Reduction	To survive or to salvage remaining assets	Change top management Reduce assets Reduce activities – products and/or markets Spin-off and manage Spin-off and sell Management buyout Franchise Liquidate	

several product development programmes with the initiation of new ones and an increase in the development budget.

He had also formulated the framework for a new corporate strategy ...

Finally, in order to facilitate the selection of an appropriate Stage 1 fundamental strategy all the strategies discussed above are presented in summary form in Table 25.

References

1   Porter, M. E., *Competitive Strategy: Techniques for Analysing Industries and Competitors*, Collier Macmillan, 1980.
2   Mikami, T., *Management and Productivity Improvement in Japan*, JMA, Tokyo, 1982.
3   Christiansen, D. R., Andrews, K. R. and Bower, J. L., *Business Policy: Text and Cases*, R. D. Irwin, 1980.
4   Argenti, J., *Corporate Collapse: The Causes and the Symptoms*, McGraw-Hill, 1976.
5   Slatter, S., *Corporate Recovery*, Penguin 1984.
6   Minolta Camera Company Ltd., Annual Report 1985.
7   Schoeffler, S., 'The Unprofitability of Modern Technology and What To Do About It', PIMSLetter, No. 2, 1980.
8   Goldberg, W. H., *Mergers: Motives, Modes, Methods*, Gower Publishing Company, 1983.
9   Doz, Y., *Strategic Management in Multinational Companies*, Pergamon, 1985.
10   Constable, J., 'Diversification as a Factor in UK Industrial Strategy', *Long Range Planning*, Vol. 19, No. 1, February 1986, pp. 52–60.
11   Stapleton, R. C., 'Mergers, Debt Capacity, and the Valuation of Corporate Loans', in Keenan, M. and White, L. J., *Mergers and Acquisitions*, Lexington Books, D.C. Heath and Company, Lexington, Mass., 1982.
12   Newbould, G. D. and Luffman, G. A., *Successful Business Policies*, Gower Press, 1978, pp. 67–9.
13   Constable, J., *op. cit.*
14   Newbould, G. D. and Luffman, G. A., *op. cit.*
15   Dickson, M., 'Signs Point to a Nail-biting Finish', *Financial Times*, 8 April, 1986, p. 22.
16   Schoeffler, *op. cit.*
17   Doz, Y., *op. cit.*
18   O'Reilly, A. F., Extracts from the statement to shareholders of H. J. Heinz Company for the year to 19 April 1987.
19   Beverage Industry Annual Manual.
20   Sobel, R., *ITT: The Management of Opportunity*, Sidgwck and Jackson, 1982.
21   Turner, G., 'Inside Europe's Giant Companies: Olivetti Goes Bear Hunting', *Long Range Planning*, Vol. 19, No. 2, April 1986, pp. 13–22.

22   Abell, D. and Hammond, J., *Strategic Market Planning*, Prentice Hall, Englewood Cliffs, NJ, 1979.
23   Mikami, T., *op. cit.*
24   Lorenz, C. 'A Painful Process of Change', *Financial Times*, 5 March 1986, p. 22.
25   Altman, E. I., 'Financial Ratios, Discriminant Analysis and the Prediction of Corporate Bankruptcy', *Journal of Finance*, Vol. 23, No. 4, September 1968, pp. 589–609.
26   Taffler, R. J. and Tisshaw, H. J., 'Going, Going, Gone: Four Factors which Predict', *Accountancy*, Vol. 88, No. 1003, March 1977, pp. 150–2.
27   Argenti, *op. cit.*
28   Slatter, *op. cit.*
29   Lorenz, C., 'How Bosch Strengthened its Defences', *Financial Times*, 2 May, 1986, p. 20.

10 Developing new strategies 2

Stage 2: The generic strategies

Once a fundamental strategy has been selected then the company should decide upon which of Porter's generic strategies it should follow. Thus the two strategy types – the fundamental and the Porter generic should complement each other and together should enable the company through offensive or defensive actions to develop a defendable position in its industry which will yield a superior return on investment.

Porter suggests that there are three broad generic strategies for creating such a position in the long run. These are overall cost leadership, differentiation and focus. Each is now discussed.

Overall cost leadership

This strategy became increasingly popular in the 1970s largely as a result of the prominence of the experience curve. A company which has a cost position lower than its competitors should yield such a company above average returns for its industry and also give it a strong and defensible competitive position.

Although expensive to achieve, once achieved, this position provides high margins which can be reinvested in new equipment and modern facilities in order to maintain leadership. Companies which have successfully followed this generic strategy include such well known examples as Black and Decker and Casio.

Although overall cost leadership has conferred major advantages on those companies that have successfully followed it, it is risky and there are many examples of failure. Such a strategy requires very heavy capital investment with no guarantee of a static environment which will yield fruits from such investment. Among the major changes which add to the risk of adopting this strategy are:

- Technological change that nullifies past investments or experience. For example, past investments in electromechanical cash register manufacturing equipment is now of relatively little value because of the development of electronic cash registers.
- Low cost learning by followers – although the leader or pioneer in the industry will have to bear the heavy development costs of a low cost strategy (R & D, building production facilities, setting up channels of distribution and mounting effective marketing campaigns) following companies may be able to achieve similar positions at a much cheaper cost. For example, the technology needed to manufacture electronic watches and calculators is now widely available and is no longer considered to be expensive.
- There may be too strong a focus on cost reduction with a consequent lack of weight given to responding to changes in the environment and the market. This was one of the reasons for the demise of the Model T Ford.
- The difference in costs between the leaders and the followers may be narrowed because of inflation, and changes in the costs of the factors of production. For example, Japanese shipyards now find it extremely difficult to compete against South Korean shipyards.

Differentiation

The objective of differentiation is that the company's products should come to be perceived, industry-wide, and by their consumers, as being unique. Usually such products are of higher quality than rival products and this cachet of quality enables them to command a premium price, i.e. the consumer is prepared to pay more than the 'normal' or average price because the item is regarded as high quality. Differentiation can be achieved in a number of ways – quality, value for money, reliability, chicness, customer service etc. Some well known examples of products that sell at a premium price because they have successfully differentiated themselves from others in the market include: Baxters' soups, Mary Quant make-up, and Volvo cars.

If differentiation is achieved it provides a strategy for earning above average returns in an industry (a higher price is usually charged) and it helps provide a defensible competitive position.

It should be noted that achieving differentiation may sometimes preclude gaining high market share as it often requires a perception of exclusivity which is incompatible with high market share. Thus mass produced large volume fashion clothes, no matter how well they are made, cannot normally be sold through a strategy of differentiation as their numbers negate such a connotation. They may, of course, be sold as a differentiated product with a higher price, if they can be differentiated by such a feature as 'up-to-dateness' which is unavailable elsewhere. In passing it is instructive to note that Japanese automobile manufacturers such as Honda appear to be moving to a strategy where they will combine low cost plus differentiation (on the basis of quality).

Just as a low cost strategy has its attendant risks, so also does a strategy of differentiation. Thus:

- The cost differential between the low cost and the differentiated competitor may become too great and consumers may not be prepared to pay the differential. Leica cameras, although almost universally admired by photographers and certainly strongly differentiated from their Japanese competitors, are now so expensive, relative to Japanese cameras, that only the most dedicated and wealthy photographers can afford them.
- The consumers of the product may no longer feel that differentiation is so important. Many businesses buy IBM 'look-alike' personal computers because, presumably, they believe that the difference between the machines is not important.
- Imitators may erode the perceived difference between the differentiated and the low cost product. This is a major problem which affects IBM's personal computers. There are now so many IBM compatibles and 'look-alikes', which frequently claim to be better than the genuine IBM that the perceived difference has been, to some extent, eroded.

Focus

A strategy of focus involves focusing on a particular buyer group, segment of the product line, or geographic market. A focused strategy can take many forms. Its basic thrust is that a company can succeed best by serving a narrow strategic target very well. Such a company will achieve differentiation through more effectively meeting the needs of the particular target, or lower costs or both – it does this only from the perspective of its narrow market target. Once again when such a strategy is successfully followed then higher than industry average returns may be earned. An example of a focused low cost strategy is the strategy followed by many Japanese companies supplying parts to large companies, while an example of a focused differentiated strategy could be specialist health food shops and specialist record shops focusing on one particular type of music.

As with the other generic strategies there are certain risks attendant upon focusing. The main risks being:

- Cost difference between the low cost producer competitor and the focused company becomes more than consumers are willing to pay. Leica cameras may be in this category.
- The differences between the focused product and the low cost product become eroded. Japanese efforts at design and quality improvement have narrowed significantly the differences between expensive focused Western cars and Japanese mass produced products.
- Non-focused large competitors may decide to focus on small market segments and use their resources to cater for these segments in a

'focused' way. It could be argued that large multiple retailers who open specialist shops within a large shop are adopting this strategy.

Stuck in the middle

Porter claims that when a company fails to develop satisfactorily one of the three generic strategies it will become 'stuck in the middle'. Such a company is too small to achieve a low cost position – it may lack market share and capital investment i.e. it does not have the critical mass necessary to compete against the major competitors; however it also cannot achieve the degree of differentiation necessary to charge premium prices as it may not have superior quality, superior reliability, chicness, or whatever attribute is necessary for differentiation. Porter asserts that a company in such a position is almost certain to have low profitability. It will also probably suffer from a blurred corporate culture and a conflicting set of organizational arrangements and motivation system. Among companies which appear to have suffered from this fate are British Leyland which neither achieved volumes of production comparable with major rivals, such as Volkswagen, nor the product differentiation achieved by companies such as BMW.

Porter suggests that a company which is stuck in the middle must make one of the following two fundamental decisions:

1   It must take the steps necessary to achieve either cost leadership or at least parity.
2   It must focus or achieve some differentiation.

The strategy selected should be determined by the environmental prospects, the nature of the competition, the company's resources, goals and culture.

Conclusions to Part Five on developing strategies

Developing strategies is the most creative and perhaps most important part of the strategic planning process. It is at this stage of the process that the long run future operations and hence destiny of the organization are decided. The next stage of the planning process is to refine the overall strategic parameters into specific responsibility centres and functional strategies which will permit their successful implementation.

Finally, because strategy development is often concerned with the selection of one or more investment projects from a number of candidates a short appendix on capital budgeting has been included at the end of this chapter.

Appendix to Chapter 10:
Capital budgeting

Capital budgeting is concerned with those long-run and frequently irreversible major investment decisions which will often determine the overall strategic direction and health of an organization. Normally the process involves the long-run commitment of resources today in the hope of expected future benefits. The constituent activities involved in this process can be grouped under the following headings:

- Planning the capital expenditures
- Evaluating and selecting projects
- Controlling capital expenditures

The first two of these activities are considered in this Appendix while the third element is considered in Part Eight.

Planning the capital expenditures

Planning the capital expenditures is concerned with planning how capital expenditures will be effected. Typically this will involve activities such as the following:

- Ensuring that the investment projects fit harmoniously with the organization's corporate goals and strategies.
- Generating a range of alternative projects so that those which are selected yield a portfolio which is optimal.
- Integrating long-range capital investment plans into the organization's annual capital budget.
- Developing procedures for ensuring that authority for capital expenditure is unambiguously assigned to those individuals who have the competence to make the decisions and who will be held responsible after implementation has taken place.

Evaluating and selecting projects

Although there are a number of approaches which can be used to evaluate proposed capital expenditures – net present value, discounted cash flow, payback and average rate of return – the net present value is strongly advocated here because: it measures costs and benefits in terms of cash flows; it deals with the time value of money; and it considers income over the entire life of a project.

Evaluating and selecting an investment proposal using the net present value method

In a situation in which an organization is selecting one investment project from a number of alternatives, the method proceeds by obtaining, for each proposed project, a net present value (NPV), by discounting its anticipated future cash flows at the weighted average cost of capital, and then selecting that project which has the highest NPV.

Although this approach can be applied to all capital expenditure decisions, it may need to be amended depending upon whether the project being considered is 'the replacement of existing equipment' type, or the 'expansion of activities' type.

The former type of investment decision is usually concerned with replacing worn-out equipment by similar new equipment, or replacing existing equipment, which has not reached the end of its economic life, but has become relatively obsolete, with more modern equipment. For both types of decision the basis upon which it ought to be made should be the same – the projected cost saving, measured in cash flow discounted to give a net present value (NPV), that the new equipment will generate.

An organization may expand its operations either through internal organic growth, acquisition or merger. The specific activities which could lead to expansion could include: an expansion of the sales of existing products through an increase in productive capacity; an increase in product range; or an increase in markets covered. Irrespective of how the expansion takes place, the basis upon which the investment decision ought to be made should be the same – the projected additional cash flows discounted to give a net present value (NPV) that the project will provide.

A hypothetical example to illustrate how a proposed investment project may be evaluated using the net present value method

Company X is successfully pursuing a fundamental strategy of organic growth and in order to sustain this growth it believes that it must purchase additional capital equipment. It is estimated that the additional equipment will cost £100,000 and that its economic life will be six years with a salvage value of £10,000. Straight line depreciation is to be used. The project's forecast after tax cash flows are computed in Table A2.

Table A1   Projected net cash flow after tax for company X's new project

Year	Projected cash income due to new equipment	Depreciation (£)	Taxable income (£)	Taxes (at 40%) (£)	Net cash flow after tax (£)
1	30,000	15,000	15,000	6,000	24,000
2	32,000	15,000	17,000	6,800	25,200
3	40,000	15,000	25,000	10,000	30,000
4	42,000	15,000	27,000	10,800	31,200
5	32,000	15,000	17,000	6,800	25,200
6	46,667	15,000	31,667	12,667	34,000
					169,600
Cash inflow from salvage value					10,000
Total					179,000

The after tax cash flows shown in Table A1 are now discounted, at the company's weighted average cost of capital discount rate, which in this case is assumed to be 12 per cent, to yield a net present value of £14,211. (See Table A2.) This indicated that the true rate of return is greater than the cost of capital discount rate and that, therefore, if this is the criterion for project selection then the project ought to be adopted.

Table A2   Net present value of cash flows from project discounted at 12 per cent

	Net cash flow after tax (£)	Discount factor (12%)	Net present value of cash flow (£)
0	100,000	1.000	100,000
1	24,000	0.893	21,432
2	25,200	0.797	20,084
3	30,000	0.712	21,360
4	31,200	0.636	19,843
5	25,200	0.567	14,288
6	34,000	0.506	17,204
Net present value =			14,211

Illustration of how a proposed investment project may be evaluated using the discounted cash flow method

In the the net present value method the discount rate is set in advance and the cash flows are discounted at this rate to yield a net present value. However in the discounted cash flow approach the objective is to determine the rate of return which would discount the projected cash inflows and outflows to zero. The rate which would achieve this is calculated using interpolation as shown in Tables A3 and A4.

Table A3 Net present value of cash flows from project discounted at 16 per cent

	Net cash flow after tax (£)	Discount factor (16%)	Net present value of cash flow (£)
0	100,000	1.000	100,000
1	24,000	0.862	20,688
2	25,200	0.743	18,724
3	30,000	0.641	19,230
4	31,200	0.552	17,222
5	25,200	0.476	11,995
6	34,000	0.410	13,940
Net present value =			1,799

Table A4 Net present value of cash flows from project discounted at 17 per cent

	Net cash flow after tax (£)	Discount factor (17%)	Net present value of cash flow (£)
0	100,000	1.000	100,000
1	24,000	0.855	20,520
2	25,200	0.730	18,396
3	30,000	0.624	18,720
4	31,200	0.534	16,661
5	25,200	0.456	11,491
6	34,000	0.390	13,260
Net present value =			(952)

Thus, in the case of Company X:

- The NPV of the cash flows discounted at 16 per cent = £1,650
- The NPV of the cash flows discounted at 17 per cent = £(952)

Therefore, the disounted cash flow rate which would discount the cash inflows and outflows to zero

$$= 16\% + \frac{1,799}{2,751}\%$$
$$= 16.65\%$$

This method, like the NPV method also considers the time value of money and the income over the entire life of the project. In addition expressing the potential return in the form of a percentage may be more meaningful to management – they can quickly relate the return to the cost of capital, or some hurdle rate of return, and also easily rank

Table A5   Computation of the payback period for Company X

Year	Actual Cash flow (£)	Cash flow needed to pay for initial investment (£)	Years
1	30,000	30,000	1
2	32,000	32,000	1
3	40,000	38,000	0.95

competing projects. However it does suffer from the drawback that the earnings are reinvested at the rate earned by the project whereas the NPV approach reinvests earnings at the cost of capital discount rate.

The payback period method

This approach simply measures the time required by the project to pay back the initial cost of the investment. In the case of Company X the payback period for the project is 2.95 years and it is calculated as shown in Table A5.

Although this approach has the advantage that it is easy to use and understand and can be used to rank projects, it does have serious limitations in that it fails to consider the time value of money, it fails to consider income after the payback has been achieved, and it fails to consider salvage values.

The average annual return on investment method

This method simply measures the average annual net profit after tax which the project is forecast to achieve and is defined as:

$$\frac{\text{Net profit after tax}}{\text{Economic life of project}} \div \text{Cost of original investment}$$

In the case of Company X this is computed as follows:

$$
\begin{aligned}
&\text{£}\\
\text{Net profit after tax and without depreciation} &= 179,000\\
\text{Less depreciation} &= \underline{90,000}\\
\text{Net profit after tax} &= 89,000
\end{aligned}
$$

Average annual rate of return on original investment

$$= \frac{£89,000}{6} \times \frac{1}{£100,000} = 14.83\%$$

Although this approach has the advantage that it considers income over the entire life of the project and is easily calculated from accounting data, it suffers from the drawback that it fails to consider the time value of money and it also cannot be used if any additional investment is made after the project has commenced.

Risk and capital investment decisions

In the interests of clarification, the above exposition of the core methods of evaluating capital projects greatly simplified the process by abstracting from the problems associated with risk. The explicit consideration of risk is of particular importance when long-term capital investment proposals are being considered. As was indicated above, these types of projects are often irreversible, involve expenditure on fixed assets, and will usually have a relatively long life. Consequently, evaluation can only be considered to be comprehensive when the risk dimensions attendant upon such projects are considered.

Although in practice explicit reference is frequently made to the degree of risk associated with a proposed project, the term is often used with great imprecision and its magnitude may be simply a subjective and intuitive reflection of the decision maker's utility function rather than a quantitative assessment. For example if a multinational company was evaluating proposals to locate new manufacturing facilities in South Africa and Sweden it would be expected that in today's political climate the South African proposal would be classed as 'high risk' and the Swedish proposal would be classed as 'low risk'. However when the degree of risk associated with an investment proposal is less stark then a clearer definition of just what risk is and a quantitative approach to its measurement may be necessary if its likely impact is to be revealed.

In the context of capital investment appraisal, the riskiness of a project could be considered to be the degree of variability which is expected in its returns*. Thus if a project is expected to have a relatively narrow band of projected annual cash flows throughout its life – for example if it is anticipated that the average annual cash flows will lie between £900,000 and £1,250,000 each year – it could be regarded as relatively low risk. If a project which is expected to have a wider band of cash flows – for example if the average annual cash flows are expected to lie between £700,000 and £1,500,000 per year – it could be regarded as being a higher risk project.

This general approach can be given greater objectivity, and its power

---

* For a detailed and comprehensive exposition of the capital budgeting process see Van Horne, J. C., *Financial Management and Policy*, Second edition, Prentice-Hall, Englewood Cliffs, N. J., 1972, Chapters 3 to 6. Much of the substance of this appendix is based on Van Horne's approach.

Table A6 The expected cash flows and their associated probabilities for two investment projects

	Proposal Number 1		Proposal Number 2	
Cash flow	*Probability*		*Cash flow*	*Probability*
£				
3,000,000	0.10		3,000,000	0.12
850,000	0.15		700,000	0.18
1,000,000	0.50		900,000	0.40
1,100,000	0.15		1,100,000	0.18
1,200,000	0.10		1,300,000	0.12
1,250,000	1.00		1,500,000	1.00

to compare alternative projects can be enhanced, if the fundamental statistical measures of location and dispersion – the mean and the standard deviation are used to measure the expected returns and their degree of variability.

Using expected values and standard deviations to assess the riskiness of capital investment projects

How expected values and standard deviations can be used to assess the riskiness of alternative investment proposals is illustrated by means of a hypothetical example. Company Q intends to expand its sales through the development of new product lines. It plans to do this internally by acquiring new plant and equipment. In the forthcoming planning period, the company has decided to develop just one new product line which will be selected from two alternative proposals which it is currently reviewing. The expected cash flows, and their associated probabilities for the next four years are shown in Table A6.

An expected cash flow value (F) and a standard deviation (σ) for each of the above probability distributions can be calculated as follows:

The expected value of the cash flows is defined as

$$\bar{F}_t = \sum_{x=1}^{n} F_{xt} \, P_{xt}$$

Where $\bar{F}_t$ is the expected value of the cash flow in period t
F_{xt} is the cash flow associated with the xth probability in period t
n is the number of probabilities in period t

Thus for Project Number 1, the expected value of the cash flows for each year of the project is:

$$\bar{F}_t = (0.10)\,(850{,}000) + (0.15)\,(1{,}000{,}000) + (0.50)\,(1{,}100{,}000)$$
$$\qquad + (0.15)\,(1{,}200{,}000) + (0.10)\,(1{,}250{,}000)$$
$$\qquad = £1{,}090{,}000$$

While for Project Number 2, the expected value of the cash flows for each year of the project is:

$$\bar{F}_t = (0.12)\,(700{,}000) + (0.18)\,(900{,}000) + (0.40)\,(1{,}100{,}000)$$
$$\qquad + (0.18)\,(1{,}300{,}000) + (0.12)\,(1{,}500{,}000)$$
$$\qquad = £1{,}100{,}000$$

Thus if project selection were to be on the basis of selecting the one with the higher expected cash flow then Project Number 2 would be selected.

In order to measure the riskiness of each project the standard deviation of each probability distribution can be calculated using the formula:

$$\sigma = \sqrt{\sum_{x=1}^{n} (F_{xt} - \bar{F}_t)^2 \, P_{xt}}$$

Thus for Project Number 1, the standard deviation of the expected value of the cash flows for each year of the project is:

$$= \sqrt{\begin{array}{l}(0.10)\,(1090 - 850)^2 + (0.15)\,(1090 - 1000)^2 + (0.50)\,(1090 - \\ 1100)^2 + (0.15)\,(1090 - 1200)^2 + (0.10)\,(1090 - 1250)^2\end{array}}$$

$$= \sqrt{11400}$$

$$= 107 \ (£000)$$

While for Project Number 2, the standard deviation of the expected value of the cash flows for each year of the project is:

$$= \sqrt{\begin{array}{l}(0.12)\,(1100 - 700)^2 + (0.18)\,(1100 - 900)^2 + (0.40)\,(1100 - \\ 1100)^2 + (0.18)\,(1100 - 1300)^2 + (0.12)\,(1100 - 1500)^2\end{array}}$$

$$= \sqrt{52{,}800}$$

$$= 229 \ (£000)$$

Thus although Project Number 2 had the higher expected return it also has a much larger standard deviation indicating that the variability of the expected cash flow, and hence the riskiness (as defined on page 233) is much higher for this project. As business decision makers tend to be risk averse it would be expected that Project Number 1 would be selected on the grounds that although its expected value is slightly lower it is a much less risky project.

In the above analyis just one time period was considered. This is unrealistic as investment projects and their associated cash flows are multiperiod in nature. The multiperiod aspect of risk analysis can be accommodated as follows.

With the assumption that the probability distributions of each of the constituent annual cash flows in a project are independent of each other, then the expected value of the project's stream of cash flows can be defined as:

$$NPV = \sum_{t=0}^{\infty} \frac{\bar{F}_t}{(1 + i)^t}$$

Where $\bar{F}_t$ is the expected cash flow in period t
i is the risk-free rate

With the maintenance of the assumption of temporal independence in the cash flows the standard deviation of the stream of cash flows can be defined as:

$$\sigma = \sqrt{\sum_{t=0}^{\infty} \frac{\sigma_t^2}{(1 + i)^{2t}}}$$

Where σ_t is the standard deviation of the probability distribution of the cash flow associated with period t.

How this approach can be applied is illustrated through reference to Company Q's Proposal Number 1. It is now assumed that the expected cash flows and their associated probabilities for the first four years of this proposal are as shown in Table A7.

The expected cash flow for year 1 is:

$$\bar{F}_t = (0.10)(850,000) + (0.15)(1,000,000) + (0.50)(1,000,000) + (0.15)(1,200,000) + (0.10)(1,250,000)$$

$$= £1,090,000$$

Similar expected cash flows can be computed for each year, and thus the expected value of the net present value of all the net cash flows is:

Expected NPV
$$= - £3,000,000 + \frac{1,090,000}{(1.12)} + \frac{1,190,000}{(1.12)^2} + \frac{1,290,000}{(1.12)^3} + \frac{1,190,000}{(1.12)^4}$$

$$= £596,365$$

The standard deviation of the expected cash flows in year 1 is:

$$= \sqrt{\begin{array}{l}(0.10)(1090 - 850)^2 + (0.15)(1090 - 1000)^2 + (0.50)(1090 - \\ 1100)^2 + (0.15)(1090 - 1200)^2 + (0.10)(1090 - 1250)^2\end{array}}$$

Table A7 The expected cash flows and their associated probabilities for proposal number 1 for four years

Year	Net cash flow	Probability	$\bar{F}_t$	σ_t
1	850,000	0.10		
	1,000,000	0.15		
	1,100,000	0.50	1,090,000	107,000
	1,200,000	0.15		
	1,250,000	0.10		
2	950,000	0.10		
	1,100,000	0.15		
	1,200,000	0.50	1,190,000	107,000
	1,300,000	0.15		
	1,350,000	0.10		
3	1,050,000	0.10		
	1,200,000	0.15		
	1,300,000	0.50	1,290,000	107,000
	1,400,000	0.15		
	1,450,000	0.10		
4	950,000	0.10		
	1,100,000	0.15		
	1,200,000	0.50	1,190,000	107,000
	1,300,000	0.15		
	1,350,000	0.10		

$$= \sqrt{11400}$$

$$= 107 \ (\text{£}000)$$

Similar standard deviations can be computed for each year, and thus the standard deviation of the expected cash flows about the expected NPV is:

$$\sigma = \sqrt{\frac{(107,000)^2}{(1.12)^2} + \frac{(107,000)^2}{(1.12)^4} + \frac{(107,000)^2}{(1.12)^6} + \frac{(107,000)^2}{(1.12)^8}}$$

$$= \text{£}163,900$$

Thus the above illustrates how the expected NPV and its standard deviation may be computed.

If the probability distributions of the expected cash flows are approximately normal then a more refined approach to risk analysis, which uses the characteristics of the normal distribution, may be used.

Thus, in the above example, if the probability distribution of the cash

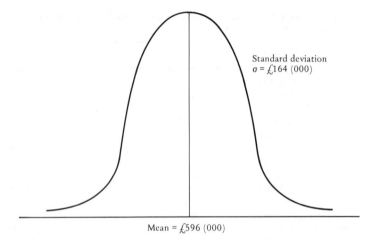

Mean = £596 (000)

Figure A1   *The probability distribution for proposal number 1's expected cash flows*

flows is approximately normal, then it could be asserted that the distribution of the expected cash flows forms a normal distribution with a mean of £596(000) and a standard deviation of £164(000) as illustrated in Figure A1.

With this information it is possible to compute the probabilities of achieving or exceeding different target NPVs. This can be achieved through converting any target expected NPV into a standard score (or Z score) and using normal distribution tables to compute the probability of achieving or exceeding this value. The procedure is illustrated below for a number of target NPVs.

1   The probability that the expected NPV will be positive (i.e. that the value of the NPV will be greater than zero) is computed as shown in Figure A2.

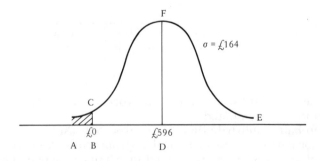

Figure A2

In Figure A2 it can be seen that the standardized normal score (i.e. the Z score) for a value of 0 is:

$$Z = \frac{0 - 596}{164}$$

$$= -3.63$$

From the normal tables the area ABC = 0.00016
Therefore the area BDEFC   = 0.9984
Therefore probability (NPV > 0) = 0.99984

Expressing this less mathematically, the probability that the NPV of the expected cash flows will be positive is 99.99 per cent.

2 The probability that the expected NPV will equal or exceed £400,000 is shown in Figure A3.

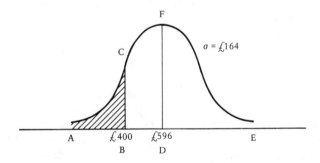

Figure A3

In Figure A3 it can be seen that the standardized normal score (i.e. the Z score) for a value of £400 is:

$$Z = \frac{400 - 596}{164}$$

$$= -1.195$$

From the normal tables the area ABC   = 0.1179
Therefore the area BDEFC   = 0.8821
Therefore probability (NPV > £400,000) = 0.8821
Expressing this less mathematically, the probability that the NPV of the expected cash flows will equal or exceed £400,000 is 88.21 per cent.

3   The probability that the expected NPV will equal or exceed £750,000 is shown in Figure A4.

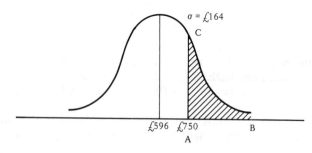

Figure A4

In Figure A4 it can be seen that the standardized normal score (i.e. the Z score) for a value of 750 is:

$$Z = \frac{750 - 596}{164}$$

$$= 0.939$$

From the normal tables the area ABC   = 0.1739
Therefore probability (NPV > £750,000) = 0.1739
Expressing this less mathematically, the probability that the NPV of the expected cash flows will equal or exceed £750,000 is 17.39 per cent.

Part Six

11 Introduction to marketing and the marketing process

Because the terms *marketing* and *selling* are frequently used interchangeably the distinction between them is made explicit below. A marketing orientation implies that the fundamental and ultimate determinant of the success of an organization, in a competitive marketplace, is the acceptance of its products or services by consumers. A competitive marketplace is necessary because in the absence of competition – for example when a company is a monopoly supplier, or in a command economy country where there is just one government supplier – the consumer cannot have a choice.

In the context of marketing, a product should not be thought of only in physical terms. A broader view is necessary so that not just its physical aspects are considered but also its associated services. Thus, for example, although the product 'domestic heating oil' could be considered as an undifferentiated commodity, many suppliers of this product have sought to differentiate their product from that offered by competitors through the provision of extra services. These services could include speed of delivery, discounts for prompt payments, willingness to make small deliveries, willingness to deliver to remote locations, friendliness of the oil delivery personnel, superior image through effective advertising etc. The supplier who provides this type of associated service changes a 'commodity' into a 'superior product'. Therefore, from a marketing perspective, it is vital to consider not just the product, but the product plus its associated services. The same type of argument in favour of taking a broader view can also be applied to services. Those organizations which most effectively adapt their goods and/or services to the needs and wishes of consumers will tend to be the most successful. Those which fail to adapt to consumers' needs and wishes will ultimately fail.

In contrast to this, a selling orientation implies that the goods or services are already in existence, i.e. their characteristics are given, and

Table 26   The contrast between a marketing and a selling orientation

Marketing orientation	Selling orientation
Products or services developed in response to consumers' needs and wishes	Consumers acquired in response to products or services

the task is how to sell them to consumers. The contrast between the two orientations is shown in Table 26.

The importance of having such an orientation has, perhaps, been expressed most clearly by Leavitt:[1]

> Every major industry was once a growth industry. But some that are now riding a wave of growth enthusiasm are very much in the shadow of decline. Others which are thought of as seasoned growth industries have actually stopped growing. In every case the reason growth is threatened, slowed, or stopped is not because the market is saturated. It is because there has been a failure of management.
>
> *Fateful purposes*
> The failure is at the top. The executives responsible for it, in the last analysis, are those who deal with broad aims and policies.
>
> The difference between marketing and selling is more than semantic. Selling focuses on the needs of the buyer. Selling is preoccupied with the seller's need to convert his product into cash; marketing with the idea of satisfying the needs of the customer by means of the product and the whole cluster of things associated with creating, delivering, and finally consuming it.

These quotations, which were first published in 1960 in the *Harvard Business Review*, were certainly true then and, as world economies and industries have internationalized are probably even more important today. The commercial benefits which can accrue from having such an orientation and applying it can be illustrated by reference to the recent economic success of Japan. In their book, *The New Competition: Meeting the Marketing Challenge from the Far East*, Kotler, Fahey and Jatusripitak,[2] argue convincingly that although there are many ingredients (culture, productivity, low cost finance etc.) which have contributed to Japanese commercial strength, it is their expertise in marketing which has been the 'coordinating capstone' of their success. They assert that:

> Japan's understanding and use of 'marketing', in our view, has been one of the key contributors to its success in the global marketplace.

and that:

When a company wants to play an offensive role in the world marketplace, the marketing edge is a key factor in determining which companies will win. In offensive marketing warfare, an indispensible ingredient is the ability to attack the opponent's mind and strategies. Japan's trade success over the past two decades is the best evidence of this. Japan realized early the crucial role of strategic market planning and made an all-out effort to study and implement the latest marketing concepts and techniques.

Recent environmental triggers which have heightened the marketing orientation

In the 1980s in most industrialized Western nations there has been a general movement towards deregulation or privatization. This movement, presumably, has been prompted by a number of basic beliefs and attitudes which include the following:

- Those nations and companies which have been most effective in marketing – notably the Japanese and the Americans – have been the most economically successful.
- Increased competition is desirable as it will confer substantial economic benefits on consumers, organizations and society.
- Consumers will be better off because they will have a greater degree of choice.
- Consumers will be better off because the goods and services will be tailored to their wishes rather than the wishes of the provider.
- Consumers will be better off because of lower prices (and/or higher quality). If free market competitive forces are allowed to reign, rather than monopoly power (either state or private monopolies) then, because of the competitive pressures which are present in such a system, prices will be driven down and/or quality will be improved.
- Those individual companies which are able to cope with the increased competitive pressure will be economically stronger because of this pressure.
- The industrial fabric of the nation will be improved because the process of competition will strengthen those organizations and industries which are internationally successful and 'shake out' those which are uncompetitive.

There are many examples, worldwide, of industries which have been transformed by this ideological shift with perhaps the clearest example being the deregulation of many of the world's national telephone networks. Thus, in 1983, the US deregulated its telephone network and broke up the almost monopoly power of A T & T into seven independent telephone companies; in 1984 the UK privatized its telephone service by setting up British Telecom and permitting the establishment of a competing rival carrier of telephone services – Mercury, and in 1986 Japan, deregulated its national telephone service NTT through offering its shares for sale on the Tokyo Stock Exchange and permitting the establishment of a total of five other carriers of telephone services.

This general movement towards a more competitive environment has developed, certainly in the UK, an attitudinal climate in business and political circles which is strongly in favour of deregulation. This move towards deregulation is much wider than simply a desire to return to the private sector state monopolies such as telephone services. It is also manifested in legislation to strip organizations, institutions and professions of those restrictive practices which are regarded as having been effective inhibitors of competition. This latter aspect of the drive towards increased competitiveness can be seen in the fundamental changes that have taken place in the UK in such diverse fields as: the opening up of hospital services such as cleaning and catering to private tenders; the granting of permission for professions such as accountants and opticians to engage in advertising; the deregulation of the London Stock Exchange; the wider roles being adopted by building societies and banks etc.

This heightened climate of competitiveness, and the actions flowing from it, have major strategic implications for institutions which previously were largely insulated from competitive forces with perhaps the most important one being that those institutions that will survive will be those whose products and services are accepted by consumers rather than those that seek to preserve their positions through regulation. Consequently, for a wide variety of organizations to survive in this new competitive world they must develop their marketing skills, i.e. they must develop their skill in adapting their products and their services to the needs and wishes of their consumers and the society in which they operate. Failure to do this will lead ultimately to organizational failure.

Marketing in society

The relationship between an organization and its markets (or consumers) is not a closed one which exists on a one-to-one basis – all such transactions take place within a broader environmental context and the influence of this environmental context is reflected in the increasing importance which is being accorded to the concept of societal marketing.

Societal marketing could be regarded as that type of marketing in which organizations attempt to market their products in a more socially sensitive or responsible fashion, i.e. societal marketing strategies. As well as having the objective of maximizing consumers' satisfaction, through responding to their needs, organizations have the additional objective of promoting (or at least not harming) the welfare of consumers of their products or services and also promoting (or at least not harming) the consumers' environment.

For example, for many years the Swedish car companies Volvo and

Saab have exceeded the UK minimum car safety requirements and have exploited this aspect of their strategy through highly effective societal marketing campaigns. Thus, both of these companies, in their promotional material, transmit messages which are much broader than the pure economic considerations which often influence buying decisions. Their promotions often emphasize the quality of their vehicles with particular reference to:

- High levels of safety.
- Security from thieves.
- Material strength.
- Quality of construction.
- Longevity and durability.

This societal approach to the marketing of their products – an approach in which the promotion is aimed not just at satisfying the needs and wishes of potential consumers but also aims to inform society in general about the 'ethical nature' of the vehicles – appears to have bestowed a distinct competitive advantage on these companies.

A more negative example of societal marketing in the UK is provided by its cigarette industry. For many years cigarette companies often marketed their products on the basis of the satisfaction that their products could bring to smokers. However, largely as a result of government pressure, a more societally responsible orientation has been developed in which cigarette marketing generally includes in its promotion information about the potentially harmful effects that cigarette smoking can have.

Although it could be argued that the societal approach to marketing is in the long-term interests of organizations (such an approach should help ensure that an organization's products have the twin attributes of matching consumers' needs and being generally accepted by society) it does appear to be the case that the strongest stimulus for the implementation of this approach has come from the pressure of environmental power groups (through direct pressure or through their influence on government) rather than through companies recognizing its commercial value.

Consumer and environmental groups have demonstrated their power to make marketing more socially responsible through their activities against those companies or products that have been engaging in, what they consider to be, societally unacceptable marketing practices. One of the most publicized examples of the power of such groups to influence is provided by the case of Nestlé's Infant Formula. In the 1970s Nestlé marketed their infant formula in Third World countries and sought, in their marketing, to influence mothers to use their infant formula to feed their children rather than using traditional breast feeding methods. Widespread criticisms of this campaign on the grounds that although consumption of the product was in the commercial interests of Nestlé it was not in the best interests of Third World consumers ultimately caused Nestlé to withdraw this product from its Third World markets.

A more recent example of having a societal approach to marketing is provided by the marketing campaigns of the UK's BNF nuclear reprocessing plant at Sellafield. Due to a series of leaks of radioactive material from the plant, exacerbated by the nuclear disaster at Chernobyl, public concern about nuclear energy became so intense in the UK in the mid-1980s that the future existence of Sellafield appeared to be threatened – public disquiet about nuclear energy was causing a questioning of the environmental acceptability of such a plant, irrespective of any claimed economic benefits. Consequently, in 1986, BNF embarked upon a societal marketing campaign designed to reduce public disquiet about the safety of nuclear fuel in general and the worthwhileness of Sellafield in particular – a campaign designed to make the activities of Sellafield more acceptable to society.

Although societal marketing has been portrayed as a practice which has either been imposed upon unwilling companies or has been employed by companies when it has appeared necessary for their continued existence, there are many examples of companies and industries which have engaged in the practice because it has been commercially advantageous for them to do so. For example, for many years most of the major oil companies operating in the UK have engaged in dual marketing campaigns comprising:

- Relatively narrow commercial marketing campaigns focusing on promoting sales of their products.
- Much broader corporate campaigns aimed at promoting the image of the oil companies as good corporate citizens through the contributions that they make in areas such as technology, balance of payments, employment and environmental improvement.

This dual approach to marketing appears to have worked successfully for these oil companies in that not only have their operations in the UK tended to have been profitable but they also appear to have enjoyed widespread social support.

In conclusion it could be argued that today, in order to be successful, in addition to being responsive to their customers' needs organizations must also, in their commercial activities – products, services, production processes, marketing practices, employment practices etc. – be seen to be societally acceptable and that if the power of external pressure groups continues to grow then the pressures to engage in societal marketing will also increase.

The marketing process

The marketing process could be described in general terms as that process through which an organization achieves its corporate goals through adapting its products and /or services to the needs and wishes of its consumers.

This general process can be subdivided into a number of linked stages: market identification; market segmentation; product positioning; and marketing mix strategy. Each of these constituent elements of the process is now discussed. In order to help clarify how each stage in the process would operate in practice a hypothetical example is considered. In the hypothetical example, it is assumed that a firm of accountants/management consultants – Accman Ltd – has developed, for its own internal purposes, integrated suites of accounting and other business software packages which run on microcomputers. The packages which it has developed are: payroll; balance sheet and profit and loss statement; data base management; simulation; forecasting; graphics; word processing; and stock control. Having found its software highly satisfactory when used for its own internal purposes Accman now believes that there may be a substantial and profitable market for this software. The marketing process – following the four stages referred to above – is considered below.

Stage 1: Market identification

In this stage the organization attempts to identify market opportunities in its environment which it may be able to exploit successfully. This is the stage at which marketing research is undertaken in order first to ascertain the extent and nature of the opportunities, and second, to assess the organization's internal ability to exploit these opportunities. At this stage there is a general lack of detail in the proposed actions – it is essentially exploratory and is really concerned with seeing if there is a possible match between the markets and the organization's capabilities including its existing (and potential) range of products and/or services.

At this stage Accman could undertake market research to provide the following information:

- The types, sizes, growth rates, locations and values of the markets for such software packages. Forecasts of future demand.
- Information on competing products. This could include information on items such as: number of competing products; number and sizes of competing companies; sales volumes; prices; growth rates; special features; methods of promotion; forecasts of future developments.
- Information on methods of distribution including customer attitudes to distribution practices.
- Profiles of customers – this could include information on items such as: uses to which currently purchased software is put; customer attitudes to existing products and service, new features sought by customers; other customer needs not satisfied by existing products;

preferred buying methods, price sensitivity; groupings of customers according to industry, region, company size, industry sector etc; forecasts of future customer demand and needs.

At this stage Accman could also undertake an internal audit of its own capability to supply the market in a satisfactory manner.

Stage 2:   Market segmentation

In this stage the organization attempts to refine the information gathered in the first stage of the process. Here, assuming that an attractive market (i.e. one in which the organization may successfully achieve its goals if it exploits it) in general terms, has been found to exist, and an appropriate match with the organization's capabilities has been identified, the general market is sub-divided or segmented into various sub-markets. It could be said that market segmentation is in the eye of the beholder in that there are no precise rules for how markets ought to be segmented other than that the segmentation should reflect the following:

- Consumers' needs.
- Locations of consumers.
- The uses to which the product or service will be put.
- The buying behaviour of the consumers.

However there are a number of bases of segmentation for consumer goods that are frequently used which include the following:

1   *Demography*:   Age, sex, family size, income, occupation, religion, race etc.
2   *Geography*:   Country, region, city, town, climate, etc.
3   *Social*:   Class, education, occupation, etc.
4   *Product function*:   Use sought, benefits sought, rate of usage etc.

It should be noted that market segmentation is often more straightforward for consumer goods than for industrial goods. This is mainly because of the greater range of uses to which many industrial goods can be put and also because there can be much greater customer heterogeneity. For example, a manufacturer of small electric motors may sell his products to customers such as automobile manufacturers, aeroplane manufacturers, small general engineering companies etc. Each of these customers has a very different set of uses and requirements.

The criteria for deciding which segments are most attractive will vary from industry to industry but in general the following tend to be considered as important influences:

1   Current and future growth rate of the segment in terms of volume and value.

2 The degree and nature of the existing competition: threat of new entrants; threat of substitutes; power of buyers; level of rivalry among existing competitors; levels of profitability.

In the case of Accman the market for its products has been segmented on the following bases:

1 *Geographical*: Location of customers – it is assumed that all customers will be drawn from the national market only. Customers are segmented into two types: proximate, i.e. within four hours driving time of the company; and remote i.e. more than four hours driving time away from the company.
2 *Type of business*: It is assumed that the following will be the only types of business that will purchase the software: small family-run businesses (less than fifty employees); large family-run businesses (fifty employees or more); small professionally managed companies (less than fifty employees); large professionally managed companies (fifty employees or more).
3 *Other customers*: Professional offices; business consulting firms; educational establishments.

When the market has been segmented, Accman can graphically link its products to the various segments that it had identified through plotting a product-market map as shown in Figure 37.

On the basis of the internal audit and the external information gathered as reflected in the product-market map, Accman must decide which of the various market segments it should enter. On this occasion it believes that its target markets should have the following characteristics:

1 Proximate markets only will be served.
2 The products which appear to offer the best prospects for success are: payroll; balance sheet and profit and loss; stock control; data base and graphics.
3 The customer groups which Accman appears to be able to meet the needs of most effectively are: small family-run businesses, small professionally managed companies and professional offices.

For Accman this set of customers most fully matches the company's capabilities and the features of its products.

Stage 3: Product positioning

Once an organization has decided upon the target markets which it intends to enter the next stage in the process is to determine how it ought to position its products in the target markets in relation to competitors' offerings. Positioning of products involves assessing how competitors' products meet customers' needs and then developing

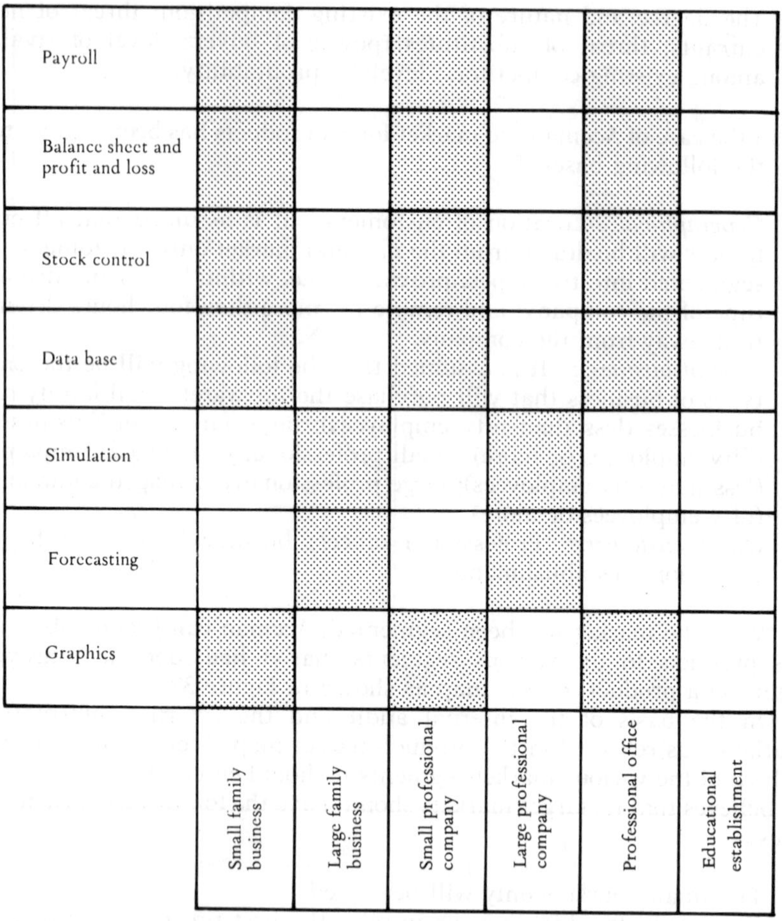

	Small family business	Large family business	Small professional company	Large professional company	Professional office	Educational establishment
Payroll	▓		▓		▓	
Balance sheet and profit and loss	▓		▓		▓	
Stock control	▓		▓		▓	
Data base	▓		▓		▓	
Simulation		▓		▓		
Forecasting		▓		▓		
Graphics	▓		▓		▓	

Figure 37   *A product market map for Accman's software packages*

marketing strategies (at the marketing mix stage) to meet customers' needs more effectively. This is a vital stage in the process, because it is here that the planners must 'see to the heart' of the reasons for competitors' success in the market and, perhaps more importantly, decide upon how they will position their products or services in order to match or exceed competitors' offerings. It is suggested that this can be accomplished in three steps.

Step 1

Decide upon the criteria that distinguish the product offerings that are currently available in the target market. These criteria will be provided by the market research undertaken in Stage 1 of the marketing process.

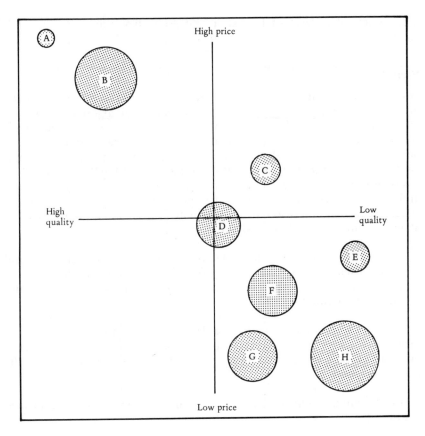

Figure 38 *A product positioning map for a consumer good*

In the case of consumer goods typical criteria could include: price, quality, durability, style etc.

Step 2

Draw up a series of product positioning maps for competitors. A product positioning map shows graphically how the various competing products in a particular market segment are positioned using two key customer criteria as axes. The products are represented by circles whose areas are proportional to their annual sales. Thus, for example, for a consumer good, two fundamental criteria could be price and quality. A product positioning map for a consumer good using these criteria is shown in Figure 38. As can be seen there are eight different types of the good available A to H. In practice, of course, a number of similar maps would be drawn up for the various criteria which emerged from the market identification stage. For a consumer good, these could include sets of criteria such as style and durability, image and reliability, etc.

Step 3

Decide upon possible positions for the organization's products on the product positioning maps. In the consumer good example shown in Figure 38 the map indicates that there are already five products with substantial sales in the 'low price/low quality' quadrant while there are only two competing products in the 'high price/high quality' quadrant. On the basis of this map alone, the company would appear to be most likely of success if it were to avoid the 'low price/low quality' quadrant and attempt to position its product in either the 'high price/high quality' or the 'high quality/low price' segment. Kotler[3] suggests that at this stage a company has two basic choices:

1   It can take a position alongside one of the existing competitors and fight to win the customers away from the existing supplier.
2   It can develop and then offer to the market a product which is not currently available.

In the example shown in Figure 38 this would imply developing a product which is 'high quality and low price'. Positioning maps, based on other criteria (taken two at a time) should also be drawn up for the consumer good.

How Accman might have carried out the three stages is summarized below.

Step 1:   Accman

Distinguishing criteria – as a result of the market research carried out in the market identification stage, Accman believes that consumers distinguish between products similar to the Accman packages on the following bases: reliability; quality; ease of use; tailored to particular needs; provision of 'free' training courses; post-purchase support; price; compatibility with other software; obsolescence; modularity (i.e. how well the units link together).

Step 2:   Accman

Product positioning maps – Four product position maps that Accman has drawn up are shown in Figures 39–42. The axes of the positioning maps are:

1   Reliability and price.
2   Post-purchase support and price.

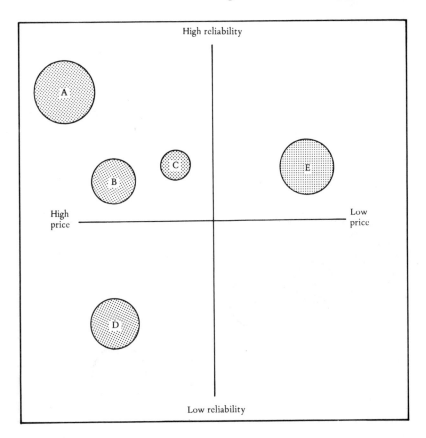

Figure 39 *A product positioning map for Accman using the criteria 'reliability' and 'price'*

3 Compatibility with other software and degree of modularity (i.e. how will the various packages be integrated).
4 Degree of tailoring to purchaser's needs and ease of use.

Step 3: Accman

Decide upon possible positions for Accman's products on the product positioning maps. On the basis of the maps, it would appear that Accman should position its products so that potential consumers perceive them to have the following attributes:

1 High reliability.
2 High quality.
3 High post-purchase support.
4 High level of compatibility with other software.

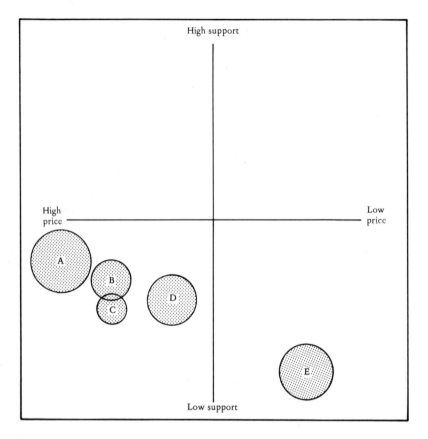

Figure 40   *A product positioning map for Accman using the criteria 'post-purchase support' and 'price'*

5   Tailored to the individual needs of purchasers.
6   Ease of use.

Characteristics 3, 4, 5 and 6 would appear to be particularly important as it is on these measures that consumers find fault with existing products.

This type of positioning may be achieved through appropriate use of the marketing mix strategies, which are now considered.

Stage 4: Marketing mix strategy

In order to position a product or service in a desired location in its target market, any organization has at its disposal a great number of instruments. These include the quality of the product, its features, its

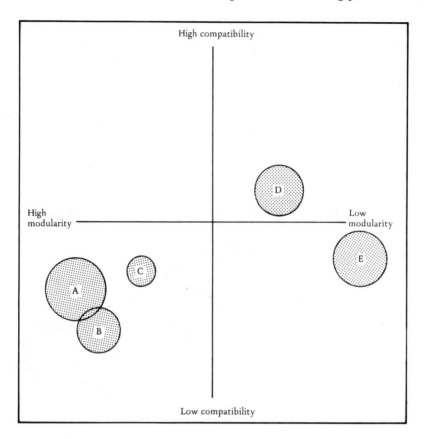

Figure 41 *A product positioning map for Accman using the criteria 'compatibility' and 'modularity'*

style, its image, its price, the associated advertising – type and volume, methods of promotion, methods of selling, methods of distribution, etc. These various instruments which an organization may use to reach its target market have been grouped together by McCarthy[4] under the four headings products, place, promotion and price and these four broader sets of strategy instruments have become known as the marketing mix. The most commonly used elements of the marketing mix are shown in Table 27.

At this stage in the marketing process, the task is to blend together various elements from the marketing mix into a combination that enables the organization to achieve its objectives in its target market. Thus the organization will position its products in its desired markets by an appropriate mix of the product, place, promotion and price variables given in Table 27. The various constituent activities which may be undertaken to achieve this are considered in Chapter 12.

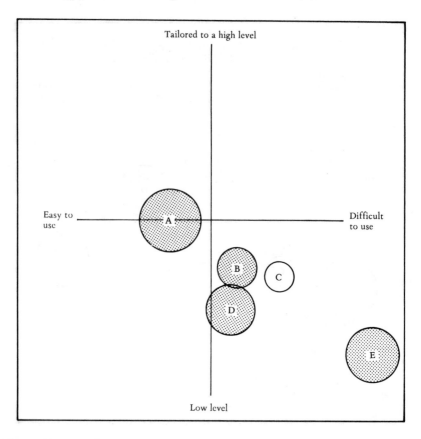

Figure 42   *A product positioning map for Accman using the criteria 'degree of tailoring' and 'ease of use'*

Table 27   **The marketing mix**

Product	Place	Promotion	Price
Quality	Distribution	Advertising	Level
Features and	channels	Personal selling	Discounts and
options	Distribution	Sales promotion	allowances
Style	coverage	Publicity	Payment terms
Brand name	Outlet locations		
Packaging	Sales territories		
Product line	Inventory levels		
Warranty	and locations		
Service level	Transportation		
Other services	carriers		

References

1 Leavitt, T., 'Marketing Myopia' in Kotler, P. and Cox, K., *Marketing Management and Strategy*: A Reader, Prentice-Hall, Englewood Cliffs, N J, 1980, pp. 3–20.
2 Kotler, P., Fahey, L. and Jatusripitak, J., *The New Competition: Meeting the Marketing Challenge from the Far East Prentice-Hall International*, 1985.
3 Kotler, P., *Principles of Marketing*, Prentice-Hall, Englewood Cliffs, N J, 1980.
4 McCarthy, E. J., Basic Marketing: A Managerial Approach, 4th ed., Richard D. Irwin Inc., 1971, p. 44.

12 The marketing mix and strategy options

Product strategy

The first element of the marketing mix to be considered is the product strategy. The 'product' activities are concerned with developing products or services which effectively satisfy customers' needs. A product is taken to mean not just the physical product but also its associated services. The term 'effectively' rather than profitably has been used because it is more general. Thus, for example, a non-profit seeking leisure centre might seek to satisfy its users' needs with no reference to the profitability involved in doing so. Among the more important dimensions which distinguish products are the following:

1 *Quality*: What is the relative quality of the product, and its associated services, in relation to other competing products which are available? *PIMS* has found that relative product quality is a fundamental influence on profitability.
2 *Features*: What particular features does the product have that distinguish it from competing products?
3 *Options*: Are there options available which are not available on competing products?
4 *Style*: How well is the product styled in relation to immediate and other non-immediate competing products?
5 *Brand name*: Does the product have a brand name with connotations?
6 *Packaging*: What is the quality of the packaging of the product in relation to that offered by competitors?
7 *Product line*: Is the product just a single offering or is it part of a wider and more comprehensive product line?
8 *Warranty*: What is the warranty period and the quality of the warranty in comparison with the warranties offered on competing products?

9 *Service level*: Is the associated level of service which accompanies the product inferior or superior to that of comparable products?

Accman's product strategies

The product strategies to be followed by Accman for all the products to be offered – payroll, balance sheet and profit and loss, stock control, data base and graphics – should have the following characteristics:

1 *Quality*: The relative product quality of each package should be regarded by consumers as higher than that provided by competing products. This quality to be reflected not just in the reliability and functions which each package can perform, but also in the attributes of ease of use, tailored to particular needs, free training and post-purchase support.
2 *Features*: The modularity of the packages and their compatibility with other software.
3 *Brand name*: The packages to be sold under the Accman brand name to emphasize a 'professional' commitment.
4 *Packaging*: High quality packaging and documentation to reflect high quality contents.
5 *Product line*: An emphasis on the extensiveness of the range of products available and how they can be linked together to provide a 'total software system' for its users.
6 *Warranty*: Longer than industry average warranty periods for the products.
7 *Service level*: Superior service to be emphasized through professional links with many purchasers, and proximity of customers to Accman's offices.

Place strategy

The 'place' activities are concerned with deciding upon where the product will be sold, the number and types of channels of distribution that will be used to move the product to the customer, and associated decisions such as the levels of inventory that will be maintained.

The distribution strategy and practices adopted by an organization should flow from its overall corporate and marketing strategies. It is important that the relationship has this direction because decisions about distribution have such far-reaching strategic implications. Among the more important implications are the following:

1 *Responsiveness to customers' needs and wishes*: The nature, quality and level of customer service will be influenced strongly by the chosen method of distribution.
2 *Profitability*: The method of distribution chosen – in most cases there is usually a choice of method – usually involves a trade-off between the costs and benefits of the alternatives.

3   *Costs*:   Distribution costs are significant in most industries. For example Christopher[1] has indicated that, on average, distribution costs are about 15 per cent of sales turnover for a typical company.
4   *Product*:   The characteristics of the product will be influenced by the method of distribution chosen. For example, a decision to distribute a product internationally may involve changing some physical aspects of it so that it conforms to international standard specifications.
5   *Pricing*:   The pricing policy adopted will be influenced not just by manufacturing and actual distribution costs but also by the nature of the distribution method adopted. Thus a decision by an organization to have broad, intensive, national distribution will tend to demand a lower price level than a decision to have limited distribution with a small number of exclusive high quality outlets.
6   *Promotion*:   The promotional requirements for a product or service are also a function of the distribution methods employed. Thus the promotional requirements for intensive national distribution are very different from those required for smaller regional sales.
7   *Relationships with other firms*:   The degree to which an organization sub-contracts out its distribution will have major long-term implications for its relationships with other firms and its flexibility for strategic change. Thus an organization which contracts out its distribution may have to enter into long-term legal contracts which cannot be changed easily.
8   *Control*:   The greater use an organization makes of intermediaries to carry out its distribution the less control it will have over the marketing of its products.

   Because of these and other strategically important aspects of distribution it is important that distribution policies reflect corporate policies rather than constrain or set them.

Place strategy for Accman

Because Accman intends to serve mainly small businesses or professional offices which are proximate to its own head office, the company has decided that it will distribute its software products using its existing consultants. Accordingly therefore the features of Accman's distribution strategy are:

1   *Responsiveness to customer needs and wishes*:   Close contact with professional staff will ensure a high degree of responsiveness.
2   *Costs*:   Using existing staff will help minimize distribution costs.
3   *Product*:   The small bulk of the product means that the physical aspects of distribution are not a major concern.
4   *Promotion*:   The promotion of the product will be through personal contact – solving clients' problems – and therefore this means of distribution will help enhance the commitment to customer service.

5 *Control*: This means of distribution will ensure a high degree of control – essential for being sensitive to customers' needs.

Distribution strategy in general

Distribution strategy is concerned with deciding upon the optimal method of transferring a product, or service, from the producer to the final consumer or customer. The adjective 'optimal' rather than phrases such as 'most profitable' or 'most efficient' or 'cheapest', is used as it is more general. Thus, optimal could have such different meanings as – 'the method that most closely meets customers' needs', or, 'the method that most closely meets customers' needs and maximizes the organization's ROI, or, 'the method that will gain the organization the largest market share', or 'the method that is most appropriate for the organization's resources'. The method of distribution which is adopted is usually known as the *distribution channel*. Distribution channels can be divided into two main classes – traditional distribution channels and vertical marketing systems (VMS).

Traditional distribution channels can be defined along two dimensions: channel length and channel breadth. The length (often referred to as the level) of a distribution channel is determined by the number of intermediaries through which the good or service must pass before it is acquired by the final customer or buyer. An intermediary is a person or organization who takes title to the producer's good or service and performs some activity on it which helps transfer it to the final customer. As shown in Figure 43 the normal length of a channel is from zero to three. There are of course distribution channels of higher levels, particularly international channels of distribution. Generally, the longer the channel is the less control the producer has over the marketing of his product or service.

The breadth of a distribution channel is determined by the intensiveness of the market coverage. Generally the more intensive and extensive the market coverage the wider the channel is said to be.

When selecting a distribution channel, the producer of a product or service should be guided by the answer to the fundamental question: Can the proposed channel of distribution meet overall corporate objectives through providing the required degree of customer service at a cost acceptable to the producer? More specifically, in selecting a channel there are various costs and benefits inherent in any selection. The main ones are summarized below.

Costs of using intermediaries

1 *Financial costs*: The payments or charges which intermediaries make for their services must, by definition, reduce the per unit value added accruing to the producer. Therefore, the greater the use of intermediaries the greater will be the reduction in the value added per unit of output. Against this, however, it ought to be the case that

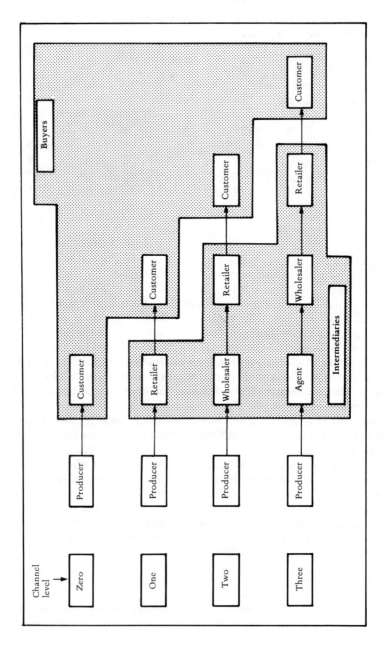

Figure 43   *Alternative lengths of distribution channels*

when intermediaries are effective, they should raise the volume of sales to the extent that the economic benefits due to the volume increases outweigh the costs due to the reduction in value added per unit of output.

2 *Control*:   The longer the chain of intermediaries the less control a producer will have over its goods or services. This lack of control can be manifested in such areas as the power to set retail prices and minimum levels of inventory to be carried, and to influence promotional levels and practices.

3 *Customer service levels*:   The use of intermediaries may reduce the level of customer service. Most intermediaries will tend to carry competing and complementary products, each of which will vie for the highest level of service possible from the intermediary. For example, a television manufacturer which distributes its products through a multiple chain of retailers has no reason to expect that its products will receive stronger promotion than rival producers' products.

4 *Strategic and operational freedom*:   Producers often enter into legally binding contracts with intermediaries. Although these agreements which may appear, when first agreed, to be in the commercial interests of both parties, it is not unusual to find that, as conditions change the agreement becomes progressively more and more commercially unsuitable for the producer (and/or the intermediary).

Benefits of using intermediaries

1 *Market knowledge*:   Normally, intermediaries will have a more intimate and extensive knowledge of the market – in terms of customer needs, market segments, market size, market trends, growth rates, market idiosyncrasies – than the producer. The payment to the intermediary is partly in payment for this knowledge which should help the producer position his products most effectively in its target markets.

2 *Market coverage*:   Intermediaries may provide a degree of market coverage which would not be achievable without them. This is particularly true in retailing. The importance of such comprehensive coverage can be demonstrated by the role that large US retailing chains such as Sears have played in helping to develop the Japanese domestic electronics industry to its current state of global pre-eminence.

> Japanese firms also focus on specific distribution channels and dealers. They will seek out those outlets that will give them large market cover. Thus many television, radio and audio equipment firms initially sold through large retail chains. Over 80 per cent of Toshiba's early television sales went through Sears.[2]

3 *Financial resources*:   Many producers simply do not have the financial resources necessary to effectively distribute their products. To

give an illustration, many smaller European companies which begin exploring the US market with a view to exporting their products are intitially horrified at what they perceive to be the very large mark-ups which intermediaries would charge for distributing their products. However, such exporters do not really have a choice if they wish to penetrate that market – they do not have the necessary financial resources to distribute their products. The relatively large level of financial resources necessary to achieve effective distribution not confined to small organizations or those engaged in international distribution. There are many large and successful organizations which could not achieve their required levels of distribution without the use of intermediaries. For example, it would be impossible for national newspapers to achieve their current levels of national sales without the use of intermediaries such as transport companies and newsagents.

4 *Risk reduction*:   The use of intermediaries may have a risk reduction effect. This may be due to two factors – first the producer does not have to finance the costs of distribution, and second, the expertise required for effective distribution may be outside the competence of the producer.

5 *Efficiency and speed*:   Intermediaries, that have substantial experience in distribution and have their distribution procedures already in place, should be able to generate effective distribution of a product more efficiently and speedily than a producer who decides to set up, and then use, his own channels of distribution. Again, Japanese companies have been adroit in exploiting this aspect of distribution in their penetration of the US market.

In the watch industry, Seiko signed up fifteen exclusive regional distributors to set up a strong nationwide marketing program instead of building its own national sales forces as its competitors did. Most of these distributors had long experience in business and had a certain position in the jewelry community that allowed Seiko to gain access to important outlets in selling watches. Through this distribution strategy, Seiko was able to gain a strong foothold in the quartz watch segment and employed it as a base for market expansion.[3]

6 *Complementary products*:   Frequently, a single product will benefit from the marketing synergy which will exist because the product is marketed as part of a range. For example, when an insurance broker, acting as an intermediary for a number of insurance companies, is selling the product 'car insurance' this product may help the sales of other insurance products – such as 'boat insurance', 'caravan insurance', 'house insurance', and 'personal insurance' – which comprise the portfolio of products which the broker is selling.

Selecting a method of distribution
The methods of distribution adopted by any organization should be the ones that most effectively meet the requirements of its strategies, are

most appropriate to the nature of its products or services and best meet customers' needs. In general, the more differentiated or exclusive the product the smaller will be the number of intermediaries used in distribution and the greater will be the degree of control exercised by the producer (for example the manufacturers of aero engines such as Rolls-· Royce, Pratt and Whitney and GE usually deal directly with their customers without using intermediaries at all) while the more extensive the degree of market coverage sought and the less differentiated the product the greater will be the number of intermediaries and the less will be the control exercised by the producer (for example a low value, largely undifferentiated product such as low cost calculators will typically be distributed through a large number of intermediaries).

Finally, although there are established channels of distribution used in most industries, individual companies can, on occasions, gain competitive advantage by adopting an unconventional method of distribution. For example although, in the UK, the traditional method employed by record companies for distribution is specialist record retailing shops or multiples, there is now a significant amount of distribution through mail order and record clubs.

Vertical marketing systems

In spite of the advantages, cited above, which are often claimed for the traditional channels of distribution they have been the subject of considerable criticism and two of the major sources of such criticism are considered below.

The producers and the intermediaries are a loosely connected federation of independent businesses. Consequently the constituent members of this federation pursue a multitude of objectives and strategies which are frequently in conflict. For example, a retailer may have a fundamental objective of responding as quickly as possible to customer needs and therefore will wish to have deliveries of stock as frequently and as speedily as possible in order to respond to these needs. In contrast the wholesaler supplying such a retailer will wish to minimize the number of separate deliveries and maximize the batch size of each delivery. Indeed, the maintenance of harmony throughout the chain is a major managerial task.

It is also alleged (see Kotler[4]) that the traditional methods of distribution encourage unnecessary duplication, fail to maximize the potential economies of scale, and are generally inefficient.

An alternative system of distribution which has been enjoying increasing popularity is the vertical marketing system (VMS). VMS is, at its simplest, a system which attempts to integrate the separate elements of 'producer' and 'intermediary (ies)' into a single vertical system which has the objective of meeting, as effectively as possible, the needs of both the producer and the customer. It is argued that the congruence of goals by the various parties within the vertical marketing system, plus the economies that can be generated, make such an approach to distribution more economically effective than the traditional channels. Three main types of VMS have developed — the corporate vertical marketing system, the contractual vertical marketing system, and the administrative vertical marketing system.

The *corporate vertical marketing system* is really a form of vertical integration — either forward by a producer or backward by a retailer so that the chain of distribution is under a single ownership. The degree of ownership may vary from total ownership of the total chain, from producer to retailer, to partial ownership of the chain where the 'owner' only has an equity stake in each of the constituent elements.

A well-known example of this type of VMS in the UK is its brewing industry. Most of the major UK brewers have substantial investments in public houses (tied to the brewer) and off licences as Table 28 illustrates.

Table 28　Major brewers' market shares, tied public houses and off licences in 1983[5]

	Market share (%)	Number of tied pubs	Approximate number of off licences owned
Bass	21	7398	1000
Allied Breweries	13.5	7500	900
Whitbread	12	6560	700
Watney, Mann, Truman (part of Grand Metropolitan	11	6500	70
Scottish & Newcastle	11.5	1500	200
Courage	9	5300	390
Guinness	7	–	–

Note:　Brewers' individual market-share figures include sales of all beer sold by them, e.g. Guinness

There is thus a vertical chain from the producer to the customer.

A *contractual vertical marketing system* is one in which independent members of the distribution chain join together to devise joint strategies which will develop their potential synergy and then enter into legal contracts to implement these strategies. There are two main types of contractual vertical marketing systems – distribution cooperatives and franchises.

Distribution cooperatives
Distribution cooperatives or voluntary groups arise where groups of individual businesses at a particular level in the distribution chain enter into an agreement to form a new business entity which will further their interests. In the UK the growth of these groups has taken place in a many areas of retailing for example, in the grocery trade the

largest groups include: Spar, Mace, VG, BOB Group, Londis, APT, Wavy Line and Maid Marian, while in the non-grocery area there are groups such as AIMS (the Association of Independent Motor Stores, car accessories) Unichem, Numark and Vantage (chemists), Intersport (sports goods) and many others.

One of the stimuli causing the growth of such groups has been the fear by independent retailers and wholesalers of the dominance of multiples – some form of cooperation is essential to withstand the competitive pressure of the multiples. The practices and procedures of the Spar group of grocery wholesalers is typical. The Spar group licenses a particular wholesaler for the wholesale distribution rights for a particular region. Then within this region, grocery retailers, on joining the Spar organization, although not required to enter into any formal agreement, are expected to make an ordinary trading arrangement with the Spar wholesaler with the request that as much business as possible is channelled through the Spar wholesaler. In return for this the retailer receives the benefits of reduced prices (because of the buying power of the Spar organization) plus a range of services from marketing and promotion to store engineering.

Empirical evidence (see McFadyen[6]) seems to indicate that when the members of such groups actively participate, rather than just use them as sources of price discounted goods, then all parties – the retailers, the wholesalers, the manufacturers and the public – benefit. The principal benefits include:

- Increased sales.
- Reduced costs due to economies of scale, greater efficiency and productivity.
- More marketing orientated distribution.
- Greater degree of harmonious communication within the distribution channel.
- Greater producer and consumer choice of retail outlets.

In summary, there is evidence (see McFadyen[7]) that group trading appears to lead to efficiencies for both wholesalers and retailers with most wholesalers, after a few years of group trading, showing an improved net profit and a higher return on capital. Similarly the disadvantages of any small loss of independence which a retailer might experience appear to be more than outweighed by the positive advantages of being a partner in a large and powerful organization.

Franchise
Franchising has been defined as:

A franchise operation is a contractual relationship between the franchisor and franchisee in which the franchisor offers, or is obligated to maintain, a continuing interest in the business of the franchisee in such areas as know-how and training; wherein the franchisee operates under a common trade name, format and or procedure owned or controlled by the franchisor, and in which the franchisee has, or will make, a substantial capital investment in his business from his own resources.[8]

One of the currently fastest growing business sectors in the US and Europe is that of the franchising of services. Euromonitor[9] estimated in 1985 that franchising would gross more than £1 billion in 1986 and that it would develop to £2 billion in 1990 with the number of franchisors growing from 400 in 1987 to 600 by 1990 with around 20,000 franchisees. Franchising now encompasses many areas within its scope. Some of the better known franchisors in the UK include the following:

- *Automotive*: Avis, Budget Rent-A-Car, Identicar, British School of Motoring.
- *Catering, hotels and food*: Burger King, Holiday Inns, Pizza Express, Wimpy.
- *Household*: Apollo Window Blinds, Dyno-Rod.
- *Business*: Kall-Kwik Printing, Prontaprint, TNT Despatch Post.

Franchising is an example of a contractual vertical marketing system as it is really a licence agreement between the owner of the business (the franchisor) and an individual or organization (the franchisee) wishing to conduct a similar business. Although, strictly speaking, franchising is simply a licensing agreement, in practice it has come to mean much more. Thus the term is now commonly taken to mean the following:

1   The granting of a licence by the owner of a business to an individual or an organization wishing to conduct a similar business.
2   The payment for this licence by the franchisee through an initial licence fee plus royalty fees.
3   The franchisee strictly conforming to the guidelines for the operation of the franchise as laid down by the franchisor.
4   The franchisor providing a total business package which normally includes the following:

- Advice on site location.
- Training for the franchisee in all aspects of the management of the business including operations, finance, marketing, and personnel.
- Continuing support, advice and help from the franchisor.
- Exclusive sales territories.
- Rights to enjoy the benefits accruing from national promotion and advertising and bulk purchasing of materials.

It could therefore he argued that franchising attempts to maximize the potential benefits available to the franchisor and the franchisee while reducing the levels of risk for both parties. Thus from the perspective of the franchisor the principal benefits that should accrue through using this form of distribution include:

1 *Risk reduction*: A major part of the financial and resource provision comes from the franchisee.
2 *Growth*: Faster growth rates may be achieved through the use of franchising than through organic growth strategies.
3 *Response to customer needs*: Most of the larger franchises are in the service sector where sensitive response to customers' needs is of fundamental importance. Franchising the business removes this task from the franchisor and assigns it, almost exclusively to the franchisee. As the franchisee's earnings are directly related to satisfying customers' needs, this is a powerful motivating influence.
4 *Control*: The difficulty of strict operational and financial control of national chains is greatly reduced as this responsibility rests, largely with the franchisee.

From the perpective of the franchisee the principal benefits should include:

1 *Risk reduction*: The 'formula' for the franchise operation has been tested and found successful in other geographical areas. With careful site selection the risks should be considerably less than a totally independent venture.
2 *Image*: The use of a prestigious name which is well established in the market will usually be a major promotional asset.
3 *Training*: The franchisor's training provision will develop in the key personnel those skills and attitudes which have been found to be necessary for the effective management of such businesses.
4 *Economies of scale*: Because of the size of the group of franchisees, individual franchisees will be able to benefit from bulk purchasing and national advertising and promotion campaigns.
5 *Exclusive rights to operate in an agreed territory*.

Although it is service-related franchising that is best known, manufacturing-related franchising is a major method used by manufacturers to distribute their goods. These type of franchises are simply licences from manufacturers to allow third parties to manufacture or distribute their goods or services. Among the best known of these types of franchise are automobile retail franchise systems (most major automobile manufacturers franchise dealers to sell their cars) and soft drinks wholesaling franchising (for example Coca Cola franchises bottlers to process its syrup and bottle it and supply local markets with bottled Coca Cola).

Athough the growth rate of franchising has been dramatic and franchising is now an established channel of distribution, it still retains an aura of uncertainty not found in the more traditional channels. This may be due to the publicity which has been attendant on unsuccessful franchise operations and also, perhaps, because of the inherent potential for adversity in the franchisor–franchisee relationship. Thus from the perspective of the franchisee there are a number of areas of potential discord which include:

1 *The size of fees payable*:   Franchisees may feel that the royalty or fee payment is disproportionate to the value of the licence which has been granted. This can occur when the franchise is particularly profitable – in which case the franchisee may feel that the rewards for the efforts which were necessary for successful development should accrue to the franchisee – or if the franchise is less profitable than expected – in which case the franchisee may feel that the royalty is exhorbitant.

2 *Degree of control*:   Franchisees may feel that the degree of control exercised by the franchisor is excessive and frustrates their own aspirations to further develop the franchise. This could arise, for example, should the franchisee wish to carry non-approved lines of goods, or to engage in non-approved promotion.

3 *Exit difficulties*:   Franchisees who wish to sell the franchise may find it more difficult to sell this type of business than a more traditional one.

4 *Lack of franchisor support*:   If the relationship between the franchisee and the franchisor is weak – whether because of conflict or lack of interest on the part of the franchisor – the franchisee may see little reasons for the continuance of royalty payments.

From the perspective of the franchisor there are a number of areas of potential discord which include:

1 *Lower profits*:   The franchisor may be taking a lower level of profits than would be achieved should the franchisor operate the franchise. This realization is often seen when franchisors make efforts to buy back their franchises.

2 *Lack of control*:   Because the franchise is legally independent the franchisor may not be able to implement developments which are not in the original contract. Additionally it may be difficult for a franchisor to remove an unsatisfactory franchisee. A further source of potential friction may arise when franchisees form associations to protect their interests and strengthen their bargaining power in relation to franchisors.

3 *Supervision*:   The actual supervision by the franchisor of how its franchises are being operated may prove to be difficult. Related to this aspect of supervision is the possibility that the full level of sales (which in many cases determines royalty paymenets) may not be declared by the franchisee.

In conclusion, it appears that franchising in the UK has shed some of the unfortunate image from which it suffered in the 1960s and 1970s. This increase in its acceptance as a mode of distribution is reflected in the high growth rates which the industry has recently enjoyed and is prompted, in part at least, by the growing number of successful franchises and the general level of satisfaction expressed by franchisees. (See Mendelsohn[10] for empirical evidence.)

The *administrative vertical marketing system* is a system in which the power of the final distributor (for example the retailer) is so great relative to its suppliers that it can command a relationship in which the suppliers and their intermediaries are so dominated by the final distributor that they act as though they were a corporate vertical marketing system. Thus the dominant final distributor has a vertical system tailored to its requirements. Major retail multiple stores, such as Marks and Spencer appear to operate a system such as this as first their power is so vast in relation to their suppliers and second they are intimately involved, through standard specifications and the provision of technical advice, in the actual production processes.

Promotion strategy

The third element in the marketing mix is promotion. This could be considered as the process through which an organization communicates with, and influences, its targeted market segments with the goal of helping to position its products or services in their desired locations and generating the desired responses from the segments. Although, from the perspective of the conventional firm making products or offering services, the promotional goal often will be, ultimately, to generate maximum sales at minimum cost, this is too narrow a view. Promotion will not necessarily have sales generation as a direct or primary goal and it may also have multiple goals. Among the more common generic promotion goals are:

Awareness

Organizations frequently wish to develop in their target audience just an awareness of their products, their brands, their services or even their existence. In commercial organizations the pursuit of this type of goal is followed when companies wish to:

1 *Develop potential customers' awareness of the existence of a new product or service*: This may be the goal when a company wishes to introduce a new product. Here the aim is not to cause the potential customer to purchase the product, but to develop an awareness of the new product's existence and inculcate a predisposition towards future purchase. For example, the advertising and promotion of management consultancy and accounting services generally does not have the goal that those influenced by the promotion will purchase the services immediately, but, rather, that they will be predisposed to do so in the future.
2 *Refresh existing customers' memories of the existence of an organization, a brand, a product, or service through reminding them of its existence*: This is often the goal behind the promotion of products which are at the mature stage of their product life cycles. This is the type of motivation which lies behind advertising of company names, products and services through diaries, calendars etc.

Attitude

The generic 'attitude' goal is somewhat similar to the 'awareness' goal in that when a promotion has such a goal its aim is to leave the targeted sector primarily with a desired attitude of mind towards a product, a service or indeed an issue, and the developed attitude may or may not result in action. For example, the promotion campaign waged in the UK in 1986 by the Department of Health and Social Services against the disease AIDS (the Acquired Immune Deficiency Syndrome) had, largely, the goal of developing attitudes:

> The aim of the campaign, says the Department of Health and Social Security, is twofold. To prevent the spread of AIDS and to allay people's fears and misconceptions about its transmission.[11]

Action

When organizations wish their promotion campaigns to lead directly to sales, then action, in the form of purchases by the targeted market segments, is the goal. Although immediate sales in response to promotion is the most frequently considered criterion for the success of a promotional campaign, there will often be lags in the process. For example, advertising campaigns designed to promote the purchase of ephemeral products such as popular records, films, plays etc. are only successes if the required number of the targeted market segments purchase almost immediately. In contrast, in the promotion of the sales of products such as housing, or industrial buildings, immediate sales are generally not expected.

Competitive signals

Organizations may use promotion to signal to their competitors, and other interested parties selected information about themselves. The information could include: strategic intentions; future goals; internal health. For example, many public companies, in order to act as a stabilizing influence in the degree of competition prevailing in their industry and also to maintain harmonious relationships with the financial community and society in general often publish, in national newspapers, their annual operating results, their achievements and their plans for the future. (See page 122.)

In general, the primary goal of any promotion strategy should be to help the organization achieve its marketing goals. More specifically it will often be the case that the promotion goals will be to use that blend of promotional devices which will achieve the maximum degree of influence in the targeted market segments at the minimum cost. Thus any promotion strategy should contribute to the marketing process through:

- Being appropriate to the product and the market segment which has been identified and is being targeted.
- Helping position the product in the desired location in the segment.
- Being appropriate to the means of distribution chosen.
- Being appropriate to the resources which the organization has.

Although there is a great variety of methods of promotion available, they can be divided into two broad types: impersonal promotion or advertising, and personal promotion or personal selling. Each of these is discussed separately below.

Impersonal promotion or advertising

Impersonal promotion or advertising takes place when an organization communicates with its targeted market segments through a communication medium. The type of advertising used can be classified under three main headings:

Medium/media used

The most frequently employed media are: television, radio, newspapers, magazines, journals, other written and printed forms including hoardings, calendars, etc. Table 29 shows the total advertising expenditure in the UK over the period 1977 to 1982 according to the main media classes.

Table 29 Total advertising expenditure by media 1977–82[12]

	1977 (£m)	1978 (£m)	1979 (£m)	1980 (£m)	1981 (£m)	1982 (£m)
By media						
National newspapers including colour supplements	251	295	347	426	467	515
Regional newspapers including free sheets	296	483	593	640	684	737
Magazines and periodicals	116	143	180	192	200	209
Trade and technical	113	169	203	214	222	247
Directories	43	50	62	82	97	124
Press production costs	73	96	119	130	146	154
Total press	1012	1236	1504	1684	1816	1986
Television, including production costs	398	482	471	692	809	928
Poster and transport including production costs	54	68	87	107	115	124
Cinema, including production costs	9	13	17	18	18	18
Radio including production costs	26	35	52	54	60	70
Total	1499	1834	2131	2555	2818	3126

As can be seen the medium which has developed most strongly over the period is commercial radio.

Geographical coverage
Local, regional, national and international.

Level of campaign
Advertising can be on the basis of a product, a product line, brand, or a corporate or institutional level.

The process of promotion

Irrespective of the media used the process followed in promotion can be considered under the following headings: goals, budget, media and evaluation.

Promotion goals
The specific goals which a promotion or advertising campaign has, should flow from the overall marketing goals and be linked to the other elements in the marketing mix. Irrespective of the goals pursued and the media used, the effects of any advertising campaign should be capable of being measured within a specified period of time. The most difficult campaigns to evaluate are those in which the primary objective is to develop awareness or attitudes. In this type of promotion evaluation of the effectiveness can be assessed by tracking the targeted segments through market research. Those campaigns which have the goal of action in the form of purchase, are the most amenable to objective appraisal as the success of the campaign will be reflected in the lagged level of sales.

Budget
The budget allocation for promotion will be a fundamental determinant of its nature and extent and although a scientific approach to promotional budgets is frequently advocated (see Kotler[13] and Lavidge and Steiner[14]), in practice the allocation is often subjective and judgemental. Apart from this arbitrary method of setting the promotion budget, three other means are often used.

1 *Tradition and practice in the industry*:   This approach takes the view that the collective wisdom of the industry is the best guide for setting promotion budgets and this collective wisdom is reflected in the actual promotion budgets of the various competitors in the industry. Therefore the appropriate budget level is one which conforms to industry norms. For example if in an industry the average amount spent on promotion is 4 per cent of turnover, then this is the appropriate amount for any company. The major drawback with this approach is that the 'collective wisdom' may be a poor guide to setting an individual promotion budget as industry averages can be

misleading – different competitors may vary greatly in their use of promotion as a lever in the marketing mix.

2 *Per cent of sales method*:   In this approach it is assumed that the appropriate promotion budget should be a fixed percentage of sales, i.e. when the marketing expenses are broken down, for every one pound of sales there should be an expense of, say, three pence, for promotion. Although this approach has the advantage that it is easy to monitor and control it assumes that the appropriate relationship between marketing and the promotion budget is fixed. It therefore ignores such dynamic aspects of marketing as the stage that a product is at in its life cycle and the nature of competition.

3 *Market driven method*:   In this approach it is assumed that the size of the promotion budget should be determined by the marketing goals, i.e. for any product the starting point of the budget calculation should be the target sales volume and market position and the ending point should be the budget required to achieve this position. This approach involves a number of discrete steps and is illustrated below by means of a hypothetical example. The substance for this approach is taken from Kotler[15] page 529. Company XX has decided to introduce, in the next year, a new product, Product X, which will compete with existing products already available in the market. Product X is a consumer product which is bought regularly by most households. An appropriate 'market driven' marketing budget could be set as follows:

(a) *Set the volume of sales required*:   This volume should reflect fundamental marketing goals and could be determined by factors such as: the break-even volume; the volume necessary to earn a given ROI; the volume necessary to achieve a certain rate of growth, etc. These figures are of course developed iteratively, i.e. the break-even figure cannot be determined until the costs of the advertising promotion have been included. Therefore some estimate of the promotion budget must be used in the initial calculation and when the 'true promotion costs' have been computed the process of setting the budget can recommence with a more accurate estimate of promotion costs.

In the case of Product X, the desired volume for the forthcoming year is 400,000 units.

(b) *Estimate the total size of the targeted market segment(s) for this type of product.*

It is estimated that each year 10,000,000 units of this type of product are purchased.

(c) *On the basis of (a) and (b) translate the volume required into a percentage market share figure.*

For Product X, the desired market share is

$$\frac{400,000}{10,000,000} \times 100 = 4 \text{ per cent.}$$

(d) *Decide upon the type of media most suitable for positioning the product in its target segment.*

The medium which is considered most suitable for the promotion of this product is national tabloid newspapers.

(e) *Obtain the costs of using each selected medium.*

Three tabloid newspapers are chosen as being most suitable and the preferred form of advertisement is a full page mono in each. Each newspaper will receive an equal volume of advertising. The readership and cost per full page mono advertisement in each newspaper are:

Newspaper A: 11,500,000 readers and £22,000 per page
Newspaper B: 9,500,000 readers and £21,000 per page
Newspaper C: 6,350,000 readers and £14,000 per page

(f) *Estimate the conversion rate, i.e. the proportion of those consumers who, when they have been persuaded to try the product, will switch to become regular consumers.*

Pilot market research has indicated that one in three consumers who try Product X will switch to become regular consumers. Therefore the conversion rate is 0.33.

(g) *Estimate the number of advertising exposures necessary to achieve a 1 per cent trial rate in the targeted market segments.*

It is estimated that a 1 per cent trial rate will be achieved if a total of twelve advertisements are placed, i.e. four advertisements in each newspaper. Therefore the cost of a 1 per cent trial rate will be:

£22,000 × 4 = £88,000
£21,000 × 4 = £84,000
£14,000 × 4 = £56,000
Total = £228,000

(h) *Convert the cost of obtaining a 1 per cent trial rate into the cost of obtaining a 1 per cent market share rate:* This is obtained by dividing the cost of the advertising necessary to achieve a 1 per cent trial rate (step g) by the conversion rate (step f).

For Product X this is: cost of twelve advertisements (cost of achieving a 1 per cent trial) ÷ 0.33 (conversion rate), i.e.

$$\frac{£228,000}{0.33} = £690,909$$

This is the cost of achieving a 1 per cent market share.

(i) *Estimate the cost of achieving the desired market share**.
In this case the desired market share is 4 per cent which will cost:

$$4 \times £690,909 = £2,763,636$$

This is the 'market driven' promotion budget.

Media
The media chosen for a particular promotion strategy should be a function of:

1 *The goals of the promotion strategy*: For example if the organization has a goal of high volume sales of an undifferentiated product on a national basis it will use media of mass communication – for example relatively simple instant cameras are advertised nationally on television and in mass circulation tabloid newspapers. In contrast to this manufacturers of very expensive strongly differentiated 'professional' cameras will use media channels such as speciality photographic journals.

2 *The costs of the media*: Tables 30 and 31 show the costs of selected television and national newspaper advertising (the most common media employed) in the UK in 1984. Although there is enormous variety in the costs of the different media, it is important to view the costs of using a particular medium not in absolute terms but in terms of its relative power to influence the target market segment. This power tends to be measured using two indices: cost per thousand exposures and effect. Cost per thousand exposures is the cost of exposing the advertisement to one thousand people in the target market segment. For example if a consumer goods company bought a full mono page advertisement in *the Daily Telegraph* the cost per thousand exposures in 1982 would have been £19,500 ÷ 3,357 = £5.81 while the cost of an equivalent advertisement in *The Financial Times* would have been £13,440 ÷ 705 = £19.06. The complementary index of assessing media cost is its effect, where effect is measured by the advertisement's power to generate the desired response. Media effectiveness varies from medium to medium – for many consumer goods television advertising is more effective generally, than other media – while advertising of services or products in the journals of the professions will normally bestow,

---

* This assumes that the relationship between the number of exposures and the trial rate is linear.

Table 30   Television – peak weekday spots in 1984

Television company	10 seconds	Spot duration 20 seconds	30 seconds
	£	£	£
Thames Television	17,500	28,200	35,000
Granada Television	9,000	14,400	8,000
Anglia Television	4,000	6,400	8,000
Scottish Television	3,500	5,600	7,000
Ulster Television	1,133	1,813	2,200

Table 31   Press – national newspapers in 1984

Newspaper	Full page £
Daily Mirror	24,500
Daily Telegraph	22,400
The Independent	7,500
The Times	14,000

because of the nature of the journal and its profession, a cachet of integrity which will enhance the effectiveness of the advertisement. The higher cost per thousand rate of *The Financial Times* reflects this newspaper's power of effect.

3 *The resources of the organization*:   The absolute level of resources that the organization has at its disposal will influence the choice of medium used. For example, multinational companies with international products – such as Coca Cola – are able to amortize their enormous advertising costs over very large volumes of sales.

4 *The targeted market segments' use of the media*:   Generally the greater the targeted market segments' use of the chosen media, the greater will be the likelihood of generating the desired response. For example, specialist car magazines, tend to contain technical information plus a very large amount of advertising of products and services of interest to such car enthusiasts.

5 *Audience quality*:   The quality of the audience could be defined as having the characteristics desired in the target segments. For example, specialist car magazines would normally have, from the advertisers' perspective, a high quality audience as their interest in the area will tend to make them interested in the products whereas the television audiences for programmes of a general interest, tend, from an advertising perspective to be much more heterogeneous and therefore of lower quality.

Conclusion on impersonal promotion or advertising
The degree and type of impersonal promotion or advertising varies greatly from industry to industry and indeed from company to com-

pany. Although various efforts have been made to scientifically select optimal total budgets for advertising and optimal allocations of those budgets among the various media (see Naert and Leeflang[16]) effective advertising still remains a branch of marketing where quantitative analysis requires considerable complementary managerial judgement.

Personal promotion or personal selling

Personal promotion, or personal selling, is considered to be the process in which a representative of an organization, through face-to-face contact with existing or potential customers, promotes the marketing goals of his organization. (Telephone contact is also regarded as a form of personal selling.) This view of personal selling casts it in a much broader context than the more traditional view which is that it is concerned, almost exclusively, with 'selling' and the criterion for success is the volume and/or the value of the sales. Here it is suggested that personal selling is just one element in the total marketing process and it is likely to be most effective when it is planned in this fashion and its success is assessed on a more comprehensive set of criteria that just sales targets. Therefore, personal selling is seen as the final and vital link in matching an organization's goods or services with existing and potential customers' needs. Consequently, it is regarded as a two way communication process between the organization and customers and is therefore an important element in the overall promotional mix.

As personal selling is an element within the promotional mix, the activities to be undertaken in this function should be determined by major influences such as: the marketing goals; the nature of the products or services; the channels of distribution used; and the methods of promotion employed. Within this context the personal selling function can be planned in the following stages: goals; sales force organizational structure; motivation and compensation; and evaluation. Each of these is now discussed.

Goals

The goals that are set for personal selling have two major linked levels – the overall goals to be achieved by the total personal selling effort and the goals to be achieved by individual sales personnel. Personal selling goals which are frequently employed are considered below under two main headings: quantitative goals and qualitative goals. Quantitative goals, which are often called targets or quotas, are the more common type and it will normally be the case that salespeople will be required to meet a number of these goals such as:

Quantitative sales goals:

- *Value of sales goals* – here the sales staff have a goal of achieving a certain value of sales within a specified period of time. This type of goal has the major advantage that it is simple to understand and measure but it suffers from the drawback that it takes no account of the benefits to be derived from selling other products which may make a greater profit contribution, may build up buyer loyalty, or may enhance the image of the company.

- *Product goals* – the requirement here is to meet specified sales targets for particular products or groups of products – usually the most profitable items.
- *Profit goals* – when this type of goal is employed the salesperson is trying to maximize the sales of those products which will yield the greatest level of profit (which could be defined as gross margin). Although this approach has the advantage, in theory, that each unit sold will contribute most to the organization's level of profitability, it assumes that profitability is the most important criterion to satisfy (market share may be more important) and also tends to remove discretion about pricing from the salesperson.
- *Costs and expenses goals* – normally it will be the case that a selling goal will be to minimize the cost of generating the sale.

Quantitative information goals: Ideally sales personnel should act as two way information conduits. They should be able to gather quantitative information about customers, target and other potential markets, their territories, and sensitize their organizations to developments taking place. Similarly they should have the type of information about their organization and its products or services which will stimulate the buying propensity of existing and potential customers. The type of quantitative information sought under this heading can be further subclassified as follows:

- *Information about existing customers* – on the basis of contact with customers and subsequent record keeping and analysis, sales personnel should be able to provide information on topics such as mix of customers according to: size of account; promptness of payment; seasonality of purchases; geographical spread etc.
- *Information about new customers* – normally sales personnel have a goal of developing new customers and the type of information provided here could include: number of new customers sought and acquired during a particular period; percentage of sales to new and existing customers; incidence of success (i.e. percentage of occasions on which new customer solicitations resulted in actual purchases) in attempts to acquire new customers.
- *Information on products* – under this goal sales staff could provide information on topics such as: breakdown of sales according to product lines; individual products; age of products etc.
- *Information on territory* – the provision of information on the changing nature of the territory served. This could include for example, demographic, industrial, economic, social, and cultural trends.
- *Information on competitors* – this goal would aim to provide the organization with information on topics such as: the number of

competitors; competitors' sales of similar products by product line; volume, value, price, age of products; competitors' coverage of the market etc.

Qualitative personal selling goals: These are often much less explicit than the quantitative ones and are generally less amenable to objective measurement. They are also concerned more with the transmission of information and the generation of attitudes than direct sales targets. In spite of the inherent difficulty in measuring how well such goals are being met, they are important influences in the selling process and the following are the types of qualitative goals that are frequently set.

Qualitative information goals: These could include information about concerns such as:

- *Customer information* – first the attitudes of existing customers to the existing range of products and services; their attitudes to the organization in general; their triggers to purchase and their triggers not to purchase. Second the nature of new and potential customers, according to size, business, location etc., their attitudes, their future sales potential, credit rating, triggers to purchase etc.
- *Product information* – transmitting to existing and potential customer information on the products which will help develop their propensities to purchase – this type of information could include evidence of quality, value for money, high technical specifications, attractive future developments.
- *Territory information* – gathering qualitative information on the changing nature of the territories being served. This could include assessments of demographic, industrial, economic, social, and cultural changes.
- *Distribution information* – this could include information about the customer perceived quality and efficiency of the channels of distribution being used.
- *Competitor information* – this could contain diverse information on topics such as the changing nature of competitors in terms of their goals and the competitive strategies which they are employing.

Sales force organizational structure
The organization structure adopted for a sales force should be such that it enables the organization to achieve its marketing goals at a minimum cost. It follows therefore that the way in which the sales force is structured is a function of:

- The product or service.
- The method of distribution.
- The promotion mix.
- The pricing strategy.

- The resources of the organization.
- The location of the organization.

  The most common forms of sales force organization structure are given below.

1 *Exclusive geographical territory*:   In this type of structure each sales person is given an exclusive geographical territory and is responsible for all personal selling of all product lines to all customers within that territory. This type of structure tends to be most appropriate when the organization's products are relatively simple, relatively limited in range, relatively homogeneous and the market is also relatively homogeneous. For example, this is often the type of structure adopted by manufacturers of packaged grocery goods who distribute through wholesalers – each sales representative has a region or territory to which they have exclusive rights for all sales to all wholesalers. This type of structure has the major advantage that it is simple to understand and administer and also it is easy to evaluate the performance of the salesperson.

2 *Exclusive product line*:   In this type of structure a salesperson is given the exclusive rights to sell to all customers, irrespective of their characteristics, a particular product or service line. This type of structure is likely to be most prevalent in conditions where there is variety in the products or services provided by the organization, the product or service being sold is of relatively large value, is technically sophisticated, and may need to be tailored to the purchaser's requirements. This type of sales force structure has the advantage that the salesperson, because of his deep knowledge of the product or service, can provide the customer with detailed information on its use; however, it does have the major disadvantage that when such a structure is used by a multiproduct company it may lead to excessive duplication with many salesmen calling upon a single customer.

3 *Exclusive customer account*:   When an organization has customers which make extremely large purchases of their products they may have a sales force structure in which a salesperson has the exclusive rights to sell the company's products to a single customer. For example, the Digital Equipment Company in Reading, UK, because it engages in such a volume of international travel, has a travel agency located within its premises for its exclusive use. The exclusive customer structure has the major advantage that the producer should develop a close relationship with the customer which should make the producer sensitive to customer needs and reqirements. However, it can be an expensive method of selling which may be prone to duplication.

4 *Matrix sales force structures*:   A matrix sales force structure is one in which one or more of the above (or indeed other) axes of structure are combined into a more complex structure. For example, a company may wish to have a matrix structure on the basis of geo-

graphical territory and product line. In general this type of structure is most likely to be adopted in situations where the organization produces a wide variety of products or services and has a wide variety of customers. In conclusion there are no firm guidelines for the appropriate sales force structure that an organization should adopt – it is a function of the elements listed on page 283 and its operational effectiveness. However, irrespective of how the sales force is structured – whether it is on a territorial, product, customer, or matrix basis – within the structure each sub-unit which supports a salesperson should be designed so that:

- Each salesperson can achieve a satisfactory level of income in return for a satisfactory performance.
- Each sub-unit makes a positive, or satisfactory contribution to profits. (A satisfactory contribution to profits does not always have to be positive – for example a product in the development stage of its product life cycle may be making losses but this may still be considered satisfactory.)

Motivation and compensation
Having emphasized the importance to many organizations of having an effective sales force, it follows that a crucial element in achieving and sustaining such a force is that it should be sufficiently motivated to meet or exceed the goals which it is expected to achieve. A traditional view is that the major, and indeed perhaps the exclusive motivator for sales personnel is financial reward i.e. that their earnings should be tied directly to their sales. The main methods by which salespeople are remunerated are set out below.

- A salary based exclusively upon commissions earned by sales.
- A fixed salary not related to sales performance.
- A combination comprising a fixed salary element plus a commission element related to sales achievements.

Even though performance-related financial reward is often considered the primary motivator which will lead to increased sales, there is considerable empirical research see Doyle and Shapiro[17] and Bagozzi[18] to indicate that salespeople are motivated more strongly by other factors such as feelings of achievement and feelings of self-esteem.

In passing, it should be noted, perhaps as a result of the experiences of companies using non-financial motivators, that in the UK there has been a trend in recent years to packages of compensation and non-financial motivators to boost sales. For example, in 1985 the Prudential Insurance company, which has around 13,000 agents throughout the UK who are paid a basic salary plus a commission which is directly related to sales, engaged a firm of consultants to help motivate their agents in a sales promotion campaign. The campaign designed by the consultants set specific sales targets, provided feedback for the agents, awarded points for achievement of the targets and encouraged team-work. Those agents whose sales reached or exceeded specified numbers of points qualified for any prize of their choice up to a specified value. In evaluating this method of motivating their salespeople the Prudential was of the opinion that 'the new business far exceeded the results that would normally have been expected'.

There is no single best standard method of sales compensation. In deciding which method ought to be employed cognisance should be taken of influences such as the marketing and sales objectives, traditions within the industry and company, competitors' practices, the availability of suitable personnel etc.

Accman's promotion strategy

Accman's promotion strategy could have the following goals for the forthcoming planning period:

1 *Awareness*: To develop in potential clients an awareness of these new software products, their capabilities and the associated services which Accman will provide.
2 *Attitudes*: To develop in clients an attitude towards the company and its products which will predispose potential customers to purchase.
3 *Action*: Purchase of the software products.
4 *Signal*: To signal to clients and other competitors that Accman has developed strong expertise in the applications of computer systems to smaller companies in particular.

Accman intends to employ three main types of promotion.

- *Personal selling 1*: This will be the main type of promotion and Accman will use its existing professional staff to promote the packages as an aspect of their normal work with clients.
- *Personal selling 2*: Promoting the products through Accman staff providing free seminars on the use of computers in business.
- *Impersonal selling*: The development of high quality promotional literature.

Price strategy

Traditional economic theory asserts that in a situation of perfect competition where there is perfect knowledge and perfect substitutes are available, price is the primary basis of competition and the primary determinant of demand. Empirical evidence (see Schoeffler[19]) and casual observation suggests that such a situation rarely accords with reality.

Rather, although price may strongly influence demand, and may be an important factor in determining the nature and the degree of competition, it is only one of many factors. From an organizational perspective, price is just one element from the marketing mix which an organization may use to achieve its marketing objectives. Indeed, there is now evidence to suggest that although producers often still accord price the number one rank as the determinant of demand for a product, the demand for most products is strongly influenced by a vector of other elements drawn from the marketing mix. Indeed Porter[20] has argued that any competitive strategy based upon price competition alone is inherently dangerous:

> Some forms of competition, notably price competition, are highly unstable and quite likely to leave the entire industry worse off from the standpoint of profitability. Price cuts are quickly and easily matched by rivals, and once matched they lower revenues for all firms unless industry price elasticity of demand is high enough. Advertising battles, on the other hand, may well expand demand or enhance the level of product differentiation in the industry for the benefit of all firms.

This quotation highlights a characteristic of price that makes it fundamentally different from each of the other elements in the marketing mix – the speed with which any organization can unilaterally make a price change. This characteristic makes heavy reliance upon price alone as a method of gaining competitive advantage rather risky. A more satisfactory approach is to use price in conjunction with other complementary elements – product, place and promotion – in the marketing mix.

The objective of any price strategy should, generally, accord with overall corporate strategies and be integrated, as an enabling mechanism, in the marketing process for achieving marketing goals. Thus any pricing strategy should:

1 Help the organization achieve its overall corporate goals in such areas as profitability, market share, growth, range of products etc.
2 Help the organization achieve its more specific marketing goals such as market share, market growth rate, etc.
3 Materially contribute to the marketing process through:

   • Being appropriate for the market segment which has been identified and is being targeted.
   • Helping position the product in the desired location in the segment.
   • Being appropriate to the means of distribution chosen.
   • Being consistent with the means of promotion chosen for the product.

In most organizations pricing strategies and practices tend to be dominated by one or more of the following major sets of influences:

demand influences; competitive influences; and cost influences. Each of these particular orientations is now discussed.

Demand influences

The demand for a product is a fundamental influence on pricing strategies and the price of a product is a fundamental influence on the demand for it. The two are mutually dependent. Generally, the higher the price charged for a product the less will be the volume of demand and vice versa. Consequently, when planning price strategies for products which have a high price elasticity of demand (such as international air travel) particular attention must be paid to the consequences of price changes.

When a demand orientation to price is employed it assumes that the price of the product or service is entirely within the control of the organization and that the level at which it is set, together with an appropriate blend of the other elements of the marketing mix, will determine the volume of demand. In practice, therefore, the use of this approach requires accurate sales forecasts or simulations of the demand consequences that different pricing strategies are likely to have. Consequently, organizations which have products or services for which there is high price elasticity of demand must have the ability to make accurate sales forecasts. Although there are many tools available to achieve this – formal statistical techniques, simulations and market empirical market research — it is an area of high uncertainty and prone to error, especially when sales estimates are being made for new products.

Competition influences

Most products and services are not unique – they must compete with rivals or substitutes. Consequently effective pricing strategies will normally require a recognition of the nature of the competition which a product or service faces. A pricing strategy based on competition influences is one where the price charged for a product or a service is in some way determined by, and related to, the price charged by existing competitors for identical or similar products and services rather than by internal costs. This does not imply that the price charged should be identical to that charged by competitors, but rather, as stated above, it should be related to it, i.e. the price set, in relation to competitors' prices, should help position the product in the desired market segment. Thus when an organization has this approach as its primary pricing orientation, it should, through market research and analysis, analyse the price levels and price structures which obtain in the targeted market segment and set its prices at levels which will signal its position within the segment. The price set may be higher than the generally prevailing price – signalling that the product is differentiated in some way, or it could be set at lower than the prevailing price – signalling 'value for money'. Thus, for example, in all the market segments in which it competes, Mercedes Benz tends to charge higher prices than its direct competitors. Apart from the commercial benefits of being able to command superior prices, this strategy also helps generate in the market the message of the very high quality of the products. In contrast to this, cut-price airline companies such as People Express and Virgin Atlantic signal to their targeted market segments that they will offer superior value for money.

The degree of influence which the competitive environment has on the pricing strategy for a product or a service will depend upon the nature of the product or service and the industry. Among the more important determinants are the following:

1 *Market position*: Those organizations which enjoy the greatest dominance in their markets will tend to be less influenced by external competitive forces as they may be so powerful that they have the power to unilaterally determine price levels and price structures for the entire market. The two basic methods for achieving market dominance are strategies of: 'high volume low cost' resulting in large relative market share – until recently, the price of automobiles in the US market (see page 292) was determined largely by the price set by the world's largest producer, General Motors; or through 'product differentiation' resulting in leadership of the quality segment of the market – the prices of men's Savile Row suits would not appear to be influenced by the price of men's suits in multiple stores. In contrast to organizations which are dominant in the market, non-dominant organizations have little choice but to adapt their pricing structures to the prevailing pattern.

2 *Market segment*: In general, those market segments which are at the lowest end of the quality spectrum tend to compete on price rather than other features. Consequently the closer a product is to commodity status the more likely it is that the price will be determined by external competitive forces. For example, the price of pencils is largely determined by competitive forces.

3 *Market structure*: Generally the larger number of equally sized competitors in the target segment the greater will be the degree of price competition. For example, British Telecom which has only one rival domestic telecommunications carrier – Mercury – would appear to be relatively free of the competitive influences in comparison with, say, car sales companies.

4 *Threat of new entrants*: Generally the greater this threat the greater will be the tendency for competition to be the dominant pricing influence. For example, contract typing services for businesses compete almost exclusively on price which is determined by the interaction of competitors. There are very low entry barriers in this 'business'.

5 *Threat of substitutes*: Substitutes place a ceiling on the price that can be charged for a product or a service and the greater the prevalence or threat of substitutes the more closely will a producer need

to follow a competition orientated pricing strategy. In domestic travel the prices charged by the substitute modes: rail, road and air, all interact and influence each other.

It could be argued that this is the most 'marketing orientated' approach to pricing as its starting point is that price is externally determined by the competitive influences in the environment and that an organization should adapt its prices so that they fit with its environment and achieve corporate objectives.

Cost influences

The cost of manufacturing a product or providing a service should be a fundamental influence on pricing strategies. Non-subsidized organizations which continuously sell their products or services below the cost of producing them will go out of business eventually. Organizations which sell their products at prices greatly in excess of the costs of production may be adversely affecting their profitability, encouraging new entrants and stimulating customers to use substitutes.

A pricing strategy based on cost influences is one where the price charged for a product or a service should in some way be determined by, and related to, the cost of its production. The main types of cost based pricing strategies are cost plus pricing, target pricing and marginal cost pricing.

Cost plus pricing

A cost plus pricing strategy involves determining the total cost per unit produced and then arriving at a price by adding to that cost a certain fixed percentage for profit margin. The total cost per unit is normally composed of the variable costs of production and marketing, plus an allocation of overhead to cover fixed costs. In practice the allocation of a fair overhead may be difficult to ensure for a single product and it is not unusual in such circumstances for a single percentage of total variable costs to be added to cover fixed costs and profit.

Cost plus pricing has a number of claimed advantages which include the following:

- It is an extremely simple method of pricing and easily understood.
- Where it is the predominant mode of pricing used in an industry, and when individual companies in the industry have similar costs, it tends to promote competitive stability as the basis of competition will be factors other than price.
- It often appears to be a fair method of pricing to buyers and suppliers.
- It guarantees that costs are indeed covered.

However, there may be certain problems associated with such a strategy which include the following:

- Although suitable for the pricing of standard products, it is more difficult to apply to complex products. For example in pricing for services, professionals such as accountants would find it difficult to use this a mode of pricing.
- By focusing on the essentially internal costs of production, the organization may lose sight of the greater strategic reality – the competitive market. As a consequence, although the pricing strategy may be appropriate from the point of view of covering costs, it may not be appropriate to the external competitive environment. The view that a company is operating profitably as long as prices exceed costs is not always valid. This approach to pricing strategy was employed by the UK motorcycle industry – UK manufacturers set prices to cover their costs. However, in the competitive marketplace they continuously lost market share to Japanese competitors with ultimately disastrous consequences. In contrast to this pricing strategy – where price was set at too high a level – in the 1970s the UK car manufacturer Jaguar set its prices on a cost plus basis which gave their products a price which was lower than the market would have borne. Consequently a 'black market' in Jaguar cars developed where cars were bought from dealers at the recommended price, and then resold at a higher price – the price that the market would bear.

Target pricing
The kernel of this strategy is that the price to be charged for a product should be set by meeting a predetermined return on the capital employed to produce and market it. Thus if an organization has a policy that its return on capital employed should be 20 per cent then all products should be priced so that they generate this rate of return. In practice, target prices can be set for different volumes of sales using the formula below:[21]

$$P = DVC + \frac{F}{X} + \frac{rK}{X}$$

where;

P   = the target price
DVC = direct variable costs per unit
F   = fixed costs
X   = standard unit volume
r   = desired profit rate of return
K   = capital employed

For example if a hypothetical company had a target rate of return of 20 per cent on capital employed, then, using the above formula and the internal cost data, as shown in Table 32 it could build up a schedule of prices and volumes which, if achieved, would enable it to meet its required rate of return. The final step, before deciding upon a produc-

Table 32 Target prices and required volumes for a hypothetical company to achieve a return on capital of 20 per cent

X Volume (thousand of standard units)	DVC Direct variable costs per unit (£)	F Fixed costs (£000)	r Target rate of return (%)	K Capital employed (£000)	P Target price (£)
200	30	1,000	20	3,500	38.50
300	27	1,000	20	3,500	32.67
400	25	1,000	20	3,500	29.25
500	24	1,000	20	3,500	27.40
600	23	1,000	20	3,500	25.83
700	22	1,000	20	3,500	24.43

tion schedule and a target price would be to estimate, through market research, the volumes that it would be likely to sell at the various target prices and then select that combination of price and volume which would be most likely to be achieved.

Target pricing has an underlying assumption that the organization setting the target price has the power to see that it is indeed followed in the industry. Consequently this type of pricing stategy tends to be adopted successfully only by organizations which have this degree of power. This type of pricing strategy is often adopted by national monopolies and public utilities where the organization's monopoly power guarantees its ability to implement its pricing decisions.

Perhaps the best known example of a public company following this type of pricing strategy is General Motors. Until the advent of the strong import penetration of its domestic market in the US by the Japanese in the 1970s, GM set its automobile prices by a target pricing strategy and the rest of the US automobile industry tended to follow the GM pricing lead. However, with the relative diminution of GM's US market power because of the success of the Japanese manufacturers, GM has been obliged to abandon this approach and adopt pricing strategies which are more strongly influenced by competitive forces.

Marginal cost pricing
Marginal cost pricing occurs when an organization has a pricing strategy where all the variable costs of production and marketing are covered, but the fixed costs are not fully covered. The fixed costs may be partly covered or not covered at all. There are a number of situations in which this type of pricing strategy may be particularly appropriate.

1   *Overcapacity*: In industries which are running at less than full capacity and have high levels of fixed assets, i.e. in PIMS terminology are 'investment intensive', marginal cost pricing is often followed. For example this type of pricing strategy is often used by

hotels in their non-holiday seasons. In this industry, which has relatively high levels of fixed assets (the hotels), off-season prices are often set to cover just the variable operating costs plus some proportion of fixed costs.

2 *Seasonal fluctuations*: Industries which are prone to seasonal fluctuations in demand may attempt to offset this seasonality through marginal cost pricing. Examples of industries which practise this are: telephone companies – cheaper calls after 1.00 p.m. and at night to help balance daily seasonality; airline companies – cheaper weekend flights to offset weekly seasonality; fuel companies – cheaper summer fuel charges to offset annual seasonality.

3 *Experience influenced industries*: In industries where costs follow experience curves, it may be more appropriate to build the strategic position of a product through a pricing strategy which is based upon reaping the benefits of reduced costs through maximizing market share rather than pricing on a marginal cost basis only. (For detailed information on those types of strategies see McNamee[22] Chapter 3.)

4 *Multiple product lines*: In companies which have multiple product lines it may be appropriate for selected lines or products to be priced on a marginal cost only. For example, when a company introduces a new product at the growth stage of the product life cycle, in order to stimulate the market penetration of the product, it may be appropriate to price on a marginal cost basis, while retaining a full cost pricing basis for products at later stages in their life cycles.

Although a marginal cost pricing strategy can make significant contributions to the strategic health of an organization there is the inherent danger that such a strategy may become overused and may, through failure to include overhead in costs, drain the organization of its resouces.

Although the influences of 'demand', 'competition', and 'cost' on price have been described above separately, all three orientations are interrelated and interdependent and the three perspective should be employed when pricing strategies are being developed.

Pricing new products or services

The effects of the influences of 'demand', 'competition', and 'costs' are most easily discernible when considering products which are already in existence or new products which are related to existing products. However, when a new product is unique, then setting an appropriate price for it tends to be more difficult. A unique new product does not have the benchmarks of demand and competition – the only element known with certainy are the costs. In such a situation the following approach could be used:

1 Assume that the price of the product will at least cover marginal costs.

2   Through market research – this could be by test marketing, analysis of substitute products and estimation of the competitive reactions of the producers of substitutes – make estimates of the likely demand for the new product at different price levels, with different means of distribution and with alternative methods of promotion.
3   On the basis of the market research decide upon a pricing structure, methods of distribution and methods of promotion.

Although there is an infinite variety of pricing structures that could be followed for most unique new products, two pricing strategies – skimming pricing and penetration pricing – which represent opposite ends of the pricing spectrum are often employed.

Skimming pricing
With this strategy a relatively high price is set for the new product with the hope that the consumers will be sufficiently price insensitive to pay the set premium price. The philosophy behind this approach strategy is that super profits will be earned from the top price-insensitive segments of the market before the product becomes more widely available (through increased production either by the original producer of the product or new entrants) as it cascades through the progressively more price sensitive lower segments.
   This type of strategy is most appropriate when:

- The buyers are price insensitive.
- The product can be kept proprietary.
- Substitutes are not available.
- The high price acts as a signal of quality.
- The costs of smaller volumes are not disproportionate.
- The high price does not act as a price umbrella which will permit new entrants to flourish.

Penetration pricing
Under this stategy the price is set at a relatively low level for the new product with the hope that large numbers of consumers will purchase the product in very large volumes. The philosophy behind this approach is that long-term market power (measured by relative market share) is more important than short-term profits and consequently the most important consideration in setting price is to set it at a level which will stimulate the market to develop rapidly. This type of strategy is most appropriate when:

- The buyers are price sensitive.
- The product cannot be kept proprietary.
- Substitutes are available.
- Significant cost reductions can be effected through the large volumes of production, i.e. the product is experience related.
- The low price acts as a deterrant to new entrants, i.e. because of the

low price, and the consequent relatively low profit margins achieved by the original producer, new entrants will not have the scale economies enjoyed by the original producer and consequently the business will not appear financially attractive.

Although for most products and services price is regarded by consumers to be the strongest and clearest signal of value – and hence a fundamental lever for positioning a product within a targeted market segment – any marketing strategy based upon exclusive reliance price carries great dangers – price is only one element in the marketing mix.

In general, any pricing strategy should be integrated with all the elements in the marketing mix and the price structure itself should be regarded as a variable which dynamically responds to its changing internal and external circumstances, particularly the following:

Internal: The resources which the organization has available to pursue its chosen price strategy.
The relationship between the pricing strategy and the costs of production and marketing.
External: The product's stage in the product life cycle.
The level and the nature of competition.
The price elasticity of demand for the product.

Accman's price strategy

Accman has two major goals which it hopes the sales of its software will achieve – first a contribution to the profitability of the organization and second an enhancement of its image as a progressive consulting company. Its pricing strategy must reflect these goals and in addition also reflect:

1 *The demand influences*:   Demand for this type of product in the targeted sectors has been growing rapidly and is likely to continue to do so.
2 *The competition influences*:   Accman is a new entrant and in volume and resources terms is a very small competitor in relation to major existing competitors. However, it already has a high reputation for quality among its existing clients and hopes to differentiate its products from competitors on the basis of excellent service to specific market segments.
3 *The cost influences*:   As the software was developed for its own internal uses, in this sense the development costs have been minimal. The major costs are therefore promotion costs.
4 *The strategy*:   The pricing strategy aims to reflect these influences and therefore the company has decided to enter the market with a skimming price strategy where prices will be at least equal to, but not significantly above those of existing products.

Conclusions on the marketing process
This part has shown how the four major stages of the marketing
process – market identification, market segmentation, product positioning and marketing mix strategy can all be blended together to form a
coherent set of actions which will enable overall strategic goals to be
achieved.

References

1 Christopher, M., *The Strategy of Distribution Management*, Heinemann, 1986.
2 Kotler, P., Fahey, L. and Jatisrupitak, J., *The New Competition:
Meeting the Marketing Challenge From the Far East Prentice-Hall
International*, 1985.
3 Kotler, P., Fahey, L. and Jatisrupitak, J., *op. cit.*
4 Kotler, P., *Principles of Marketing*, Prentice Hall, Englewood Cliffs
1980.
5 McNamee, P. B., *European Cases in Competitive Strategy*, Forthcoming.
6 McFadyen, E., *Voluntary Group Trading: 6 Case Studies*, HMSO,
1971.
7 McFadyen, E., *op. cit.*
8 Mendelsohn, M., *The Guide to Franchising*, Pergamon, 1985.
9 Franchising, a report by Euromonitor, 1985.
10 Mendelsohn, M., *op. cit.*
11 McEwan, 'Too Little and Too Late?' *Financial Times*, 14 August
1986, p. 18.
12 The Advertising Association, *Marketing Pocket Book*, 1986.
13 Kotler, P., *op. cit.*
14 Lavidge, R. J. and Steiner, G. A., 'A Model for Predicting Measure-
ments of Advertising Effectiveness', *Journal of Marketing*, October
1961, pp. 59–62.
15 Kotler, P., *op. cit.*
16 Naert, P. A. and Leeflang, P. S. H., *Building Implementable Marketing Models*, Martinus Nijkoff, Leiden/Boston, 1978.
17 Doyle, S. X. and Shapiro, B., 'What Counts Most in Motivating your
Salesforce?', *Harvad Business Review*, May–June 1980, pp. 133–40.
18 Bagozzi, R. P., 'Performance and Satisfaction in an Industrial
Salesforce: An examination of their Antecedents and Simultaneity',
Journal of Marketing, Spring 1980, pp. 65–77.
19 Schoeffler, S., 'The Nine Basic Findings of Business Strategy',
PIMSLetter, No. 1, 1980.
20 Porter, M. E., *Competitive Strategy: Techniques for Analysing Industries*, The Free Press, 1980.
21 Monroe, K. B., *Pricing: Making Profitable Decisions*, McGraw Hill,
New York, 1979.
22 McNamee, P. B., *Tools and Techniques for Strategic Management*,
Pergamon, 1985.

13 Selected topics in marketing

This chapter sets out three topics – buyer behaviour, the PIMS studies and marketing and non-profit making organizations – which it is believed are important elements of study for a comprehensive understanding of marketing.

Buyer behaviour

The commercial success of any non-subsidized organization is ultimately determined by buyers purchasing its products or services – organizations which produce products or services which buyers do not wish to purchase will wither. Consequently, understanding the buying process is of fundamental strategic importance. Although the process is often complex, for the purposes of strategic analysis it can be considered to involve the following stages: understanding the nature of the buyer; understanding how existing and potential buyers can be influenced; and understanding the actual buying process.

Understanding the nature of the buyer

Although the variety of buyers is almost infinite it is traditional to divide them into two broad classes: consumer buyers, i.e. buyers who purchase goods or services for personal consumption, and industrial buyers, i.e. buyers who purchase goods or services on behalf of their organizations. Buyers are segmented on this basis because, in the total buying process, consumer and industrial buyers usually exhibit differences in their motivations, their perceptions, the forces influencing their buying decisions, their purchase procedures, the sizes of their purchases and how they evaluate their purchases.

In addition to this fundamental division of buyers, both sets can be further sub-divided according to the comprehensiveness of their buying processes where the degree of comprehensiveness is determined by one or more of the following factors:

1   *Size of purchase:*   Generally the larger the value of purchase the more comprehensive will be the process leading to the buying decision and its subsequent evaluation.
2   *Importance:*   Generally the more important the purchase the more comprehensive will be the buying decision and its evaluation.
3   *Risk:*   Generally the greater the degree of risk attached to the purchase the more comprehensive will be the buying decision and its evaluation.
4   *Frequency:*   Generally the more infrequently a purchase is made the more comprehensive will be the buying decision and its evaluation.

Influences on the consumer buying process

Although the actual purchase of a good or service by a consumer is normally carried out by a single individual, the process leading to that action often involves three major sets of influences: the individual who makes the purchase; immediate influencers; and general environmental influences. Each of these influences is now discussed.

The individual
The buying behaviour of an individual is strongly influenced by his or her totality, where totality is considered to be that complex pattern of influences which makes each individual unique. These influences are commonly categorized under the following headings: sex; age; family; personality; personal needs or drives; occupation; income level; social status; lifestyle; culture; attitudes; past experiences; religion; hobbies or interests.

Except in the most trivial of purchases, one or more of these influences will usually strongly sway the buying decision.

Immediate influences
The immediate influences on a buying decision are considered to be those influences which in some way can be linked directly to a purchaser or to a particular product or service being purchased. These influences can prevail at any of the stages in the buying process (which is outlined on page 300) and the most common ones can be classified as:

1   *Immediate family and friends:*   This group of influencers will often be extremely powerful when major purchases are being contemplated. For example, for most people the largest single purchase they undertake is a house. When this decision is being made frequently the buyer will seek advice from, and be strongly influenced by, the advice and opinions of family and friends.
2   *Peer groups:*   Most people perceive themselves as being members of

both defined and undefined groups in society. Defined groups could include: religious denomination; profession; occupation; earnings group; family status; age group; political affiliation; type of house; geographical location; recreation group etc. Undefined groups are not so clearly delineated and could include groupings according to: wealth – 'a member of the wealthy section of society'; social class – 'a member of the upper middle classes'; age class – 'a young professional person'; attitude classes – 'a member of the Yuppie class', 'a member of the liberal thinking class' etc. Individuals often find it extremely important to be seen to be members of their groups and may publicly strive to be seen to conform to the norms of their groups. Consequently peer groups can have major influences on the buying decisions of the individual. The power of this type of influence on buyer behaviour can be seen particularly clearly in the area of fashion clothes. Today, visible designer or manufacturer labels on casual clothes have become such a powerful signal of belonging to particular fashion groups that identical clothes without such labels will not sell to this market segment at all or will only sell at a lower price.

3 *Role models:* People often attempt to relate to, or indeed model themselves on, well-known public figures in many fields such as business, politics, sport and entertainment. These well-known figures can often be powerful influences on buyer behaviour. This influence is used particularly in the area of the promotion of sports goods, where endorsement by a leading professional is often essential for the success of a product in its target markets.

4 *Marketing campaigns:* Effective marketing campaigns which are designed to lead to the purchase of a product or a service ought, by definition, to influence the buying decision. Therefore the particular marketing mix used by the producer of the product or service should be tailored to provoke the desired response in a potential buyer. (However, not all marketing campaigns have this goal – see page 273.)

General environmental influences
All buyers and potential buyers are influenced to some extent by more general environmental factors. These environmental factors can be grouped together under the headings that were used in Part Two. Thus the main factors which may influence buyers are briefly considered below:

1 *Competitive influences:* The number of competitors and the nature of the competition will influence buyers. For example, in a period of excess capacity in industries which have high exit barriers (such as the European car industry) there will be strong price competition which will stimulate buyers to try to take advantage of the situation.

2 *Marketing influences:* The trends within the market and its stage of development will often influence buyers. Thus when a product is at the development stage of its product life cycle there will often be

buyers who will pay a premium price for a new product and there are other potential buyers who will not wish to purchase until the product has been more widely accepted. These attitudes can be seen when a new car model is introduced.

3 *Economic influences:* The general state of the economy should influence buyer behaviour with the propensity to buy increasing in times of relative prosperity.

4 *Legal/government influences:* Government legislation can have fundamental influences. For example, a government decision on the tax relief available for company cars will fundamentally affect buying decisions.

5 *Technological influences:* Technological change influences buying decisions not just in terms of making existing products obsolete, but, in industries which are subject to continuous cost reductions, such as computers, the buying decision may be deferred in the hope of benefiting from hoped-for future price reductions.

6 *Geographical influences:* Events in foreign countries may influence domestic buying behaviour. For example, the continuance of the practice of apartheid in South Africa has caused many UK consumers not to buy South African goods.

7 *Social influences:* Prevailing social attitudes can have fundamental influences. For example, the general social hostility towards cigarette smoking has been dramatic in influencing people not to buy cigarettes.

8 *Other influences:* This category includes random or unexpected influences not captured by the above, for example, the weather.

The buying process

There is no single or standard buying process, rather, there is a continuum of complexity from the simple instantaneous purchase generally made with little thought (for example the purchase of a commodity such as salt) to a detailed and complex analysis (for example the purchase of a foreign holiday). Generally the more important and infrequent the purchase the more complex the analysis will be and the more the consumer will be affected by the various influence groups described above. Various writers and researchers (see Kotler[1], Bluell[2] and McCarthy[3]) have argued that the process can be divided into stages similar to those shown in Figure 44 and described below.

Need
At this stage the buyer perceives a need for the product or service. This need could be generated internally or be the result of one or more of the influence groups described above (perhaps an advertising campaign) triggering the feeling of need. The nature of this need could vary from a realization of a need to purchase an essential commodity such as salt to feeling the need to purchase, say, a foreign holiday.

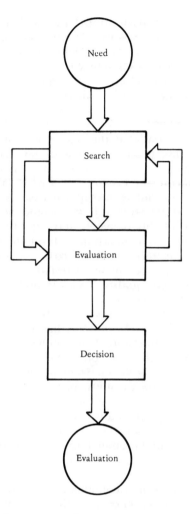

Figure 44 *Stages in the consumer buying process*

Search
At this stage the buyer will search for alternative methods of fulfilling the need. This will often involve searching for competing products or services and trying to find substitutes. At this stage the consumer is reducing the degree of uncertainty in the proposed purchase by increasing his knowledge of the target product, rival products and substitutes. The extensiveness of the search is a function of the complexity, importance and frequency of the proposed purchase. Once again the influence groups may provide the buyer with information which will assist in the search stage. In the above case the search for alternatives to salt and

further information on salt, for most people, will be minimal. The search activities undertaken prior to the purchase of the foreign holiday are likely to be rather more detailed and will probably include seeking out information from various influence groups – family, friends, peer groups, travel agents, television travel programmes etc. – on the holiday chosen and also alternative holidays.

Evaluation
When the buyer has completed the search for information about the product and competing products, he will then evaluate the various alternatives. Once again, the complexity and importance of the purchase will help determine the extent to which influence groups will impinge upon the decision. In the above case the evaluation of the alternative ways of purchasing the salt would normally be straightforward and would probably be based upon just two criteria: price and packet size. However, the evaluation criteria for the foreign holiday would include many criteria such as: cost; location; facilities; other people's previous experiences in the alternative locations; methods of transport; quality of food; quality of accommodation etc.

Decision
Once the evaluation of the alternatives has been completed then the consumer will decide upon, and then purchase, a particular product. The product purchased will be the one which most closely accords with his own, and perhaps the significant influence groups', preference maps. In the case of the decision to buy a particular packet of salt, this is straightforward. In the case of the foreign holiday, the holiday chosen will have to satisfy, better than any other holiday available, the preferences of the buyer and perhaps the preferences of significant immediate interest groups (for example, other family members).

Evaluation
After the purchase has been made, and the product has been used, it is often the case that the wisdom of the purchase will be evaluated. In the case of the purchase of salt, this evaluation, if it takes place at all, will be minimal. In the case of the foreign holiday, the evaluation (post-mortem perhaps) may comprise a comparison with other holiday-makers who have taken comparable alternative holidays.

The nature of the industrial buyer

As indicated on page 217 the industrial or organizational buyer is considered to be distinctively differentiated from the consumer buyer. This distinction is based on the observation that the two groups frequently exhibit major differences in: motivation, perception, generic influences on buying decisions, the purchase procedures, and the sizes of the purchases. Each of these sources of difference is considered below.

Motivation
For consumer buyers the primary motivation is satisfying the needs of the individual. For industrial buyers the primary motivation is satisfying the needs of the organization. At the lowest level in the organization this could involve a decision to purchase additional raw materials for inventory when a certain predetermined minimum threshold level has been reached. In this case the buying motives are clear – to avoid a stock out – and there are usually well-established buying guidelines and procedures. However, at the highest level in the organization, it will often be the case that the purchase decisions are much more important (in terms of size, risk and infrequency) and the motivation leading to the purchase of specific products or services will be of fundamental importance in achieving corporate goals. For example if the corporate goals of an organization were:

- Profit maximization, then the primary buyer motive could be cost minimization.
- Technology leadership, then the primary buyer motive could be advanced technical specification.
- Growth, then the primary buyer motive could be purchases that promote that goal.

Perception
The perception of the industrial buyer will tend to be somewhat different from the consumer buyer as prospective purchases will often be viewed from both an organizational perspective (what will best satisfy the needs of the organization) and from an individual perspective (what will best satisfy the needs of the individual responsible for making the purchase). Therefore, industrial buyers may have a broader set of perspectives than consumer buyers. Of course, it should be noted that the reverse may also be true – if industrial purchasing procedures are set inflexibly (as they often are) then the only perspective that will prevail in the purchasing decision is that of the organization.

Generic influences on buying decisions
Irrespective of whether the industrial buying is carried out by a group or an individual, the decision is often subject to the following major sets of influence: the individual, organizational relationships, general organizational factors and general environmental factors. Each of these sets of influence is considered below.

1 *The influence of the individual*: Whether industrial purchase decisions are carried out by individuals or groups, it may be important to take cognisance of the behavioural complexion of the individual or the group responsible. This complexion may be influenced by factors similar to those considered to be influential on consumer buying behaviour and considered on page 298. These are: sex, age,

family, personality, personal needs or drives, occupation, income level, social status, lifestyle, culture, attitudes, past experiences, religion, hobbies or interests. In assessing the buying behaviour of an organization it is important to understand how these forces influence the individual or group responsible for buying as they will help determine the criteria used in buying decisions. For example, if an individual with the organizational responsibility for buying has the attitude that parsimony should be exercised in buying behaviour, then it is likely that prospective purchases will be evaluated on the basis of cheapest price and value for money. In contrast, if an organizational buyer has the attitude that reliability and durability are of primary importance, then it is likely that the issue of quality will be more important than that of cost.

2   *General organizational influences*: Organizations differ greatly in their attitudes, procedures, and decision-making processes when making purchases. When making purchases the organizational process is often a function of factors such as the following:

- *Goals*: As indicated above, the goals followed by an organization will often have a fundamental influence in shaping the criteria used in purchase decisions.
- *Strategies*: The strategies being followed will influence buyer behaviour. For example, in a period when retrenchment is the fundamental strategy and cost reduction is deemed to be of paramount importance, then it would be expected that purchase decisions would be characterized by: buying on the basis of the cheapest price, buying minimum quantities, seeking superior credit terms, deferring purchases, etc.
- *Structure*: The overall structure of the organization and the particular structure of the department responsible for purchasing, will influence the buying process. Thus, in relatively small organizations, where there is no purchasing department at all, purchasing decisions will tend to be made on a personal basis by personnel who, by definition, have other functions. The purchase decisions in this type of organization will tend to be relatively informal. In such situations personal relationships between the supplier and the decision maker will often be extremely influential. In contrast to this type of structure, large centrally-controlled organizations will often have centralized purchasing through a purchasing department which buys goods and services on behalf of all parts of the organization. The purchase decisions in this type of organization will tend to be much more formal and will follow established purchasing procedures. The type of structure that an organization has affects both internal and external aspects of purchasing. Thus, from an internal perspective, in large centralized organizations there is often a formal 'purchasing chain' which separates the individual, or department, which expresses the need for the product or service, from the

individual or group who makes the final purchase decision. Thus, by way of illustration, should the marketing department in a large centralized organization express the need for a micro-computer, often, although the marketing department would draw up a specification for the computer, it would be the pur-chasing department which would be principally involved in the buying process. Similarly, from an external perspective, sup-pliers of computer equipment might target their promotion so that it influences both the groups in the organization – final users (the marketing department) and the decision makers (the pur-chasing department).

- *Resources*: Clearly, the resources which an organization has at its disposal are a major determinant of its buying practices. Organ-izations which are scarce of resources will tend to be more price conscious than those which are well endowed.

- *Culture and past experiences*: These two influences interact and are considered as a single factor which helps shape buyer prac-tices. For example, if an organization has had a buying strategy of purchasing at the cheapest available price and has experi-enced poor post-purchase support, this may cause a reorientation towards quality of service as a primary criterion in buyer selec-tion. Often organizations have particular buyer orientations which help shape their purchasing decisions. Among the more common are: *minimum cost* – this attitude suggests that when alternatives are being evaluated the crucial concern is the cheapest price; *value for money* – this may or may not be the same as minimum cost. It implies that the dominant criterion is a function of the cost of the good or service, the quality of its service and its durability; *supplier relationship* – often organiza-tions build up relationships with suppliers which prove valuable to both parties. This 'value' may be assessed on many scales including quality of service, flexibility, quality of delivery etc; *barter relationship* – organizations may develop strong relation-ships with suppliers who are also final customers, so that the market for the end product helps determine buyer selection.

3 *Organizational relationships*: In most cases, organizations are not cultural deserts functioning exclusively on facts and bereft of indi-vidual and group relationships. Consequently, those individuals and groups who are engaged in the purchasing process, will develop particular relationships – which are often influential in the buying decision – with other internal and external groups who are in the 'purchasing chain'. Understanding, or cultivating these rela-tionships, can be a valuable way for a supplier to increase a target purchaser's propensity to buy.

4 *General environmental influences*: As was the case for consumer buyers, all industrial buyers are influenced to some extent by the more general environmental factors considered in Part Two and reconsidered briefly below:

- *Competitive influences*: The nature of the competition will influence buying behaviour. For example, if competition is based upon technological leadership then a buying strategy which supports this could be expected.
- *Marketing influences*: Market prospects will tend to influence buying behaviour. For example, if the market for a product is expected to decline then this will be translated into decreased demand from suppliers and a heightening of pressure on suppliers.
- *Economic influences*: The general state of the economy will influence buying confidence and the propensity to buy.
- *Legal/government influences*: Government policies and legislation can fundamentally affect buying practices. For example, subsidies on the purchase of fixed assets will often substantially affect the price of production equipment.
- *Technological influences*: The influence of technological progress may be a significant spur to increasing the rate of scrapping and new investment.
- *Geographical influences*: The new mobility of the factors of production has, for many industries, invalidated traditional models of international trade and caused suppliers to be conscious of how multinational buyers may switch sources on a global basis.
- *Social influences*: Prevailing social attitudes can influence industrial buying in areas such as buying from political regimes which have, in Western society, socially unacceptable work practices.
- *Other influences*: This category includes influences not captured by any of the above.

The industrial buying process
There is no single or standard industrial buying process. Instead, there is a continuum of complexity which, although like the consumer buying process is a function of the importance of the purchase is also, additionally determined by the nature of the organization. This additional dimension of complexity is imposed by the size and structure of the organization on whose behalf the buying is carried out and is generally directly related to size and degree of centralization.

The industrial buying process can be divided into stages similar to those shown in Figure 45 and described below.

1 *Need:* At this stage an individual, or a group of individuals within the organization, perceives a need for the product or service. This need could be for a product or service necessary for the continued running of the business – say the purchase of fuel, or for its development – say the installation of a new market research information system and it could be generated as a result of internal stimuli, external stimuli, or both.
2 *Communication of the need*: In organizations which have a relative-

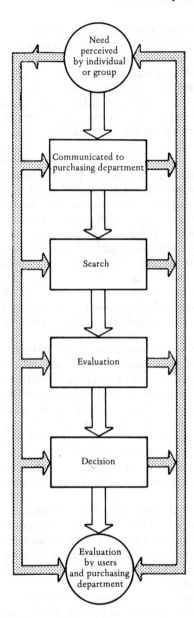

Figure 45 *Stages in the industrial buying process*

ly simple structure the buying process will be undertaken, largely, by the individual or group which is experiencing the need. In this situation the buying process is similar to the consumer buying process. However, in more complex organizations it is normal for the need to be communicated to a purchasing department which will then be responsible for all the other stages in the buying process. The purchasing department confers a significant difference on the industrial buying process – the process is more complex because those experiencing the need must communicate it to a third party which will purchase on their behalf; and second the purchasing department will have professional, experienced buyers whose primary task is to buy to satisfy their organization's goals. Although in this model of the purchasing process it is assumed that the purchasing department is the sole agency within the organization responsible for all stages in the buying process (apart from initiation of the purchase), in practice it will often be the case that many other individuals and departments (the originators of the need, the end users, and senior personnel) will participate actively and be influential in all the stages of the buying process.

3   *Search:*   At this stage the purchasing department will solicit proposals from alternative suppliers and search for the optimal methods of fulfilling the need. This will normally involve searching for competing products or services, trying to find substitutes and reducing the degree of uncertainty. The extensiveness of the search is a function of the complexity, importance and frequency of the proposed purchase.

4   *Evaluation:*   When the purchasing department has completed the search for information about the product or service and rivals, then the various alternatives will be evaluated. Again, the complexity and importance of the purchase will help influence the extent to which influence groups will impinge upon the decision.

5   *Decision*:   When the evaluation of the alternatives has been completed then the purchasing department will decide upon, and then purchase, a particular product or service. The product purchased will be the one which most closely accords with the organization's purchasing policies and the judgement of the purchasing department.

6   *Evaluation*:   After the purchase has been made, delivered to the user and used, then it is normal for it to be evaluated by both the user and the purchasing department. The nature of organizational evaluation tends to be different from that of consumer evaluation – it is often much more objective, rigorous and formal and may involve a performance review.

7   *The purchase procedures*:   Consumer buyers tend to appraise the cost of potential purchases on the basis of a, usually informal, consideration of price. In industrial buying the pricing of goods and services is often much more complex through the use of devices such as written quotation, written tenders and legal purchase contracts which may include performance specifications. Additionally, unlike consumer purchases where payment is usually in the form of cash or credit, the payment may be in the form of leasing or some form of barter.

8 *The sizes of purchases*: Purchases by organizations tend to be on a much larger scale than consumer purchases by individuals. This scale effect reflects the relative size of commercial operations and their relative concentration, i.e. in most industries there is a 'Pareto effect' so that small numbers of companies produce most of the output.

Conclusion on buyer behaviour

Understanding the process by which a buyer of an organization's products or services, whether a consumer or an industrial buyer, is a crucial element in the marketing process – if an organization does not understand the process then it is unlikely that any organization will be able to consistently respond to consumers' needs and wishes.

The pervasiveness of marketing

Although the importance and influence of marketing is usually seen most clearly in the context of consumer goods, in most industrialized Western societies it is becoming a progressively wider and more pervasive influence which is being experienced increasingly in the industrial, non-profit seeking and service sectors of society. How marketing affects each of these sectors is now discussed.

Marketing in the industrial sector

Perhaps the most objective and comprehensive evidence of the power of marketing as a strategic lever is provided by the PIMS studies, some findings of which are summarized below.

History of the project

One of the ways in which the Japanese developed their expertise in marketing was through the study and the subsequent implementation of the marketing practices of leading large US companies. The relative importance accorded to the marketing function can be seen, in general, from the business practices in larger US corporations. One corporation in particular, General Electric (GE) has researched the area deeply and some of its better known contributions are considered below.

In 1960 GE set up a research project to investigate, on behalf of its various SBUs, the relationship between market share and operating economies; the factors that determine ROI; and methods of strategically managing GE's diverse set of SBUs. This research project was based upon the premise that if sufficient hard quantitative information about the operations of its SBUs could be gathered then the analysis of this data would provide the 'laws of the marketplace' which would be a guide to strategic planning and, in the process, reduce the subjectivity of strategic planning and help turn it into an applied science. After several years, GE had developed a comprehensive computerized data base and through analysis of this data, had built quantitative cross-sectional models for its strategic planning.

In 1972 the project was established at the Marketing Science Institute, in Cambridge, Massachusetts and the scope of the data base was widened to include businesses other than GE's. Additionally the staff were expanded to include academics from the Harvard Business School as well as staff from GE. This enabled the original GE findings and models to be verified, tested and developed on a wider cross-section of businesses.

In 1975, in order to change its orientation from that of an academic research centre to that of an operating entity, the Institute was restructured and renamed. It was named the Strategic Planning Institute (SPI) and the major programme and set of research studies which SPI now manages is called the PIMS programme. PIMS stands for the Profit Impact of Market Strategy.

Today SPI is a non-profit making, autonomous corporation governed by its member companies. In 1985 PIMS had over 300 member corporations, mainly from the USA and Europe, and had data on over 3000 business units. Each business unit had 200 items of information for a minimum period of five years. This makes the PIMS data base the largest and most comprehensive data base ever assembled.

The main objectives of the PIMS programme include the following:

- To have an up-to-date data base of its member companies which accurately reflects their business experiences.
- Through analyses of the data base to discover the 'laws of the marketplace'.
- To make the research findings available to member companies.
- To help member companies in their strategic planning through consultancy and the provision of advice based on findings from the research into the data base.

How PIMS operates is illustrated in Figure 46.[4]

The major publicly available findings of the PIMS programme are the *Reports on the General Principles of Business Strategy* and of these reports perhaps the best known is the *Nine Basic Finding on Business Strategy*.[5] Some of the more important elements of this report are summarized below.

Finding I: Business situations generally behave in a regular and predictable manner
This asserts that the operating results achieved by any business are determined by the 'laws of the marketplace' and that therefore it is

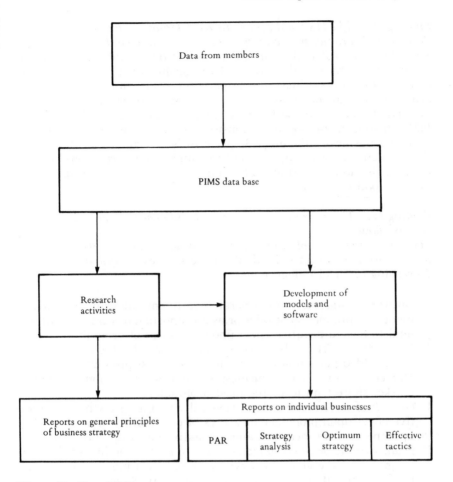

Figure 46 *How PIMS operates*

possible for a strategist to make accurate estimates of the future performance of individual businesses if he understands and takes account of 'the laws of the marketplace' (as determined empirically through the PIMS data base)

Finding II: All business situations are basically alike in obeying the laws of the marketplace
This suggests that individual businesses will tend to behave in the same way in similar business circumstances and therefore a trained strategist should be able to operate equally effectively in any business in any industry as it is the characteristics of the marketplace that largely determine the performance of a business and not its particular products or services.

Finding III: The laws of the marketplace determine about 80 per cent of the observed variance in operating results across different businesses
This claims that it is the particular competitive circumstances i.e. the nature of the market, the nature of the business itself and the nature of the competitors – that are 80 per cent responsible for the results achieved by any business. This implies that management is a less important influence on performance than is often believed. According to PIMS, management is only responsible for 20 per cent of the performance of a business – the other 80 per cent is determined by the laws of the marketplace. An implication of this finding for career development is that it is more important to be in a strategically good business than to be a good manager.

Finding IV: There are nine major strategic influences on profitability and net cash flow
These nine major influences are responsible for almost 80 per cent of the performance of an individual business. These major influences, in decreasing order of influence, are:

1 *Investment intensity:* In general investment intensity (i.e. investment as a proportion of sales or as a proportion of value added) will tend to have a negative effect upon measures of profitability.
2 *Productivity:* Those businesses which have the highest levels of value added per employee tend to be the most profitable.
3 *Market position:* Those businesses which have the highest relative market share tend to be the most profitable.
4 *Growth of the served market:* Generally market growth has a positive effect upon monetary measures of profitability, a neutral effect upon percentage measures and a negative effect upon cash flow.
5 *Quality of the products and/or services offered:* The higher the level of quality of the goods or services offered by a business the higher tends to be all its measures of profitability. Indeed, quality and market share are partial substitutes for each other i.e. a business which cannot reap the profitability advantages which accrue through having a large relative market share, may alternatively reap similar advantages through pursuit of a strategy of high quality.
6 *Innovation/differentiation:* Strong efforts in the area of innovation/ differentiation tend to have a positive effect upon operating performance if the business already has a strong strategic position.
7 *Vertical integration:* Vertical integration tends to have a positive effect upon businesses which are in mature and stable markets. Otherwise it tends to have a negative effect.
8 *Cost push:* The effects of wage/salary increases and raw material increases have complex impacts and their effect is partially determined by the ability of the business to pass on the increased costs to consumers.
9 *Current strategic effort:* A change in direction of any of the above factors may often have an effect which is the opposite of what might

be expected. For example, although having a strong market share would be expected to boost profitability, the efforts needed to gain market share may have a negative effect upon profitability

Finding V: The operation of the nine major strategic influences is complex
This indicates that the major strategic influences do not always operate in the same direction, i.e. one influence may be having a positive influence on operating results while another may, simultaneously, be having a negative effect. What is important is the resulting net effect.

Finding VI: Product characteristics don't matter
This suggests that what determines the performance of a business is not the actual products of the business, but its overall strategic position. For example, it may be a mistake for a small garment manufacturer, which is a 'captive'* supplier to a large retail multiple, to compare its strategic position and performance with that of a large 'independent' garment manufacturer. Their products may be similar and they may be in the same industry, but the strategic fundamentals of their businesses are very different. It may be much more appropriate for the small garment manufacturer to compare its position with a small 'captive' supplier of prepared foods to a large retail multiple. Although the products may be different, the 'fundamentals' are similar.

Finding VII: The expected impacts of strategic business characteristics tend to assert themselves over time
This asserts that when a change in the fundamental characteristics of a business takes place – for example if it becomes more investment intensive through the purchase of relatively large amounts of plant and equipment – then its operating results would be expected to move towards the expected norm for this set of strategic circumstances. A second aspect of this finding is that if the performance of a business deviates from the expected performance norm for the particular set of strategic circumstances in which the business lies, then, over time, the performance will move back towards the expected norm.

Finding VIII: Business strategies are successful if their 'fundamentals' are good, unsuccessful if they are unsound
For success, a strategy must accord with the fundamental laws of the marketplace.

Finding IX: Most clear strategy signals are robust
This implies that moderate errors in assessing how well a strategy is working don't invalidate the signal.

---

* A captive supplier is considered to be one who is (a) extremely small in relation to the purchaser and (b) relies so strongly on purchases from a single purchaser that the business would be in jeopardy should the purchaser cease to be a customer.

Conclusions on the PIMS studies
Although there have been considerable criticisms of the PIMS studies
(see Anderson and Paine[6] and Lubatkin and Pitts[7]) they have made, and
continue to make, a fundamental contribution to strategic thinking and
planning. The data base is, after all, the largest and most comprehensive data base ever assembled and it seems rational to base theories of
strategic management upon empirical analyses of this vast pool of
information. Additionally the PIMS studies have helped planners focus
on the importance of the market (and hence the marketing function) as
the fundamental determinant of ultimate success or failure.

Marketing and non-profit making organizations

Increasingly, government and other non-profit making organizations
are employing marketing techniques which, traditionally, have been
regarded as business tools reserved primarily for the profit making
sector of society. Table 33 shows that in 1984 in the UK, HM Government had, in fact, the fourth highest level of expenditure on advertising.
(In 1982 it was ranked fifth.)

Table 34 shows a selection of non-profit making organizations which
engage in marketing and lists typical issues which their campaigns seek
to promote.

Although many reasons have been advocated for the above types of
institutions increasing their commitment to marketing (see Riley[9] and
Kotler[10]) the following appear to be among the major stimulants.

Failure to satisfy stakeholders
In many of the above institutions the public is the major stakeholder –
it is both the owner of the institution and also the recipient of its
services – and there appears to be evidence (see Windle[11]) to suggest
that the public is, in many cases, being disappointed on both counts.

Table 33   Top holding companies' advertising expenditure 1984[8]

Rank	Holding company
1	Unilever
2	Mars
3	Procter and Gamble
4	HM Government
5	Allied Lyons
6	Imperial Group
7	British Telecom
8	Cadbury Schweppes
9	Nestle
10	Rowntree Mackintosh

Table 34 Non-profit making organizations who engage in marketing

Type of institution	Topic and typical issues
Central government:	*Health:* Information on health services, the importance of healthy living, how to cope with emergencies *National security:* The role of national security, recruitment *Unemployment:* Schemes to reduce it *Social security:* How to claim benefits and how to assess entitlement *Education:* Promoting education, alternative education routes and information about availability *Safety:* Promoting safety consciousness at home, in public and at work *Energy:* Conservation, acceptability of nuclear power *Industrial development:* Promoting inward investment, promoting exports
Local government:	As for central government with a local orientation, for example, promoting the use of: local leisure centres; local transport systems; local welfare schemes; community help, etc.
Other users: hospitals, trade unions, political parties, charities, clubs, societies, universities, colleges, schools, professional associations, churches	Various campaigns to promote the use of their services

Thus, from an ownership perspective the public (often as represented through government) has been expressing concern about the 'value for money' that many of the non-profit making institutions are providing. In a complementary fashion, from a consumer perspective, the public, as recipients of the services, have increasingly questioned the quality of the services provided by non-profit making organizations. These dual pressures have caused the decision makers in such organizations to justify, often with the aid of marketing, their activities.

Failure to achieve objectives
Although it is normally the case that non-profit making organizations have a wider, and less quantifiable set of objectives than profit making organizations the former are coming under increasing pressure to meet specified quantitative objectives. For example, a crucial quantitative objective in the university sector is meeting certain staff–student ratios (i.e. a ratio obtained by dividing the number of full-time equivalent students in a university by the number of full-time equivalent staff in

the university). It is argued that failure to achieve specified staff student ratios adversely reflects upon the efficiency of the university. Consequently, in order to improve their staff student ratios, many universities have engaged in marketing campaigns to *attract* students. This marketing orientation can be seen particularly clearly in the contrast between the slick student prospectuses which many universities produce today and those which were produced in the student-bountiful days of the 1960s.

General increase in environmental uncertainty
The general increase in the level of environmental uncertainty prevailing today which has been postulated by Ansoff[12] tends to heighten most organizations' feelings of uncertainty about their future directions or indeed their continuing existence. Such feelings may cause organizations to become more aware of the needs and wishes of those who consume their services so that they can respond most effectively. Such a predisposition tends to cause organizations to develop their marketing orientations.

Increase in the speed of environmental change
Similarly the increasing speed of environmental change which Ansoff has postulated is now occurring may be causing organizations to lag behind and therefore be less synchronized with their users' needs and requirements. A marketing orientation can help reduce such lags.

Increased levels of competition for services
In today's environment of increased competitiveness and deregulation (described on pages 245-6) organizations which are funded by state resources no longer have the same guarantee of continuing support if they fail to provide services which satisfy their consumers or their paymasters. For example, in the UK the trend towards the privatization of hospital services reflects partly an ideological commitment by government to privatization and also a belief by government that the most effective stimulus for the improvement of services and maximizing value for money is that of the threat of competition.

Marketing is effective
For many non-profit making organizations, marketing may be seen as the most effective, or indeed, the only means of achieving their objectives. For example, charities, which compete with each other for limited amounts of money must be effective in their marketing if they are to generate the funds which they need to implement their objectives. Similarly, health programmes which have a preventative objective (for example programmes to prevent the spread of Aids) will often be most effective and efficient if they proactively use marketing to promote their objectives rather than relying upon passive compliance by target groups.

The marketing process for non-profit making organizations

The marketing process for non-profit making organizations could be described as that process through which the organization achieves its goals through adapting its services and/or products to the needs and wishes of its consumers and although it is, in most respects, similar to that employed by profit making organizations, there tends to be one major difference – the goals of non-profit making organizations tend to be somewhat dissimilar to the goals of profit-seeking organizations, and consequently the criteria by which the effectiveness of marketing is assessed also differs.

In most profit-seeking organizations goals tend to be couched in hard, financial, easily measurable terms such as: achieving target levels of sales; achieving target levels of profits; achieving target levels of earnings per share etc. In contrast the goals which obtain in non-profit making organizations tend to be more diffuse and less amenable to quantification. For example, an urban leisure centre could have as its goals:

- Improving the health of the community.
- Heightening community awareness of the importance between sport and health.
- Acting as a social centre for the community.
- Providing leisure services for the disadvantaged.
- Furthering the careers of sportspeople of outstanding ability.
- Maximizing the numbers of users of the centre.
- Maximizing the revenue of the centre
- Providing as wide a range of leisure services as possible.
- Minimizing the costs of running the centre.

By definition, many of these goals are incompatible and, in addition, a number of them cannot be measured precisely. Such a diffusion of goals can complicate the marketing process and make the assessment of the success of a non-profit making organization's marketing strategies difficult.

However, bearing in mind the above complications, the marketing process for non-profit making organizations can follow the same stages advocated for profit-seeking organizations set out on pages 248 to 309.

Conclusions to Part Six

The objective of Part Six was to provide the complementary marketing orientation which is necessary for effective strategic management. As was indicated above, today it is increasingly important for all organizations – in the private sector, the public sector, the manufacturing sector and the service sector – to have a knowledge of the marketing process which will enable them, first, to understand those external marketing-related forces in the environment and, second, to develop and implement strategies which will enable their organizations to achieve their goals.

References

1   Kotler, P., *Principles of Marketing*, Prentice-Hall, Englewood Cliffs, 1980.
2   Bluell, V. P., *Marketing Management: A Strategic Planning Approach*, McGraw-Hill, 1985.
3   McCarthy, E. J., *Basic Marketing: A Managerial Approach*, R. D. Irwin, Homewood, Ill., 1971.
4   The PIMS Program, Planning Institute, Cambridge, Mass.
5   Schoeffler, S., 'The Nine Basic Findings of Business Strategy', *PIMSletter*, No. 1, 1980.
6   Anderson, C. and Paine, F. 'PIMS: A Re-examination', *Academy of Management Review*, July 1978, pp. 602–12.
7   Lubatkin, M. and Pitts, M., 'PIMS: Fact or Folklore?', *Journal of Business Strategy*, Vol. 30, No. 5, May/June 1978, pp. 3–20.
8   The Advertising Association, *Marketing Pocket Book*, 1985.
9   Riley, B. 'The Marketing Men Flex their Muscles', *Financial Times*, 25 November 1985, p. 38.
10 Kotler, P., *Marketing for Non-profit Organizations*, Prentice-Hall, Englewood Cliffs, 1975.
11 Windle, R., *The Public Good*, Market Research Society Survey, Spring 1988, pp. 26–7.
12 Ansoff, I., *Strategic Management*, Macmillan 1979.

Part Seven

14 An overview of implementation

Although for effective strategic management implementation is essential, it isn't easy. Frequently there can exist an unbridgeable gap between a strategic aspiration (the strategy) and its fulfilment (the implementation). Thus although the UK automobile manufacturer Austin Rover has often *formulated* apparently winning strategies, it has yet to successfully *implement* them.

By way of contrast, a strategy that, in 1986, was widely agreed to have been implemented successfully was that devised by Robb Wilmot for the rejuvenation of the UK computer company ICL. The success of Wilmot's strategy which was a reorientation of the company from that of a 'technology led broad range computer manufacturer' to that of a 'marketing-led specialist manufacturer' was due, first, to having a strategy that was appropriate to the company and the environment which it faced and, second, to having a commitment to effective implementation. The latter being a long, expensive, and arduous task:

> ICL's struggle to create a competitive organisation has been far from easy. As well as requiring charismatic leadership and vision, it has involved considerable frustration and strain for everyone involved. The inner workings of a company undergoing radical change are seldom smooth ...
> ... ICL's own outlay has certainly been heavy. Between mid-1983 and the end of 1984 it spent £3m a full 10 per cent of its then measly profits. One of the largest items was an intensive 'mind-shift' programme for the company's top 200 managers. After the initial hump of education and training, ICL's annual spend has now settled down at just under £1m.[1]

In the model of strategic management used in this book implementation is defined as the process through which the aspirations of the fundamental/generic strategy developed in Part Five are transformed into operating realities i.e. where strategy goals are transformed into operational functional targets and where long-run strategies are refined into day-to-day procedures.

Although in the implementation of a strategy the focus will be within the organization the emphasis will be on ensuring that there is congruence between the strategy and the goals, leadership, culture, functional policies, resources and structure of the organization – a broad cognisance of the external environment should always be present to ensure that the strategy being implemented retains its original external validity.

The effective implementation of any strategy poses a fundamental dilemma for strategic planners – it requires the accommodation, in the organization, of two fundamentally opposing forces: those leading to organizational integration and those leading to organizational segmentation.

Thus, implementation is usually most effective if, somehow, the strategy can be communicated throughout the organization so that at all levels and in all departments:

- There is a clear recognition of what the strategy actually is.
- Each department understands the role that it ought to play in implementing the strategy.
- There is consensus at all levels, and in all departments, about the wisdom of pursuing the strategy and this consensus is reflected in an organization-wide unity of purpose.

Clearly this type of organization-wide commitment is most likely to occur if the process of implementation attempts to integrate the work of the organization at all levels and in all departments.

On the other hand, for effective implementation it is usually necessary to disaggregate a fundamental strategy into relatively small and simple constituent elements so that departments, especially those at the lowest levels in the organizational hierarchy, have clear operating targets to which they can relate. When, as part of the strategy implementation process, each department is asked to meet precise operating targets, or budgets, with the criterion of 'success' being 'meeting the targets', this will predispose each department to view itself as separate and unique. Thus, in the strategy implementation process there are likely to be 'departmental forces' which will tend to have a segmenting influence.

Therefore, it is suggested that effective implementation requires, on the part of planners, a recognition of this 'integration–segmentation' dilemma and subsequent provision for the fruitful accommodation of these, frequently opposing, forces. This provision can be effected through sensitive communication (which recognizes the aspirations and triggers of motivation of each level and department) of the strategy and sensible use of the organization power structure.

The process of implementation is multidimensional and complex. Figure 47 provides a flowchart which shows it in skeleton form. In

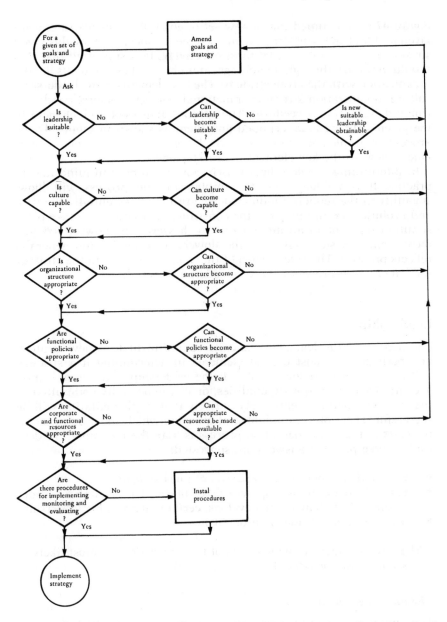

Figure 47 *A flowchart showing schematically how a strategy may be implemented*

Figure 47 it is assumed that a new set of goals and a new strategy are given and that the only strategic management concern is how this given strategy can be implemented most effectively. It is suggested that this should be done through matching a number of key elements in the organization with the given strategy. The key elements being leadership, culture, organization structure, functional policies, resources and control and evaluation procedures. The appropriateness of each element to the given strategy is ascertained and then, as shown in Figure 47 the process of implementation proceeds largely as planned or there is amendment to the key element or the strategy.

In interpreting the flowchart it is important to bear in mind that in practice it is unlikely that the implementation process will 'flow' smoothly in the sequence indicated. The process is essentially iterative and evolutionary and many of the constituent activities may take place simultaneously or in a different order – however the flow of 'key elements' and decisions given in the flowchart is logical and generally reflects practice. The role of each of these 'key elements' in the strategy implementation process is now considered in detail.

Leadership

The quality of the leadership and its commitment to a new strategy are, perhaps, the most crucial elements in determining if a strategy will be implemented successfully. If the leadership of an organization does not have the requisite qualities, or if it is not fully committed to the strategy, then it is extremely unlikely that implementation will be successful. Therefore, a fundamental question which must be raised at the start of the implementation process is 'Can the incumbent leader* lead?' Three possible answers are suggested:

- 'Yes', and the incumbent leader continues as leader.
- 'Yes, if leadership development takes place.' The incumbent leader continues but changes, or develops, certain facets of his leadership.
- 'No', and a new leader is brought in.

The circumstances in which each of these situations is most likely to prevail are now considered in greater detail.

The incumbent leader continues

This situation is most likely to occur if the incumbent leader is regarded by key personnel and external stakeholders as having successfully led the organization in the past and the new strategy is not a major break

---

* Although the term 'leader' is used it should be taken to mean either an individual leader or the group of top people which is regarded, collectively, as the leadership of an organization.

with the past. For example, if the new strategy is a continuation of a past successful strategy of conservative growth in similar markets with similar products then it is likely that the incumbent will continue as leader. In such circumstances the leader, because of past success, should enjoy cultural support from the organization, have the approval of external stakeholders and should have in place power structures which also support him. In this situation there is no need for a new leader and furthermore it is likely that there would be considerable internal and external opposition to such a change.

The incumbent leader continues with leadership development

This situation is most likely to occur if the incumbent leader is regarded by key personnel and external stakeholders as having led the organization successfully in the past but the new strategy is a major break with the past. When such strategic discontinuity occurs, even though there may be general internal and external respect for the incumbent's past achievements, there may also be a questioning of his power to implement the new strategy. When this occurs it may be possible for the leader to develop his claim to continued leadership through the development in himself of those skills considered necessary to implement the new strategy, or by expanding the leadership through recruiting to it additional personnel who possess the required attributes. When there is doubt about an incumbent's future potential as the leader this doubt will frequently pivot around the following issues:

Intellectual knowledge and skills
If the new strategy requires a set of intellectual knowledge or skills which is fundamentally different from the set required in the past this may cause doubts to arise about the leadership. For example, should an organization decide to diversify, on a relatively large scale, either through acquisition or organically, into an unrelated technology, then there may be a questioning of the incumbent's ability to provide the required technical leadership in this new area.

Vision
One aspect of the intellectual skills or knowledge that is perhaps worthy of special mention is that of vision. For effective implementation it is often necessary for the leader to have the width and depth of vision, first, to see the strategic challenges facing the organization in a distinctive and informed light and, second, (and often simultaneously) to be able to see and attend to the small details throughout the organization which must be considered if implementation is to be effective.

Japanese companies are extremely adroit at strategy development and implementation and on aspect of their management development practice which contributes significantly to their powers of vision in implementation is their use of job rotation. Thus, in contrast to the usual practice in Western companies, many large Japanese companies, in their management development process, place great emphasis on developing managers who are generalists and have skills in all the functional areas rather than specialists with the bulk of their skills in just one area. Top Japanese managers develop this broad view of management by having management career structures which are characterized by job rotation, i.e. typically, when a new manager enters such a Japanese organization he will spend a number of years in, say, production, then he will move to, say, marketing, then he will move to, say, finance etc. A consequence of this job rotation is that when such a manager has reached a senior level he has a balanced knowledge of all the functional areas of management which contributes to his width of vision in strategic decision making and implementation.

Behavioural or attitudinal skills

If the new strategy requires a different behavioural attitude from the leader this may cause problems for the incumbent. For example, if in the past an organization has always had a production/engineering orientation – i.e. good knowledge of, and enthusiasm for, excellence in engineering has been synonymous with good leadership – and it proposes a new strategy in which the organization's orientation shifts towards marketing, then there may be a questioning about whether the incumbent can develop the necessary behavioural perspectives and attitudes to implement this new orientation.

Related to this behavioural aspect of implementation are features of leadership such as style and attitudes. For example, a leader who has, during his tenure, led in an autocratic fashion may find himself unable to change sufficiently, if a strategy requiring a consensual style of leadership, is adopted. Similarly a leader who has led his organization through a strategy of continuous aggressive growth may find it difficult to feel committed to a new strategy of conservative growth.

Finally, it is not unusual to find that a leader who has been instrumental in inventing or developing a successful product, may in the process, have developed such an emotional attachment to it that it prevents him from taking a wider and more commercially rational view of the product's potential and the appropriate strategies for its commercial development.

Thus, in a series of articles in the *Financial Times* in 1986 on successes and failures in British technology, Marsh[2] found that, generally, those companies which had been started by entrepreneurial engineers and had successfully developed into high growth successful manufacturers had, in the process of their development, added to the initial founding leadership with non-technical experts.

In every case, the engineers who started the (successful) companies are still firmly in control. They have, however, recruited into key positions specialist managers, for instance with marketing skills, to supply non-technicial expertise not possessed by the founders.

In contrast to the successful companies, those which failed to make the transition from small entrepreneurial companies to larger commercial successes often failed, not because of the quality of their products, but because the founders were engineers who, although they had strong emotional attachment to the products which they had developed, did not possess that wider vision of the commercial considerations necessary for success.

The age of the leader

When the age of the leader is considered to be a problem it is usually of the form that the incumbent is considered to be too old for the arduous tasks of implementation. This is not always so. This type of problem tends to occur very often in family owned and run businesses where the leader 'father or grandfather' is unwilling to 'surrender' the leadership to a later generation. It may also be the case that a relatively youthful incumbent may be inappropriate because his goals, interests or ambitions are inappropriate to the strategy or he does not have the experience for effective implementation.

In all the above situations, it is postulated that whether the incumbent continues as leader or ought to be replaced depends upon whether the leader has the necessary attributes or is capable of developing them. If these attributes are present, or will be developed, then he should continue, if not he should be removed. In practice, however, this may not be the case. Even though, on the basis of rational economic arguments, a leader ought to be replaced, frequently this does not happen for a variety of reasons which may include the following: the leader has erected a power structure around himself which enables him to prevent his removal; there is a cultural impediment to leadership change – if the incumbent has been a leader for a considerable time it conditions others to regard him as the leader irrespective of his suitability; there are no other suitable potential leaders available; or the rewards for leadership are not sufficient.

A new leader is brought in

There are two main circumstances under which a new leader is brought in. The first is when the existing leader departs voluntarily, a new leader takes over, and there is no major strategic or operational change. In this situation the new leadership is new largely in name only and the organizational effects of the change tend to be relatively minor. Of course a 'voluntary' departure does not always mean a willing departure. For example, when in a family firm, the leader, it is generally agreed, is at the retirement stage, it is not always the case that he will retire without protest. Similarly when an organization has been achieving results which are not entirely satisfactory (but are still not severely damaging to the organization) a power struggle will often be necessary in order to remove such a leader.

The second circumstance occurs when, as detailed in Chapter 5, the organization faces a crisis which is so severe that its existence is threatened. In this situation often the existing leader is forcibly removed and a new leader, who can come from within or outside the organization is installed.

Motivation to implement

In the above consideration of the role of leadership in implementation it was assumed throughout that the leader actually did wish to implement the strategy. For various reasons this may not always be so. Thus leaders may be unenthusiastic about implementing a given strategy for a number of reasons including:

- They disagree with the corporate wisdom of pursuing a strategy, i.e. they feel that wholehearted pursuit of the strategy is not in the best interests of the organization or their SBU.
- They feel that they do not receive adequate compensation for the additional tasks which implementation is going to impose.
- They feel that successful implementation will be a threat to their future.
- They feel they do not have the skills or resources to implement the strategy.
- They feel that the benefits of implementation will accrue to others and not themselves.
- They feel that they do not have the energy needed to implement the strategy.

Therefore, in the implementation stage it is important for planners to be aware of these potential motivational impediments to implementation and to have means of reducing them.

Culture

Because the culture of an organization is not usually stated explicitly in the way that, say, its organizational structure is, it may appear that it is not an important consideration in the implementation stage of a strategy. This is not so. When the details of how a strategy will be implemented are being considered there should be a recognition that its ultimate success will be related to the degree of cultural acceptance and support which it receives in the organization. It is postulated here that the problem of achieving congruence between a proposed strategy and the culture of an organization is directly related to the magnitude and the speed of the proposed strategic change. For the purposes of assessing the cultural aspects of implementation strategic change can be divided into two main types – minor strategic change and major strategic change.

Minor strategic change

When the new strategy is a minor break with the past – for example a quantitative adjustment in goals, or relatively minor additions or deletions to products and markets or other relatively minor functional adjustments – then it is likely that the implementation of such a strategy will not encounter strong cultural problems. Normally, the existing leadership and the existing power groups in the organization will see the new strategy as confirmation of the correctness of their approach in the past will not feel threatened by it, and the existing status quo will be likely to continue. Additionally, people at all levels in the organization will tend to feel 'comfortable' with the new strategy, as they will be familiar with similar operations in the past and, generally, will believe that the success attendant upon the past will continue in the future.

Major strategic change

However, when the new strategy is a major break with past strategies, attempts to implement it (irrespective of how worthwhile it is) may encounter severe cultural resistance. As has already been discussed, when the major change in strategy has been provoked by a severe crisis then cultural resistance to the change may be minimal as the disparate interest groups submerge their cultural and political differences and unite in the common fight for survival.

However, when the strategic change is a major break with the past, and, when the organization is not perceived by its various interest groups to be in crisis, then the implementation of this type of strategy may encounter severe cultural and behavioural impediments. This resistance to strategic change will be especially strong if the change is to be implemented rapidly and there is little time for adjustment. The most commonly found major sources of this resistance are as follows:

Natural resistance
In many organizations there prevails an organization-wide view that those strategies and practices which have worked in the past will continue to work in the future – in other words there is a natural disinclination to change which must be overcome. This disinclination to change, which Ansoff[3] calls 'systemic social inertia', is not a fault or an organizational vice, rather, it is a natural phenomenon and in planning how a strategy should be implemented, provision should be made for it.

Cultural resistance
Normally major strategic change will threaten existing power relationships and preferences and those groups who are most threatened by the proposed strategic changes will tend to resist them most fiercely. This resistance can occur at many levels: organization-wide, hierarchical, or departmental.

1 *Organization-wide resistance:* This may occur when there is general agreement within the organization about the overall strategic direction that it has been taking and the proposed new strategy is at variance with this. This type of situation could arise, when an SBU is required by corporate headquarters to change strategy. For example, if an SBU which had, historically, pursued a strategy of high growth was then required by corporate headquarters to pursue a strategy of consolidation or reduction of its assets, it is likely that there would be strong cultural resistance throughout the SBU to this new, and previously unthinkable, strategy.

2 *Hierarchical resistance:* Hierarchical resistance may occur when the implementation of the new strategy involves a change in the status, or the power, or the influence strength, of the different levels in the hierarchy. For example, if a new strategy requires an organization-wide commitment to quality improvement and in order to achieve this there must be a general development of the communication links between management and 'the shop floor' and if, as part of the implementation process, it is proposed that shop floor and management have common dining and washroom facilities then there may be managerial resistance to such a move as management may see this as an erosion of its status.

3 *Departmental resistance:* Frequently the implementation of major strategic change will involve a change in interdepartmental power relationships. This type of change is likely to be resisted by those departments who perceive their power to be diminished. For example, it is often the case (see Murray[4]) that potentially successful businesses develop difficulties during periods of rapid growth because minimal attention is given to financial control. When, in order to return such organizations to health, there is a major strategic change of direction, which often involves the appointment of additional financial staff to senior positions and the imposition of stringent financial controls, it is not unusual to find that such actions are strongly opposed by personnel in the marketing function.

Developing cultural change

Ansoff has linked types of strategic change to the anticipated cultural and political impact within an organization. As Table 35 shows, those strategies which are the most politically threatening are likely to generate the greatest resistance while those which are most politically welcome are likely to generate the greatest degree of acceptance.

As can be seen from Table 35, the degree of cultural change necessary for effective implementation of a strategy is a function of the magnitude and speed of the strategic change from the past. Although there are no proven procedures for developing cultural change, there are certain activities which have been found (see McGregor[5], Sather[6] and Wilkins[7]) to have helped the process. Baker[8] has suggested that among the more important stimuli are the following:

Table 35 Relation of social inertia to power and culture

	Politically threatening	Politically neutral	Politically welcome
Change in culture	Greatest resistance	Depends on size of cultural change	Depends on size of cultural change
Culturally acceptable	Depends on size of threat	Least resistance	Positive reinforcement

Role modelling by leaders

When the leadership of an organization requires a change in cultural attitudes it is important that they themselves reflect this change. For example, if the strategy calls for financial restraint, this restraint should be seen in the behaviour of the leaders.

Positive reinforcement

There should be positive reinforcement of those individuals, and those departments in the organization which are perceived to be adopting the new strategy and its new culture. The most potent method of reinforcement being the allocation of resources, i.e. those departments which are most successfully following the new strategy receive the greatest rewards.

Negative reinforcement

In contrast to using positive reinforcement as an agent to promote cultural change negative reinforcement may be used. In this situation the stimulus to change is the threat of the consequences of not changing. It should be pointed out, however, that the use of this approach tends to develop a much lower level of commitment than the positive reinforcement approach and also for this approach to be feasible there must be a power structure in existence which is actually capable of enforcing it.

Promotion

Linked to the lever of positive reinforcement is that of promotion, i.e. change can be effected through ensuring that those individuals who are displaying the desired cultural attributes are promoted most rapidly and their influence extended.

Communication

Effective communication, both explicit and implicit, is essential for cultural change. The explicit communication can take the form of verbal and written directives, targets, budgets, etc. The more subtle, implicit communication can take many forms and is displayed through the actions, rather than just the words, of the leaders. For example, a directive from the managing director, emphasizing the importance of good organization-wide communication, issued through his remote office by an assistant will probably have less effect than if the managing director were to meet with personnel at all levels to discuss how communication could be enhanced.

Recruitment
Careful recruitment of new staff, who have the attributes necessary for the implementation of the new strategy can be an effective method of effecting cultural change. Indeed, in some cases it may be the only way.

Organizational design
The organizational structure and the organizational practices can have significant cultural effects. For example, in a company which has a pyramidal hierarchical structure within which all important decisions can be, and are, scrutinized by the top management, it is unlikely that individual flair and risk-taking will flourish in such a structure.

Physical design
The physical design and layout of an organization can have cultural effects. This can be seen in the case of one of the UK's most successful companies – JCB, the excavator manufacturing company. Under the guidance of its chairman, J. Bamford, this company has very open offices, populated in places by stuffed jungle animals. One of the reasons is to encourage a culture of creativity.

Effecting major cultural change is never easy and may, even in the face of imminent failure, prove to be impossible to achieve. The difficulty of achieving change is well illustrated by the case of the prestigious UK luxury automobile manufacturer, Rolls-Royce Motors which suffered a bitter five week strike, for the first time in twenty-three years, in 1983.

> What struck observers most was not that the 2800 shopfloor workers downed tools for five weeks. It was the sullenness outside the factory gates and the animosity towards the company bubbling to the surface in every conversation.
> Something was very wrong in an enterprise where resentment sought such expression and where the management had conspicuously failed to carry the workforce with it during a very difficult period of the company's life ...

The major external problem facing the organization was insufficient sales:

> As a result, Rolls-Royce, a Vickers subsidiary, has been forced to take a long look at itself and try to begin the transformation into a marketing rather than production led company more willing to cut its inflated manufacturing costs, replace ineffectual pay systems, address the problem of workflow in the company's complex machine shop and modify its culture.
> Thus the old patrician flavour of management has been at least diluted. George Fenn, Perry's (chief executive) predecessor, who took early retire-

ment in 1984, was once described by George Ellis, the plant convenor, as an absolute gentleman, but was hardly ever seen on the shopfloor.

Change is coming only slowly and slower than some observers believe is necessary. But change there is.

Much of this has come as something of a culture shock. Modern workflow systems 'contradict every culture here,' says Hill (director of personnel and systems).

The whole of society is changing and we have to change with it, says Perry. Deeply entrenched and frequently acid divisions between foreman and lineworkers, who, until recently, were required to eat in separate canteens, between manual staff employees and between rather remote directors and the shop floor are being partially removed. One self-service cafeteria now replaces three levels of canteen. Shop stewards and foremen are sent off together on training courses, an unheard of approach in a once tightly stratified company.[9]

Structure

The most common types of organizational structure have already been discussed in Part One. Consequently below, only the role of structure in the implementation process is considered.

The particular structure that an organization has at any particular point in time should not be thought of as static, but rather, as something which can be changed and which evolves and develops in response to the strategic challenges that the organization faces.

If an organization has been achieving results which are considered by the stakeholders to be satisfactory and if the new strategy does not represent a major break with the past then the structural changes necessary at the implementation stage are likely to be relatively minor. If, however, the new strategy is significantly different from the past, then structural alterations may be necessary in order to achieve a strategy and a structure which are synchronized.

The relationship between strategy and structure

The first exhaustive investigation of the links between strategy and structure was published by Chandler[10] in 1972. Chandler investigated the relationship between strategy and structure in seventy large American corporations and found that the structure that an organization had was a reflection of its strategy. In other words, it tends to be the case that structure is developed as a result of strategy, i.e. structure follows strategy. If this is so, then it follows, that at the implementation stage an organization's structure should be examined to see if it is synchronized with its strategy. Although, the direction of this relationship, i.e. that structure follows strategy, is still regarded by strategists as correct, Ansoff has pointed out that in certain circumstances the reverse relationship, i.e. that strategy follows structure, may obtain. Ansoff asserted that when, as a result of environmental turbulence top management

introduced sophisticated long-range planning and environmental surveillance systems these new approaches frequently appeared threatening to managers. However, in spite of this if these new systems were
maintained long enough by top management so that lower managers
had to learn to use the system they developed a new capability to devise
new strategies. These new strategies were a result of the structure and
hence, argued Ansoff, strategy follows structure.

A clear example of the importance which is attached to effecting a
match between strategy and structure is provided by the structural
changes that were announced in the German 'vehicle manufacturer'
Daimler Benz in July 1986. Between 1984 and 1986 there was a fundamental change in the strategy of the company. During this period the
company, which had previously been engaged almost exclusively in
vehicle manufacture, rapidly diversified, through a series of major acquisitions into engines (MTU), aerospace (Dornier) and electricals (AEG)
to become West Germany's largest industrial concern. The total spent
on these acquisitions was approximately DM2.6 billion and in the process Daimler Benz changed from being a 'vehicle manufacturer' to
being a highly diversified high technology company. In order to implement its new strategies the company changed its structure. Perhaps the
most significant overt structural change was the change in the composition and responsibilities of the executive board. The previous board
comprised of nine people who had mainly functional responsibilities,
was expanded in July 1986 and the responsibilities of members changed
from a functional orientation to a product grouping orientation, i.e.
instead of having responsibility for areas such as sales, production etc.,
board members had responsibility for product groupings such as cars,
engines, aerospace. This was a significant structural change carried out
in order to implement a new strategy.

The measurement of the 'match' between strategy and structure can
be considered from two perspectives.

First, is the existing structure such that the new goals and strategies
can be achieved? For example, if an organization which manufactures
and markets consumer products which are sensitive to local tastes
decides on a new strategy of expansion outside its domestic market into
international markets and it is structured in a pyramidal fashion with
all relatively important decisions being taken at the apex of the pyra-
mid, then this type of structure may be inappropriate for the new
strategy. The new strategy may require a more decentralized structure
which passes a greater degree of control to local units so that they are
in a position to respond to local market conditions.

Second, the structure of the organization will tend to have an influence on how resources are distributed. Thus, if an organization is
structured on an SBU basis with the SBUs being determined by the
product ranges that they produce, then resources will tend to be allocated on the basis of competition among the claims of each SBU. The
pattern of resource allocation that this type of structure will generate is
likely to be substantially different from that which would arise in a
functionally structured organization.

In conclusion, there is no one structure that is best. Rather, the structure adopted should be that which will enable the organization's strategy to be implemented most successfully, will enable the organization to achieve its goals and will ensure that resources are directed to those areas which most need them, if the organization's goals are to be achieved.

References

1 Lorenz, C., 'Metamorphosis of a European Laggard', *Financial Times*, 12 May 1986, p. 18.
2 Marsh, P., 'British Technology,' a series of articles in the *Financial Times* on 9, 11 and 13 June, 1986.
3 Ansoff, H. I., *Strategic Management*, Macmillan, 1979.
4 Murray, J., 'Strategic Behaviour in the New Venture', *IBAR*, Vol. 6, No. 1, 1984.
5 McGregor, D. M., *The Human Side of the Enterprises*, McGraw-Hill, New York, 1960.
6 Sather, V., 'Implications of Corporate Culture: A Manager's Guide to Action', *Organizational Dynamics*, Autumn 1983, pp. 5–23.
7 Wilkins, A. L., 'The Culture Audit: A Tool for Understanding Organizations', *Organizational Dynamics*, Autumn 1983, pp. 24–38.
8 Baker, E. L., 'Managing Organizational Culture', *Management Review*, July 1980, pp. 9–13.
9 Garnett, A. D., 'Pulling Slowly Out of a Patrician Past', *Financial Times*, 9 June 1986, p. 20.
10 Chandler, A. D., *Strategy and Structure*, MIT Press, 1972.

15 The detail of implementation

The hierarchical nature of strategy implementation

In this book the process of implementation is assumed to take place in the context of an organization whose structure is shown schematically in Figure 48. This organization is assumed to have a holding company type of structure in which the relationships between the corporate level and the SBU level are mainly financial and there is minimal corporate control and guidance of individual SBUs. Consequently the exposition will concentrate on how strategy is implemented at the SBU and the functional levels, i.e. it will be assumed that overall corporate goals and strategies and SBU goals and strategies have been largely determined and the major concern is with the translation of the given corporate goals into effective functional operations.

The flow of the implementation process

The organization's corporate strategy is implemented in a hierarchical fashion i.e. the top level goals and strategies are progressively refined and made more operational as they are communicated throughout the company and cascade downwards through the organizational structure. The implementation process is assumed to take place at three levels – the corporate, the SBU, and the functional. The hierarchical nature and flow of the process is shown in Figure 49.

As Figure 49 shows, the top level (corporate) management set the corporate goals and strategies for the corporation as a whole – these are the parameters within which the lower levels in the hierarchy must operate. These corporate goals and strategies are then communicated to, and subsequently refined by, the top managers at the next level in the hierarchy (the SBU level) into SBU goals and strategies. These SBU goals and strategies are then communicated to, and subsequently refined by, the functional managers at the third level in the hierarchy (the functional level) into a set of functional targets and plans.

The initial set of functional targets and plans developed for the SBU is then appraised by the SBU top managers to see if it conforms to SBU

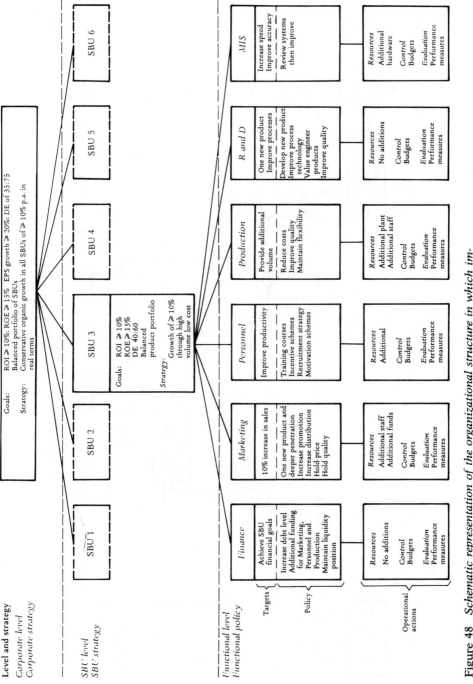

Figure 48 *Schematic representation of the organizational structure in which implementation is assumed to take place*

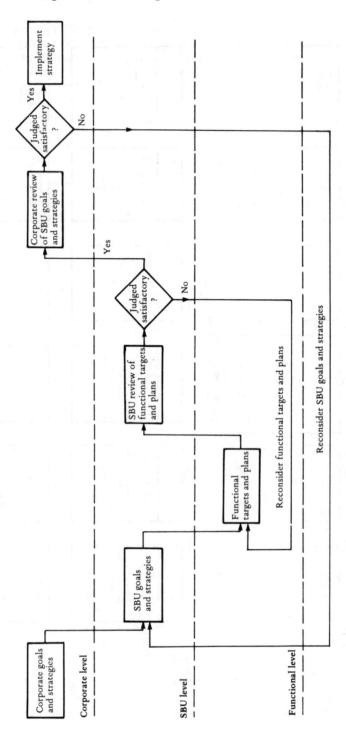

Figure 49   *The hierarchical process of strategy implementation*

goals and strategies. If the proposed functional targets and plans do not conform then they are adjusted by the functional managers and resubmitted. This process continues until an agreed congruence between functional plans and targets and SBU goals and strategies is achieved. When this has been achieved the SBU goals and strategies are then submitted to the corporate top management for approval. If these SBU goals and strategies do not meet with corporate approval they are then reviewed and amended by SBU management until agreement with corporate top management is achieved. Thus the process of planning the implementation is one of progressive refinement and adjustment in order to comply as closely a possible with corporate directives.

In spite of the differences caused by the different degrees of aggregation at each level in the organizational hierarchy, the implementation process will have the following common sequence of activities:

1 *Goals or targets* are set.
2 *Strategies or policies* are formulated which will enable the chosen goals or targets to be achieved.
3 *Projections* to see the effects of following alternative strategies are made and then the strategies which most closely meet the formulated goals are chosen.
4 *Resources are allocated* to enable the chosen strategies to be followed. (See page 349.)
5 *Control and evaluation* systems are set up to provide *feedback* so that progress in the implementation of the chosen strategies can be monitored.

Although, for the purposes of exposition the above elements in the implemention process are separated out and considered independently, in practice they all interact with, and impact upon, each other and therefore an iterative approach to implementation is necessary. Consequently the precise quantitative consequences of following alternative strategies should evolve only after projection, review, discussion and amendment of their cross impacts upon each other. This mutual dependence of the elements is portrayed graphically in Figure 50.

Implementation at the corporate level

At the top level in the hierarchy, the corporate, the goals and strategies tend to be couched in mainly financial terms and to a lesser extent in marketing terms. Typical corporate goals and strategies could include the following:

Corporate goals – financial and marketing

- Achieve a return on investment of at least 10 per cent each year.
- Achieve a return on equity of at least 15 per cent each year.

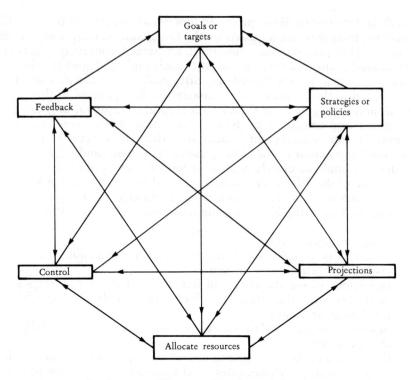

Figure 50   *How the elements of functional implementation interact*

- Achieve a growth in earnings per share of at least 15 per cent each year.
- Maintain a debt to equity ratio of 35:75.
- Achieve a growth in sales of at least 10 per cent in real terms each year.
- Continue environmental surveillance for suitable acquisitions which will strengthen the portfolio of SBUs.

Corporate goals – portfolio

Maximize the returns from the portfolio of SBUs while keeping the cash flows in balance and minimizing the risk profile of the portfolio. The corporate portfolio to be (a) augmented by acquisitions which have the potential to contribute to financial and marketing goals and (b) reduced through the disposal of those SBUs which are failing to meet corporate financial goals and show no prospect of doing so.

Corporate strategy

Conservative organic growth in sales of at least 10 per cent, in all SBUs, in real terms, for each of the next three years.

Corporate projections

At this level it is suggested that projections should be based upon consolidations of individual SBU projected income statements, cash budgets, sources and applications of funds statements, balance sheets and ratios and that the wisdom of pursuing particular strategies should be determined by measuring how well alternative consolidations meet corporate goals. If the financial results of the consolidated initial set of strategies of all the SBUs fail to meet corporate goals, then individual SBUs can be required to amend their strategies until the projected results provide an acceptable corporate portfolio of strategies. Corporate management has the ability to effect such strategic changes in its SBUs because of its power over resources.

Although corporate projections tend to be based mainly on financial data, it is important to complement such data with appropriate marketing information. This can pose considerable difficulties in larger organizations. In such organizations, because of the very large amounts of data generated, corporate planners may find it difficult to develop a clear overall view of the activities of the constituent SBUs and how they individually, and in total, contribute to corporate goals. It is suggested here that the quality of corporate perception can be greatly enhanced through the use of two-dimensional matrices of the type discussed in Part Four. Thus, when the consolidated projected income statements, cash flow statements and balance sheets are considered jointly with a related projected Product Market Portfolio Matrix or a Directional Policy Matrix (both of which relate the individual SBUs to each other and the portfolio of SBUs to their environments) then a comprehensive picture of the projected strategy can be provided which combines:

- Financial information on each SBU.
- Marketing information on each SBU.
- Financial information on the portfolio of SBUs.
- Marketing information on the portfolio of SBUs.

Resources

In this model of strategic management it is assumed that the only resource which corporate management has under its control is finance. It therefore has the task of determining which SBUs should receive additional funding, perhaps to support anticipated growth, which should be allowed to remain cash neutral (i.e. they neither contribute to corporate funds nor do they receive any) and which SBUs ought to contribute to corporate funds. These decisions can be made on the basis of the projected SBU statements outlined above plus additional SBU information on their market positions and market prospects.

In the corporate resource allocation process although in theory corporate resource allocation decisions ought to be made on the basis of quantitative assessments of the potential contributions of individual SBUs to corporate goals (the two dimensional matrices can be of considerable help in this process) in practice the judgement and experience of the top corporate management will often be of extreme importance and may override the quantitative dimensions of the decision.

Control and evaluation

Ensure that devices which will enable the finally agreed strategies to be monitored are in place. This is considered more fully in Part Eight.

Implementation at the SBU level

At this level in the hierarchy each SBU will formulate a set of goals and strategies which will enable it to comply with, or exceed, the higher level corporate goals and strategies. In this example, in order to simplify and help clarify the exposition, the set of goals and strategies for just one SBU have been made explicit. Similar sets of goals and strategies would obtain for each other SBU in the organization.

SBU goals – financial and marketing

- Achieve a return on investment of at least 10 per cent each year.
- Achieve a return on equity of at least 15 per cent each year.
- Maintain a debt to equity ratio of 30:70.
- Achieve a growth in sales of 15 per cent in real terms each year for each existing product.
- Introduce two new but related products into the existing markets.

SBU goals – portfolio

Maximize the returns from the portfolio of products while keeping the cash flows in balance and minimizing the risk profile of the portfolio. Ensure the future viability of the portfolio by introducing two new related products in the forthcoming year. Monitor the performance of existing products to ensure that their current and future contributions are satisfactory.

SBU strategy

Exceed corporate strategy parameters through pursuing a strategy of conservative organic growth in sales of 15 per cent, in real terms, for each of the next three years. This growth to be achieved by continuing to follow the generic strategy of high volume low cost with the same product lines, introducing two new related products, using the same channels of distribution in the same markets.

SBU projections

At this level it is suggested that implementation decisions should be based upon projected SBU income statements, cash budgets, sources and applications of funds statements, balance sheets and ratios, and that the wisdom of pursuing particular strategies should be determined by measuring how well alternative projections meet SBU goals. If the projected results of the initial set of strategies fail to meet SBU goals, then the functional policies contributing to these results should be reviewed and amended. Although SBU projections tend to be biased towards financial data and information, there is, in comparision with the corporate level, an increasing degree of influence from the other functional areas upon decision making. Therefore when SBU strategies are being projected the projections should include summary information from each functional area. Once again when the SBU financial data is complemented with two-dimensional matrices of the type discussed in Part Four then additional insights can be achieved by SBU managers. Such an approach can provide managers with a comprehensive picture of the implications of the projected strategy which combines:

- General financial information on the overall performance of the SBU: income statements; balance sheets; cash flow statements; sources and applications of funds statements; and ratios.
- Financial information on each function, product, channel of distribution and sales region.
- Marketing information on each product, as revealed by the product market portfolio.
- Marketing information on the portfolio of products, as revealed by the product market portfolio.

Resources

In this model of strategic management it is assumed that financial resources are provided (or are taken) by corporate management and that the SBU top managers are free to use these financial resources to purchase the resources which they feel are necessary to achieve SBU goals. SBU top managers therefore have the task of allocating the limited resources among the competing functional claimants. Again, although in theory resources should be allocated on the basis of quantitative assessments of the potential contributions of each functional area to the achievement of SBU goals, in practice, the judgement and experience of the SBU's top management will often significantly influence the decisions.

Control and evaluation

Ensure that devices which will enable the finally agreed strategies to be monitored are in place. This is considered more fully in Part Eight.

Implementation at the functional level

The overall objective of functional implementation is to refine the corporate and SBU goals and strategies into targets, policies and actions that will guide and control each functional area in ways that will ensure that implementation of the adopted strategy actually takes place.

A general approach to implementation in each functional area is set out below and a specific case study example is given in Part Eight.

The functional activities are determined by the overall SBU goals and strategies and typical implementation issues for each functional area are now presented. It is natural that functional implementation in the marketing function is considered first because, as indicated on page 9, it is assumed that it is this function which 'drives' the organization towards its goals. However, even though sales or marketing strategies are considered to be the starting point of the strategic process, the financial targets for many organizations will be set, at the corporate or SBU level, prior to the setting of the functional marketing targets. Therefore the process requires an ability of planners to 'look two ways at once' – upwards towards the apex of the hierarchy to see the financial goals which must be achieved and downwards towards the base of the hierarchy to see the actions in the marketplace, in which the organization must engage, if it is to achieve its goals.

Implementation in the marketing function

Targets
In order to achieve the given growth goal, for the forthcoming year what are the sales targets in terms of the following:

- Total sales volumes and values?
- Return on sales?
- Sales volumes and values broken down by product line, channel of distribution, location of sales, and customer type?
- Contribution margins by product line, channel of distribution, location of sales, and customer type?

Policies
Given the SBU objective of growth and the marketing targets that have been set above, the following policy issues must be resolved.

- What are the markets for the products – new markets or existing ones?
- How should the markets be segmented?
- What are the desired product positions for each market segment?
- What are the marketing mix policies necessary to achieve desired goals through having the organization's products appropriately positioned in the desired segments.
- Specifically what are the: product policies?, distribution policies?, pricing policies?, promotion policies?

Projections
When the functional marketing policies have been decided, then, together with other relevant information from each of the other func-

tional areas, the effects of the implementation of a particular set of marketing policies can be projected and the consequences ascertained. The projections can be set out in terms of: proforma income statements and balance sheets; departmental budgets; cash flow budgets; sources and applications of funds statements; break-even statements; and financial ratios. This type of assessment of the effects of a particular set of policies enables an assessment to be made of their likely impacts throughout the organization. On the basis of these results, if the initial policies are considered to be unsatisfactory they can be amended, and then, using the amended policies, further projections can be made in order to try to 'steer' the organization towards its desired goals. This process can be continued until an optimal set of policies has been devised.

Resources
On the basis of the policies decided upon, determine the resources necessary to implement these policies and establish budgets which will then allocate such resources.

Control and evaluation
Ensure that devices which will enable the finally agreed policies to be monitored and evaluated are in place. This is considered in Part Eight.

Implementation in the finance function

Targets
Although this model assumes that the sales or marketing strategies are the starting point of the strategic process, the financial targets for an organization are usually the terms in which goal achievement is measured.

In order to achieve its given growth goal and its given financial goals for the forthcoming year the financial targets could be set in terms of the following:

- The target ROI.
- The target ROCE.
- The target debt to equity ratio.
- Target debt structure.
- Target levels of equity.
- The target ROE.
- Target levels of dividends.
- Target levels of liquidity.

Policies
Given the SBU goal of growth and the marketing policies that have been suggested the financial policies can be considered under the headings: financing policies; dividend policies; and liquidity policies.

1 *Financing policies:* Assuming that additional finance will be require to support the growth of the organization will these additional funds come from external or internal sources? If external sources are used then:

- Will debt or equity or a combination of both be used?
- What capital structure ought the organization to have?
- What are the ownership implications?

If internal sources are used then:

- Should it be retained earnings?
- Should it be more stringent control of such elements as working capital, debtors, creditors or stock?

What should be the balance between long term sources of finance and short term? Irrespective of the source of the finance at what time(s) of the forthcoming year should it be sought?

2 *Dividend policies:* What is the level of dividend payout which will satisfy shareholders and also achieve financial targets?

3 *Liquidity policies:* What are the cash balances that should be maintained?

Projections

The proposed financial policies should be included in the 'marketing projection' outlined on page 344 and the financial consequences of the alternative policies can be ascertained. As with the marketing policies, if the results are deemed to be unsatisfactory, then the financial variables can be changed to try to achieve more satisfactory results.

Resources

On the basis of the policies decided upon determine the resources necessary to implement these policies and draw up budgets to allocate these resources.

Control and evaluation

Ensure that devices which will enable the finally agreed policies to be monitored and evaluated are in place. This is considered more fully in Part Eight.

Implementation in the production function

Production requirements are directly determined by the proposed sales schedules and so production targets and policies are sales dependent variables.

Targets
For the forthcoming year what are the production targets in terms of:

- Total volume of production according to product types?
- Capacity utilization?
- Costs?
- Quality?
- Stock levels?

Policies
Given the SBU objective of growth and the marketing targets that have been set above the following policy issues must be resolved.

- What is the production capacity necessary for the given volumes of sales?
- How should the production capacity be increased – by new factories, additional plant, additional personnel, longer working with existing plant?
- What proportion of the production should be made by the organization and what proportion should be bought in?
- What policies are being adopted to meet cost targets: automation; special purchasing arrangements; value engineering; product and process redesign; minimize stock levels?
- What policies are there for quality improvement: quality circles, feedback from sales personnel and customers, comparison with rival products?
- Policies toward suppliers: How can the relationships with suppliers be enhanced so that both parties benefit economically.

Projections
The production data is integrated with data from the other functional areas and projections are made to calculate break-even and safety stock levels and to see the broader consequences of the proposed policies. After projection, policies may be amended if necessary to help achieve SBU goals.

Resources
On the basis of the policies decided upon, determine the resources necessary to implement these policies and draw up budgets to allocate these resources.

Control and evaluation
Ensure that devices which will enable the finally agreed policies to be monitored and evaluated are in place. This is considered more fully in Part Eight.

Implementation in the personnel function

The personnel requirements are directly determined by the proposed sales and production schedules and so personnel targets and policies are dependent variables.

Targets
For the forthcoming year what are the personnel targets in terms of:

- Numbers of personnel broken down according to functions?
- Skills, motivation, days lost, productivity?
- Total labour costs and unit labour costs?

Policies
In order to meet the sales and production schedules:

- Is the labour force adequate in terms of: numbers; skills; location?
- What recruitment and training programmes will be necessary to provide the required labour force?
- What is the level of motivation or commitment to the organization and what policies should be adopted to maintain or improve it – training, incentives, salaries and wages, conditions etc?
- Is compensation linked to results?
- What is the current level of absenteeism?

Projections
The personnel data is combined with other functional data to help provide integrated projections for the SBU.

Resources
On the basis of the policies decided upon determine the resources necessary to implement these policies and draw up budgets to allocate these resources.

Control and evaluation
Ensure that devices which will enable the finally agreed policies to be monitored and evaluated are in place. This is considered more fully in Part Eight.

Conclusion on functional implementation

Functional implementation* is the final link in translating a strategic aspiration into an operating reality and effective functional policies ensure that the detail necessary for success is present.

Allocating resources

It could be argued that the crucial distinction between a 'real strategy' and a 'signal of intention' is the allocation of resources – until the

---

* Note that the process of functional implementation with MIS Function has not been considered. It may be carried out in a similar fashion to that used in the other functions.

resources which are necessary for the implementation of a strategy are allocated, the strategy has only the status of a written or verbal signal and will have been a minimal cost to the company.

This section provides a methodology for ensuring that the resources are provided at the appropriate times and in the appropriate amounts so that each functional area can successfully implement its set policies and thus achieve its targets.

Generally, the types of resources which companies can use to achieve their goals can be summarized under the headings: financial; human; and physical. Thus resource allocation, at the sub-SBU level, is concerned with ensuring that each functional area has sufficient of those resources to enable it to meet the targets which have been specified for it.

How resources should be allocated

As it is normally the case that the demands for resources exceed their availability, judgements must be made about how they ought to be allocated. Considerations which ought to influence the allocation process include the following:

1 *Allocations should reflect strategic priorities:* Generally, the allocation of resources to the different functional areas should reflect the priorities given to the different functions when the functional targets were set. These targets should reflect the weighting given to strategic goals. Thus, for example, if absolute priority was given to achieving an increase in sales of 10 per cent per year in real terms, and in order to achieve this increase, the marketing department required extra resources, then it would be expected that this department should receive priority in the allocation of resources.

2 *Allocations should fit with existing resource realities:* The amounts of resources which are allocated to particular functions should reflect the existing and potential stock of resources which the SBU has. For example, should an SBU decide that in the next year if will double the resources – manpower, finance and the value of physical assets – of its marketing department, and it does not have the financial resources (or the ability to raise the necessary finance) to do this, then clearly, this is an infeasible and therefore inappropriate pattern of resource allocation.

Impediments to effective resource allocation

Although in theory the above is how resources *ought* to be allocated, in practice, as discussed in the section concerned with the role of culture in the implementation process, this is frequently not the case. Resource allocation is affected by forces other than logic or conformity with strategy guidelines, and so when planning resource allocations cognisance must be taken of potential impediments to optimal allocations. Among the principal impediments are the following:

Resistance to change
If there is a change in the traditional pattern of allocations of resources among departments there will tend to be resistance from those departments which have had their absolute, or relative, allocations reduced.

Failure to communicate the strategy
If the strategy is not communicated effectively throughout the organization and managers, charged with the responsibility of implementation, are unsure of what exactly is required of them, this uncertainty may be reflected in a sub-optimal allocation of resources.

Failure to understand the nature of the business
If the top managers (especially in large diversified companies) do not adequately understand the nature of the business of the SBU whose resource allocations they are considering, this may result in pressures for allocation stemming from the sectional interests rather than flowing from the strategy. Additionally, a failure to understand the resource implications of a particular strategy may result in a misallocation based on erroneous figures. For example, when companies commence exporting they frequently miscalculate the very high costs of entry into foreign markets and consequently fail to allocate sufficient resources to ensure effective implementation.

Managerial concern with day-to-day problems
It is often the case that managers are so engrossed in meeting the day-to-day, short term, pressures of managing their departments that they do have the opportunity to reflect upon longer term and wider strategic issues. This type of pressure may also help thwart optimal resource allocations.

A methodology for effective resource allocation

Although there are many procedures which could be followed to ensure effective allocations, a five step methodology is suggested below.

Step 1: Develop an inventory of the resources which are currently available and which it is feasible to acquire. This inventory can be drawn up under the headings: financial; human and physical.

Step 2: Determine what resources are required by each department in order to meet the given strategy targets.

Step 3: Iteratively amend the functional allocations, or the targets, to obtain as good a match as possible between what is required and what is feasible.

Step 4: Decide upon appropriate actions to overcome the cultural/behavioural impediments to the desired resource allocations.

Step 5: Allocate the resources using budgets.

Budgets

A budget could be described as a detailed plan which is expressed in financial or other quantitative measures. It shows how resources will be acquired and used in a specified period of time, in most cases for a period of one year or less, and it can be used as a device for the planning, implementation, and control of strategy. Ideally a budget should be a detailed set of guidelines for the activities which each responsibility or profit centre in the organization must follow if the chosen strategy is to be implemented successfully. Additionally all the various budgets for all such centres should, when summed together, provide a detailed, coordinated, and integrated plan of activities for the entire organization. This coordinated plan is known as the master budget.

Budgeting in the implementation process

Figure 51 shows diagramatically a typical budget structure and also how the various budgets can be linked together to implement strategies. As can be seen the master budget can be disaggregated into three major types: operating budgets; financial budgets and the capital expenditure budget.

Operating budgets
Operating budgets or functional budgets are really projected income statements which should provide the expected revenues and expenses for each responsibility or profit centre for the forthcoming year. They are usually computed for monthly or quarterly time periods.

Financial budgets
Show the movements of cash into and out of the organization. The operating budgets are normally prepared on the basis of revenues and expenses, i.e. accruals. However, for planning and control purposes it is necessary to convert these accruals into cash inflows and cash outflows and this can be effected through the cash budget which is normally computed on a monthly time period basis and through the sources and applications of funds 'budget' which is computed on an annual basis.

Capital expediture budget
This budget is concerned with analysing, choosing, and then allocating funds to those competing projects which will involve the organization in long-term commitments. Typical types of projects which could be included in this type of budget include:

- Acquisition of new businesses.
- Acquisition of new plant and equipment.
- Projects involving the expansion of productive capacity.
- Product lines or markets.
- Cost reduction projects.

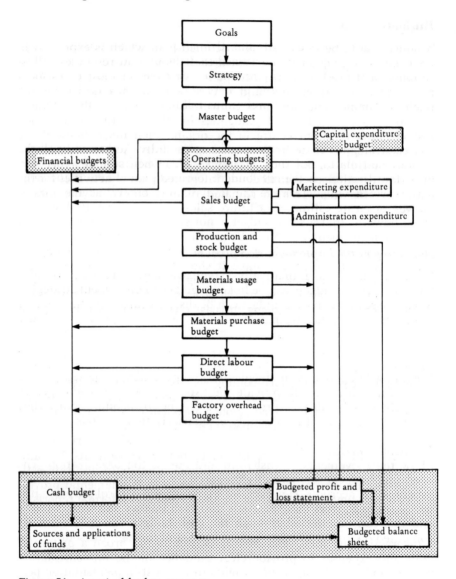

Figure 51 *A typical budget structure*

(Note that the shaded rectangle at the bottom of Figure 50 contains those budgets and statements which are most useful for strategic management, i.e. the budgeted profit and loss statement, the budgeted balance sheet, the cash budget and the sources and applications of funds statement.)

The budgeting process

How each of these budgets is linked in the budgeting process is now discussed. In Figure 51 it is assumed that the organization's goals and strategy for the forthcoming planning period have been set and that the only concern in the budgeting process is how to implement the given strategy. The process could proceed as follows:

The sales budget
The starting point of the process is the sales budget. This budget shows the sales estimates and their expenses for the forthcoming year. It is important that this is the first budget to be computed as it is the sales figures which will determine the levels of the other budgets. Consequently accurate estimates of future sales are necessary. It should be noted however that a sales budget is not simply a sales forecast – it is an active instrument which can be used to influence results. For example, should the sales forecast appear to be too small to satisfy company goals, then at the planning stage it should be possible to positively affect final sales volumes through altering the elements of the marketing mix, through, say, increasing the promotion budget. When sales for the forthcoming year are being forecast one or more of a number of techniques tend to be used:

1 *Mathematical extrapolation of past trends:* When this approach is used it is assumed that the historical pattern of sales will continue and a forecast for the forthcoming year is made on this assumption with the model taking account of environmental variables. This type of forecast could be based upon a forecasting approach such as: regression, time series, exponential smoothing etc.
2 *Empirical market research:* Market research could be carried out by personnel from the organization or by outside consultants. The aim of the research is to provide the organization with accurate estimates of its market for the forthcoming year. Fundamental providers of this type of information are the formal and informal reports of sales people.

In practice the total sales budget is usually too broad a picture of sales and expenses to provide clear guidance in the implementation process and useful diagnostic insights in the post-implementation performance evaluation stage. Accordingly therefore, the total sales budget is often broken down into smaller constituent sales budgets such as: sales by product line; sales by region; sales by channel of distribution; and sales by customer. This sub-division assists in implementation and evaluation.

The expense budget
Commercial expenses can be classified either under the heading of primary accounts (which is probably the simplest) or by functions. The latter approach is generally superior for strategic and control purposes

as it enables judgements to be made about how well the various departments or cost centres in the organization are performing. Generally, expenses can be grouped into two main categories: marketing expenses – selling, warehousing, transportation, advertising, credit and collection and general accounting; and administrative expenses.

Production and stock budget
The next budget to be computed is that for production and stock. This budget is set in response to the sales estimates and aims to keep production and stock levels in line with sales estimates. In practice this budget should be completed before the final acceptance of the sales budget so that the production capacity is synchronized with sales.

Materials usage budget
This budget contains the estimates, made by personnel in manufacturing and assembly, of the amounts and costs of the materials needed to meet the planned production schedules.

Materials purchase budget
This budget details the quantities and costs of materials to be used and shows, often on a monthly basis, the funds that will be necessary to purchase these materials. This budget is prepared by the purchasing department.

Direct labour budget
The direct labour budget enables the structure and cost of the amount of direct labour necessary to meet the production schedule to be estimated.

Factory overhead budget
The production budgets and the direct labour budgets together show the planned amount of work for the various production centres as well as the amounts of work which it is anticipated will consequently be required from the maintenance and other factory overhead departments.

The projected income statement
The sales figures in this statement are the sales projected by market research and analysis for the forthcoming year and this is the variable which 'drives' the process. The sales figures are complemented with information from the various budgets, as shown in Figure 50, and on the basis of the total information, future net profit is estimated. This projected income statement can be used to assess the quality of the supporting budgets and the causes of variances as the strategy is implemented.

The cash budget
This budget provides detailed information on cash inflows and outflows

in the budget period and is an essential planning device – organizations can confer considerable competitive advantage upon themselves through the careful and creative use of cash.

The sources and applications of funds
While the cash budget is essentially concerned with helping to plan short-term financial needs and opportunities, the sources and applications of funds statement is more concerned with medium and longer term financial movements. These statements can be extremely useful in estimating the effects of plans upon liquidity and in evaluating an organization's methods of financing the 'budget' which is computed on an annual basis.

The budgeted balance sheet
The budgeted balance sheet or pro-forma balance sheet is a statement of the organization's assets and liabilities position at the end of the budgeting period should the planned strategies be implemented.

Like any other element in the strategy process the usefulness of budgets as an instrument of implementation depends upon the circumstances in which they are used and how they are used. Thus, when properly employed, budgets can be of fundamental importance in planning, controlling, providing feedback and highlighting areas of strength or weakness within the organization. However, budgeting practices can also develop features which inhibit the effective implementation of potentially successful strategies. Among the more common problems associated with budgeting are:

1 *Misallocation of resources:* Resources may be allocated on the basis of tradition rather than on the basis of the needs of the current strategy.
2 *Time and cost:* The development of budgets can be an extremely time-consuming and costly operation whose results may not justify the effort.
3 *Inflexibility:* Budgets may be set inflexibly and then resolutely adhered to. This type of inflexibility may be costly for the organization if it prevents the rapid adaptation of the organization's strategy to changed circumstances. Related to the inflexibility is the concept of certainty. Budgets often appear to assume a world of certainty. This view is often at variance with reality.
4 *Behavioural aspects:* If budgets are rigorously and inflexibly applied they may come to be regarded as a threatening and coercive device by many departments and may therefore inculcate negative attitudes towards the organization and be sources of demotivation.
5 *Unrealistic budgets:* Organizations often develop attitudes towards the levels at which budgets should be set so that setting budget estimates may develop into a type of game in which departments submit budgets which although they are related to the tasks they

will be undertaking, are strongly influenced by departmental views on how the individual allocations will be made. Thus, it is not unusual to find in many organizations a predisposition to inflate budget estimates, in the belief that the budget committee will reduce them to more realistic levels.

Requirements for effective budgeting

Although the number, frequency and nature of the budgets which any organization has will be a function of its industry, its goals, its strategy and its structure there are nonetheless a number of fundamental guidelines which should be considered when structuring the set of budgets in an organization. These include the following:

1 *Organizational structure:* The set of budgets which an organization has, should be built upon its internal organizational structure with the scope of the budgets based upon responsibility or profit centres. This type of budget structure enables responsibility for ensuring implementation to be allocated to the managers responsible for each centre and thus provides a mechanism for subsequent evaluation of performance.
2 *Budget committee:* The traditional method of planning and integrating the budgeting process is through the budget committee. Typically the budget committee comprises the managers who are responsible for profit or responsibility centres. These managers constitute a committee which has the responsibility for coordinating the budgeting activities and ensuring consistency.
3 *Consensus:* A major function of the budget committee is to try to generate consensus among the various departments whose budget estimates may be competing for scarce, and consequently rationed, resources.

Management by objectives

Management by objectives (MBO), as its name implies, is an approach to management which asserts that the most effective way to manage any organization is through the use of objectives, i.e. if an organization can make all its individuals aware of its objectives and persuade them to see a congruence between these objectives and their own personal objectives then this compatibility can be harnessed and used for the benefit of both parties.

MBO is therefore used predominantly as an aid to the implementation of strategy. It seeks to do this through two main routes: clarification and motivation.

Clarification

MBO asserts that strategy implementation is most likely to be effective if all individuals within the organization are completely clear about what is expected of them. Therefore, the approach seeks to clarify for all managers at all levels, and in all functions, what their exact organizational goals are, the key tasks they will need to perform in order to achieve these goals, the time span available in which to do this, the bases upon which their performance will subsequently be evaluated, and the consequences of achieving, or not achieving, the specified targets. This process is explicit and formal and has the objectives of ensuring that:

- Organization-wide, the corporate plan is disaggregated into precise quantitative and qualitative targets and tasks for individual managers which, when summed, will achieve corporate objectives.
- Corporate plans are implemented vertically throughout the organization, i.e. from corporate to SBU to functional levels, and in the process foster hierarchical communication.
- Corporate plans are implemented horizontally throughout the organization, i.e. at the functional level across the marketing, finance, personnel and production functions and in the process foster horizontal communication.
- The performance of the individual managers and their departments for which objectives have been set are evaluated on the bases agreed.
- At all levels, perspectives develop which encourage individual managers to perceive their tasks in terms of longer run strategies and plans rather than short run budgets.

Thus as Figure 52 shows, MBO can be considered to be a device which complements and role of budgets in the communication, implementation, and evaluation of strategy throughout the organization.

Motivation

As the MBO process commences at the top of the organizational hierarchy, it can be employed in two fundamental ways – it can be imposed coercively or it can be agreed creatively.

If the MBO system is imposed coercively the goals and standards of performance expected from each individual or department at a particular level in the hierarchy are determined, predominantly unilaterally, by the supervising level in the hierarchy. When this approach is used the primary motivation will tend to be fear of failure with the main concern being the size of the penalty for failing to meet targets. (This approach is often used with sales personnel – failure to meet imposed sales targets may result in dismissal.) Therefore, when the MBO approach is coercive the role of the setter of the objectives and targets becomes, largely, that of a controller and inspector. Although this approach will often ensure that corporate strategies are implemented it may cause managers to comply with corporate targets rather than to enthusiastically pursue them, and it may also result in alienation with a consequent lack of organizational loyalty. Therefore, any assessment of

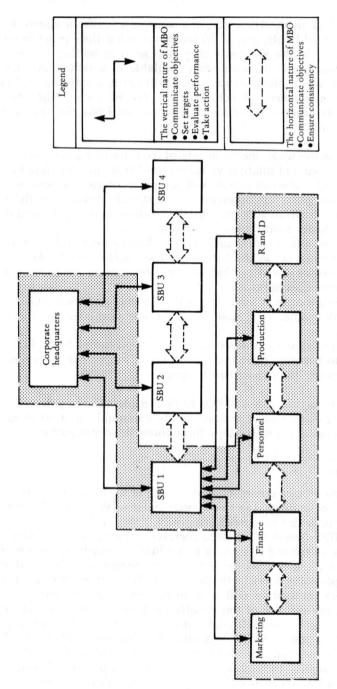

Figure 52   *An illustration of the vertical and horizontal nature of MBO in one SBU in a divisionalized organization*

the degree of success which an organization has in using this approach should be tempered with an assessment of the costs of the demotivating influences it may have.

In contrast, the creative agreement of goals and standards approach proceeds by each individual or department head, through a process of consultation and discussion, agreeing goals and standards of performance with its supervising level in the hierarchy. The goals and performance standards are still 'imposed' by the supervising level, and detailed evaluations of individuals will still take place, but the process is sensitive to the needs and goals of the individual and seeks to accommodate them within the organizational goals. This approach has been strongly advocated by McGregor[1] who has asserted that when managers, through consultation with superiors, develop joint goals and targets which satisfy organizational requirements and their own personal aspirations, then there is likely to be an enhanced level of commitment to the organization and its strategies, and consequently superior levels of performance. Therefore, when this approach is employed the role of the supervisor is less of an inspector and more of a leader and counsellor to a group.

The process of MBO

Although a variety of approaches can be employed in the implementation of MBO, the following set of steps is set in general terms which can be tailored to the circumstances facing specific organizations.

Stage 1:   Explicit commitment by senior personnel
The process should commence at the most senior level in the organizational hierarchy with an explicit statement of commitment to it. This first step is an organization-wide signal of the importance of the process.

Stage 2:   An organizational analysis
The commitment to the process can be manifested through the analysis which should precede the formal implementation. The analysis will be concerned with determining the scope of responsibility of, first, individual departments, or units, and ultimately, individual managers. The quality of this analysis is extremely important as individual managers should only be assessed on the basis of performance for which they have direct responsibility and influence. In this stage an analysis should cascade through the organization from the top level down to the lowest level individual manager so that a total integrated pattern of goals, targets, activities and reporting systems, for each manager can be developed.

Stage 3:   Set measures of performance
Following this analysis, measures of performance for each individual are provisionally set.

Stage 4:   Agree measures of performance and evaluation procedures
The provisionally set measures of performance, the time period in which targets are to be achieved, the reporting system, the criteria for evaluation and the consequences of not achieving agreed targets are then discussed, perhaps amended, and then agreed with individual managers.

Stage 5:   Operations take place
A period of performance then takes place and the results are formally recorded.

Stage 6:   Analysis of performance and feedback
The performance of each individual is analysed and feedback is provided. This may prompt individuals who are failing to meet agreed targets to take action to do so before formal evaluation.

Stage 7:   Action on performance
On the basis of the feedback on performance the following types of action may be taken:

1   The original targets may be reconsidered and, depending upon the degree of achievement, new targets for the next period set. Although the new targets would primarily reflect the actions necessary to achieve corporate goals, they would be influenced by the experience of the previous period. For example, if there had been universal under-achievement of targets, then perhaps the targets were set unrealistically high and a lower level for the forthcoming period might be more appropriate.
2   Rewards for achievement or over-achievement may be dispensed. These could include:

  • Financial rewards, for example salaries, bonuses, or other non-financial rewards such as cars etc.
  • Accelerated promotion.

3   Actions to rectify under-achievement may be taken. These could include:

  • Dismissal.
  • Financial sanctions, for example no salary increment, no bonus or other non-financial measures.
  • Decelerated promotion or demotion.
  • Change of job within the organization.
  • Compulsory attendance on training programmes to improve performance.

Conclusions on MBO

Although MBO is not a standard practice – it has many different forms – there appears to be some evidence to show (see Humble[2]) that in spite of the large amount of effort required to set up and maintain, it, it can bestow substantial economic benefits. The financial benefits flowing principally from MBO's power to:

- Clearly communicate corporate strategy and achieve integrated implementation throughout the entire organization.
- Act as an effective mechanism for ensuring the continuous monitoring and control of the total organization.
- Motivate individual managers and departments to achieve specified targets.

Conclusions to Part Seven

Part Seven provided a framework through which strategy can be implemented in an organization. The framework is multidimensional in that it explicitly recognizes that for implementation to be effective there must be a broader range of concerns than simply the refining of corporate goals into functional targets. In addition to this necessary element cognisance must also be taken of the behavioural elements which must be handled for the process to be effective.

References

1 McGregor, D. M., *The Human Side of the Enterprise*, New York McGraw-Hill, 1960.
2 Humble, J., 'Corporate Planning and Management by Objectives', *Long Range Planning*, Vol. 12, No. 4, 1969, p. 36.

Part Eight

16 General framework for control and evaluation

The final element in the strategic planning model is that of control and evaluation and it is concerned with appraising how well the chosen strategy is being implemented with the basis of the appraisal being how well the actual results achieved during the operation of the strategy compare with the results which were forecast prior to implementation. The evaluation stage thus provides management with the opportunity to examine how well goals and objectives are being achieved, to monitor the progress of the implementation of the strategy, and to take corrective action should the level of achievement be considered unsatisfactory.

Control and evaluation is particularly important at the corporate or strategic level as the operations which are evaluated at this level tend to be long run and relatively major. It is at this level that the composition of the organization's fixed assets may be changed through, for example, the acquisition of a new company or the disposal of an SBU. Consequently the success or failure of corporate or strategic plans is a fundamental determinant of the future success of the entire organization.

This is in contrast to the impact of failure at the operational level. At this level, failure to achieve an operating target – for example daily sales – does not mean catastrophe for the organization. This type of failure frequently occurs and remedial action is often relatively simple.

Tracking the environment

Evaluation should not be confined to issues internal to the firm. Rather a comprehensive system of evaluation should also track the environment so that the organization can shift its strategy and its structure in response to organizationally significant environmental changes. The importance of environmental surveillance is a function of the nature of the industry. For example, all successful companies in the computer manufacturing industry must constantly evaluate the technological developments which competitors in this technology-driven industry are pursuing – failure to do so may lead to extinction.

Tracking organizational performance

Performance, at all levels in the organizational hierarchy, will not automatically conform to the targets which have been set in corporate, SBU, and operational plans. Deviations from preordained standards or goals will naturally occur as different departments either fail to meet, or exceed, targets. Control and evaluation mechanisms are necessary to monitor and appraise the impact of deviations and to ensure that actions are taken which will ensure organization-wide compliance with the strategies that have been adopted.

Providing feedback

In most organizations feedback about the effectiveness of strategies is an important ingredient in ensuring that adherence to an approved strategy continues. Control and evaluation provide a mechanism for doing this.

Acting as a motivator

The process of control and evaluation can be a strongly motivating force (either as a negative reinforcer where failure to meet targets results in some form of sanctions, or as a positive reinforcer where success in achieving targets results in some form of rewards) within an organization. Individuals at all levels who are aware of the criteria by which they will be judged will have clear personal targets which should help motivate them to achieve organizational objectives.

Acting as a sensitizer

An effective control and evaluation system should be sensitive to internal and external stimuli and should enable the organization to respond quickly and appropriately to relevant external and/or internal changes.

Impediments to effective control and evaluation

Although the necessity for having mechanisms for control and evaluation is widely accepted, their power can be greatly diminished if they have the following characteristics.

Coerciveness

Coercive control and evaluation mechanisms, which cause personnel to experience the feeling of constant threatening appraisal, can have demotivating effects which are ultimately harmful to the organization as personnel seek to avoid sanctions rather than strive to achieve organizational goals.

Systems that encourage cheating

Related to the coercion effect is the element of cheating. In organizations in which there are severe penalties for failing to meet targets there may be an inclination for personnel to submit false figures of achievement in order to avoid the penalties associated with failure. Such an attitude can corrupt the organization's data and consequently greatly reduce the value of control and evaluation procedures.

Timeliness

A fundamental determinant of the effectiveness of control and evaluation is the timeliness of the information provided. This timeliness can be considered to have two related aspects. First, if information is provided only after significant landmarks in the strategic implementation process have been passed then it does not provide the feedback to guide subsequent implementation. This type of information provision merely records such landmarks and contributes little to control. For example, should the sales department of an organization experience a sudden and significant decline in its sales, the more speedily this information is communicated through the organization the more speedily can a recovery strategy be planned and implemented.

Second, if the control and evaluation process is merely mechanical, i.e. it takes place at regularly preordained intervals, rather than continuously and dynamically then adherence to the timetable for evaluation may thwart its diagnostic and prescriptive powers. This is not to say that control and evaluation should take place at random intervals. Rather, in addition to regular reports, there should also be a complementary continuous control and evaluation process so that deviations from planned goals or targets are spotted as speedily as possible.

Costliness

The costliness of providing information can be measured in terms of two major resources – personnel time and money. Thus, relatively large amounts of time spent on control and evaluation may be less fruitful than time being spent on more creative activities. Similarly, if the monetary cost of providing information for control and evaluation is high then the benefits derived from the process may not justify the expenditure.

The objectives of control and evaluation

In general the objectives of control and evaluation will be:

- To set standards for achievement – these are the goals or targets for the strategy.
- To measure organizational performance, i.e. how well the goals or targets are being achieved.
- To make comparisons between the set standards and the actual performance achieved – this is the evaluation of the performance.
- To take action when appropriate – this is the dynamic aspect of the process which attempts to ensure that the strategy being followed continues to meet organizational goals.

Types of measures

Generally two types of measures – qualitative and quantitative – may be used. The qualitative measures express descriptively the quality of organizational performance and how well goals are being achieved, for example 'the organization's sales growth has been satisfactory'. Quantitative measures attempt to give a precise numerical measure of organizational performance and goal achievement, for example 'the organization's sales revenue grew by 11.1 per cent last year'. Because of the subjective nature of qualitative measures of performance, it is normally considered that the utility of such measures is greatly enhanced if they can be complemented by quantitative ones. For example, if in evaluating the performance of a product in a market against competing products the qualitative assessment is that 'the product has performed better than competitors' products in terms of sales and consumer acceptance' then this assessment would be greatly enhanced if it were to be accompanied by quantitative assessments such as 'the product's relative market share changed from 0.10 at the start of the year to 0.20 at the end of the year – this increase in relative market share of 100 per cent was much superior to the next best performing competitor which was only able to increase its relative market share by 25 per cent'.

The dual focus

In most evaluations a dual focus will be necessary, i.e. there must be a consideration of those factors internal to the organization and those external elements, both of which may be influencing the level of performance and goal achievement.

Information quality

The quality of the control and evaluation process will be directly determined by the quality of information upon which the assessments are based – poor information will generally lead to poor control and evaluation and vice versa. Generally information should be:

- Correct
- Timely

- Concise
- Relevant

Assignment of responsibility

Effective control and evaluation requires that the responsibility for activities should be assigned unambiguouly to particular individuals. Therefore any control and evaluation system should be based on the existing set of responsibility centres and should reflect the type of responsibility which is vested in each centre (i.e. a cost centre should be evaluated on its 'cost performance', an investment centre on its 'investment performance' and a profit centre on its 'profit performance').

Action orientation

Control and evaluation procedures which do not lead to action being taken, when necessary, are merely paper exercises – for the process to be effective it must lead to action being taken.

Future or historical orientation

Although control and evaluation is usually considered from a historical perspective, i.e. the process is concerned with appraising the effectiveness of a past strategy, it can also have a future orientation. Thus the techniques outlined on pages 372–434 which may be employed in control and evaluation can be used both as devices for assessing the anticipated future impact of different strategic options *before implementation*, and as devices for reviewing the *historical performance* of an organization *after* a strategy has been followed. How the techniques are applied is identical in each case – the projected or the historical performance is judged against the goals or targets which were set and, depending upon the degree of congruence between the projected or achieved performance, action is taken. How the process of control and evaluation is effected is now considered.

The general results of control and evaluation

When the operation of any strategy is being evaluated just two results are possible – either the goals are being achieved or the goals are not being achieved.

The goals are being achieved

In this circumstance the strategy is being implemented successfully, i.e. preordained goals and targets are being met, and therefore, assuming that the original strategy is still optimal, it should continue to be implemented as before.

The goals are not being achieved

If an organization is failing to achieve its goals or targets it may be due to one or both of the following reasons. First the external environment may have changed resulting in the original strategy no longer being appropriate. In this case it is likely that a change of strategy will be required so that the organization can adapt to the changed environmental circumstances. For example, a significant environmental change could be the entry of new and aggressive competitors into the market. Such an event would usually require a strategic realignment which explicitly considers how the organization would need to change in order to meet this increase in competitive pressure. Drucker[1] has suggested that in this type of situation (i.e. where the environment has changed) that the organization's current strategy is lacking in *effectiveness* and that a change of *strategy* is required. (Alternatively the organization's structure may no longer be appropriate.)

The second possible cause of an organization failing to achieve its goals is that the internal operations of the organization are being carried out in an unsatisfactory fashion. In this type of situation it is likely that, rather than a change of strategy, a change in operations or procedures is required. For example, if an organization was experiencing unsatisfactory levels of sales because of a lack of communication between the marketing department and the production department then the appropriate changes would involve actions to improve communication between the two departments with the original strategy continuing to be implemented. Drucker has suggested that in this type of situation the organization's strategy is lacking in *efficiency* and a change in *operations* is needed.

The nature of control and evaluation

In the control and evaluation of strategy, there is a spectrum of possible actions which ranges from 'doing nothing' other than fine-tuning the existing strategy (i.e. the strategy is working satisfactorily and little change is required) to fundamental changes in the strategy (i.e. the strategy is failing and unless action is taken corporate failure will occur). The degree of strategy change will be determined by the size of the variances from strategic goals and also the cause of the variances, i.e. is it due to ineffectiveness or inefficiency.

Control and evaluation at the corporate, SBU and functional levels

For the purpose of control and evaluation it is suggested that it is more appropriate to 'invert' the organizational hierarchy outlined on page 337 and consider the process from a 'bottom-up' rather than a 'top-down' approach. This is suggested first because it is the consolidation of the results at the lowest levels of the hierarchy that usually determine overall corporate results, second, the time horizons in which lower level targets or goals must be achieved are shorter and therefore results, which should indicate the degree of success of strategies, are available sooner, and finally, lower level results tend to be expressed in more precise quantitative terms (for example 'total sales of £232,000 in the second quarter of the year') and are therefore more easily measured.

For the purposes of control and evalation, the organization has been divided into two levels – the combined SBU and functional level' and 'the corporate level'. The SBU and the functional levels have been combined because, for the purposes of control and evaluation, it is somewhat artificial to separate them as the overall performance of an SBU is often mainly the sum of its functional performances. However, the evaluation of corporate strategies is considered separately because, as was pointed out in Part One, the nature of corporate strategies is fundamentally different from those SBU strategies – at the corporate level it is assumed that strategy is primarily concerned with deciding upon the mix of *businesses* in which an organization should be operating, while at the SBU level, strategy is primarily concerned with the *products and markets* in which the SBU is operating.

The process of control and evaluation

Irrespective of the level in the organizational hierarchy at which control and evaluation of strategy is being carried out, the process can be considered under three main headings: evaluation of the degree of achievement of goals or targets; evaluation of functional strategies and performance; and evaluation of the organizational structure.

References

1   Drucker, P., *Management*, Heinemann, 1974.

17 Control and evaluation

Control and evaluation at the SBU and the functional levels is considered through the medium of a hypothetical company Siva, details of which are given below.

Siva: A case study to illustrate control and evaluation

Company background

This is a new company called Siva which is about to commence operations on 1 January 1987. The time is now early December 1986 and the board of Siva, comprising the managing director and each of the functional managers, is meeting to fine-tune the proposed strategies for the forthcoming year.

Products and production

Siva has just two product lines – product line 1 (PL1) and product line 2 (PL2) and the company's production process is a standard one in which PL1 and PL2 are bought in and finished in the company. Therefore there are only variable manufacturing costs.

Finance structure

At the time of the commencement of operations Siva will have the following financial structure:

Fixed assets:	£60,000
Current assets:	£25,000
Share capital:	£ 5,000
Retained earnings	£45,000

Long-term liabilities: £25,000
Number of shares: £ 5,000

Organizational structure
The company is organized on the functional structure basis outlined on pages 21–36 – it can be considered to be an SBU.

The markets
For the forthcoming planning period, i.e. for the year 1987 Siva intends to market PL1 and PL2 in four markets or regions: North, South, East and West.

Distribution
In each marketing region PL1 and PL2 will be distributed through two channels of distribution: Channel 1 (Ch1) and Channel 2 (Ch2).

The environment

The environment in which Siva's products will be sold is considered to be stable and enjoys steady economic growth. Consequently the demand for PL1 and PL2 types of products has been shown, through the success of rival competitors already in existence, to be growing steadily at rates in excess of 10 per cent per year in volume terms. Existing competitors are profitable and although competition is not severe, sales are strongly influenced by the prices at which the products are set. Siva's marketing department has estimated that for PL1 the price must lie between £15 and £20 per unit and for PL2 the price must lie between £17 and £24 per unit. More precisely, Siva's market research indicates that for the forthcoming year PL1 and PL2 will have the price/demand schedules shown in Table 36 and 37.

Table 36   Price/demand schedule for PL1

Price interval (£)		(£)	*Demand range*
	<	15.0	3500+
15.0	<	15.5	3152–3499
15.5	<	16.0	2772–3151
16.0	<	16.5	2484–2771
16.5	<	17.0	2191–2483
17.0	<	17.5	1811–2190
17.5	<	18.0	1426–1810
18.0	<	18.5	946–1425
18.5	<	19.0	848–945
19.0	<	20.0	468–847
	more than	20.0	0–467

Table 37   Price/demand schedule for PL2

Price interval (£)		(£)	Demand range
	<	17.0	3528+
17.0	<	17.5	3400–3527
17.5	<	18.0	2902–3399
18.0	<	19.0	2593–2901
19.0	<	20.0	2384–2592
20.0	<	21.0	2281–2383
21.0	<	22.0	2175–2280
22.0	<	23.0	2074–2174
23.0	<	24.0	1654–2073
24.0	<	25.0	518–1653
	more than	25.0	0–517

Siva's goals and strategies

For the forthcoming year Siva has provisionally adopted the following set of goals and strategies:

Goals: financial and marketing

- Achieve a return on investment of at least 15 per cent for the year.
- Achieve a return on equity of at least 25 per cent for the year.
- Do not let the debt to equity ratio exceed 30:70.
- Achieve total sales of at least £800,000 by the end of the year.
- Have sales approximately equally distributed among the four target sales regions North, South, East and West.

Goals: Portfolio

Maximize the returns from both products while keeping the cash flows in balance and minimizing the risk profile of the portfolio. Try to ensure the future viability of all aspects of the strategy by continuously evaluating the financial and marketing contributions of each product. Continue to scan the environment for suitable new related products which may complement the existing range.

Strategy

Pursue a strategy of organic growth in sales to a level in excess of £800,000 for the year in the first year and then to grow at least 20 per cent in monetary terms for each of the next two years. This growth to be achieved by continuing to follow the generic strategy of high volume low cost with the same product lines, with new related products being introduced if market opportunities are discovered and if internal resources permit. Continue to use the same channels of distribution and serve the same markets. Evaluate and control success in the market on a quarterly basis and continuously check consistency of internal operations with Siva's goals.

Table 38 Projected price quantity and revenue data for Siva for 1987

	Product line 1 (PL1)				*Product line 2 (PL)*		
Date	Price per unit (£)	Quantity (units)	Total revenue (£)	Date	Price per unit (£)	Quantity (units)	Total revenue (£)
Jan 1987	17	1811	30,787	Jan 1987	18	2593	46,674
Feb 1987	17	1811	30,787	Feb 1987	18	2593	46,674
Mar 1987	17	1811	30,787	Mar 1987	18	2593	46,674
Apr 1987	17	1811	30,787	Apr 1987	18	2593	46,674
May 1987	17	1811	30,787	May 1987	18	2593	46,674
Jun 1987	17	1811	30,787	Jun 1987	18	2593	46,674
Jul 1987	17	1811	30,787	Jul 1987	19	2384	45,296
Aug 1987	17	1811	30,787	Aug 1987	19	2384	45,296
Sep 1987	17	1811	30,787	Sep 1987	19	2384	45,296
Oct 1987	17	1811	30,787	Oct 1987	19	2384	45,296
Nov 1987	17	1811	30,787	Nov 1987	19	2384	45,296
Dec 1987	17	1811	30,787	Dec 1987	19	2384	45,296

The projections

On the basis of the marketing information available, the planners at Siva have decided that the price for PL1 should be set at £17.00 for the whole of 1987, while the price of PL2 will be set at £18 for the first six months (i.e. up to and including June 1987) and that its price should then be increased to £19.00 for the remainder of the year.

On the basis of this set of prices plus the marketing information given above, Table 38 gives the projected sales revenues for 1987.

On the basis of the projection shown on Table 38 Siva's planners anticipate that additional financial resources will be required to sustain the projected level of operations and also to conform to strategic goals. The planners have tentatively agreed that there should be two debenture issues – one of £50,000 in April 1987 and one of £40,000 in July 1987. In addition there should be a share issue of £30,000 around June 1987.

On the basis of all the above information the quarterly and annual income statements and balance sheets for the company are calculated and are shown in Tables 39 and 40.

Evaluation of the degree of achievement of goals or targets

This aspect of control and evaluation is concerned with ascertaining how well the SBU's overall goals and targets have been met. Although any evaluation will need to be tailored to the actual goals and targets which a particular organization has set, it is often the case that most goals will be contained in a standard ratio analysis. The exposition of

Table 39   Siva's projected quarterly income statement with annual total for 1987

	Quarter 1 (£)	Quarter 2 (£)	Quarter 3 (£)	Quarter 4 (£)	Total for 1987 (£)
Sales	232,383	232,383	228,249	228,249	921,264
Cost of goods sold	125,427	125,427	123,360	123,360	497,574
Gross Profit	106,956	106,956	104,889	104,889	423,690
Less					
Administration expenses	45,000	45,000	45,000	45,000	180,000
Marketing expenses	46,476	46,476	45,651	45,651	184,254
Interest	0	1,500	2,241	2,241	5,982
Profit before tax	15,480	13,980	11,997	11,997	53,454
Tax	6,966	6,291	5,400	5,400	24,057
Profit after tax	8,514	7,689	6,597	6,597	29,397
Dividend payable	0	0	0	5,345	5,345
Unappropriated profit	8,514	7,689	6,597	1,252	24,052
Retained earnings	53,514	61,203	67,800	69,052	69,052

Table 40   Siva's projected quarterly balance sheet with annual total for 1987

	Quarter 1 (£)	Quarter 2 (£)	Quarter 3 (£)	Quarter 4 (£)	Total for 1987 (£)
Employment of capital					
Fixed assets	200,000	240,000	265,000	265,000	265,000
Accumulated depreciation	40,000	40,000	40,000	40,000	40,000
Total fixed assets	160,000	200,000	225,000	225,000	225,000
Current assets					
Closing stock	20,904	20,560	20,560	20,560	20,560
Debtors	116,191	116,191	114,124	114,124	114,124
Bank	0	11,717	40,229	52,226	52,226
Total current assets	137,095	148,468	174,913	186,910	186,910
Creditors					
Creditors	54,352	54,008	53,456	53,456	53,456
Overdraft	42,263	0	0	0	0
Tax payable	6,996	13,257	18,657	24,057	24,057
Dividend payable	0	0	0	5,345	5,345
Total current liabilities	103,581	67,265	72,113	82,858	82,858
Net current assets	33,514	81,203	102,800	104,052	104,052
Total net assets	193,514	281,203	327,800	329,052	329,052
Financed by					
Share capital	115,000	145,000	145,000	145,000	145,000
Retained earnings	53,514	61,203	67,800	69,052	69,052
Long-term liabilities	25,000	75,000	115,000	115,000	115,000
Capital employed	193,514	281,203	327,800	329,052	329,052

ratio analysis set out below is based upon the projections which have been made for Siva for 1987.

Ratio analysis can provide internal and external dimensions to control and evaluation. Thus, from an internal point of view, the technique can be used to measure how well SBU goals are being achieved during any planning period and also to analyse the trends that are taking place in the various ratios over time. While, from an external point of view, the ratios of a particular firm can be compared with competitors' ratios or industry averages so that a judgement can be made about that firm's competitiveness. This type of information can easily be obtained from publications such as ICC, Mintel etc. For example, ICC[1] in its *Industry Sector Reports* series, provides commentaries on the industry being examined plus ratios such as return on capital, return on assets, profit margin, asset utilization, stock turnover, quick ratio, return on investment, growth rates of sales, profits, etc. This information is provided for the industry as a whole and also for individual companies.

Although ratio analysis can be a very quick and effective way of obtaining insights into an organization's operations and performance, care must be exercised when applying it as the quality of the analysis is determined by the quality of the information upon which it is based. If this information is unsound then the resulting ratios will also be unsound. It should therefore be used in conjunction with complementary analytical tools and other supporting qualitative information.

The ratios which are most frequently used in this type of analysis are now set out in five main categories which tend to provide the most effective strategic insights.

- *Profitability ratios:* These measure a management's overall performance and show the returns which management has been able to achieve for the various stakeholders in the organization.
- *Liquidity ratios:* These measure the organization's ability to meet its short-term obligations.
- *Gearing ratios:* These measure the extent to which the organization has been financed by debt and by shareholders' funds.
- *Activity ratios:* These measure how well the organization has been using its resources.
- *Growth ratios:* These show the potential that exists for growth in the organization.

How each of these sets of ratios can aid the evaluation of an organization's historical or projected performance is now considered through the medium of Siva. In passing it should be noted that in addition to the actual ratios which are computed below for Siva, industry average ratios are provided so that external comparisons can be made.

Profitability ratios

Because profitability is often thought to be the fundamental measure of an organization's performance, the profitability ratios are considered

Table 41   Selected measures of profitability and their strategic uses[2]

Measure	Definition	Use
Gross profit margin	$\dfrac{\text{net sales} - \text{cost of sales}}{\text{net sales}}$	How well are costs being controlled? How effective is marketing?
Net profit margin	$\dfrac{\text{net profit}}{\text{net sales}}$	Shows return on sales. How effective is marketing?
Return on investment	$\dfrac{\text{net profit}}{\text{total assets}}$	Cash show how effective marketing and production are
Return on equity	$\dfrac{\text{net profit}}{\text{equity}}$	A crucial measure for shareholders, management and financial institutions – shows performance and indicates financial for growth
Earnings per share	$\dfrac{\text{earnings available}}{\text{average number of shares}}$	Of interest to shareholders and financial institutions

first. The most commonly used measures of performance and the principal analytical uses to which they are put are set out in Table 41.

Siva's projected profitability ratios for 1987 are considered below.

Gross profit margin
Gross profit margin can be defined as net sales minus cost of sales divided by net sales. The projected gross profit margins for Siva for 1987 are shown below.

$$\text{Gross profit margin} = \frac{\text{net sales} - \text{cost of sales}}{\text{net sales}}$$

Gross profit margins:

1Q 1987
$$\frac{£232{,}383 - £125{,}427}{£232{,}383} = 46.0 \text{ per cent}$$

2Q 1987
$$\frac{£232{,}383 - £125{,}427}{£232{,}383} = 46.0 \text{ per cent}$$

3Q 1987
$$\frac{£228{,}249 - £123{,}360}{£228{,}249} = 45.9 \text{ per cent}$$

4Q 1987
$$\frac{£228{,}249 - £123{,}360}{£228{,}249} = 45.9 \text{ per cent}$$

All 1987
$$\frac{£921{,}264 - £497{,}574}{£921{,}264} = 45.9 \text{ per cent}$$

Industry average = 35 per cent

Comments
Over the year Siva is expected to have a higher and improving gross profit margin than the industry in general. Therefore, these margins could be considered as highly satisfactory and would seem to indicate that the overall marketing function and the control of costs are both being managed effectively.

Net profit margin
Net profit margin, or return on sales, could be defined as net profits before taxes divided by net sales. The projected net profit margins for Siva for 1987 are shown below.

$$\text{Net profit margin} = \frac{\text{net profit before tax}}{\text{net sales}}$$

Net profit margins:

1Q 1987
$$\frac{£15,480}{£232,383} = 6.66 \text{ per cent}$$

2Q 1987
$$\frac{£13,980}{£232,383} = 6.01 \text{ per cent}$$

3Q 1987
$$\frac{£11,997}{£228,249} = 5.25 \text{ per cent}$$

4Q 1987
$$\frac{£11,997}{£228,249} = 5.25 \text{ per cent}$$

All 1987
$$\frac{£53,454}{£921,264} = 5.80 \text{ per cent}$$

Industry average = 4 per cent*

Comments
The net profit is above the industry average and seems to provide further evidence that the company is being effective in its marketing. Siva is generating a net profit in excess of 5 pence of each £1 of sales whereas in the industry as a whole the average net profit per £1 of sales is only 4 pence.

Return on investment
Return on investment (ROI) is obtained by dividing net profits before taxes by total assets and measures how effectively the company's assets have been managed. The projected return on investment ratios for Siva for 1987 are shown below.

---

* Industry average performance measures in all the following analyses are for the last year available, i.e. 1986.

$$\text{Return on investment} = \frac{\text{net profit before tax}}{\text{total net assets}}$$

Return on investment:

1Q 1987		2Q 1987	
$\dfrac{£15,480}{£193,514}$ = 8.00 per cent		$\dfrac{£29,460}{£281,203}$ = 10.48 per cent	

3Q 1987		4Q 1987	
$\dfrac{£41,457}{£327,800}$ = 12.64 per cent		$\dfrac{£53,454}{£329,052}$ = 16.24 per cent	

All 1987

$\dfrac{£53,454}{£329,052}$ = 16.24 per cent

Industry average = 14 per cent

Note: The 'net profit before tax' figures for 2Q, 3Q and 4Q are the sums of the accumulated net profits before tax for each preceding quarter.

Comments
ROI is frequently advocated by strategists (see Ansoff[3]) as the fundamental or core measure of organizational performance as it expresses most effectively the returns that an organization is generating on its assets. Consequently Siva's ROI should be regarded as highly satisfactory as it is above the industry average and also exceeds the level set in the company goals statement.

Return on equity
Return on equity measures the return which shareholders are obtaining and is calculated by dividing net profits before taxes by stockholders' equity. The projected returns on equity for Siva for 1987 are shown below.

$$\text{Return on equity} = \frac{\text{net profit before tax}}{\text{stockholders' equity}}$$

Return on equity:

1Q 1987

$$\frac{£15,480}{£168,514} = 9.19 \text{ per cent}$$

2Q 1987

$$\frac{£29,460}{£206,203} = 14.29 \text{ per cent}$$

3Q 1987

$$\frac{£41,457}{£212,800} = 19.48 \text{ per cent}$$

4Q 1987

$$\frac{£53,454}{£214,052} = 24.97 \text{ per cent}$$

All 1987

$$\frac{£53,454}{£214,052} = 24.97 \text{ per cent}$$

Industry average = 22 per cent

Note: The 'net profit before tax' figures for 2Q, 3Q and 4Q are the sums of the accumulated net profits before tax.

Comments
As with most other measures of profitability Siva's projections indicate that it will outperform the industry. However, the return is marginally less than has been set in the company goal statement (minimum of 25 per cent).

Earnings per share
Earnings per share measures the earnings of each share during the period being considered, and is calculated by dividing the earnings available for common stockholders by the average number of shares outstanding. The projected earnings per share for Siva for 1987 are shown below.

$$\text{Earnings per share} = \frac{\text{profit after tax}}{\text{average number of ordinary shares outstanding}}$$

Earnings per share:

1Q 1987

$$\frac{£8,514}{£115,000} = £0.07$$

2Q 1987

$$\frac{£16,203}{£145,000} = £0.11$$

3Q 1987

$$\frac{£22,800}{£145,000} = £0.16$$

4Q 1987

$$\frac{£29,397}{£145,000} = £0.20$$

All 1987

$$\frac{£29,397}{£145,000} = £0.20$$

Comments
The earnings per share ratio has increased steadily throughout 1987 and should be considered to be satisfactory.

Comments on Siva's overall profitability
Siva's projected profitability ratios indicate that if the proposed strategy is adopted then its profitability performance, in relation to its financial goals and in comparison with the average performance in the industry, will be highly satisfactory irrespective of which measure is used.

Liquidity ratios

Liquidity shows the ability of an organization to meet its short-term obligations, i.e. those which are due within one year. Organizations tend to try to meet such obligations by using their current assets, i.e. those assets which can quickly and easily be converted into cash. Adequate liquidity is particularly important in times of high inflation and at the start-up stage of a new business. Closely related to the state of liquidity of an organization is its cash flow position. Consequently a more comprehensive picture of liquidity can be provided when, as shown on page 418 funds flow statement and monthly cash budget statement analyses are also carried out.

The main ratios which can be used to measure liquidity are set out below.

Current ratio
The current ratio is defined as current assets divided by current liabilities. Siva's projected current ratios for 1987 are shown below.

$$\text{Current ratio} = \frac{\text{current assets}}{\text{current liabilities}}$$

Current ratios:

1Q 1987
$$\frac{£137,095}{£103,581} = 1.32$$

2Q 1987
$$\frac{£148,481}{£67,265} = 2.21$$

3Q 1987
$$\frac{£174,913}{£72,113} = 2.42$$

4Q 1987
$$\frac{£186,910}{£82,858} = 2.25$$

All 1987
$$\frac{£186,910}{£82,858} = 2.25$$

Industry average = 2.2

Comments
The current ratio should show steady improvement throughout the year and by the year end should be above the average for the industry.

Quick ratio
A complementary measure of liquidity often employed is the quick ratio, or acid test ratio. This can be defined as current assets minus average stock divided by current liabilities. (Average stock = (Opening stock minus closing stock) divided by 2.) This ratio, rather than the current ratio may be used because it could be claimed that the inclusion of stock (some of which may be obsolete and difficult to sell) in the current ratio may overstate an organization's ability to meet its short-term obligations. The projected quick ratios for Siva for 1987 are shown below.

$$\text{Quick ratio} \;=\; \frac{\text{current assets} - \text{average stock}}{\text{current liabilities}}$$

Quick ratios:

1Q 1987
$$\frac{£137,095 - £20,900}{£103,581} \;=\; 1.12$$

2Q 1987
$$\frac{£148,468 - £20,732}{£67,265} \;=\; 1.90$$

3Q 1987
$$\frac{£174,913 - £20,560}{£72,113} \;=\; 2.14$$

4Q 1987
$$\frac{£186,910 - £20,560}{£82,858} \;=\; 2.01$$

All 1987
$$\frac{£186,910 - £20,569}{£82,858} \;=\; 2.01$$

Industry average = 1.8

Comments
In general a quick ratio of 1 is considered satisfactory as such a ratio indicates that an organization can meet its current liabilities quickly. In this case the quick ratio is improving and can be considered to be conservatively high – immediate liquidation would easily allow all current liabilities to be met.

Average collection period
Although debtors come under the heading of current, and therefore liquid assets in the balance sheet, this overstates the degree of liquidity

that debtors possess. Debtors only become liquid assets when the money they owe can be obtained quickly. A measure of the speed with which this is being carried out is the average collection period which is defined as debtors multiplied by the number of days in the year divided by net sales. This ratio expresses the average number of days for which debtors are outstanding. The projected average collection period for Siva for 1987 is shown below.

$$\text{Average collection period} = \frac{\text{debtors} \times \text{days in year}}{\text{net sales}}$$

Average collection period (days):

1Q 1987
$$\frac{£116,191 \times 365}{£232,383} = 182.5$$

2Q 1987
$$\frac{£116,191 \times 365}{£464,766} = 91.25$$

3Q 1987
$$\frac{£114,124 \times 365}{£693,015} = 60.11$$

4Q 1987
$$\frac{£114,124 \times 365}{£921,264} = 45.21$$

All 1987
$$\frac{£114,124 \times 365}{£921,264} = 45.21$$

Industry average = 40 days

Comments
The important figure is the figure for the whole year – the quarterly figures are distorted because the debtors figure is being divided into less than one year's sales. As can be seen the projected figure for Siva is just a little above the industry average and greater efforts should be made to reduce the collection period.

Debtors turnover ratio
Closely related to the average collection period is the debtors turnover ratio – this ratio shows how many times per year debtors are being turned over and can be defined as net sales divided by debtors. The projected debtors turnover ratio for Siva for 1987 is shown below.

$$\text{Debtors turnover ratio} = \frac{\text{net sales}}{\text{debtors}}$$

Debtors turnover ratio:

1Q 1987

$$\frac{£232,383}{£116,191} = 2.00$$

2Q 1987

$$\frac{£464,766}{£116,191} = 4.0$$

3Q 1987

$$\frac{£693,015}{£114,124} = 6.07$$

4Q 1987

$$\frac{£921,264}{£114,124} = 8.07$$

All 1987

$$\frac{£921,264}{£114,124} = 8.07$$

Industry average = 9.1

Comments
This measure is equivalent to the average collection period (it can also be obtained by dividing 365 days by the average collection period) and therefore the comments given above for the average collection period also apply here.

Creditors ratio
This ratio shows the number of days credit that are being taken by the company and the average age length of credit being taken, in days, can be computed from the formula creditors divided by purchases, multiplied by 365 days. The projected creditors ratio for Siva for 1987 is:

$$\text{Creditors ratio (days)} = \frac{\text{creditors} \times \text{days in year}}{\text{purchases}}$$

Creditors ratio (days)

1Q 1987

$$\frac{£54,352 \times 365}{£146,331} = 135.57$$

2Q 1987

$$\frac{£54,008 \times 365}{£271,414} = 72.63$$

3Q 1987

$$\frac{£53,456 \times 365}{£394,774} = 49.42$$

4Q 1987

$$\frac{£53,456 \times 365}{£518,134} = 37.66$$

All 1987

$$\frac{£53,456 \times 365}{£518,134} = 37.66$$

Industry average = 45 days

Comments
The above ratios show that Siva will be paying its creditors in a shorter number of days than obtains on average for the industry. The primary advantage of this could be that such a policy could help establish strong relationships with suppliers.

Comments on Siva's overall liquidity
It does not appear to be the case that Siva will have short-term liquidity problems – all the measures are moving in directions which will increase liquidity. Perhaps the projected strong current ratios and quick ratios should cause Siva's financial planners to question having such high levels of liquidity. The funds flow and cash flow statements should help answer this question.

Gearing ratios

This set of ratios show the sources of the organization's capital i.e. shareholders or outside agencies such as banks and therefore these ratios show the organization's overall level of indebtedness.

Debt to equity
This is probably the most commonly used gearing ratio and is calculated by dividing total long-term debt by the total of stockholders' equity. The projected debt–equity ratios for Siva for 1987 are shown below.

$$\text{Debt–equity ratio} = \frac{\text{total long-term debt}}{\text{total equity}}$$

Debt–equity ratio:

1Q 1987	2Q 1987
$\dfrac{£25,000}{£168,514} = 14.84$ per cent	$\dfrac{£75,000}{£206,203} = 36.37$ per cent

3Q 1987	4Q 1987
$\dfrac{£115,000}{£212,800} = 54.04$ per cent	$\dfrac{£115,000}{£214,052} = 53.73$ per cent

All 1987
$$\frac{£115,000}{£214,052} = 53.73 \text{ per cent}$$

Industry average = 48 per cent

Comments
Siva's debt to equity ratio will increase over the year and be well outside the goals laid down in the strategic plan. Although this will

increase the overall risk of the company, it should be borne in mind that such a high level of debt to equity will in this period of growth help enhance Siva's return on equity and hence its propensity for sustained growth.

Debt coverage
Debt coverage shows an organization's ability to cover its fixed charges and is defined as profit before tax divided by interest expense. The projected debt coverage for Siva for 1987 is shown below.

$$\text{Debt coverage} = \frac{\text{profit before tax}}{\text{interest expense}}$$

Debt coverage:

1Q 1987	*2Q 1987*	*3Q 1987*
$\frac{£15,480}{0*} = 0$	$\frac{£13,980}{£1,500} = 9.32$	$\frac{£11,997}{£2,241} = 5.35$

4Q 1987	*All 1987*
$\frac{£11,997}{£2,241} = 5.35$	$\frac{£53,454}{£5,982} = 8.9$

Industry average = 7.5

Comments
Siva will, at the end of 1987, have a higher than industry average debt coverage ratio. However, the company will be trading profitably and servicing this level debt should not prove a problem.

Comments on the overall level of gearing
Although Siva is more highly geared than the strategic plan suggested and is also above the industry average this is not necessarily to the company's disadvantage. Indeed in this period of growth it may well be that such a capital structure confers competitive advantage through enhancing the company's return on equity.

Activity ratios

This set of ratios attempts to express how effectively an organization is using its resources – the more frequently its assets are being turned over the more effectively they are being used.

---

* Indicates no interest payable in this quarter

Total asset turnover
The total asset turnover ratio measures how well management is using all the organization's assets and is calculated by dividing net sales by total net assets. The projected total asset turnover ratio for Siva for 1987 is shown below.

$$\text{Total asset turnover ratio} = \frac{\text{net sales}}{\text{total assets}}$$

Total asset turnover ratio:

1Q 1987	2Q 1987	3Q 1987
$\frac{£232,383}{£297,095} = 0.78$	$\frac{£464,766}{£348,468} = 1.33$	$\frac{£693,015}{£399,913} = 1.73$

4Q 1987	All 1987
$\frac{£921,264}{£411,910} = 2.24$	$\frac{£921,264}{£411,910} = 2.24$

Industry average = 3

Comments
As Siva's anticipated use of assets is less than the average prevailing for the industry it may be fruitful to examine means of increasing their usage.

Fixed asset turnover
The fixed asset turnover ratio measures how well management is using the organization's fixed assets and is calculated by dividing net sales by total net fixed assets. The projected fixed asset turnover ratio for Siva for 1987 is shown below.

$$\text{Fixed asset turnover ratio} = \frac{\text{net sales}}{\text{net fixed assets}}$$

Fixed asset turnover ratio:

1Q 1987	2Q 1987	3Q 1987
$\frac{£232,383}{£160,000} = 1.45$	$\frac{£464,766}{£200,000} = 2.32$	$\frac{£693,015}{£225,000} = 3.08$

4Q 1987	All 1987
$\frac{£921,264}{£225,000} = 4.09$	$\frac{£921,264}{£225,000} = 4.09$

Industry average = 4.6

Comments
As with the assets turnover ratio Siva's anticipated use of fixed assets is less than the average prevailing for the industry. The reasons for this should be investigated.

Stock turnover times
The stock turnover times ratio measures how many times the organization's stock is turned over each year and is calculated by dividing the cost of goods sold by the closing stock. In general the greater the stock is turned over the more quickly it is being turned into sales. The projected stock turnover times ratio for Siva for 1987 is shown below.

$$\text{Stock turnover times ratio} \quad = \quad \frac{\text{cost of goods sold}}{\text{stock}}$$

Stock turnover times ratio:

1Q 1987	*2Q 1987*	*3Q 1987*
$\frac{£125,427}{£20,904} = 6.00$	$\frac{£250,854}{£20,560} = 12.20$	$\frac{£374,204}{£20,560} = 18.20$

4Q 1987	*All 1987*
$\frac{£497,574}{£20,560} = 24.20$	$\frac{£497,574}{£20,560} = 24.20$

Industry average   =   23.4

Comments
Siva's stock turnover rate is marginally better than the industry average which seems to indicate that the company may be relatively efficient in rapidly fulfilling orders and maintaining low levels of stock or both.

Comments on the overall levels of activity
Siva's management seems to be achieving superior results from its management of short term-assets – stock – rather than its longer-term assets. It may be worthwhile investigating the capacity utilization of the company.

Growth ratios

Frequently, a fundamental strategy of many organizations is growth. Growth is normally considered to be determined by environmental forces – such as the growth of the market, the intensity of competition, etc. However, the financial policies followed by an organization can significantly influence its growth rate. Among the more important financial determinants of the sustainable growth rate that an organization can achieve are: its dividend policy; its rate of return; the proportions of debt and equity in its capital structure. These are strategic variables which can be used to influence the rate of growth of an organization.

Earnings retention ratio
The earnings retention ratio shows the proportion of net profit after interest, but before tax, which is retained by the organization. Generally the greater this ratio, the greater the growth potential of the organization. This ratio can be computed by expressing the dividend payable as a fraction of the profit before tax. The projected earnings retention ratios for Siva for 1987 are shown below.

$$\text{Earnings retention ratio} \quad = \quad 1 - \frac{\text{dividend payable}}{\text{profit before tax}}$$

Earnings retention ratio:

1Q 1987

$$1 - \left(\frac{£0}{£15,480}\right) = 100 \text{ per cent}$$

2Q 1987

$$1 - \left(\frac{£0}{£13,980}\right) = 100 \text{ per cent}$$

3Q 1987

$$1 - \left(\frac{£0}{£11,997}\right) = 100 \text{ per cent}$$

4Q 1987

$$1 - \left(\frac{£5,345}{£11,997}\right) = 55.45 \text{ per cent}$$

All 1987

$$1 - \left(\frac{£5,345}{£53,454}\right) = 90.00 \text{ per cent}$$

Industry average = 65 per cent

Comments
The projection shows that Siva will retain a greater proportion of its earnings than the industry average. Following such a policy should help boost Siva's long-term growth prospects.

Return of equity
This has already been discussed on page 380.

Earnings per share
This has already been discussed on page 381.

Dividend per share

The dividend per share ratio shows the amount of dividend that each share should receive. In general there is an inherent tension in setting the level of dividends – the wishes of shareholders will frequently be to maximize the dividends payable to them, whereas management may wish to reduce the level of dividends payable in order to help fuel future growth.

$$\text{Dividend per share} \quad = \quad \frac{\text{dividend payable}}{\text{number of shares outstanding}}$$

Dividend per share:

$$\begin{array}{cc}
\textit{1Q 1987} & \textit{2Q 1987} \\
\dfrac{£0 \times 100}{£115,000} = 0.00\text{p} & \dfrac{£0 \times 100}{£115,000} = 0.00\text{p}
\end{array}$$

$$\begin{array}{cc}
\textit{3Q 1987} & \textit{4Q 1987} \\
\dfrac{£0 \times 100}{£145,000} = 0.00\text{p} & \dfrac{£5,345 \times 100}{£145,000} = 3.69\text{p}
\end{array}$$

$$\begin{array}{c}
\textit{All 1987} \\
\dfrac{£5,345 \times 100}{£145,000} = 3.69\text{p}
\end{array}$$

Comments

The proposed dividend to be paid does not appear to be excessive.

Dividend cover

Dividend cover measures the number of times the dividend can be paid out of the profit before tax, and is therefore a measure of an organization's ability to meet its dividend promises. The projected dividend cover for Siva for 1987 is shown below.

$$\text{Dividend cover} \quad = \quad \frac{\text{profit before tax}}{\text{dividend payable}}$$

Dividend cover:

$$\begin{array}{ccc}
\textit{1Q 1987} & \textit{2Q 1987} & \textit{3Q 1987} \\
\dfrac{£15,480}{£0} = 0 & \dfrac{£13,980}{£0} = 0 & \dfrac{£11,997}{£0} = 0
\end{array}$$

$$\begin{array}{cc}
\textit{4Q 1987} & \textit{All 1987} \\
\dfrac{£11,997}{£5,345} = 2.24 & \dfrac{£53,454}{£5,345} = 10.00
\end{array}$$

Comments

Dividend cover appears adequate.

Comments on overall growth potential

The company seems to possess good potential for growth. First, external or environmental circumstances appear to be conducive and second the internal financing policies of the company also appear to be conducive to promoting it.

Conclusions on goal achievement

On the basis of the analyses carried out above it appears to be the case that the strategies which Siva has provisionally adopted will lead to a high level of goal achievement except for the goal of not letting the debt to equity ratio exceed 30:70. However, it could be the case that allowing the ratio to drift may be to the benefit of the company as it should help boost its growth rate.

References

1   ICC Business Ratios, ICC Information Group Ltd, London.
2   McNamee, P. B., *Tools and Techniques for Strategic Management*, Pergamon, 1985.
3   Ansoff, H. I., *Strategic Management*, Macmillan, 1979.

18 Control and evaluation of marketing and financial strategies

Marketing strategies and performance

The control and evaluation of marketing strategies and performance can be carried out at two levels: first at the level of overall marketing performance and second, at the level of the quality of the performance of the constituent elements within the marketing function. How to assess the effectiveness of marketing at each of these levels is now considered.

The quality of overall marketing performance

Overall marketing performance can be assessed in terms of the degree of achievement of overall marketing goals and also the strength of the organization's competitive position. The latter element causes this aspect of evaluation to have a strong external orientation – marketing performance must be judged not just in absolute terms, but also in terms of performance relative to that of competitors. It is difficult to overstate the importance of measuring performance in relative as well as absolute terms – absolute measures alone may give a false, and often an overly-optimistic impression of achievement. For example, if an organization had a sales goal of 'growth in real terms of 12 per cent per annum' and it comfortably exceeded this target by growing at 16 per cent per annum, it might, if it relied exclusively on this measure, evaluate its performance as 'satisfactory'. However, if three major competitors in the same market were achieving annual growth rates of between 20 per cent and 40 per cent then, in relative performance terms, it could be argued that the organization had been performing rather poorly. The main measures which can be used to assess overall marketing performance are set out below.

Total sales revenue
It could be argued that this is the most important measure of marketing performance or competitiveness as it shows an organization's absolute level of achievement in its markets. Failure to achieve specified total sales targets could be due to lack of effectiveness (in which case the strategy ought to be reappraised) and/or lack of efficiency (in which case internal operations ought to be examined).

Market share
A measure closely related to total sales revenue is that of market share, where an organization's market share is defined as its percentage share of the total market revenues available. Market share shows how effective the organization has been in meeting the challenges from competitors. Thus, if an organization has been experiencing increases in market share over a period this tends to indicate that the current overall strategy and supporting marketing mix strategies have conferred some competitive advantage on the organization, with the opposite being true for decreases in market share.

Relative market share
Relative market share, as defined on page 152 measures the performance of an individual organization in the marketplace relative to its most important rivals. It shows whether an organization is gaining or losing market share in relation to its most important competitors and therefore indicates the relative effectiveness of marketing strategies in the marketplace. An organization which is losing relative market share is losing to at least one competitor and such a situation should provoke an investigation into the reasons why this has happened.

Return on sales
Return on sales measures the overall profitability of the marketing function and generally the higher the figure the greater will be the resulting cash flow and consequently the greater will be the resources, and consequently the scope that the organization has for defending its position or employing aggressive strategies against competitors.

Total volume sold
The total volume sold, in absolute terms, gives a measure of the organization's productive capacity as well as its success in the market. Perhaps the most useful aspect of this measure is that it can be used to calculate unit costs and hence relative unit costs.

Unit costs and relative unit costs
Unit costs can be calculated by dividing total costs by total volume sold. The resulting unit costs can then be compared with competitors' unit cost figures to develop a relative cost per unit position, so that an organization can make a judgement about its relative competitive strength in the area of costs. An organization which is conducting such

Table 42 The behaviour of relative unit costs for Company A and three others over a three year period

	Company A	Company B	Company C	Company D	
Total volume (units)	100.0	80.0	140.0	50.0	
Total costs (£)	1,000.0	960.0	1,330.0	650.0	
Cost per unit (£)	10.0	12.0	9.5	13.0	
Relative cost	1.0	0.83	1.05	0.77	1 year ago
Total volume (units)	80.0	80.0	120.0	50.0	
Total costs (£)	800.0	900.0	1,164.0	680.0	
Cost per unit (£)	10.0	11.25	9.7	13.60	
Relative cost	1.0	0.88	1.03	0.73	2 years ago
Total volume (units)	75.0	80.0	115.0	44.0	
Total costs (£)	675.0	800.0	1,012.0	616.0	
Cost per unit (£)	9.0	10.0	8.80	14.0	
Relative cost	1.0	0.9	1.02	0.64	3 years ago

an evaluation can define its relative unit costs as being equal to 1.00 and calculate each competitor's costs as follows:

$$\text{Relative unit cost} = \frac{\text{the organization's unit costs per unit}}{\text{competitor's unit costs per unit}}$$

This is illustrated by means of a hypothetical example, Company A, which has estimated the relative units costs of its three main competitors over the past three years, as shown in Table 42.

Table 42 shows that over the period, competitor C, which has consistently had the largest volume of production, has enjoyed the lowest unit costs, and has actually increased its cost advantage relative to A from 1.02 three years ago to 1.05 one year ago. Although competitor D has been improving its cost position relative to A, it has improved from 0.64 three years ago to 0.77 one year ago, it is still very much a follower and not a serious threat to competitor A. Finally, competitor B has performed worse than A in controlling unit costs – B's relative unit costs have deteriorated from 0.90 three years ago to 0.83 one year ago. Therefore, in conclusion, although A is falling behind the leader in relative costs, and is also failing to control its costs as well as D, it is steadily improving its cost position relative to competitor B.

Finally, when all other things are equal, then in general, the lower an organization's relative unit costs are, the greater its competitive advantage ought to be.

Unit prices
Unit prices can be calculated by dividing sales value by sales volume and thus seeing how a particular organization's prices relate to those of

competitors. Examining how prices for all competitors have changed over time should reveal the extent to which price has been used as a competitive weapon in the market and should enable an assessment of the appropriateness of the organization's pricing strategy to be made. For example, if an analysis of unit prices indicates a continuous period of strong price erosion by major competitors this could indicate that in order to continue to be effective, i.e. retain market share, a competitor must develop strategies and plans of action that will enable it to at least match the reducing price levels. This could be achieved through volume expansion strategies to reduce costs, asset reduction strategies to reduce costs, changing the basis of the pricing strategy through, for example, reducing the target level of profits for a pricing strategy based on preset profit targets, or, for example, changing the pricing strategy from one of 'cost-plus' to one of 'what the market will bear', etc. (See page 286 for alternative pricing strategies.)

Unit profit
Unit profit levels can be determined by subtracting unit costs from unit prices in order to determine the gross profit per unit. Determining the value of an organization's gross profit per unit in relation to competitors should give some insight into the organization's overall efficiency and also indicate resources that a rival might have at its disposal for the purposes of engaging in severe rivalry. Those organizations which have the greatest unit profit levels should have the greatest scope for such rivalry.

Quality of product range
This indicator is concerned with assessing the strength of the organization's product range in product life cycle terms. Although this type of assessment is frequently made only in qualitative terms, i.e. through verbal qualitative assessment, a more objective approach can be achieved by relating the organization's sales to the age of its products. Table 43 shows the sales for a hypothetical company, Company X, for 1987 broken down according to the year in which the products were first introduced.

As Table 43 shows Company X has not had any successful product introductions in 1987 and 1986 and indeed more than 50 per cent of its sales come from products introduced before 1981. This would seem to indicate that, recently, Company X has suffered from a lack of success-

Table 43   Age profile of Company X's sales

Total sales in 1987 (£)	Percentage of sales by value from products introduced in										
	1987 (%)	1986 (%)	1985 (%)	1984 (%)	1983 (%)	1982 (%)	1981 (%)	1980 (%)	1979 (%)	1978 (%)	Before 1978 (%)
2,600,000	0	0	5	10	10	8	6	16	10	8	27

ful product innovation. Care must be taken however in reaching such a conclusion on this information alone as the optimal rate of successful product innovation is often a function of the nature of the industry or the segment within the industry in which the organization is operating. Thus, in some relatively static industries such as, for example, traditional furniture manufacturing, new products tend to be introduced relatively infrequently, whereas in an innovative industry, such as consumer electronics, the frequent introduction of new products tends to be a feature of the most successful companies. There is a clear distinction to be drawn between 'product innovation' and 'successful product innovation'. Thus 'product innovation' can be measured by the numbers of *new products* introduced over a period of time, whether or not they were successful in the market, whereas 'successful product innovation' is measured by the *actual sales of new products' introduced* over a period of *time*. When making this type of assessment, relative performance as well as absolute performance should be considered. The importance of relative performance is illustrated in Table 44 by reference to Company Y. Company Y competes with Company X in the same industry and markets and is the industry leader in terms of sales, growth and profitability. As Table 44 shows the age profile of Company Y's products is significantly younger than Company X's and such a pattern should cause Company X to question its ability to continue to compete successfully when it has such a relatively old product range. In passing, it should be noted that this approach must be used with circumspection and due regard to the strategic philosophy of the organization being assessed. For example, the highly successful German automobile company Porsche has a philosophy that its automobiles should be regarded as durable, high quality engineering products not subject to fickle and ephemeral fashion trends. Consequently the age profile of its sales would be significantly older than that of most other automobile manufacturers. In contrast to this, one of the major problems which confronted BL in the late 1970s and early 1980s was the age profiles of its product range. In comparison with its competitors BL had a disproportionate amount of its sales from aged products.

Table 44 Age profile of Company Y's sales

| Total Sales in 1987 (£) | *Percentage of sales from product introduced in* | | | | | |
	1987 (%)	1986 (%)	1985 (%)	1984 (%)	1983 (%)	before 1983 (%)
12,000,000	5	10	25	30	20	10

Conclusions on the control and evaluation of overall marketing performance

As the above has shown there are many measures which can be used to assess overall marketing effectiveness – the choice of measures must be tailored to the particular circumstances facing the organization. Table 45 presents a summary of the various measures together with a brief indication of their uses.

Control and evaluation of the elements of the marketing function

This aspect of control and evaluation is concerned with measuring the performance of the major marketing elements within the marketing function of an organization. This can be achieved through disaggregating the function into its major constituent segments: product lines; channels of distribution; marketing regions; and methods of promotion, and assessing the contribution that each of these segments is making to the organization's overall marketing goals and profitability. In other words this type of evaluation is concerned with evaluating how effective the marketing mix strategies have been in placing the organization's products or services in the desired market segments and soliciting the desired responses. This can be achieved through a profitability and cost analysis of the organization's product, place, promotion and pricing strategies.

In the analyses carried out below the objectives are the same in each case – to ascertain the overall cost that the segment has been and the contribution that it has made to the organization's marketing goals, to estimate the costs and contributions of elements within each segment, and to take appropriate action to ensure compliance with goals.

The segments can be divided into two broad sets – those segments that may be analysed through developing an income statement and those which are analysed by other methods.

Segments which may be analysed using income statement approaches

The main segments which tend to be analysed using this approach are the product lines, channels of distribution and marketing regions. Irrespective of the segment being analysed the approach will have the following general format: an income statement is developed which shows the performance of the segment under analysis, the achieved income statement results are then compared with the marketing targets, variances are noted, and, where appropriate, remedial action is taken.

There are two basic approaches to this type of analysis which tend to be employed – the full cost approach and the contribution margin approach. Each of these is now considered.

The full cost approach to segment cost and profitability analysis

This is the more frequently used approach and the objective of the analysis is to ascertain the profit contribution that the segment under consideration is making through drawing up an income statement for it and charging it with the actual costs it has incurred plus other costs which are allocated. The approach can be carried out in a number of discrete steps:

Table 45 A summary of the measures of overall marketing performance

Measure of overall marketing performance	Units	Definition/source	Purpose/use	Comments
Total sales revenue	£	From income statement	Measures degree of goal achievement	Ultimate measure
Market share	%	Sales revenue Total market sales	Measure sales relative to all competitors	Overall strength in market
Relative market share	Index	Company's market share Share of largest competitor	Measures market strength relative to largest competitor	Shows if company is relatively stronger or weaker than competitors
Return on sales	%	Net profit sales	Overall profitability	Overall effectiveness of marketing strategy
Total volume	Units	Production data	Physical size	Compare with competitors
Unit cost	£	Total costs Total volume	Measures unit costs	Compare with competitors
Relative unit cost index		Unit costs Competitors' unit costs	Measures costs relative to competitors	Ability to control costs
Unit price	£	Sales values Sales volumes	Shows industry price patterns	Shows type of price strategies
Unit profit	£	Unit price – unit cost	Measures profit per unit	Shows efficiency and room for manoeuvre
Quality	%	Percentage of sales plotted with year of introduction	Measures degree of quality/innovation	Shows dependence on 'new' and 'old' products

1 The natural expenses should be classified according to their marketing function, and each function, plus its expenses, should be made the responsibility of a departmental head. Typical expenses will normally include items such as salaries, insurance, heating etc. and a typical functional classification of marketing costs could be selling, warehousing, transport, advertising, credit and collection and general accounting for marketing.
2 Assign these functional expenses to the marketing segments under analysis.
3 Allocate fixed and variable, direct and indirect expenses associated with marketing to each segment.
4 On the basis of the segment's activities and the expenses assigned, an income statement for each segment can be developed.
5 These income statements can be the basis for the cost and profitability analyses of each marketing segment.

How this approach can be implemented is illustrated in Table 46 which provides an example of a full cost analysis, by product line, for a hypothetical company with two product lines.

As well as showing the profit margins for each product line this type of statement also enables each product line's expenses to be monitored and controlled. Thus, in the above example although the gross profits which the product line are generating are roughly the same, Product Line B's marketing and administrative expenses are disproportionately

Table 46 A product line profitability and cost analysis by product line using a full cost approach

	Product line A (£)	Product line B (£)	Total (£)
Net sales	273,000	120,000	393,000
Cost of goods sold	200,000	95,000	295,000
Gross profit	73,000	25,000	98,000
Marketing expenses:			
Selling	16,000	7,000	23,000
Warehousing	3,000	1,600	4,600
Transport	1,900	850	2,750
Advertising	1,000	600	1,600
Credit and collection	700	200	900
General accounting	1,100	1,000	2,100
Total marketing expenses	23,700	11,250	34,950
Administrative expenses	6,000	6,000	12,000
Total marketing and administrative expenses	29,700	17,250	46,950
Net profit before tax	43,300	7,750	51,050
Return on sales (%)	[15.9]	[6.5]	[12.9]

high. It would therefore appear to be prudent to investigate the reasons for this, particularly the allocation of equal amounts for 'administrative expenses' to each product line.

The contribution margin approach to segment cost and profitability analysis
An alternative method for analysing segment profitability is to use a contribution margin approach. This approach is advocated when only variable manufacturing costs can be accurately estimated and allocated. When using such an approach just variable costs are deducted from each segment's sales to provide a figure which shows each segment's gross contribution margin. This figure can be used for assessing the segment's contribution to profitability. The element 'fixed expenses' is shown separately and is not allocated at all unless it can be directly and specifically charged to the segment under analysis.

The analysis attempts to ascertain the profit contribution that the segment under consideration is making through drawing up an income statement for it and charging it only with the variable marketing costs that can be directly and unambiguously attributed to it.

The approach can be carried out by following a number of discrete steps.

1 The natural expenses should be classified according to their marketing function, and each function, plus its expenses, should be made the responsibility of a departmental head. Typical expenses will normally include items such as salaries, insurance, heating etc. and a typical functional classification of marketing costs could be selling, warehousing, transport, advertising, credit and collection and general accounting for marketing.
2 Assign these variable functional expenses to the marketing segments under analysis.
3 On the basis of the segment's activities and the expenses assigned, an income statement for each segment can be developed.
4 These income statements can be the basis for the cost and profitability analyses of each marketing segment.

How a contribution margin approach can be used to control and evaluate strategies is now provided through an analysis of the projected results of the hypothetical company Siva for 1987.

Profitability and cost analysis of product strategy using a contribution margin approach
When products can be grouped according to product line or brand line and when functional costings are applied, a product line income statement can be prepared. This type of statement enables assessments to be made of the levels of marketing expenses which each product line has incurred as well as the contribution that product line is making to

Table 47   Projected product line profitability and cost analysis for SIVA for 1987

	PL1 (£)	PL2 (£)	Total (£)
Sales	369,444	551,820	921,264
Variable costs	199,538	298,036	497,574
Gross contribution margin	169,906	253,784	423,690
Less:			
Variable marketing expenses			
Selling	18,426	27,636	46,062
Warehousing	12,534	18,792	31,326
Transport	7,374	11,052	18,426
Advertising	18,426	27,636	46,062
Credit and collection	11,058	16,584	27,642
General accounting	5,898	8,838	14,736
Variable marketing expenses	73,716	110,538	184,254
Contribution margin	96,190	143,246	239,436
Product controllable margin to sales (%)	[16.29]	[12.91]	[14.27]
Less:			
Product line fixed expenses	36,000	72,000	108,000
Margin available for common fixed expenses and profit	60,190	71,246	131,436
Common fixed expenses			77,982
Net profit before tax			53,454

profitability. Table 47 shows a projected product line income statement for Siva for 1987.

As the Table 47 shows the more profitable line, in terms of product controllable margin to sales, will be PL1 and this is due to it having a relatively lower level of product line fixed expenses.

Profitability and cost analysis of channel of distribution strategy using a contribution margin approach

When sales are split according to identifiable channels of distribution, channel expenses can be allocated and an income statement which shows the contributions that each channel is making can be developed. Table 48 shows a projected channel of distribution income statement for Siva for 1987.

As Table 48 shows Channel 1 will have a much superior contribution. This is due to one main factor – its variable marketing expenses will be disproportionately lower than those for Channel 2.

Table 48 Projected channel of distribution profitability and cost analysis for Siva for 1987

	CH1 (£)	CH2 (£)	Total (£)
Sales	737,010	184,254	921,264
Variable costs	398,058	99,516	497,574
Gross contribution margin	338,952	84,738	423,690
Less:			
Variable marketing expenses			
Selling	32,244	13,818	46,062
Warehousing	21,930	9,396	31,326
Transport	12,894	5,532	18,426
Advertising	32,244	13,818	46,062
Credit and collection	19,350	8,292	27,642
General accounting	10,314	4,422	14,736
Variable marketing expenses	128,976	55,278	184,254
Contribution margin	209,976	29,460	239,436
Controllable contribution by channel (%)	[16.77]	[4.26]	[14.27]
Less:			
Channel fixed expenses	86,400	21,600	108,000
Margin available for common fixed expenses and profit	123,576	7,860	131,436
Common fixed expenses			77,982
Net profit before tax			53,454

Profitability and cost analysis by region
This is perhaps the most fundamental and also the simplest type of cost and profitability analysis. When sales are split according to easily identifiable regions it is relatively easy to assign regional expenses and thereby develop an income statement which shows the costs and contributions that each geographical region is making. Table 49 shows a projected regional income statement for Siva for 1987.

As Table 49 shows the region which will make the strongest contribution is the Northern while the weakest contribution will come from the Southern one – the cause of the disparity is due to the higher product line fixed expenses which the Southern region will incur.

Comparison between using a contribution margin approach and a full cost approach
Although, for the analysis of segment performance, the contribution margin approach is less frequently used than the full cost approach it

Table 49   Projected sales region profitability and cost analysis for SIVA for 1987

	North (£)	South (£)	East (£)	West (£)	Total (£)
Sales	285,594	202,674	193,464	239,532	921,264
Variable costs	154,249	109,464	104,490	129,371	497,574
Gross contribution margin	131,345	93,210	88,974	110,161	423,690
Less:					
Variable marketing expenses					
Selling	14,280	10,134	9,672	11,976	46,062
Warehousing	9,708	6,888	6,576	8,148	31,326
Transport	5,712	4,056	3,870	4,794	18,426
Advertising	14,280	10,134	9,672	11,976	46,062
Credit and collection	8,568	6,078	5,802	7,182	27,642
General accounting	4,566	3,246	3,096	3,834	14,736
Variable marketing expenses	57,114	40,536	38,688	47,910	184,254
Contribution margin	74,231	52,674	50,286	62,251	239,436
Controllable contribution by region (%)	[19.69]	[3.78]	[16.69]	[14.72]	[14.27]
Less:					
Region fixed expenses	18,000	45,000	18,000	27,000	108,000
Margin available for common fixed expenses and profit	56,231	7,674	32,286	35,251	131,436
Common fixed expenses					77,982
Net profit before tax					53,454

nonetheless has certain attributes, which are outlined below, that may make it a superior tool when the primary objective of the analysis is the accurate analysis and subsequent improvement of marketing performance. Some of the arguments for and against the approach (see Matz[1] and Solomons[2]) are set out below:

- A primary objective of marketing cost control and evaluation is to be able to see the true marketing cost structures of the various constituent elements in each marketing segment. However, marketing costs are composite and contain direct and indirect, fixed and variable elements and this complexity makes accurate allocations difficult and subject to error. Indeed it is not unusual to find that organizations simply allocate costs in a rule of thumb type, arbitrary manner. However, if only variable manufacturing costs, which can be accurately estimated and allocated, are deducted from each segment's sales then a figure which shows each constituent element's gross contribution margin can be calculated and this figure can be used for assessing the segment's contribution to profitability. The element 'fixed expenses' is shown separately and is not allocated at all unless it can be directly and specifically charged to the segment under analysis. This aspect of the contribution margin approach raises the question about situations in which a segment contributes nothing to the recovery of fixed expenses, i.e. there is a pricing policy based on marginal rather than full costing. A contribution margin type of income statement should reveal such a situation and provoke appropriate managerial action.

- The contribution margin approach has as its focus the importance of profit, and not sales volume, i.e. the success of a marketing strategy should be evaluated not in terms of the volume of goods sold, but rather in the profit contribution that they make. This shifts the focus of evaluation away from what is 'good for the marketing department (sales)' to 'what is good for the organization (profitable sales)'.
- Because only directly attributable costs are assigned to segments managers who are responsible for the segments can be more easily appraised – there is no scope for managers attributing an unsatisfactory performance to having had to meet obligations – for example overhead – over which they do not have control. In other words in this context managers are assessed solely on the contribution of their segment.
- Unlike the full costing approach in which reported income is affected by the physical size of the finished goods inventory, in the contribution approach reported income is a function of sales volume. This shows more clearly the relationship between income and sales volume.
- Contribution margin approach is more useful for marketing managers than the full costing approach in that it enables them to appraise their performance more objectively.
- It does need a highly efficient management information system and the advent of low-cost computer systems should help stimulate further interest in the approach.
- However, it should be borne in mind that the approach is only acceptable for internal accounting purposes.

Irrespective of whether a full cost or a contribution margin approach is used, market segment income statements can be used to evaluate the quality of an organization's product strategy, its distribution strategy and its effectiveness in its chosen marketing regions.

The evaluation of promotion

In Part Six promotion was sub-divided into two broad types – impersonal promotion and personal selling. How each of these types of promotion may be evaluated is now considered.

The evaluation of impersonal promotion

Irrespective of the nature of the type of impersonal promotion being evaluated (for example, a television advertising campaign, a newspaper advertising campaign, participation in a trade show, etc.) the fundamental criterion upon which the evaluation ought to be based should always be the same – the extent to which promotional goals or objectives are being achieved. Impersonal promotion campaigns can be subdivided into two main types: first, those which do not directly lead to action – for example campaigns to develop awareness, to develop attitudes, or to signal to rivals, and second, those which are designed to lead to action – for example an advertising campaign which aims to increase sales.

Evaluating promotion campaigns which do not lead to action poses problems in that it is usually difficult to measure with precision the effects that such campaigns may have had. For example, in the case of the corporate advertising campaigns which the major oil companies run in the UK there are no clear quantitative measures of their impact. However, one approach which may be employed to evaluate the effectiveness of a 'non-action' promotion campaign is to use market research techniques, after the campaign has ended, to question representative samples of people drawn from the populations which were the targets of the campaign. For example, if a fast-growing conglomerate, which had achieved its growth through the rapid acquisition of unrelated companies, was concerned about developing the image of being a 'financial predator' rather than that of being 'an economic force restructuring industry to bring economic benefit to society as a whole' it might engage in a corporate advertising campaign to promote the latter image. The conglomerate could assess the effectiveness of its campaign through using interview teams to sample, and then question, target segments of the campaign (existing investors, potential investors, trade unionists, banks, politicians, etc.) to ascertain the extent to which they have been influenced by it.

Although promotion campaigns which lead to action such as sales appear to be more amenable to evaluation – if there is an increase in sales after a campaign then it could be argued that the relationship between the cost of the campaign and the subsequent increase in sales is a measure of its effectiveness – this may be too superficial a view. Such a view assumes that there is a direct link between a promotion campaign and subsequent sales. However, promotion campaigns are not the only influences on buying decisions. Other factors such as price, quality, the activities of competitors and general economic influences may influence, or even swamp, the influences that a promotion campaign may have. Therefore, when a promotion campaign is being evaluated on the basis of the direct effects that it has had upon sales, any conclusions should be tempered with a consideration of the effects of other non-promotional influences. In general it is suggested that there are three core methods by which a promotion campaign which leads to action may be evaluated and each is considered below.

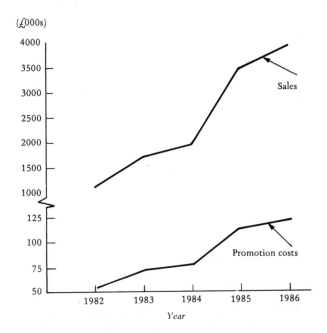

Figure 53   *The relationship between the costs of a promotional campaign and sales*

A historical approach to evaluating the effects of a promotion campaign
This is the simplest approach and can be carried out by estimating the
total costs of promotion and correlating these, on a time series basis,
with subsequent sales. This correlation will usually be on a lagged
basis, i.e. it will take some time for the effects of the campaign to be
reflected in sales. Figure 53 shows how the relationship may be plotted
so that the influence of time can be seen. The relationships shown are
based upon total costs and total sales. If, however, total costs are
divided by total sales a ratio which shows 'the costs of promotion per
£1 of sales' results. Such ratios enable the effectiveness of promotion
campaigns to be evaluated first on an annual basis – the value of
sales generated by each £1 of promotion in 1985, 1986, and 1987 – and
second in relation to competitors – how well does the value of sales
generated by each £1 of promotion compare with the achievements of
competitors.

Evaluating the effects of promotion through varying its intensity
Even in promotion campaigns in which the link between the campaign
and the resultant sales is clear, it is not always immediately apparent
what the optimal intensity of a campaign ought to be. For example, if a
company were running a newspaper advertising campaign which comprised a half-page advertisement once per week in regional newspapers
how would it determine if this was the optimal intensity or frequency

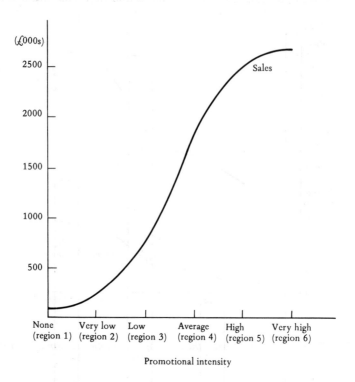

(£000s)

Sales

Promotional intensity

None	Very low	Low	Average	High	Very high
(region 1)	(region 2)	(region 3)	(region 4)	(region 5)	(region 6)

Figure 54   *Measuring the effects of promotion intensity on sales*

i.e. would it be in the company's commercial interests to run the campaign on the basis of the same advertisement one day per fortnight, or two days per week, or three days per week? One approach to answering this type of question is to divide the company's market into a number of similar regions and to vary the intensity of the campaign in each region. In the above example this could be achieved by selecting six regions which had similar market characteristics, running an identical campaign with different frequencies (say, very high, high, average, low, and very low) in each region, and then relating the subsequent sales to the intensity of the campaign. The results could then be plotted as shown in Figure 54.

Figure 54 suggests that the effectiveness of the campaign is greatest when the intensity is 'low' and 'average' and that the marginal increases in sales when the campaign assumes a 'high' or 'a very high' intensity are much lower.

Evaluating the effects of alternative methods of promotion
Just as there may be an optimal level of intensity for a given method of promotion, so there may also be an optimal method of promotion or an optimal mix of methods. For example, if a company had been using a

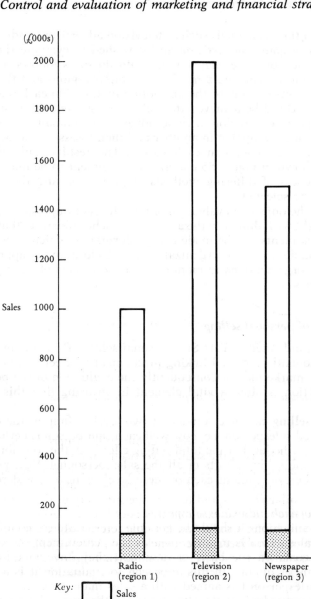

Figure 55   *Measuring the effects of alternative methods of promotion*

mix of promotional channels such as television advertising, radio advertising and newspaper advertising and it wished to evaluate the effectiveness of each of these channels, it could do so as follows. It could
divide its total market into a number of similar regions and then vary
the method of promotion, or the promotion mix, within each region. In
this case this could be achieved through running a television advertising campaign in one region, a radio advertising campaign in another
and a newspaper campaign in another and then assessing the costs and
effects of each campaign in each region. The results could then be
plotted as shown in Figure 55 enabling a judgement to be made about
the effectiveness of differing methods of promotion and the optimal
methods to be selected.

Although the objective evaluation of the effects of impersonal promotion is fraught with difficulty the above approaches illustrate that quantitative assessments can be made using information which is normally
freely available in most organizations. Therefore these approaches
should help organizations to monitor the effectiveness of their promotion strategies.

Evaluation of personal selling

As has been indicated in Part Six, personal selling, for many organizations, is frequently the final linking mechanism between the organization and its marketplaces. Consequently the evaluation of the personal
selling function is often a vital element in ensuring that this link is
effective.

Personal selling can be evaluated at two levels – first, at the level of
the individual salesperson, i.e. how well each salesperson is performing,
and second at the level of the total selling effort, i.e. the contribution of
the sum of the selling efforts of all the sales personnel. How personal
selling can be evaluated at each of these levels is now considered.

Evaluation of each individual salesperson

In most organizations it should be possible to evaluate the contribution
that each salesperson is making towards the achievement of sales and
marketing goals on the basis of how well they have met their set
targets, goals or quotas. In this approach to evaluation it is assumed
that each salesperson has agreed with a sales manager or a marketing
manager an individual set of targets for the forthcoming planning period
(depending upon the circumstances this planning period could be one
week, one month, one quarter, or one year). Consequently salespeople
will tend to be evaluated on how well they have met targets such as:

- *Sales or revenue targets* – total value of sales.
- *Product targets* – numbers and value of sales of each product line.
- *Profit targets* – total gross profit and gross profit for each product
  line.

- *Customer targets* – customer types: size, new customers, existing customer, etc.
- *Activity targets* – number of calls made.
- *Expenses targets* – the control of expenses incurred in carrying out selling tasks.

The sources of information on which the evaluation can take place are the salespeople's individual sales or call reports. These reports, which are often completed on a daily basis, aim to provide information on the activities which the salespeople have engaged in during that day and to chart each individual's progress towards meeting targets. Activities often included in such reports include information on:

- Prospecting for new customers.
- Soliciting orders from existing customers.
- Explaining why customers have been lost.
- Details of expenses incurred.
- Perhaps, reports on areas of interest such as rival products, competitors' behaviour, market conditions, and market opportunities.

The above information is normally recorded under headings such as:

- Number of calls made.
- Breakdown of calls according to type e.g. prospecting, soliciting.
- Number of sales made.
- Details of individual orders placed (information on customer, product, value).
- Volume of sales transacted.
- Value of sales transacted.
- Customer names and types.
- Travel and other expenses incurred.

When the reports have been completed then each salesperson's performance can be assessed along three dimensions:

- How well have agreed targets been met for the time period under consideration?
- What has been the historical performance of the salesperson over a number of time periods?
- How does the salesperson's performance, in the period under consideration, compare with the performance of other salespeople in the organization?

How this type of evaluation can be effected is illustrated by means of a hypothetical example.

A hypothetical example to illustrate the evaluation of sales personnel
The Riva Company has two products – Product A (A) and Product B (B) and its sales personnel sell direct to the customers. The total market is

divided into a number of approximately equally sized sales territories with one salesperson having the exclusive rights for each territory. The sales performance over three years of one salesperson – J. Wilson – and an evaluation of his performance is given in Table 50.

As can be seen salesperson Wilson's performance is in some ways highly satisfactory and in other ways not so satisfactory. Thus if Wilson is evaluated upon the criterion of meeting his agreed targets for the last time period or if a purely *historical* perspective is taken, it can be seen that he has consistently been close to, or indeed exceeded, the targets which have been set for him – a satisfactory performance.

However, if an *average* perspective is applied, it can be seen that, in terms of his 1986 performance Wilson is performing below the company average in all measures of sales performance.

This example illustrates the importance of applying multiple measures to this type of evaluation. Thus, even though Wilson's current average performance is below company average, there may be good reasons for it, for example, the territory which Wilson has may be inferior to that of the average salesperson – there may be less propensity on the part of potential consumers to purchase A and B, the expenses in making calls in the territory may be greater, the products may face more severe competition from competing products in this territory, the company may be a relative newcomer to this territory and may still be experiencing considerable competition from incumbent sellers etc.

Evaluation of the sum of the contributions of all sales personnel
It is relatively easy to sum the above type of individual salesperson's sales performance reports and thus evaluate the total contribution that all staff involved in personal selling are making. Although the time period for this type of evaluation is determined by the nature of the organization and its industry it is relatively common to find such an evaluation being carried out on a rolling monthly or quarterly basis. This type of evaluation tends to rely on summary information of the type shown in Table 51.

Table 51 shows the necessity of considering multiple measures of performance. The sales force has failed to achieve many targets for the year – total sales, total gross profit, control of expenses, gross profit per customer etc. However some measures of performances had positive variances during the year and it might be worth questioning the assumptions behind the annual and quarterly target levels of sales and expenses.

The evaluation of sales personnel and the total selling function is often seen as a negative device for the control of salespeople. This may be too narrow a view. Although control is an important element in the evaluation of this function it should be regarded just as one element. A more comprehensive view suggests that the evaluation process, in addition to providing information about performance, can also be used as a positive instrument to encourage sales personnel to plan sales campaigns which will bring greatest benefit to themselves and their organization. For example, the above type of analysis may highlight the

Table 50 Sales performance of J. Wilson

Year	1984 (£)	1985 (£)	1986 (£)	Company averages for 1986 (£)
Sales targets A	42,000	47,000	58,000	75,000
Sales targets B	245,000	238,000	280,000	300,000
Total target sales of A and B	287,000	285,000	338,000	375,000
Actual sales of A	45,200	51,000	57,000	72,000
Actual sales of B	220,000	235,000	250,000	285,000
Actual sales of A and B	265,200	286,000	307,000	357,000
Variance for A (%)	+3,200 (108)	+4,000 (108)	(1,000) (98)	(3,000) (96)
Variance for B (%)	(25,000) (90)	(3,000) (99)	(3,000) (90)	(15,000) (90)
Gross profit targets A	6,000	6,800	8,300	10,800
Gross profit targets B	39,000	46,500	58,000	71,250
Total profit targets A and B	45,000	53,300	66,300	82,050
Actual gross profit A	6,400	7,200	7,200	10,100
Actual gross profit B	35,600	45,400	57,500	69,500
Actual gross profit A and B	47,300	52,600	67,700	79,600
Variance for A (%)	+400 (107)	+400 (106)	(1,100) (87)	700 (94)
Variance for B (%)	(3,400) (90)	(1,100) (98)	(500) (99)	2,450 (97)
Selling expenses	6,630	7,214	7,300	6,400
Number of customers	76	83	120	96
Number of calls	420	477	490	632
Calls per day*	2.10	2.38	2.45	3.16
Cost per call	15.79	15.12	14.89	10.13
Sales per customer	3,489.47	3,445.78	2,558.33	3,718.75
Gross profit per customer	622.37	633.73	564.17	829.17

* Based upon 200 selling days sales per year.

Table 51 Summary of 1986 performance of a total of eight sales personnel on a rolling quarterly basis

Time	Quarter 1 (£)	Quarter 2 (£)	Quarter 3 (£)	Quarter 4/ total for year (£)
	£000	£000	£000	£000
Total sales targets	600	1,200	2,100	3,000
Actual sales	476	1,190	1,914	2,856
Variance	(124)	(10)	(186)	(144)
Gross profit targets	131	263	460	656
Actual gross profit	106	265	426	637
Variance	(25)	+2	(34)	(19)
Target selling expenses	11	22	33	44
Actual selling expenses	10	20	46	51
Variance	+1	+2	(13)	(7)
Target number of orders	187	375	562	750
Actual number of orders	140	290	482	768
Variance	(47)	(85)	(60)	+18
Target number of calls	1,300	2,600	3,900	5,200
Actual number of calls	1,010	2,030	3,545	5,056
Variance	(290)	(570)	(355)	(144)
Target cost per call	8.46	8.46	8.46	8.46
Actual cost per call	9.90	9.85	12.98	10.09
Variance (%)	(1.44)	(1.39)	(4.52)	(1.63)
Target number of customers	187	375	562	750
Actual number of customers	140	290	482	768
Variance	(47)	(85)	(73)	18
Target sales per customer	3,208.56	3,200.00	3,736.65	4,000.00
Actual sales per customer	3,400.00	4,103.45	3,970.95	3,718.75
Variance (%)	191.44	903.45	234.30	281.25
Target gross profit per customer	700.53	701.33	818.50	874.67
Actual gross profit per customer	757.14	913.79	883.82	829.42
Variance (%)	56.61	212.46	65.32	(45.25)

differing gross profit contributions of different territories or types of customers and may be used to encourage sales personnel to pursue sales most vigorously in those areas which seem to offer the greatest gross profit potential.

Financial strategies and performance

The control and evaluation of financial strategies and performance can be carried out at two levels – first the effectiveness of overall financial strategies and performance, and second, the effectiveness of the performance of the constituent elements within the finance function.

The quality of overall financial performance

The overall financial performance of an organization can be assessed in terms of the degree of achievement of overall financial goals and also the quality of the organization's financial performance relative to its competitors' performances. Both of these elements of performance have already been considered in the context of the case study Siva on page 372. Thus, to recapitulate, the overall effectiveness of various strategies can by measured by the following means.

- *Investment strategies* can be measured by: return on investment, return on capital employed.
- *Financing strategies* can be measured by: debt to equity ratio, creditors ratio, debtors ratio.
- *Dividend strategies* can be measured by: return on equity, payout ratio dividend growth rate.
- *Liquidity strategies* can be measured by: current ratio, quick ratio.

Although there is almost an infinite number of issues which could be worthy subjects for control and evaluation within the finance function, for the purposes of exposition and analysis it can be useful to group these issues into two major categories:

- The control and evaluation of long-term strategies – this is mainly concerned with monitoring and evaluating capital expenditures.
- The control and evaluation of shorter-term strategies – this is mainly concerned with monitoring and controlling the organization's cash position.

The control and evaluation of capital expenditures

The control and evaluation of capital expenditures is primarily concerned with monitoring the achieved and projected cash flows associated with capital projects to ensure that target net present values (NPVs) or rates of return are achieved. Thus control and evaluation of the performance of projects involving capital expenditure has three elements – monitoring achieved performance, revising forecasts of future expected cash flows as implementation of projects proceeds, and deciding upon actions which will keep projects on course to achieve targets.

There are two major reasons why a capital project may fail to achieve targets which were considered to be realistic when it was initiated – the

Table 52 Net present value of cash flow from project discounted at 12 per cent

	Net cash flow after tax (£)	Discount factor (12%)	Net present value of cash flow (£)
0	100,000	1.000	100,000
1	24,000	0.893	21,432
2	25,200	0.797	20,084
3	30,000	0.712	21,360
4	31,200	0.636	19,843
5	25,200	0.567	14,288
6	34,000	0.506	17,204
		Net present value =	14,211

revised forecasts of future expected cash flows are less than had been originally anticipated, and/or the rate at which the cash flows ought to be discounted is greater than the discount rate which was initially forecast. How the impact of each of these factors can be assessed is now considered through reference to the capital investment project of Company X which was set out on page 229. The initial evaluation of the project is set out in Table 52.

It is now assumed that the project has been implemented for one year and its performance to date and revised forecast of future performance are being re-evaluated. Two scenarios are considered. In the first the future cash flows turn out to be less than was originally forecast and in the second the discount rate is greater than was originally forecast.

Scenario number 1: The future cash flows are less than was originally forecast
Table 53 shows the results achieved and revised forecast of the project's expected cash flows one year after the project has commenced.

As can be seen the revisions have reduced the anticipated NPV substantially and if management is dissatisfied with this level of return it must consider steps which will improve it. Generally, failure to achieve forecast net cash flows can be due to one or both of the following reasons:

• The environment is less attractive than had been forecast because of influences which could include: a lower than forecast rate of economic growth; a lower than forecast rate of growth of the market; a higher than forecast level of competition, etc.
• The organization's internal costs associated with the project – for example labour costs, R and D cost, promotion costs, etc. are greater than had been anticipated and this is reducing the net cash flow.

When the causes of the reduction in cash flow have been ascertained

Table 53 Revised net present value of cash flows from project discounted at 12 per cent

	Net cash flow after tax (£)	Discount factor (12%)	Net present value of cash flow (£)
0	100,000 (Actual)	1.000	100,000
1	22,000 (Actual)	0.893	19,646
2	23,100	0.797	18,411
3	27,500	0.712	19,580
4	28,600	0.636	18,190
5	23,100	0.567	13,098
6	31,200	0.506	15,787
		Revised net present value =	4,712

Table 54 Revised net present value of cash flows from project discounted at 15 per cent

	Net cash flow after tax (£)	Discount factor (15%)	Net present value of cash flow (£)
0	100,000	1.000 (Actual)	100,000
1	24,000	0.869 (Actual	20,856
2	25,200	0.756	19,051
3	30,000	0.657	19,740
4	31,200	0.572	17,846
5	25,200	0.492	12,524
6	34,000	0.432	14,688
		Revised net present value =	4,705

then it may or may not be possible to take steps to improve it. For example, if the reduction is due to external causes such as a lower than forecast rate of economic growth, it may be beyond the power of the company to overcome this. However, if the fundamental cause is internal and is due to a failure to control the costs associated with the project then the company should be able to take remedial action.

Scenario number 2: The discount rate is greater than was originally forecast
Table 54 shows the results achieved and revised forecast of the project's expected cash flows one year after the project has commenced under the assumptions of the second scenario.

As can be seen the increased discount rate has reduced the anticipated NPV substantially and if management is dissatisfied with this level of return it must consider steps which will improve it. Generally, an increase in the discount rate can be due to one or both of the following reasons:

- The general rate of interest and therefore the rate at which future cash flows must be discounted has increased.
- Although the general rate of interest has not changed, the organization's own weighted average cost of capital has increased* and it must apply this new rate when discounting.

If the increased discount rate is due to the former reason there is little remedial action that can be taken. However if it is due to the organization's weighted average cost of capital increasing then steps may be taken to investigate and then remedy the causes.

The control and evaluation of shorter term financial strategies: cash management

At the opposite end of the time spectrum from the control and evaluation of capital budgeting strategies is the control and evaluation of cash strategies and activities. These analyses are concerned with ensuring that the flow of cash into and out of the organization effectively supports its operations and also gives stakeholders (internal and external) confidence in its continuing existence and future. From a strategic point of view the monitoring of cash flows can be extremely important as cash movements are essentially short term and adverse cash flows are often one of the earliest signals of strategic failure. For the purposes of strategic control it is suggested that two core statements may be used – the cash flow statement and the funds flow statement.

The cash flow statement

This is a fundamental managerial tool for planning, control and evaluation. A cash budget shows cash flows into and out of an organization over a specified period of time and provides management with a profile of net cash balances. This information is essential for such managerial tasks as the raising of finance to support operations, payments to stakeholders, and the exercising of control over cash and liquidity. A cash flow statement rather than an income statement or a balance sheet statement is used because sales do not lead to an immediate cash flow (in most organizations some sales will be paid for by cash, some after one month's credit, some after two months' credit etc.) and conse-

---

* There are of course many reasons why this might occur. Poor results, an increase in the gearing levels, a risky portfolio of investments, a top management scandal, a structural change, the entry of a new and aggressive competitor are all reasons why lenders would tend to regard the company as having increased its risk profile and this increased risk is often reflected in an increased cost of borrowing and hence increased weighted cost of capital.

quently income statements or balance sheet statements, which rely upon the accrual system of accounting, cannot be used for cash planning.

Although the actual time period of such a statement is specified at the discretion of the user and his perceived needs (for example the time interval could be weekly, monthly, or quarterly) the most frequently used time interval is monthly and this is the time period which has been adopted below for Siva.

Developing a cash budget statement can be divided into three major stages: the sale forecast, the cash inflows, and the cash outflows.

1 *The sales forecast:* The starting point for cash budgets in most commercial organizations is the projected level of sales for the forth-coming planning period. The sales estimate is the basis upon which receipts from sales will be based and therefore, for most organizations, this will normally be the main determinant of cash inflows. Consequently, the accuracy of sales estimates (and, of course, how quickly sales are paid for and therefore turned into cash receipts) is a fundamental determinant of the accuracy and consequent usefulness of the derived cash budget forecasts. As suggested on page 369, rather than constructing a single cash budget based upon a single sales forecast a superior and more realistic approach is to generate a number of projected cash budgets based upon alternative sales forecasts and internal policies, and then, on the basis of these simulated results adopt those strategies which most closely meet corporate goals and strategies.

2 *The cash inflows:* When the sales forecast has been obtained, the sales figures are translated into anticipated cash receipts (i.e. the cash receipts from sales are lagged by the anticipated delay in payment) and these receipts, together with other anticipated cash inflows, such as for example, the issue of shares of debentures are summed to give the anticipated cash inflows.

3 *The cash outflows:* As detailed on page 351 the sales forecast determines the production schedule and the various expenses associated with meeting this schedule, (labour costs, raw materials, marketing, etc.) together with other expenses such as capital expenditures, dividends, taxes etc. are summed to provide the anticipated cash outflows.

The cash inflows and outflows are then combined to provide net cash flows. The projected cash flow statement for Siva for 1987 is shown in Table 55.

Table 55 shows that for the first five months of the proposed strategy the monthly cash flow position for Siva will be mainly negative. However, after June 1987 monthly cash flow becomes, and remains, positive and grows. This cash flow trend could raise the following strategic issues:

- Assuming that this strategy is adopted what should be done with the positive cash balances that are being generated? For example should they be invested, should the level of debt be decreased?
- Is Siva's marketing/pricing strategy optimal? For example, it would appear that Siva could reduce its prices, and thus increase its market share and strengthen its competitive position, and still have positive cash balances.

Funds flow analysis

A funds flow statement and analysis can be extremely useful in strategic planning through providing managers, and other stakeholders (shareholders) with information on how an organization has used its funds over a period of time and also how it has raised those funds. Such statements can be used to analyse the historical performance of an organization or to evaluate the consequences of following particular strategies.

A funds flow statement aims to show the net flow of funds throughout an organization between any two points in time. The time interval normally chosen is one year, with the dates coinciding with the dates of the annual balance sheet. However, the planner may choose any time period which suits his purposes. Thus, in the case of Siva, because it is a start-up company and there is interest in seeing how the funds will flow over the first year, a quarterly funds flow statement has been developed.

Although there are many bases upon which funds flow statements may be computed the two most common are: statements based upon cash and statements based upon working capital. Below, the working capital basis has been used as this approach takes a longer time perspective and therefore complements the essentially short-term perspective that monthly cash budget analysis provides.

Developing a funds flow statement can be divided into four major stages: the sales forecast; the sources of funds; the applications of funds; and the changes in working capital.

1 *The sales forecast:*   The starting point for a funds flow statement, in most commercial organizations, is the projected level of sales for the forthcoming planning period. The sales estimate is the basis upon which income from operations will be based and for most organizations, this will normally be a major source of funds. As was the case for the cash budget analysis above the accuracy of the sales estimates is of primary importance and it is suggested that a number of alternative projections be developed and used in the same manner as was suggested for the cash budget.

2 *The sources of funds:*   The sources of funds will be the sum of elements from the income statement and balance sheet such as the income from the operations of the organization together with other sources such as share issues, debenture issues and disposals.

3 *The applications of funds:*   This element shows how the funds raised have been used and normally includes items such as the acquisition

Table 55 Projected cash flow statement for Siva for 1987

	Jan 87	Feb 87	Mar 87	Apr 87	May 87	Jun 87	Jul 87	Aug 87	Sep 87	Oct 87	Nov 87	Dec 87
Inflows												
Receipts from sales	–	38,731	77,461	77,461	77,461	77,461	77,461	76,772	76,083	76,083	76,083	76,083
Share issue						30,000						
Debenture issue				50,000			40,000					
Total inflows	–	38,731	77,461	127,461	77,461	107,461	117,461	76,772	76,083	76,083	76,083	76,083
Outflows												
Payments to creditors	–	43,899	48,080	41,809	41,809	41,809	41,568	41,224	41,120	41,120	41,120	41,120
Marketing expenses	15,492	15,492	15,492	15,492	15,492	15,492	15,217	15,217	15,217	15,217	15,217	15,217
Cash administrative expenses	15,000	15,000	15,000	15,000	15,000	15,000	15,000	15,000	15,000	15,000	15,000	15,000
Additions					40,000		25,000					
Interest paid				500	500	500	747	747	747	747	747	747
Dividends paid												
Tax paid												
Total outflows	30,492	74,391	78,572	72,801	112,801	72,801	97,532	72,188	72,084	72,084	72,084	72,084
Cash balance	(£5,492)	(£41,152)	(£42,263)	£12,397	(£22,943)	£11,717	£31,646	£36,230	£40,229	£44,228	£48,227	£52,226

Table 56   Projected funds flow statement for Siva for 1987

	Quarter 1 (£)	Quarter 2 (£)	Quarter 3 (£)	Quarter 4 (£)	Total for 1987 (£)
Income from operations	15,480	13,980	11,997	11,997	53,454
Other sources					
Share issue	0	30,000	0	0	30,000
Debenture issue	0	50,000	40,000	0	90,000
Disposals	0	0	0	0	0
Total sources	15,480	93,980	51,997	11,997	173,454
Applications					
Additions	0	40,000	25,000	0	65,000
Tax paid	0	0	0	0	0
Dividends paid	0	0	0	0	0
Total applications	0	40,000	25,000	0	65,000
Surplus or deficit	15,480	53,980	26,997	11,997	100,454
Caused by Increase (decrease)					
Debtors	116,191	0	(2,067)	0	114,124
Creditors	(54,352)	344	552	0	(53,456)
Stock	20,904	(344)	0	0	20,560
Cash balance	(67,263)	53,980	28,512	11,997	27,226
Change in working capital	15,480	53,980	26,997	11,997	108,454

of fixed assets, the payment of tax and the payment of dividends.
4   *The changes in working capital:*   The differences between the sources
    and the applications of funds will be reflected in working capital, i.e.
    debtors creditors, stock and cash.

The projected funds flow statement for Siva for 1987 is shown in
Table 56.
Table 56 shows the projected movements of the major items on Siva's
balance sheet over 1987. It can be seen that Siva's major source of funds
has not been its operations, but the issue of debentures and shares and
that it has invested substantially in fixed assets (additions) – this may
be adversely affecting turnover ratios. Additionally the company now
has a substantial cash balance which should perhaps be reduced.

Conclusion on financial control and evaluation

The above types of analyses should enable multidimensional evaluations to be made about the financial effectiveness of an organization's
strategies. Thus the evaluations should be multidimensional in the
senses of:

- Having external and internal dimensions.
- Being concerned with the long-run aspects of strategy.
- Being concerned with ensuring that the shorter term cash management aspects of effective strategy implementation are not neglected.

References

1 Matz, A. and Usry, J., *Cost Accounting Planning and Control*, South Western Publishing Company, 1971.
2 Solomons, D., *Divisional Performance: Measurement and Control*, Financial Executives Research Foundation, Irwin, 1968.

19 Control and evaluation at the corporate level

In this section it is assumed that the organization under analysis is structured on a corporate–SBU basis and that corporate planning is exclusively concerned with determining, controlling and evaluating strategies for its portfolio of SBUs which will achieve corporate goals.

At the corporate level it is assumed that the principles of control and evaluation previously considered at the SBU and functional levels still apply, but the level of aggregation is different. Therefore, with the assumption that the type of information provided for control and evaluation at the SBU level, is also available at the corporate level, the process of control and evaluation can be considered under headings similar to those used for the assessment of SBU performance given on page 372. These are evaluation of the degree of achievement of corporate goals, evaluation of financial performance, and evaluation of the individual SBUs.

Evaluation of the degree of achievement of corporate goals

This element is concerned with assertaining how well the organization's overall corporate goals have been met. Although any evaluation will need to be tailored to the actual goals which a particular organization has set, it will often be the case that most goals will be contained in a standard ratio analysis of the type set out on pages 375–92. Therefore, with the assumption that the consolidated income statements, cash flow statements and balance sheets from the individual SBUs which comprise the organization are available, a ratio analysis can be carried out to reveal the organization's degree of goal achievement in the areas of:

- Profitability

- Liquidity
- Leverage
- Activity
- Growth potential

Evaluation of the corporate risk position

Frequently organizations will have a corporate goal of seeking to mini-mize their risk exposure. Although the above analysis will reveal, through the leverage ratios, the total corporate risk position from a finance perspective it will not reveal the corporate risk from a business portfolio perspective, i.e. the risk to which the organization is exposed from the point of view of the age balance, or the life cycles, or the cash usage of its constituent SBUs. Insights into this position can be gained from developing a corporate product market portfolio with the level of aggregation being that of the SBU and considering the following types of issues.

The degree to which the portfolio has internal balance

By this is meant that the distribution of SBUs in each quadrant of the matrix is such that:

- *There are a small number of problem children* – although these types of SBUs may offer excellent prospects for the future they will nor-mally require large amounts of cash to develop sufficiently strong market positions to become stars. Furthermore, even if they are provided with this cash, there is no guarantee that they will become stars. Consequently a relatively large number of problem children will tend to indicate exposure to risk.
- *There are a small number of dogs* – dog SBUs have poor prospects and are frequently absorbers of cash. Consequently a portfolio with a relatively large number of dog SBUs could indicate that the organization is suffering severe cash outflows with little prospect of any future return.
- *There are cash cows* – these SBUs usually provide the greatest pro-portion of the cash inflows and so a portfolio with no cash cows will probably be prone to having overall negative cash flows. From another perspective, it also increases the risk exposure of an orga-nization if it has a relatively large number of cash cows. Thus, although such a portfolio may generate large cash inflows at the present time, because cash cows tend to be at the mature stage of their life cycles, a relatively large number of them in a portfolio may indicatate that insufficient thought has been given to developing SBUs which will be the cash generators of the future.
- *There are stars* – these SBUs may have neutral, negative, or positive

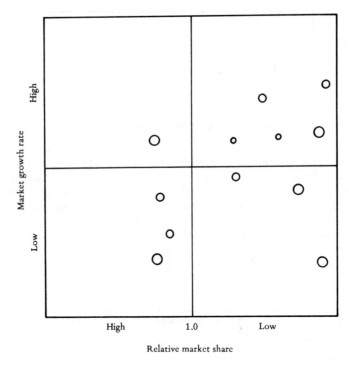

Figure 56 *An unbalanced product market portfolio*

cash flows. A portfolio which does not have stars is lacking in SBUs which will be the cash cows of the future.

The degree to which the portfolio has financial balance

By this is meant that the sum of the cash flows (normally positive from the cash cows and perhaps the stars, and normally negative from the dogs and the problem children) from each SBU plus cash flows from external sources is in balance. If the portfolio of SBUs does not have a sufficient number of cash generators then there is a risk of problems of liquidity or excessive debt developing.

Figure 56 shows a product market portfolio which is unbalanced from the point of view that it appears to have an insufficient number of cash-generating SBUs to sustain its cash-absorbing SBUs, while Figure 57 shows a more balanced portfolio.

The external strength of the portfolio

Corporate portfolio performance also has an external dimension which can be evaluated using product market portfolios to assess an organization's performance relative to that of its competitors. This could be

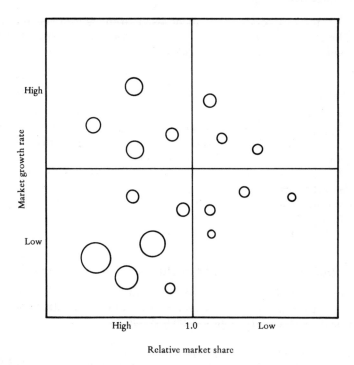

Figure 57 *A more balanced product market portfolio*

achieved by an organization drawing up product market portfolio matrices for its major competitors for a number of time periods and then analysing the movements of competitors' SBUs within these matrices. Such analyses provide some insights into the strategies that are being employed by these competitors and should enable an assessment to be made of the organization's relative performance and the riskiness of its strategies. For example, if an organization had a problem child SBU which was receiving considerable corporate resources, and this SBU had three major competitors, then analyses of the competitors' product market portfolios could reveal the strategies and likely future strength of the rival SBUs. Thus, if the analyses revealed that each competitor was devoting relatively large resources to the development of these rival SBUs then it might be prudent for the organization to question the wisdom of strongly supporting an SBU which is facing, and will continue to face severe competition.

Evaluation of financial performance

Because the only standard unit in which performance throughout the entire organization can be measured is money, financial measures are

frequently the only ones that can be used to measure overall performance. The measures that may be used are essentially those used at the
SBU level and are summarized below.

The quality of overall financial performance

The overall performance of the organization can be assessed in terms of
the degree of achievement of overall financial goals and the quality of
its financial performance relative to competitors. This effectiveness, as
set out on page 415 can be measured by:

- Investment strategies
- Financing strategies
- Dividend strategies
- Liquidity strategies

The control and evaluation of constituent financial elements

This can be sub-divided into two parts: the control and evaluation of
long-term strategies – capital expenditures; and the control and evaluation of shorter term strategies – cash control.

The control and evaluation of capital expenditures
This may be effected in the same manner as detailed on page 415 for the
control and evaluation of such expenditures at the SBU level. The major
difference is that instead of being concerned with the evaluation of the
projected discounted cash flows associated with particular projects this
type of control and evaluation is concerned with evaluating and monitoring the projected discounted cash flows emanating from the individual
SBUs.

The control and evaluation of cash
Once again, this can be effected through the use of cash budgets and
sources and applications of funds using the same techniques outlined on
pages 418–23. The major difference in the approach is that the cash
flows considered are those associated with the individual SBUs rather
than individual projects.

Evaluation of organizational structure

The objective evaluation of the effectiveness of an organization's particular structure is fraught with difficulty because there is no established rigorous methodology for doing so. However, a general approach
which could be applied to most organizations is set out below.

When the appropriateness of an organization's structure is being
evaluated just two results are possible.

1 *The goals are being achieved and the strategy implemented success-fully*: In this circumstance, assuming that the original strategy is still optimal, the structure is appropriate and it should not be changed.

2 *The goals are not being achieved and the strategy is not being im-plemented successfully*: If this type of failure has a structural cause it may be due to one or more of the following reasons: change in the external environment; change in the organization's strategy, poor internal performance.

Change in the external environment

In this case the external environment has changed, the original struc-ture is no longer appropriate, and a change of structure will be required if the organization is to successfully adapt to the changed environmen-tal circumstances. For example, the Dutch electronics company Philips has had to make many rapid and fundamental changes to its organiza-tional structure in order to remain competitive in the rapidly changing and volatile electronics industry as the following quotation illustrates.

> In line with the required integration of products and systems we are merg-ing product divisions where this is appropriate. For example, we have implemented organizational moves to meet the demands of the forthcoming markets for home interactive systems. This will certainly require an inte-grated approach, combining activities in the fields of video, audio and communications. A new product group, Home Interactive Systems, has been established to set up this new organization. Similarly, business com-munications and data systems have been merged to optimize our approach to the office systems market.
>
> At the same time, for certain activities we are shifting from a geographic-al structure towards a more product-oriented structure. In product groups with complicated products or systems and highly specialized customers (for instance, in scientific and industrial applications) it is vitally important to establish a direct link between the local situation and the product group. In these cases, we have integrated the sales function completely into the product organization.
>
> In the rest of our professional sector the sales functions are still localized in the National Sales Organizations. But here, too, it has been necessary to achieve a more integrated co-ordination and feedback with everyone in-volved along the product axis. For the relevant product/market combina-tions, organizational units are created with integral entrepreneurial responsibility.[1]

Change in the organization's strategy

In this case the organization's structure is no longer synchronized with its strategy and a change of structure will be required if the strategy is to be implemented successfully. Although there are many circum-stances under which this will occur, this type of structural inadequacy can be seen particularly clearly when an organization attempts to change from having a national strategy (i.e. where the focus is on serving a single or a number of national markets) to having a global strategy (i.e. where the focus is on serving the world viewed as a single market). Leontiades[2] has documented the issue well:

> The old style multinational addressed this aspect of doing business abroad through the simple expedient of allowing its foreign subsidiaries virtual autonomy, so much so that its 'global strategy' was largely the sum of distinct and separate national strategies. The parent firm was in effect an international holding company. It was the classic example of simplification and conflict avoidance through decentralization.
>
> This worked well enough when national barriers insulated industry in one country from its competitors in others. Today, the diminished effectiveness of such barriers makes this fragmented country-by-country approach appear suboptimal. Globalization requires that management find a new balance between responsibility and control at the local operating unit level and the wider perspective of international headquarters which has responsibility for global strategy. The task is complicated by the enormous pressure on all companies to reduce overhead costs and give maximum responsibility to operating units in direct contact with customers. Many firms have organized themselves into strategic business units (SBUs) specifically for this purpose. The question facing managers here is how to retain the benefits of the SBU structure and decentralization while adopting a global strategic approach which looks beyond national boundaries. All too often the answer to this has relied extensively on organization change. Formal organization reporting relationships were altered shifting authority away from the local level. Such changes do indeed provide management with powerful tools. But in this context it has often proved counter-productive.

In both of the above cases, i.e. when an organization has an inappropriate structure, it can be instructive to consider restructuring along the lines adopted by more successful competitors.

Poor internal performance

In this case the organization's structure is appropriate to its environment and its strategy, but the performance of the organization's constituent departments is unsatisfactory. Insights into the causes of such a situation can be achieved through quantitatively measuring the performances of all departments. As money is the only universal unit of measurement which can be used throughout the organization comparisons of departmental performance must be made in financial terms.

The starting point for assessing performance of any department on a financial basis should be the type of responsibility which has been assigned to the department. Thus, following Part One departmental responsibility can be divided into the types: investment, profit and cost. How each of these types of centre can be evaluated is now considered.

Evaluation of the performance of investment centres

This type of centre should be evaluated in terms of its investment performance and this can be measured by a variety of techniques which include return on capital employed, where this is defined as:

$$\frac{\text{net profit before tax from the investment centre}}{\text{capital employed in the investment centre}}$$

Although this is perhaps the measure most widely used to assess centre performance it does suffer from a number of drawbacks including the following:

True responsibility

In many organizations an investment centre will not have complete control over the capital it employs. For example, decisions about relatively large investment projects are often taken at a higher level in the organization, and imposed upon the centre. Similarly in most organizations there will be a shortage of central funds and investment centre managers will be constrained in their demands for capital. Thus frequently, the amount of capital employed by an investment centre will be decided, not by the centre itself, but by a higher authority, and so in these cases, the task of the investment centre changes to the maximization of return on a *given* amount of capital.

Measurement difficulties

There are various ways in which ROCE can be measured and the measures used can advantage or disadvantage an investment centre. For example, profit could be measured on a pre- or post-tax basis. It could be argued that assessment should be on a pre-tax basis as tax should be paid on the basis of the performance of the total organization rather than a single centre. However it could also be argued that it should be on a post-tax basis in that if a centre received a cash grant for its investment then it should be credited with this. Similarly assets could be valued on a historical cost basis or on a replacement cost basis. Those investment centres which have relatively old assets will tend to favour assessment on a historical basis, as the denominator for ROCE will be smaller if this basis is used and hence their apparent return will be boosted. In contrast, investment centres which have relatively new assets will favour a replacement basis to be used as their apparent return relative to other centres will be adversely affected if the historic cost basis is employed.

The allocation of costs

A fundamental determinant of ROCE is the level of costs which the investment centre incurs. If common costs, joint costs and central services costs are allocated by central management and the basis of the allocation is not influenced by the investment centre then these managers do not have control over these costs and their apparent performance may be adversely affected.

Failure to maximize owners' wealth

If an investment centre is being assessed on the basis of its ROCE this may cause investment projects which, in isolation, are attractive and worthwhile to be rejected when considered as part of the centre's portfolio of investments. How this can occur is illustrated through a hypothetical example.

Investment centre X has as its primary goal the maximization of its ROCE. The centre's cost of capital is 15 per cent and it currently has a total amount of capital of £500,000 on which it is earning profits of £120,000, i.e. its ROCE is 24 per cent. If the centre now has a new investment project which will cost £200,000 and earn profits of £36,000, yielding an ROCE for this project of 18 per cent it may reject this investment opportunity even though the returns from it exceed the cost of capital. Its reason for rejection would be that if the project were to be accepted it would reduce centre X's ROCE from 24 per cent to 22 per cent and the centre would be failing to maximize its ROCE. If this were to happen then the owners of centre X would have missed a wealth-creating opportunity as the return on the new investment project covered its costs.

This above exposition helps illustrate the dangers of adhering exclusively to a single measure of performance and it also indicates a major shortcoming of a ratio or percentage measure – it ignores the element of size or scale.

Residual income

An alternative to the ROCE approach is to set the investment centre the goal of maximizing its residual income where residual income is defined as: net profits from the investment centre less an interest charge for the capital employed. (For further details see Solomons[3].)

How the approach can be applied is illustrated through reference to investment centre X. If the criterion for evaluation of the centre's performance is now the maximization of residual income, then, assuming an interest charge of 15 per cent a different decision concerning the new investment project will be made. Under this criterion the residual income of the centre *without* the new project would be:

	£
Profit from centre	= 120,000
Minus the charge for the capital employed, 15 per cent of £500,000	= 75,000
Giving a residual income of	45,000

The residual income of the centre *with* the new project would be:

	£
Profit from centre £120,000 + £34,000	= 154,000
Minus the charge for the capital employed, 15 per cent of £500,000 + £200,000	= 105,000
Giving a residual income of	49,000

This type of approach to the evaluation of centres promotes growth in the centre and also growth in the organization as a whole and will encourage the adoption of new investments as long as the returns from the additional investment are greater than the cost of capital.

Evaluation of the performance of profit centres

In this type of centre because, in the short run, managers can only have control over revenues and variable costs it is suggested that performance should be evaluated using the contribution margin approach advocated on pages 401–5.

Evaluation of the performance of cost centres

Cost control can be evaluated by a variety of accounting techniques including:

- Comparisons of unit costs, over time and with competitors.
- Comparisons, using variance analysis, between actual costs and budgeted costs.

Conclusion on the evaluation of organizational structure

The above shows a number of approaches that can be employed for the evaluation of performance on a structural basis. However, is should always be borne in mind that strategy and structure are intimately linked and that for a comprehensive evaluation both elements must be considered.

Conclusions to Part Eight

Although control and evaluation of strategy can be regarded as the final link in the strategic management process, it is perhaps more constructive, as the strategic model diagram on page 5 suggests, to regard this element not as the final one but rather as the link which completes the 'strategic management loop'. This view suggests that strategic management is most effective in helping an organization align with its environment, if it is practised as a continuous rolling process with each element being fine-tuned in response to the feedback provided by control and evaluation. It is because of this positive pervasive influence that control and evaluation ought to have that makes it such a crucial ingredient in creative strategic management.

References

1 Dekker, W., 'Managing a Global Electronics Company in Tomorrow's World', *Long Range Planning*, Vol. 19, No. 2, April 1986, pp. 31–7.
2 Leontiades, J., 'Going Global – Global Strategies vs. National Strategies', *Long Range Planning*, Vol. 19, No. 6, December 1986, pp. 96–104.
3 Solomons, D., *Divisional Performance: Measurement and Control*, Financial Executives Research Foundation, Irwin, 1968.

Part Nine

20 A wider view

This chapter has been called 'A wider view' because this title reflects the benefit that both of its major topics ought to bring. Thus it is hoped that the strategy model which is detailed in this chapter will help readers appreciate the width of perspectives that computer modelling can bring to strategy formulation, planning, implementation, communication, and evaluation. Similarly, the second major section of the chapter – the case method – aims to provide an approach which will help readers to analyse the strategic performance and potential of an organization from a similarly wide set of perspectives.

Models and strategic management

If a model is defined as a means of summarizing and representing reality so that important relationships can be clearly seen and the use of the model provides a means of understanding the present, and predicting the future, then it could be argued that in one guise or another models which have the potential to aid strategic management have been in existence as long as the subject itself. Thus, if the above definition is employed then all of the following would be considered to be models which can in some way contribute to strategic management.

- Financial statements.
- Mathematical forecasting techniques such as regression econometrics, exponential smoothing, time series etc.
- Simulation forecasting methods such as Monte Carlo.
- Mathematical programming models.
- Network analysis.
- Queuing techniques.
- Markov Chain techniques.

While all of the above types of models have indeed made contributions to strategic management it is really only since the advent of computers that modelling, which has as its specific focus the strategic process, has had the power and flexibility to accommodate the width of views necessary to contribute to effective strategic decision making. Consequently this chapter will only consider this type of model.

Types of computer models

Irrespective of the exact functions which a model is designed to carry out, it could be argued that there are three main approaches which can be used to integrate computing power into strategy. These are:

1 Large complex models written by computer experts in a computer language and tailored to the unique needs of the organization commissioning the model. These types of models tend to be run on mainframe computers and although the planners have been involved in their development they tend not to be built by them and there is some evidence to show that their contribution to strategic planning has been less than planners initially expected.
2 Small tailored models developed by strategists written in a computer language which run on microcomputers. These type of models have the advantages that they reflect the needs of the strategists who develop them, and run on easily accessible desktop micros. However, generally they cannot be amended by personnel who do not have expertise in the language in which they are written, and also they are limited by the programming skill of the strategists who build them.
3 Comprehensive strategy models developed by planners, based on off-the-peg, easy-to-use spreadsheet type software, written in English, or near equivalent, and run on microcomputers. Because of the great advances in the power and the ease of use of off-the-peg software it is suggested here that this approach to modelling appears to offer planners the greatest potential for developing sophisticated models which are tailored to their particular needs. The next section shows how a strategy model was developed using this approach.

Using Javelin to build models for strategic management

Javelin* is a relatively new software package which appears to offer unique opportunities for planners who do not have computing skills to

---

* Javelin is a product of the Javelin Software Corporation and the product is distributed in the United Kingdom through Ashton Tate.

build extremely realistic strategic models. These models have the potential to be major aids in the development of new strategies, and the control and evaluation of existing strategies. Perhaps most importantly the Javelin-based strategy models appear to offer great potential as devices for simulating the effects that changes in assumptions about the market, or changes in strategy, will have upon a company's levels of goal achievement.

One of the major contributions which Javelin makes is that it enables planners themselves who may have no experience of, knowledge of, or indeed interest in, computer programming to build *their own* planning models on personal computers rather than relying on specialist computer personnel.

Consequently the orientation and sophistication of these models should be a direct function of the interests and skills of the planner building the models. Expressing this from another perspective – if a planner has an issue which he wishes to model and he can express the relationships of the issue in English, then he should be able to model it on Javelin.

A strategy model

In order to reflect the contribution that the above type of model can make to strategic management, a strategy model, based upon Javelin was developed on an IBM PC XT to complement this book. The data upon which the model is based is that of the Siva Company which was set out in Chapter 17. As was detailed in Chapter 17 it is assumed that the time is early December 1986 and the board of Siva is meeting to fine-tune the proposed strategies for the forthcoming year. On this occasion however they have a computer-based strategy model to assist them in their deliberations. This model can be used to alter the environmental conditions which have been forecast for the company for 1987 – for example the rate of interest may be changed – and to experiment with alternative strategies – for example changing the prices charged for the products, or changing the amount of financial disposals and acquisitions – so that the effects of these changes upon financial statements and ratios can be speedily calculated and communicated to the board. Note that the assumptions, goals, strategies and results obtained from the model are the same as the results obtained by manual calculations in Chapter 17 although there may be small discrepancies due to rounding errors or slightly different methods of calculation.

The primary aim of the model is to show how changes in the marketplace or changes in strategy can affect:

- The achievement of corporate goals.
- Marketing performance.
- Financial performance.
- General operating results.

Additionally the model aims to:

- Simulate the effects of *proposed* strategies upon performance, i.e. project the effects of proposed strategic changes.
- Simulate the effects of different future environments upon performance.
- Monitor and evaluate the effectiveness of current and past strategies.
- Show how marketing and finance are combined in strategic management.

Finally it is hoped that the model will stimulate planners and accountants who are not computer specialists to develop their own planning models.

Assumptions underlying the model

The more important assumptions upon which the model is based are set out briefly below.

1   Although organizational performance is determined by many external and internal factors this model assumes that the primary determinant of the performance of any company is its performance in the market. Therefore the 'marketplace' is assumed to be the 'source' from which all other elements of the model spring, i.e. the marketplace is the driver of the model and the primary source of information.
2   Because of the width of issues which it covers the strategy model is too unwieldy if viewed as a single unit. Consequently it has been broken down into a number of discrete 'sub-models' or building blocks, each of which, when linked together, provides a comprehensive strategic planning model.
3   Input data is provided on a monthly basis. The model uses this data to calculate output data which may be on a monthly, quarterly or annual basis.

The model comprises a series of sub-models (henceforth simply called models) linked together as shown in Figure 58.

Building the model

An overall plan for a one year strategy model was first developed and then the detailed construction of each constituent model was undertaken. All the constituent models are integrated and all calculations must take place in the sequence shown in Figure 57 otherwise the strategy model will be corrupted. In the calculation process each model

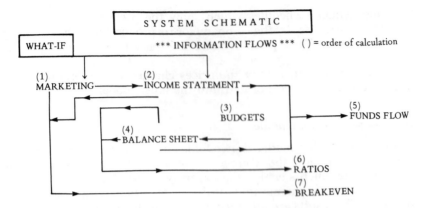

Figure 58 *The strategy model's sub-models and their linkages*

imports data from one or more preceding model and uses this data in its calculations. When a particular model has completed its calculations its output data will, when requested, be exported to other models in the sequence. For example the income statement model imports data from the what-if model and the marketing model in order to calculate its income statements. Later, when requested, the income statement model will export its calculated results to other models such as the budget model, the balance sheet model and the funds flow model.

Each of the models is now briefly described below.

The what-if model

As its name implies, the what-if model attempts to permit the planner to simulate in the strategy model the effects of changes in circumstances which are internal and/or external to the company. The changes permitted are:

- Changes in the monthly interest rate.
- The addition or disposal of fixed assets.
- Changes in the rate of growth of the markets for the products in the model.
- The issue of shares and/or debentures.

These changes may be introduced singly or jointly, so by varying these elements a planner can simulate the effects of differing environmental and internal circumstances.

The marketing model

The objective of this model is to incorporate the effects of change with the marketplace into the strategy model. The model presents plan price and demand schedules which show the predicted relationships between the prices set by the company for its products and the resulting levels of demand. (These price-demand relationships are specified in the model.)

The planner may then vary the prices charged for its products and these effects will be incorporated into the other models.

The income statement model

The objective of this model is two-fold. First to provide standard income statements for the company's operations over the planning period. The statements enable the company's sales, levels of profitability, its dividend payments and its levels of retained earnings to be monitored. The results are provided on a quarterly and an annual basis.

Second to develop insights into the profitability of some of the major segments – the product lines, the channels of distribution and the regions or territories – within the marketing function. This is achieved through the provision of income statements which provide the contribution margins according to product line, channel of distribution and region. The results are provided on a quarterly and an annual basis.

The budget model

The objective of this model is to provide information on the company's cash flow position. A monthly cash flow giving cash inflows, cash outflows and the cash balance position is provided. Additionally users may vary the relationship between receipts and payments so that the cash implications of policy changes in this area can be seen.

The balance sheet model

The objective of this model is to show the changes in assets and liabilities that have occurred over the period. The information is provided in standard UK balance sheet format with the results provided on a quarterly and an annual basis.

The funds flow model

The objective of the funds flow statement is to show, on an annual basis, the sources of the company's funds and the applications to which these funds were put.

The ratios model

The objective of the ratios model is to provide a set of financial ratios which will provide comprehensive diagnostic insights into the effectiveness of the company's current or proposed strategies.

Ratios which analyse profitability, liquidity, gearing, activity, and growth and potential are presented and the results provided on a quarterly and an annual basis. As there may be debate about the bases of the formulae used to compute the ratios, a list of the actual formulae used can be inspected on the screen

The break-even model

The objective of this model is to simulate the consequences for break-even and margins of safety of varying the price. The model will show these values for any month selected by the user.

It is hoped that when all the models are integrated together that they provide comprehensive strategic insights into how environmental changes and changes in proposed strategies affect the operations of a company. Additionally the model should also help in the monitoring of existing strategies.

The input to and the output from the model

When the model was being developed it was specified that the input and the output should be in forms which would aid comprehension by non-specialist personnel. Accordingly therefore the input and output do not always conform to the standard layout used by accountants and, in order to aid the communication of the model's output, there are a number of optional graphical formats.

The most important input and output screens from the various models are reproduced below. Limited explanations or interpretations are provided as the analysis of the output has already been provided for the manual calculations given in Part Eight.

Introduction to the models

Screens 1, 2 and 3 introduce the user to the overall model and provide information about how to operate the model.

The what-if model

Screens 4 to 10 are concerned with the 'what-if model'. Thus screens 4 and 5 provide an explanation of how this model can be used. Screen 6 shows the monthly rate of interest that has been assumed for 1987 – it is assumed that it will be 12 per cent from January to June and then it will fall to 10 per cent for the rest of the year. Screen 7 shows the additions that are projected for the year – it is assumed that fixed assets of £40,000 and £25,000 will be acquired in May and July respectively. Screen 8 shows that the growth rate assumed for both products has been set at 7 per cent. Screens 9 and 10 show that there will be a share issue of £30,000 in June and two debenture issues of £50,000 and £40,000 in April and July.

The marketing model

Screens 11, 12 and 13 show how the marketing model may be used. Thus screen 12 shows that the price for PL1 has been set at £17 for all of 1987, and screen 13 shows its monthly demand schedule for prices ranging from £15 to £20.

All the above models together provide the input information for the other models which are illustrated below.

The income statement model

Screens 14 to 19 show how the income statement model may be used. Thus screen 15 shows the standard income statement for 1987 while screens 16, 17 and 18 show a profitability analysis according to product line, region and channel of distribution. Finally screens 19 and 20 show how selected elements of the profitability analysis information may be shown graphically.

The budgeting model

Screens 20 and 21 show the monthly cash budgets.

The balance sheet model

Screens 22 and 23 show the balance sheet.

Funds flow model

Screens 24 and 25 show the funds flow for the year.

Ratio analysis model

Screens 26 and 27 show the ratios that have been projected for the forthcoming year. In addition screens 28 to 30 show optional graphical displays of the ratios.

The break-even model

Screens 31 and 32 show a break-even analysis for product line 1 and product line 2 for January 1987.

The above screens provide the results obtained from just one set of assumptions. It is extremely easy to alter the assumptions – for example changing the rate of interest – and re-run the model to see the effects that the changes have on the company's projected operating results. Additionally, the nature of the relationships among the variables may be changed – for example the relationship between price and demand could be changed from the relatively simple one specified where demand falls in response to price increases to a more complex function in which demand is influenced by lagged promotional expenditures – and the effects of these changes can be projected.

Finally it is hoped that this model will provide a flavour of the potential which spreadsheet-based computer models have to aid strategic decision making.

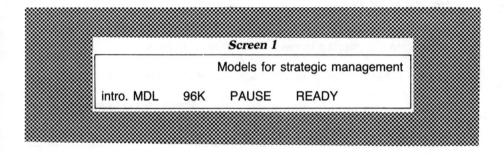

Screen 1

Models for strategic management

intro. MDL   96K   PAUSE   READY

Screen 2

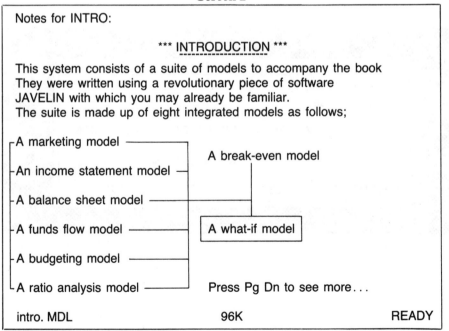

Notes for INTRO:

*** INTRODUCTION ***

This system consists of a suite of models to accompany the book
They were written using a revolutionary piece of software
JAVELIN with which you may already be familiar.
The suite is made up of eight integrated models as follows;

- A marketing model
- An income statement model
- A balance sheet model
- A funds flow model
- A budgeting model
- A ratio analysis model

A break-even model

A what-if model

Press Pg Dn to see more...

intro. MDL   96K   READY

Screen 3

Notes for INTRO:

For a detailed explanation of the nature of the integration please read the user manual.

Below is an outline of the way the models are linked:

Entry to any part of the system is via the menu you read at the start. You can invoke this menu at any time by holding down the key marked ALT and pressing M for menu.

*NB. If any changes are made to input variables then it is important to recalculate the affected models in the given sequence.

See the schematic below for the sequence of information flows!

Press Pg Dn to see more...

Intro. MDL   96K   READY

Screen 4

Press the F7 key to continue
Notes for model:

MODELS FOR STRATEGIC MANAGEMENT

The what-if model

WHATIF. MDL   83K   PAUSE   READY

Screen 5

Notes for what if:

This model allows the user to input information about a new strategy and to build in assumptions of projected changes in the environment within which the company operates. All of this new information can then be reflected in the other models and the resultant outcomes evaluated.

Press ALT M for menu

WHATIF. MDL   84K   READY

Screen 6

0.12
Notes for interest rate:

Enter the annual interest rate for any month. Javelin will convert it to the monthly equivalent.

Press ALT M to return to the menu.

Interest rate = < Monthly data: January 1987 – December 1987 >

Jan 1987............. 0.12	Sep 1987 .... 0.1	May 1988......
Feb 1987 .... 0.12	Oct 1987 .... 0.1	Jun 1988.......
Mar 1987 .... 0.12	Nov 1987 .... 0.1	Jul 1988........
Apr 1987 .... 0.12	Dec 1987 .... 0.1	Aug 1988 ......
May 1987............ 0.12	Jan 1988......	Sep 1988 ......
Jun 1987............. 0.12	Feb 1988	Oct 1988.......
Jul 1987 .... 0.1	Mar 1988	Nov 1988 ......
Aug 1987 .... 0.1	Apr 1988	Dec 1988 ......

WHATIF. MDL   84K   READY

Screen 7

Notes for additions:

Enter the amount in the table press ALT M for the menu.

Additions = < Monthly data: January 1987 – December 1987 >

Jan 1987 0	Sep 1987 0	May 1988 ......
Feb 1987 0	Oct 1987 0	Jun 1988 ....
Mar 1987 0	Nov 1987 0	Jul 1988 ....
Apr 1987 0	Dec 1987 0	Aug 1988 ......
May 1987 40000	Jan 1988	Sep 1988 ......
Jun 1987 0	Feb 1988	Oct 1988 ....
Jul 1987 25000	Mar 1988	Nov 1988 ......
Aug 1987 0	Apr 1988	Dec 1988 ......

WHATIF. MDL   84K   READY

Screen 8

Product growth rate: 0.07

Growth rate
                                              *
Product growth rate   7.00%*   < – – – – –   Enter the new
                                                    annual growth rate
                                                    as a decimal

For PL1

Press ALT A to calc the new demand

For PL2

Press ALT B to calc the new demand

WHATIF. MDL   84K   READY

Screen 9

Notes for share issue:

Enter the amount of the issue in the appropriate month.

Press ALT M to return to the menu.

Share issue = < Monthly data: January 1987 – December 1987 >

Jan 1987 0	Sep 1987 0	May 1988 ......
Feb 1987 0	Oct 1987 0	Jun 1988 ....
Mar 1987 0	Nov 1987 0	Jul 1988 ....
Apr 1987 0	Dec 1987 0	Aug 1988 ......
May 1987 0	Jan 1988	Sep 1988 ......
Jun 1987 30000	Feb 1988	Oct 1988 ....
Jul 1987 0	Mar 1988	Nov 1988 ......
Aug 1987 0	Apr 1988	Dec 1988 ......

WHATIF. MDL   84K   READY

Screen 10

Notes for debenture issues:

Enter the amount of the issue in the appropriate month.

Press ALT M to return to the menu.

Debenture issue = < Monthly data: January 1987 – December 1987 >

Jan 1987 0	Sep 1987 0	May 1988 ......
Feb 1987 0	Oct 1987 0	Jun 1988 ....
Mar 1987 0	Nov 1987 0	Jul 1988 ....
Apr 1987 50000	Dec 1987 0	Aug 1988 ......
May 1987 0	Jan 1988	Sep 1988 ......
Jun 1987 0	Feb 1988	Oct 1988 ....
Jul 1987 40000	Mar 1988	Nov 1988 ......
Aug 1987 0	Apr 1988	Dec 1988 ......

WHATIF. MDL   84K   READY

Screen 11

```
┌─────────────────────────────────────────────────────────────────────┐
│      PL1 price = < Monthly data: January 1987 – March 1988 >          │
│                                                                       │
│  Jan 1987 ............... 17    Oct 1987 ............... 17   Jul 1988 .........  │
│  Feb 1987 ............... 17    Nov 1987 ............... 17   Aug 1988 .......   │
│  Mar 1987 ............... 17    Dec 1987 ............... 17   Sep 1988 .......   │
│  Apr 1987 ............... 17    Jan 1988 ............... 17   Oct 1988 ........  │
│  May 1987 ............... 17    Feb 1988 ............... 17   Nov 1988 .......   │
│  Jun 1987 ............... 17    Mar 1988 ............... 17   Dec 1988 .......   │
│  Jul 1987 ............... 17    Apr 1988 ........            Jan 1988 ........  │
│  Aug 1987 ............... 17    May 1988 .......            Feb 1988 .......   │
│  Sep 1987 ............... 17    Jun 1988 ........           Mar 1989 .......   │
│                                                                       │
│                   p11 demand = ROUND (P1 DEMAND, 0)                   │
│                                                                       │
│  2400                                                                 │
│  2000                                                                 │
│  1600   **********************                                        │
│         **********************                                        │
│  1200   **********************                                        │
│         **********************                                        │
│   800   **********************                                        │
│         **********************                                        │
│   400   **********************                                        │
│     0   ------------------------------------------------------------  │
│         J F M A M J J A S O N D J F M A M J J A S O N D J F M A M J J A S │
│         87                      88                      89            │
│                                                                       │
│  MARKET. MDL*                    94K                    CALC READY    │
└─────────────────────────────────────────────────────────────────────┘
```

Screen 12

Top of interval:
To return to diagram view, press [Esc]. To interpolate rates, press [F9].

			Lookup table: PL1 demand		
	Input interval		Output value		
	Over	But not over	Base amount	Rate (optional)	
	–	15	0		
	15 –	15.5	3152	−760	
	15.5 –	16	2772	−576	
	16 –	16.5	2484	−586	
	16.5 –	17	2191	−760	
	17 –	17.5	1811	−770	
	17.5	18	1426	−960	
	18 –	18.5	946	−196	
	18.5	19	848	−760	
	19 –	20	468	−468	
over 20			0	0	

MARKET. MDL*   93K   CALC READY

Screen 13

Press for model:

Models for strategic management

Income statement model

Ress ALT M for menu

Screen 14

	Standard income statement				
	1 Q 1987	2 Q 1987	3 Q 1987	4 Q 1987	1987
Sales	£232,383	£232,383	£228,249	£228,249	£921,264
Cost of goods sold	£125,427	£125,427	£123,360	£123,360	£497,574
Gross profit	£106,956	£106,956	£104,889	£104,889	£423,690
Less					
Admin expenses	£45,000	£45,000	£45,000	£45,000	£180,000
Marketing expenses	£46,476	£46,476	£45,651	£45,651	£184,254
Interest	£0	£1,500	£2,241	£2,241	£5,982
Profit before tax	£15,480	£13,980	£11,997	£11,997	£53,454
tax	£6,966	£6,291	£5,400	£5,400	£24,057
Profit after tax	£8,514	£7,689	£6,597	£6,597	£29,397
Dividend payable	£0	£0	£0	£5,345	£5,345
Unappropriated profit	£8,514	£7,689	£6,597	£1,252	£24,052
Retained earnings	£53,514	£61,203	£67,800	£69,052	£69,052

Screen 15

Product line profitability analysis			
1987	PL1	PL2	TOTAL
Sales	£369,444	£551,820	£921,264
Variable costs	£199,538	£298,036	£497,574
Gross contribution margin	£169,906	£253,784	£423,690
Less			
Variable mktng exps			
Selling	£18,426	£27,636	£46,062
Warehousing	£12,534	£18,792	£31,326
Transport	£7,374	£11,052	£18,426
Advertising	£18,426	£27,636	£46,062
Credit and collection	£11,058	£16,584	£27,642
General accounting	£5,898	£8,838	£14,736
Variable marketing expenses	£73,716	£110,538	£184,254
Contribution margin	£96,190	£143,246	£239,436
Product controllable margin to sales %	16.29%	12.91%	14.27%
Less			
Product line fixed expenses	£36,000	£72,000	£108,000
Margin available for common fixed exps and profit	£60,190	£71,246	£131,436
Common fixed expenses			£77,982
Net profit before tax			£53,454

Screen 16

Sales region profitability analysis					
1987	NORTH	SOUTH	EAST	WEST	TOTAL
Sales	£285,594	£202,674	£193,464	£239,532	£921,264
Variable costs	£154,249	£109,464	£104,490	£129,371	£497,574
Gross contribution margin	£131,345	£93,210	£88,974	£110,161	£423,690
Less Variable mktng exps					
selling	£14,280	£10,134	£9,672	£11,976	£46,062
Warehousing	£9,708	£6,888	£6,576	£8,148	£31,326
Transport	£5,712	£4,056	£3,870	£4,794	£18,426
Advertising	£14,280	£10,134	£9,672	£11,976	£46,062
Credit and collection	£8,568	£6,078	£5,802	£7,182	£27,642
General accounting	£4,566	£3,246	£3,096	£3,834	£14,736
Variable marketing expenses	£57,114	£40,536	£38,688	£47,910	£184,254
Contribution margin	£74,231	£52,674	£50,286	£62,251	£239,436
Controllable contribution by region	19.69%	3.78%	16.69%	14.72%	14.27%
Less Region fixed expenses	£18,000	£45,000	£18,000	£27,000	£108,000
Margin available for common fixed exps and prof	£56,231	£7,674	£32,286	£35,251	£131,436
Common fixed expenses					£77,982
Net profit before tax					£53,454

Screen 17

Profitability by distribution channel			
1987	CH1	CH2	TOTAL
Sales	£737,010	£184,254	£921,264
Variable costs	£398,058	£99,516	£497,574
Gross contribution margin	£338,952	£84,738	£423,690
Less			
Variable mktng exps			
Selling	£32,244	£13,818	£46,062
Warehousing	£21,930	£9,396	£31,326
Transport	£12,894	£5,532	£18,426
Advertising	£32,244	£13,818	£46,062
Credit and collection	£19,350	£8,292	£27,642
General accounting	£10,314	£4,422	£14,736
Variable marketing expenses	£128,976	£55,278	£184,254
Contribution margin	£209,976	£29,460	£239,436
Controllable contribution by channel	16.77%	4.26%	14.27%
Less			
Channel fixed expenses	£86,400	£21,600	£108,000
Margin available for common fixed exps and profit	£123,576	£7,860	£131,436
Common fixed expenses			£77,982
Net profit before tax			£53,454

Screen 18

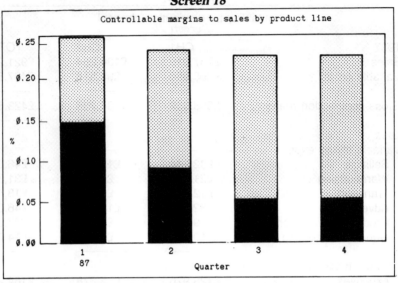

Screen 19

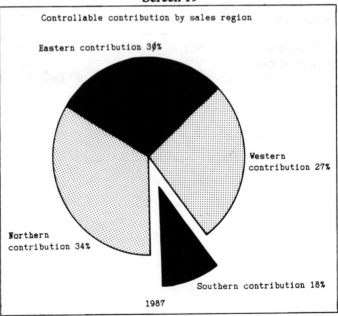

Screen 20

Notes for model:

Models for strategic management

The budgeting model

Press ALT M for menu

Screen 22

Notes for model:

Models for strategic management

Balance sheet model

Press ALT M for menu

Screen 21

Cash flow statement for 1987

	Jan 1987	Feb 1987	Mar 1987	Apr 1987	May 1987	Jun 1987	Jul 1987	Aug 1987	Sep 1987	Oct 1987	Nov 1987	Dec 1987
Inflows												
Receipts from sales		38,731	77,461	77,461	77,461	77,461	77,461	76,772	76,083	76,083	76,083	76,083
Share issue				50,000								
Debenture issue						30,000	40,000					
Total inflows		38,731	77,461	127,461	77,461	107,461	117,461	76,772	76,083	76,083	76,083	76,083
Outflows												
Payments to creditors		43,899	48,080	41,809	41,809	41,809	41,568	41,224	41,120	41,120	41,120	41,120
Marketing expenses	15,492	15,492	15,492	15,492	15,492	15,492	15,217	15,217	15,217	15,217	15,217	15,217
Cash admin expenses	15,000	15,000	15,000	15,000	15,000	15,000	15,000	15,000	15,000	15,000	15,000	15,000
Additions					40,000		25,000					
Interest paid				500	500	500	747	747	747	747	747	747
Dividends paid												
Tax paid												
Total outflows	30,492	74,391	78,572	72,801	112,801	72,801	97,532	72,188	72,084	72,084	72,084	72,084
Cash balance	(£5,492)	(£41,152)	(£42,263)	£12,397	(£22,943)	£11,717	£31,646	£36,230	£40,229	£44,228	£48,227	£52,226

Screen 23

Annual balance sheet

Employment of capital	1 Q 1987	2 Q 1987	3 Q 1987	4 Q 1987	1987
				Figures are scaled down by a factor of 100 for presentation	
	£00s	£00s	£00s	£00s	£00s
Fixed assets	2000	2400	2650	2650	2650
Accumulated depreciation	400	400	400	400	400
Total fixed assets	1600	2000	2250	2250	2250
Closing stock	209	206	206	206	206
Debtors	1162	1162	1141	1141	1141
Bank	0	117	402	522	522
Total current assets	1371	1485	1749	1869	1869
Creditors	544	540	535	535	535
Overdraft	423	0	0	0	0
Tax payable	70	133	187	241	241
Dividend payable	0	0	0	53	53
Toal current liabilities	1036	673	721	829	829
Net current assets	335	812	1028	1041	1041
Total net assets	1935	2812	3278	3291	3291
Financed by	£00s	£00s	£00s	£00s	£00s
Share capital	1150	1450	1450	1450	1450
Retained earnings	535	612	678	691	691
Long-term liabilities	250	750	1150	1150	1150
Capital employed	1935	2812	3278	3291	3291
Diff	0	0	0	0	0

Screen 24

Notes for model:

Models for strategic management

Funds flow model

Press ALT M for menu

Screen 26

Notes for model:

Models for strategic management

Ratio analysis model

Press ALT M for menu

Screen 25

	Funds flow statement				
	1 Q 1987	2 Q 1987	3 Q 1987	4 Q 1987	1987
	£00s	£00s	£00s	£00s	£00s
Income from operations	155	140	120	120	535
Other sources					
Share issue	0	300	0	0	300
Debenture issue	0	500	400	0	900
Disposals	0	0	0	0	0
Total sources	155	940	520	120	1,735
Applications					
Additions	0	400	250	0	650
Tax paid	0	0	0	0	0
Dividends paid	0	0	0	0	0
Total applications	0	400	250	0	650
Surplus or deficit	155	540	270	120	1,085
Caused by					
	£00s	£00s	£00s	£00s	£00s
Inc dec					
Debtors	1,162	0	(21)	0	1,141
Creditors	(544)	3	6	0	(535)
Stock	209	(3)	0	0	206
Cash balance	(673)	540	285	120	272
Change in working capital	155	540	270	120	1,085
Difference	0	0	0	0	0

Screen 27

	Ratio analysis report				
	1 Q 1987	2 Q 1987	3 Q 1987	4 Q 1987	1987
		Quarterly			Annual
	. . . .	Ratios		. . . .	Ratios
Profitability					
Total sales	£232,383	£232,383	£228,249	£228,249	£921,264
Gross profit margin	46.03%	46.03%	45.95%	45.95%	45.95%
Net profit margin	6.66%	6.02%	5.26%	5.26%	5.26%
Return on investment	8.00%	10.48%	12.65%	16.24%	16.24%
Return on equity	9.19%	14.29%	19.48%	24.97%	24.97%
Earnings per share	2.47	2.15	1.73	1.68	1.68
Liquidity					
Current ratio	1.32	2.21	2.43	2.26	2.26
Quick ratio	1.12	1.90	2.14	2.01	2.01
Average collection					
period	182.50	91.25	60.11	45.22	45.22
Debtors turnover ratio	2.00	4.00	6.07	8.07	8.07
Creditors ratio	135.57	72.63	49.42	37.66	37.66
Gearing					
Debt to equity	14.84%	36.37%	54.04%	53.73%	53.73%
Debt coverage	0.00	9.32	5.35	5.35	5.35
	NOTE: IF DEBT COVERAGE = 0				
	THEN THERE IS NO DEBT IN THAT PERIOD				
Activity					
Total asset turnover	0.78	1.33	1.73	2.24	2.24
Fixed asset turnover	1.45	2.32	3.08	4.09	4.09
Stock turnover times	6.56	13.13	19.58	26.04	26.04
Growth and potential					
Earning's retention ratio	100.00%	100.00%	100.00%	55.45%	88.86%
Sustainable growth rate	1949.92%	749.85%	566.13%	259.13%	881.26%
Return on equity	9.19%	14.29%	19.48%	24.97%	24.97%
Earnings per share	2.47	2.15	1.73	1.68	1.68
Dividend per share	0.00	0.00	0.00	3.69	3.69
Dividend cover	0.00	0.00	0.00	10.00	10.00

Screen 28

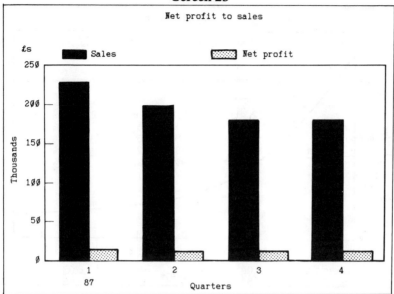

Screen 29

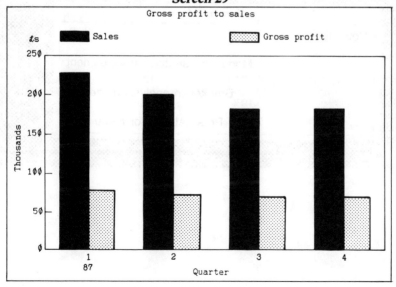

Screen 30

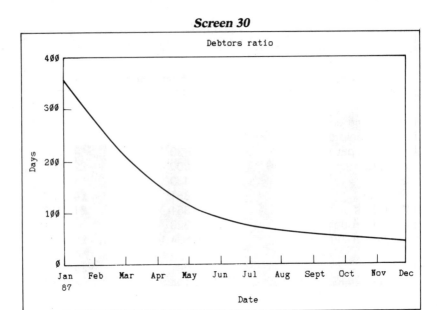

Screen 31

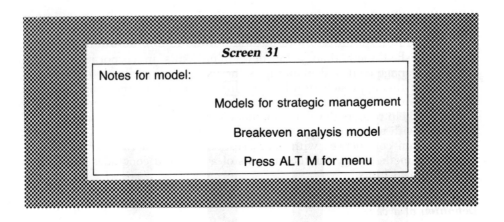

Screen 32

Enter a date e.g JAN87, 1Q87, 1987 !

	Break-even analysis	
Q 1987	PL1	PL2
Market selling price	£17.00	£18.00
Market variable cost	£13.62	£12.58
Contribution per unit	£3.38	£5.42
Fixed costs	£18,000	£27,000
Units sold	5433	7779
Contribution	£18,351	£42,129
Profit or loss	£351	£15,129
Breakeven in units	5329	4985
Breakeven in turnover	£90,594	£89,739
Les	£92,361	£140,022
Margin of safety	104	2794

Ven. MDL   84K

Units

CALC READY

The case method

The established methodology for developing skills in corporate or strategic management and planning is the use of case analyses – it is argued that this approach simulates reality and develops the range of skills and width of vision necessary for effective strategic management. In order to help readers develop a methodology in this area this chapter concludes with a section on case study analysis.

The section commences with a description of what a case is, then develops a methodology for the analysis of a case and concludes with some practical hints.

Definition of a case

A case is a written description of a company or an organization (throughout this section the word company will be used) and it may contain information on topics such as:

- The environment in which the company operates.
- The value systems of the company's owners and top decision makers.

- The goals or objectives of the company.
- The strategic plans that the company has been following.
- The internal operations of the company.
- The history of the company.
- The future plans and prospects of the company.

Cases are based on material from real life although frequently names of companies, personnel and locations may be changed in order to provide the companies and the individuals with anonymity. This, however, does not affect its underlying reality.

A note to the student

A case analysis is a splendid opportunity for you to develop and display the knowledge, skills and abilities which are prerequisite to a successful management career. More specifically in a case presentation you have the opportunity to:

- Draw upon previously studied subjects – for example economics, accounting, quantitative analysis, marketing, personnel, behavioural science etc. and integrate them into a convincing set of arguments to support your analysis.
- Develop your research skills through obtaining, classifying and using data from sources outside the case.
- Develop your ability to cogently and confidently present an analysis to a group.
- Show your ability to work as a member of a team or group.

A note to the instructor

For some students a verbal presentation to a group may be a potentially terrifying experience, so encouragement rather than criticism (however constructive and well intended) should be the prevailing atmosphere for initial presentations.

Types of presentations

Students may be required to give a variety of types of presentation both verbal and written. Among the main types are:

- Individual presentation.
- Small group presentation.
- Large group presentation.
- Role playing presentation.
- 'Devil's advocate' presentation.

This section will be addressed to the individual verbal presentation to a group, but its suggestions can be applied to all types of presentation.

Analysing the case

There are, of course, many approaches that can be used and the following is one which the author has found to be relatively successful.

1   Read the case attentively for the first time. In analysing a case there is usually more than just one issue to be considered and analysed – indeed, in some instances even identifying the issues may not be easy. For this reason a concentrated first reading – i.e. one where you do not skip paragraphs or ignore tables and diagrams – is necessary. At this stage you should underscore areas which appear to be important and take short notes on what appear to be important issues. Be especially careful in analysing charts, diagrams and other exhibits. This could be called the stage of informal analysis – i.e. as you proceed try calculating a few statistics – say financial ratios, sales forecasts etc. to give you a feeling of what the 'direction' of the case is.

2   After the first reading set the case aside and attempt to collate these initial impressions. Use the instructor's case questions and the analysis guidelines given under the 'step by step method of analysis' below to help you.

3   Discuss these initial impressions with some colleagues and through this discussion try to crystallize some of the issues and decide upon areas for further investigation.

4   Read the case again and this time focus your attention on the areas which you think are of greatest importance. Commence your detailed analysis of the data and marshall the information to enable you to proceed to step C of the 'step by step method of analysis'. During this stage you should be able to support your assertions with hard quantitative data.

5   Bearing in mind the company's 'current strategic position' generate a number of strategies which you feel the company could now adopt. Follow each strategy through and work out, as far as you can, the implications of each. For example, if the company has a strategy of grabbing market share, what are the implications for the marketing, production, personnel and accounting departments; how will competitors react, etc. When you have done this for each possible strategy decide upon a strategy which:

(a)   Most closely meets the company's goals.
(b)   Is a good fit with the environment.
(c)   Is feasible for the company, given its resources.

6   Work out in detail the actions which must be taken (and by whom they should be taken) to operationalize your chosen strategy.

7   Work out the procedures which will allow you to monitor, evaluate, and if necessary amend, the chosen strategy.

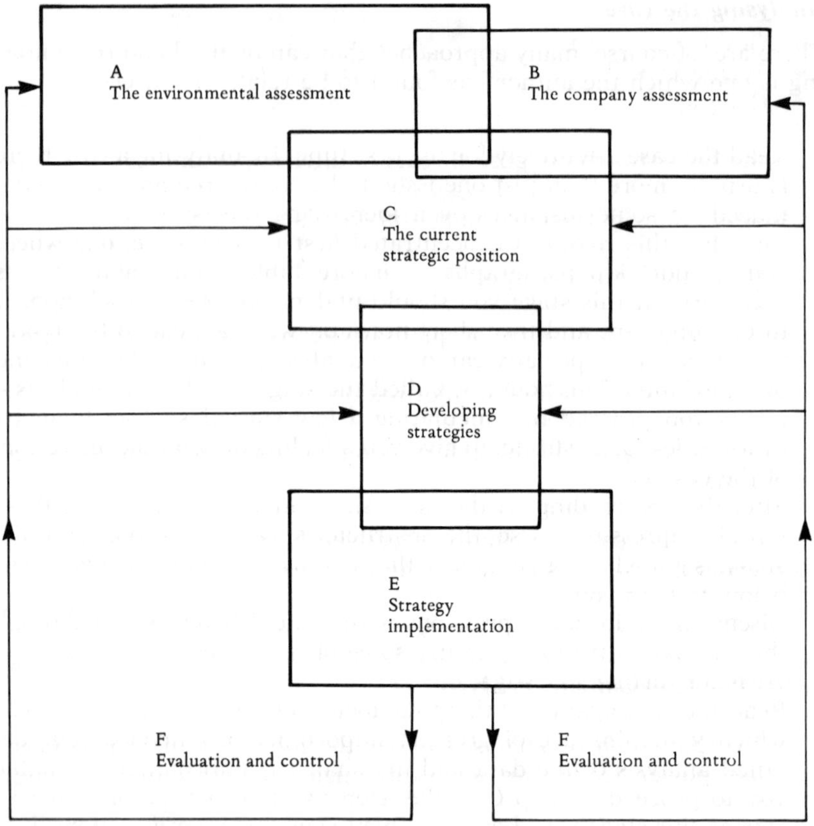

Figure 59 *A summary of the step by step method of analysis*

A step by step method of analysis

This analysis is presented in a step by step fashion but remember that the various steps are all linked together in many dimensions so your completed analysis should be a multidisciplinary integrated whole. This interdependence of the steps is indicated by the overlapping shapes in Figure 59.

Step A – The environmental analysis

Which segments of the environment are relevant to the company?

- Competitive
- Marketing
- Economic

- Social/cultural
- Government/legal
- Technological
- Geographical

Do these environments pose threats of offer opportunities?

Can you quantify the environmental trends?

What are the future prospects?

Can you make quantitative or qualitative forecasts about the future?

Can you bring in additional information?

Can you summarize all this information on an environmental assessment diagram?

How can the company most effectively limit its environmental threats and exploit its environmental opportunities?

Step B – The company analysis

The company can be analysed under the following main headings: culture, power, leadership, goals, organizational structure and functional strength.

The culture of the company:

- What is the culture of the company?
- Is the culture appropriate to the environment?
- Is it appropriate to the objectives?

The power structure:

- Where is power located in the company?
- How is power distributed in the company?
- What is the relative power of each of the company's constituent groups?
- How is power exercised?

The company's leadership:

- Is there leadership?
- Is it appropriate in style?
- Does it have the appropriate skills?

- Does it have vision?
- Does it have power?

The company's goals:

- Who are the company's leaders, owners, decision makers?
- What are the value systems of the top decision makers?
- What is the company's primary goal?
- What are the company's other goals?
- What are the company's short-term goals?
- What are the company's long-term goals?
- Are there discrepancies between the company's stated goals and those which are actually being followed?
- Is there consistency among the goals?
- Are goals being achieved?

The organizational structure:

- What structure does the company have?
- Is it appropriate to the environment and company goals?

Functional strengths and weaknesses:

What particular internal strengths and weaknesses does the company have in the following areas:

- Finance and accounting
- Marketing
- Production
- Personnel
- Information systems

In every element of the company analysis:

- Can you support your assertions quantitatively?
- What are the future prospects for each of these elements?
- Can you draw up a company assessment diagram which will summarize the company's position?
- How can the company most effectively reduce its areas of weaknesses and build upon its strengths?

Step C – Assessing the current strategic position

To assess the company's current strategic position it is necessary to relate the environmental analysis (Step A) to the company analysis (Step B) and assess the match. When this it being carried out the following questions should arise and be considered:

- In what business(es) is this company operating?
- What have been the strategies of the company over the period of analysis?
- How consistent have these strategies been, singly and collectively in relation to:

  - The company's goals?
  - The company's external environment?
  - The internal organization?

Step D – Developing strategies

The type of strategy you advocate should depend upon your assessment of the company's current strategic position (Step C). The strategy may be developed in the following stages: Carry out a gap analysis and then on the basis of the analysis develop a strategy using a two-stage methodology:

Stage 1: Decide upon a fundamental strategy – the basic options are:

- Conservation growth
- High growth
- Neutral
- Recovery
- Reduction

Stage 2: Decide upon a generic strategy – the basic generics are:

- High volume low cost
- Differentiation
- Focus

Remember that any major strategic shift will have immense managerial implications so before you suggest a change of strategy which is a major break with the past check that what you propose will be behaviourally feasible.

Finally, all strategies involve risk. Is the risk associated with your proposed strategy acceptable?

Step E – Strategy implementation

- Are the leaders of the company capable of implementing the strategy or must the leadership change?
- Is the culture appropriate to the strategy?

- Is the organizational structure appropriate to the strategy chosen or must changes be made?
- Are the company's resources adequate to implement the strategy?
- Have you specified the policies necessary at the sub-corporate level to ensure that strategic goals will be achieved?
- Have you built in controls to ensure that implementation will take place?
- Is the company's information system capable of handling the chosen strategy?

Step F – Evaluation and control

- What are the criteria for assessment of the success of the strategy?
- How well are the goals specified in the strategy being met?
- How effective are the functional strategies?
- How effective is the organizational structure?
- If goals are not being met, what are the reasons?
- How well is the company fitting with its environment?
- What is the internal health of the company?
- What is the company's risk position?
- In what ways, if any, should the strategy be amended?

Presenting the case

It is assumed below that the presentation will be oral. However the suggestions for presentation that are given can be applied to a written case analysis.

1 After your detailed analysis you will probably have more information than you need so you will need to carefully winnow it so that you present only that which is really important.
2 Start with a summary of what you intend to cover and end with a summary of your main recommendations.
3 Speak slowly and try to encourage a dialogue with your audience.
4 Use overhead projector slides to summarize the main points and to pictorially display quantitative data. Don't put too much information on any slide – write in large letters and use colour.
5 When you make an assertion always try to support it with hard quantitative data.
6 If you have detailed quantitative data have it printed and distribute it as a handout before your presentation.
7 Give your audience a smile.

Some things not to do

1 Do not recapitulate the case. Remember it is an analysis you should be presenting and your audience will have already read the case.

2 Do not say 'If only the case had more information.' All cases always have enough information. The detail of your analysis should reflect the detail of the information contained in the case.

3 Do not say 'If only I had had more time.' This is just an excuse.

4 Don't sit on the fence. If you say something like: 'On the one hand we are recommending a strategy of growth and on the other we are recommending a strategy of reduction', you are indeed sitting on the fence. Take a position and defend it by using the analysis you have carried out. In many cases there is no completely correct solution – stark correct answers tend to be the exception. Frequently, many alternatives will be perfectly acceptable provided the arguments are logical and presented with conviction.

5 Don't try to solve all of the company's problems. It is unlikely you will be able to do so. Restrict yourself to the major ones.

6 Don't forget that even though the strategy of 'doing nothing', i.e. continuing the strategy which has been previously followed, lacks appeal because it is unoriginal, it is frequently an appropriate course of action.

References

1 Charan, R., 'Classroom Techniques in Teaching by the Case Method', *Academy of Management Review*, Vol. 1, No. 3, July 1976, pp. 116–123.

2 Dooley, A. R. and Skinner, W., 'Casing Case Methods', *Academy of Management Review*, Vol. 2, No. 2, April 1977, pp. 277–289.

3 Faria, A. J., 'Relevancy and the Business Simulation Game', *Business and Society*, Vol. 17, No. 1, Fall 1976, pp. 277–289.

4 Mitroff, I. I. and Kilman, R., 'Teaching Managers to do Policy Analysis', *California Management Review*, Vol. 20, No. 1, Fall 1977, pp. 47–54.

Index